BEST PRACTICE

Today's Standards for Teaching and Learning in America's Schools

Third Edition

Steven Zemelman, Harvey Daniels, and Arthur Hyde

HEINEMANN
Portsmouth, New Hampshire

Heinemann
A division of Reed Elsevier Inc.
361 Hanover Street
Portsmouth, NH 03801–3912
www.heinemann.com

Offices and agents throughout the world

The authors and publisher wish to thank those who have generously given permission to reprint borrowed material:

Excerpt from *Standards for the English Language Arts* by the International Reading Association and the National Council of Teachers of English. Copyright © 1996 by the International Reading Association and the National Council of Teachers of English. Reprinted by permission.

Excerpt from *New Policy Guidelines for Reading: Connecting Research and Practice* by Jerome C. Harste. Copyright © 1989 by the National Council of Teachers of English. Reprinted by permission.

Excerpt from *A Community of Writers: Teaching Writing in the Junior and Senior High School* by Steven Zemelman and Harvey Daniels. Copyright © 1988 by Steven Zemelman and Harvey Daniels. Published by Heinemann, a division of Reed Elsevier, Inc., Portsmouth, NH. Reprinted by permission of the publisher.

Library of Congress Cataloging-in-Publication Data
Zemelman, Steven.
   Best practice : today's standards for teaching and learning in America's schools / Steven Zemelman, Harvey Daniels, and Arthur Hyde.—3rd ed.
      p.   cm.
   Includes bibliographical references and index.
   ISBN 0-325-00744-6 (alk. paper)
      1. Teaching—United States—Case studies.   2. Direct instruction—United States—Case studies.
   3. Active learning—United States—Case studies.   4. Teaching—Standards—United States.
   5. Education—Curricula—Standards—United States.   6. Educational change—United States.
   I. Daniels, Harvey, 1947–   II. Hyde, Arthur A.   III. Title.
      LB1025.3.Z46   2005
      371.102—dc22   2005005728

Editor: Leigh Peake
Production: Patricia Adams
Typesetter: Technologies 'N Typography, Inc.
Cover design: Judy Arisman, Arisman Design
Manufacturing: Louise Richardson

Printed in the United States of America on acid-free paper
09 08 07 06 05   RRD   1 2 3 4 5

Contents

Preface: Welcome to the Third Edition

This is a book about excellent teaching and powerful learning. Its principles come from authoritative and reliable sources—the major professional organizations, research centers, and subject-matter groups in American education. Its recommendations draw upon scientific research of rigorous design, both experimental and qualitative. The classroom stories woven through the book come from some of the country's most accomplished teachers. And the practices endorsed here have proven their effectiveness with students from kindergarten through high school, across the curriculum, and among learners of diverse languages, abilities, personalities, and learning styles.

In these fundamental ways, the third edition of *Best Practice* is very much like the two previous ones. And, as you would expect, we've completely revised and updated the book: we've reviewed the newest scientific evidence on effective teaching practices, shown how the standard of proficient teaching is evolving in every major teaching field, and added new classroom stories from several different states.

But since this book began its life, the school world has also changed in important, sometimes worrisome ways. For one thing, the term *Best Practice* itself has suffered from "terminology drift," a process by which useful educational ideas become overly popular, are carelessly used, and come unmoored from their original meanings. When we see "Best Practice worksheets" being sold at professional conferences, and tucked into free "Best Practice" tote bags, we get worried.

We're also concerned about the changing meaning of the term *standards*. When we wrote the first edition of this book in 1993, the three of us were pleased to be part of the newborn "standards movement" in education. Today, we're not so sure. Now, under the banner of "higher standards," forty-nine of the fifty states have developed their own often-idiosyncratic system of frameworks, targets, benchmarks, rules, and, above all, *tests* for both students and teachers. It's unfortunate. A movement that began as a sincere attempt to provide all children with first-rate teaching has mutated into a contentious, costly battle that has left everyone—kids, parents, teachers, school administrators, and the taxpaying public—bruised and confused.

Indeed, today's school reform conversations have become both so polarized and so muddled that we were briefly tempted to leave the word *standards* out of the book's title altogether this time around. But, of course, the opposite is needed. The language of school improvement needs clarification and defense now more than ever. If terms are being co-opted and misused, the abuse needs to be challenged, not winked at. So we want to begin this third edition by clarifying and affirming what the terms *standards* and *Best Practice* mean to us and to the teaching profession, and how they are evolving amid the political battles raging through education today.

WHAT DO WE MEAN BY "BEST PRACTICE"?

The expression "best practice" was originally borrowed from the professions of medicine, law, and architecture, where "good practice" or "best practice" are everyday phrases used to describe solid, reputable, state-of-the-art work in a field. If a professional is following best practice standards, he or she is aware of current research and consistently offers clients the full benefits of the latest knowledge, technology, and procedures. If a doctor, for example, does not follow contemporary standards of medicine and a case turns out badly, peers may criticize his decisions and treatments by saying something like, "that was simply not best practice."

Until recently, we haven't had an everyday term for state-of-the-art work in education. In fact, some veteran teachers would even *deny* the need for a current, research-based standard of instruction. "I just give 'em the basics," such teachers say, "It's worked just fine for thirty years, and I don't hold with any of this new mumbo-jumbo." One wonders how long such self-satisfied teachers would continue to go to a doctor who says: "I practice medicine exactly the same way today that I did thirty years ago. I haven't changed a thing. I don't pay any attention to all that newfangled stuff."

Some people insist that education as a field does not enjoy the clear-cut evolution of medicine, law, or architecture. But still, if educators are people who take ideas seriously, who believe in inquiry, and who subscribe to the possibility of human progress, then our professional language must label and respect practice that is at the leading edge of the field. So that's why we have imported (and capitalized) the term *Best Practice*—as a shorthand emblem of serious, thoughtful, informed, responsible, state-of-the-art teaching.

As you'll learn in the following pages, there is a strong consensus among the seemingly disparate subject-matter fields about how kids learn best. Virtually all the authoritative voices and documents in every teaching field are calling for schools that are more student-centered, active, experiential, authentic, democratic, collaborative, rigorous, and challenging. That's the short definition of Best Practice teaching; the rest of the book will deepen that description. But this isn't the only definition of standards around; indeed, there's a contrary, competing paradigm, one that's increasingly impinging on the lives of teachers, children, and parents.

THE DOUBLE STANDARDS MOVEMENT

Most teachers don't like the standards movement. Don't believe us? Just bring up the topic of standards with a roomful of teachers and watch what happens. Their faces immediately take on the expression of one of Dracula's about-to-be victims in those old horror movies. You half expect them to start making defensive crosses with their fingers and tossing garlic bulbs at you. What happened? How did *standards* become a dirty word—or at least one that invokes wildly mixed feelings among educators?

Back in the late 1980s, establishing curriculum standards sounded like a good idea. Wouldn't it be great if each subject taught in school (language arts, science, mathematics, history, the arts) had its own clear-cut descriptions of what to teach and how to teach it? These recommendations could be based on a meta-analysis of the latest research in the subject, consultations with top experts and theorists, and systematic reviews of pedagogy and practice. The National Council of Teachers of Mathematics was the first professional organization to attempt this process, when in 1987 it outlined a challenging curriculum that stressed math as a way of thinking and required new, highly interactive teaching strategies. The NCTM Standards were welcomed by teachers, school reformers, and politicians alike, and the idea quickly spread that every school subject field should develop parallel documents. With initial funding from the U.S. Department of Education, a dozen other professional organizations were eventually commissioned to develop similar standards for their own fields.

Trickling in over the next several years, the outcomes were uneven and asymmetrical. Some standards reports specified the content to be mastered in minute detail; others kept to broad guidelines. Some gave careful attention to teaching methodology; others hid it in the background. A few reports frontally addressed issues of access and equity, while most simply assumed that all children would have equal opportunities under new standards. Almost all the commissioned groups used their standards documents to lobby for more money, personnel, and classroom time for their own subjects, at the expense of others. Former Department of Education official Chester Finn was not far wrong when he noted the standards-setters' "gluttonous and imperialistic tendencies."

But however disparate and self-serving, the results also held a consensus. All the standards documents rejected schooling as usual. All called for classrooms filled with challenging, authentic, and collaborative work—a big break with past practice. They repudiated the coverage model of curriculum, where students go one inch deep in a thousand topics, and instead urged deeper exploration of a smaller number of subjects. In a word, these national curriculum standards, developed by the mainstream professional organizations in each field, contained a strong endorsement of progressive teaching methods and constructivist learning theory. And these standards, it is important to remember, emerged from *within* the profession. We teachers saw these as *our* standards, developed inside our profession, based on our research, and enunciated by our subject-matter experts and top practitioners, just the way best practice standards are developed among doctors, lawyers, and other professionals.

Meanwhile, outside the teaching profession, another standards movement was developing. Spurred by business groups, school privatization enthusiasts, conservative think tanks, and culture-wars pundits, the state governors and legislatures embarked on their own standards-building projects. Sometimes the states began by accepting the premises of the national curriculum standards; others started fresh. Almost all subscribed to the more-is-better school of rulemaking, generating hundreds of standards, targets, benchmarks, goals, and procedures. The resulting mandates undermined classroom practitioners' autonomy and professionalism in a variety of ways. Teachers were increasingly told by their states what to teach, when to teach it, and how—often in pre-scripted, word-for-word, "teacher-proof" programs that not only ruled out teachers' creativity, but their humanity as well. Across the country, teachers were forced to post outside their classroom doors, in arcane code, which among thousands of state standards (e.g., Reading, C.4.viii.23) they were meeting at each minute of the school day.

But the worst was the testing. By the time they were done, most states had linked their newly created curriculum frameworks to testing systems that deeply contradicted the national curriculum standards. Across the country, state tests (with a few notable exceptions that we'll celebrate in this book) predominantly favored multiple-choice, factual-recall formats that pushed teachers right back toward a superficial curriculum of coverage and time-eating test-prep. Arbitrary "cut scores" publicly labeled individual kids, ethnic groups, whole schools, and increasingly, individual teachers as "failures." States required that these often-misleading findings be published as "school report cards," which naturally became fodder for local editorial pages and stock-in-trade for competing real estate agents. In Chicago, we've now attained the apotheosis of accountability: many of our most affluent, even elite suburban schools have been placed on the state "watch list" because of technicalities, mistakes, or anomalies in complying with various accountability standards. Perhaps experiences like these explain why teachers react like vampire victims when the word *standards* comes up.

So we have two, mostly contradictory standards movements afoot in the land, and the accountability advocates currently have the loudest voice. These reformers retain their laserlike focus on systems of high-stakes testing and accountability, linked to elaborate rewards and punishments for students, teachers, schools, and districts. Though wary that federal tests might undermine local authority, these standards-seekers claim they can raise student achievement by measuring it more frequently and by constraining everyone in the educational enterprise with more extensive rules and regulations. In its reliance upon control and specification, this reform approach recapitulates the failed school efficiency fad of the 1920s and the similarly discredited "behavioral objectives" movement of the 1970s.

On the other side, feeling a little drowned out, are the curriculum reformers, composed mostly of subject-area experts, classroom teachers, discipline organizations, professional associations, and research centers. This book, while respectful of the need for school performance measures, is unequivocally part of this latter movement for school renewal through curriculum reform. Our vision of school improvement relies not on new rules and controls, but on improved instruction. We believe that schools are clinging to inefficient, ineffective teaching practices that urgently need to be replaced. We reject the idea that doing the same things harder, longer, and stronger will materially improve education. We repudiate the assumption that achievement can be elevated by giving students more and more tests, no matter how "rigorous." As one of our agriculturally savvy friends recently commented: "You can weigh the pig as many times as you want; the scale won't fatten him up."

In our lowest moments (happily, not too frequent or extended), we tend to look at the two standards movements in this way. The original curriculum standards projects were developing what were called "opportunity-to-learn" standards, statements about what kind of experiences, teaching, materials, and supports kids need in order to learn. They were basically asking the question, What can we do for kids? But the now-ascendant accountability movement mainly asks, What can kids do for us? How can American school children generate standardized tests scores that enrich test makers and publishers, provide evidence for privatization efforts, undermine left-leaning teachers unions, and help tough-sounding legislators get reelected? The accountability gang stays focused on measuring the purported outcomes of education, not on providing the inputs (like funding, smaller class sizes, better materials, and more teacher training) that might actually *improve* the results.

If we sound especially concerned with issues of equity and opportunity to learn, that's because these issues have tripped up almost all previous reform movements in America. Reform means nothing unless *all* students have genuine access to the kind of instruction that makes reaching high standards possible. We can't help commenting that the suburban town where we happen to be writing today spends over $15,000 per year on each of its high school students. Cross Howard Street into Chicago and the expenditure drops to $7,700. Like it or not, genuine school reform requires changes in accounting, not just accountability.

WELCOME TO BEST PRACTICE

Undoubtedly this debate, along with its acrimony and political chicanery, will continue long into the future. But the curriculum standards movement, and the historic documents it has generated, will continue to guide well-informed schools and teachers, especially in this impulsive and politicized era. While transient state standards and tests, like most politically driven reforms, tend to be volatile, inconstant, and self-contradictory, the curriculum and teaching standards developed inside the teaching profession by people who know content and understand kids will prevail over decades. Even now, most of the country's truly high-achieving schools, including some of our most costly and elite private schools, chart their course by the Best Practice map every day.

So this book is about the really big ideas in education, the ones with depth and staying power. You'll soon be visiting classrooms and schools where these enduring ideas are honored and their distinctive activities are enacted. And while *Best Practice* deals mostly in facts, it also has a strong, unabashed, and partisan vision: we believe (and we hope we are about to prove) that progressive educational principles can and should govern classroom practice in American schools. While some people belittle the past cycles of progressive innovation during the 1930s and 1960s as transient fads, this book shows how the current wave of curriculum-based reform connects and culminates those past eras, and offers hope of creating the strongest and most enduring school reforms this country has ever seen.

Acknowledgments

Preparing this third edition has been a labor of love: a reunion of the three authors, a feast of new ideas and stories, and a celebration of great teaching. Above all, the book reflects the brave, intelligent, and loving practice of the elementary and secondary educators we work with, many of whom appear personally in these pages. Throughout this book, you'll be invited into the classrooms of teacher-authors who are bringing alive the principles of Best Practice every day. For their well-told stories, our deepest thanks to Tina Archuleta, Pat Bearden, Diane Clark, Diane Deacy, Pat Dragan, Jim Effinger, Mary Fencl, Katie George, Wayne Mraz, Rebecca Mueller, Maureen Nolan, Sara Nordlund, Yolanda Simmons, Delois Strickland, Amy Vecchione, Ben Warner, Melissa Woodbury; Diane Gillespie and all the teachers of Huntsville Elementary School in Huntsville, Ohio; Daria Rigney and the teachers at P.S. 126 in New York City; and the teachers at the Manhattan New School, also in New York.

Over the last twenty years, we've had the privilege of gathering a family of brilliant, committed teacher-consultants who work with schools and teachers in our staff development projects. This team now includes Tina Archuleta, Linda Bailey, Pat Bearden, Jan Booth, Pat Braun, Kathy Daniels, Barbara Dress, Lynnette Emmons, Marianne Flanagan, Debra Gurvitz, Mary Hausner, Pete Leki, Barbara Morris, Diane Morrone, Toni Murff, Yolanda Simmons, Katy Smith, and Nancy Steineke. We have borrowed these amazing people from different branches of the Chicago public schools (classrooms, parent councils, computer labs) and watched with delight as they have entered hundreds of colleagues' classrooms, sharing their expertise with tact, energy, and concern. They are supported by a much larger corps of talented classroom teachers who, while still bringing the best of Best Practice to their own students every day, somehow find the energy to conduct extended workshops for colleagues after school and on weekends through the Illinois Writing Project. It's when we're working with all these dedicated professionals that we feel most confident—sometimes downright euphoric—about the prospects for reform in America's schools. We've seen schools change in deep and enduring ways when outstanding teachers like these are empowered to lead.

Over years of struggle (and some successes), we've learned from the wonderful teachers at many Chicago schools, including Washington Irving, where we first began trying to make a difference in city schools; Best Practice High School, which we helped to start and where so many talented teachers became wonderful friends; Waters School, whose K–8 arts and ecology program has become a model for the city; South Shore High School, which has led the way in reorganizing into small schools; and Federal Hocking High School in Stewart, Ohio, where principal George Wood and his faculty have created such a nurturing and thoughtful learning environment. George's book *A Time to Learn* has been an inspiration to us, and working with FedHock teachers and kids this past year has been one of the most energizing experiences of our careers.

We owe a special debt to our cherished colleague Marilyn Bizar, who has been our partner in classroom research, school reform, and staff development projects for the past fifteen years. Her deep knowledge of literacy education, cross-cultural curriculum, and school change processes—not to mention her dynamism and humor—have knitted our disparate group snugly together in a thousand critical ways. Jim Vopat, director of the Milwaukee Writing Project and founder of the Parent Project, is an old friend entangled with us in countless ways. Above all, his wisdom is strongly reflected in the ideas for parents woven throughout the book. Patrick Schwarz, chair of the Department of Special Education at National-Louis University, has shown us a whole new paradigm for working with students, moving from disability to possibility. We look forward to reading his own book on this vital subject very soon (get writing, Patrick!).

For the past sixteen summers, most of the people mentioned above and many of this volume's contributors have been gathering at the Walloon Institute. There, in a relaxing northwoods atmosphere, we spend four days with other teachers, parents, and principals from around the country, all of whom are trying to bring Best Practice teaching and learning to life in their schools. We don't know whether it's the provocative speakers, the respite from back-home pressures, the late-night dormitory debates, or the lumberjack buffets, but we always come back from Walloon smarter, stronger, and more committed than ever to progressive principles. Our thanks go to all the people who make Walloon possible each summer—with special kudos to Cherie Bartlett and Karen Belanger for handling both the back room and the front lines with such aplomb.

Between the three of us, we have now published seven books with Heinemann. Talk about repeat business! There's a reason for our loyalty: the people of Heinemann, who treat every book like a best-seller and every author like a member of the family. Our editor, Leigh Peake, has shepherded this book into its third incarnation with her usual wisdom, wit, and patient "wait time." Ever-generous elementary editor Lois Bridges offered extensive and much-needed guidance on the reading chapter. The production crew, starring production editor Patty Adams and copyeditor Sarah Weaver, not only caught most of our mistakes but also gave the book an open, attractive new look. Maura Sullivan, sage and seer, tweaked the title and showed us the big picture. Now, when Pat Carls revs up her machine, we know the book will find its readers, old and new. And Vicki Boyd will figure out more ways to take Best Practice training "live" to teachers around the country. Working with Heinemann is a constant delight; we are honored to be part of their unparalleled list of resources for progressive educators.

Some of our students at National-Louis University lent a hand in the creation of the book's inside front cover. Special thanks to Megan Lavery, Ken Finder, Jason Widdes, Ellie Sato, and Juri Park.

We also have some other, closer networks of people who support us—our families. Steve wants to thank his wife Susan for pursuing her own highly engaged teaching, consulting, and writing, with demanding standards for herself, making her a valuable and sympathetic model to follow and share with. And he has especially admired his sons, Mark and Daniel, for their unremitting struggles to find meaning and joy and achievement as they negotiated their own careers in the world of dance and music. Their searches have constantly reminded their parents about all that children can do, and about the freedoms and supports they needed as they grew up.

Harvey and Elaine's children were lucky to spend most of their formative years in Best Practice schools, particularly the Baker Demonstration School at National-Louis University. Marny is putting her splendid education to work as an artist, a voracious reader, and the hostess to frequent parental visits in Santa Fe, New Mexico. Nick, a certified pathologist's assistant in Oakland, California, is doing both surgical and forensic work while pursuing a Master's in Biological Science at the University of Minnesota.

Elaine Daniels, in addition to mothering these now-large children, teaches, advises, and supervises student teachers, and is the sweetest companion one could hope for in a newly empty nest.

Art has been blessed with a wonderfully supportive family as he has chased many a wild idea down the rabbit hole. Pam Hyde, an amazing educator in her own right, has been a constant collaborator, a partner in writing, and a sounding board for those ideas as she moved from a Best Practice teacher to a Best Practice principal. Their three children, Alicia, David, and Adam, have contributed mightily to the years of Best Practice development by being the guinea pigs for new curricular activities. Now grown adults, they continue to offer three remarkably different and insightful analyses and critiques of this work, in accordance with their personalities and talents.

Chapter 1
Renewing Our Schools:
The Progressive Consensus

This is both an exciting and disturbing time for America's schools. For twenty years we have been enduring the most intense period of educational reform this country has ever experienced. Nearly everyone has gotten into the act: politicians, parents, teachers, taxpayers, teacher-educators, social critics, journalists, and researchers—all of them passionately involved in school renewal. Education-oriented cover stories, blue-ribbon commissions, government reports, exposés, recommendations, talk shows, documentaries, conferences, jokes, gossip, and legislation abound. Indeed, we are writing this book during the reign of yet another "Education President," in a state with a self-declared "Education Governor," and in Chicago, a city famed for its drastic and occasionally effective school reforms. For the moment, at least, education is the issue of the day.

This universal worry about the health of our public schools was deliciously portrayed in a *New Yorker* cartoon. A horrifying, ten-story-tall reptile, presumably from outer space, rampages through a downtown square as crowds of citizens run for their life in every direction. One man at the head of the fleeing crowd turns to a fellow runner and comments: "Just when citywide reading scores were edging up!"

While all the heartfelt public concern about education is certainly useful, very little of this sudden interest has been admiring, pleasant, or even civil. Our national reappraisal of education began with widespread anger about urban dropout rates, worry about low test scores, and fears about the perceived slippage in American workers' global competitiveness. These worries are constantly stirred by a drumbeat of downbeat headlines, such as this morning's offering: "U.S. Slips in Education Ratings: America Falls Behind in Number of Those Who Finish High School" (Feller 2004). Not surprisingly, much school reform energy has been spent on blaming and finger-pointing: responsibility for our nation's educational disappointments has been enthusiastically and variously apportioned among TV, video games, single-parent families, ill-trained teachers, urban gangs, bad textbooks, sexual permissiveness, drugs, schools of education, and dozens of other causes.

Undeniably, the current debate about schools has included plenty of nonconstructive turmoil and rancor. Still, on balance, those of us who work in schools must welcome the scrutiny and even the fractiousness. After all, it is a rare and overdue moment when education leaps to the top of the national agenda—and it is during unstable periods like this one that true change often begins. So no matter what misgivings we might have about the current era of school reform, one thing is sure: today, millions of Americans are thinking hard and talking urgently about their schools. And that is welcome.

WHAT ABOUT LEARNING AND TEACHING?

One topic is too often missing from this loud, ongoing conversation: *what* shall we teach and *how?* At first, it seems unlikely that amid all this furor the substance of education could somehow be overlooked, but the record of the reform era so far sadly bears this out. Except for the national curriculum standards documents we'll soon be describing, most public discourse has concerned the organizational features of schooling and "accountability" for its outcomes, rather than its content and methodology. From the trendsetting *A Nation at Risk* onward (National Commission on Excellence in Education 1985), many reports, commission papers, books, and state and local reform efforts have focused on the logistics of schooling, rather than its content and process. The central concerns have been the length of the school day and year, the credentials and pay of teachers, the roles and duties of principals, the financing of schools and school reform, forging connections to the worlds of work and higher education, articulating educational policy with national defense, and, above all, the testing and measurement of school "products." Indeed, the federal government's current No Child Left Behind program challenges *nothing* in traditional curriculum or pedagogy. School-as-usual is just fine with NCLB, which promises only one direct governmental action in the name of educational renewal: more standardized tests for students, teachers, and schools, followed by more systematic labeling and punishing of the "failures."

As we have argued in the Preface, there are now two largely contradictory school reform movements in the United States, one located mainly inside the education profession and another pressing from outside it. The inside group is the curriculum standards movement, composed of subject-matter experts, educational researchers, professional associations, and classroom teachers who believe the key to school improvement lies in more authentic curriculum and revamped teaching methods. The outside group, now holding center stage, is usually called the accountability standards movement. This determined coalition of politicians from both parties, state and federal legislators, state education departments, testing companies, and conservative think tanks, along with some educators, believes that schools will improve through tighter controls, more regulation, and frequent high-stakes standardized tests with tough consequences.

This latter position is sometimes hard for parents and taxpayers to understand. How are kids supposed to pass all those new tests if something isn't done to make them smarter, more ready, more educated, *before* the test booklets hit the desk? How can you ignore subject matter and teaching practices in any serious conversation about school improvement? Writing in *Educational Leadership* more than a decade ago, our colleague James Beane addressed this peculiar imbalance in contemporary school reform debates, and what he argued still holds true: "It seems that no matter how radical restructuring talk may otherwise be, it almost never touches upon the curriculum itself. Much of what passes for restructuring is, in a sense, new bottles for old wine that has not gotten better with age. How is it that we can claim to speak of school reform without addressing the centerpiece of schools, the curriculum?" (1991).

This gap doesn't seem to bother the accountability-oriented reformers. With the exception of a few commercial purveyors of "cultural literacy" (Bennett 1993; Hirsch 1996; Ravitch 2003), surprisingly few of the accountability folks have paid serious attention to changing the *content* of schooling. If our schools indeed have failed as utterly as so many blue-ribbon commissions claim, then immediate changes in the curriculum would seem advisable. To be sure, many states have compiled compendia of mandatory subject matter, not just in weighty guidebooks, but on trillion-gigabite websites too. But the preponderance of this specified curriculum is 1950s-vintage subject matter—the same old textbook-driven, cover-everything string of factoids, digitalized for schools of the new millennium. The only thing new is the delivery system.

Similarly, the methods of teaching have been thoroughly ignored in the current debate. With notable (and valuable) exceptions like George Wood, Theodore Sizer, Alfie Kohn, and Deborah Meier, the people who write about school reform rarely focus systematically on teaching *processes*—the nature of the interactions between kids and teachers. Again, if our educational system truly has collapsed, then the careful critique and revision of instructional methods would seem an urgent priority. We should be figuring out how to re-arrange the basic ingredients of school—time and space and materials and ideas and people—to maximize student learning. Instead, the topic of teaching methods is not just ignored, it is often explicitly ridiculed by the account-ability reformers as a time-wasting distraction best left to the pea-brained teacher-educators in their despised colleges of education. This is not profes-sional paranoia talking: G. Reid Lyon, one of the our top-ranking federal ed-ucation officials, recently exclaimed: "If there was one piece of legislation I would pass it would be to blow up the colleges of education" (2002).

Sometimes the accountability reformers will even claim that progres-sive teaching methods have *already* come to dominate American class-rooms—and ruined them. But previous innovations like whole language, open classroom, or integrated curriculum, though much debated, have never been widely or faithfully implemented. Even at the height of such move-ments, the vast majority of classrooms have carried on unaffected with lecture-test instruction. Indeed, over the last century of astonishing techno-logical and cultural change, our educational institutions have arguably changed *less* in form and function than any other social structure. Indeed, if a person from the 19th century were suddenly transported ahead to their present-day home town, the only recognizable and familiar institution would probably be the old public school—even if it were located in a new building.

So, after nearly a generation of "reform" focused on everything but sub-ject matter and methodology, students are still sitting in pretty much the same classrooms with the same teachers, divided into the same instructional groups, doing the same activities, working through the same kinds of text-books and worksheets, and getting pretty much the same scores on the many new standardized tests that are the only tangible legacy of all the hand-wringing and exhortation. In a backhanded and ironic way, the accounta-bility standards movement actually has ended up *endorsing* old modes of schooling. These reformers have never really questioned the day-to-day pro-cess and content of American education; instead, they simply assume that if the same activities are conducted within an enhanced framework—with more time, more resolve, more tests—then student achievement and outcomes will improve. In this version of reform, you simply do the same things harder, longer, and stronger.

Now, this can be a perfectly fine approach if what you already are doing works well and merely requires intensification. Unfortunately, we are coming to understand that the basic things we've done in the past in American schools—what we teach and how—*don't* work: they don't empower kids, don't nurture literacy, don't produce efficient workers, don't raise responsible citizens, don't create a functional democracy. If we really want to change student achievement in American schools, we must act directly on teaching and learning. More of the same is not the answer.

REAL REFORM

While legislatures, blue-ribbon panels, and media sages have designed tests and tinkered with the logistics of education, the other, quieter school reform movement has steadily continued working. Our national curriculum research centers, subject-matter professional associations, capable researchers, and thousands of on-the-line classroom teachers have been struggling to clearly define "best educational practice" in each teaching field. These groups and individuals share a curriculum-driven view of education: they assume that if American schools are to be genuinely reformed, we must begin with a solid definition of the content of the curriculum and the classroom activities through which students may most effectively engage that content. They do not see the shortcomings of American schools as mainly logistical and administrative, but rather a failure of what we teach and how.

Our long-running school reform debate, even though it hasn't concentrated enough on instruction and curriculum, has nevertheless prodded further work in these areas. All the people in the curriculum reform movement—teachers, instructional researchers, professional associations, subject-area leaders—have been rethinking the substance, content, processes, methods, and dynamics of schooling. As a result, in virtually every school subject we now have summary reports, meta-analyses of instructional research, accounts from exemplary classrooms, and landmark professional recommendations. Some of these reports were produced with funding from the U.S. Department of Education; others were independent and self-financed. Taken together, this family of authoritative documents provides a strong consensus definition of Best Practice, state-of-the-art teaching in every critical field.

One might expect that when experts and practitioners from such disparate fields as art, science, mathematics, reading, writing, and social science sit down to define their own field's Best Practice, the results would reflect very different visions of the ideal classroom, contradictory ways of organizing subject matter, and divergent models of what good teachers do. But in fact, such polarities do *not* characterize these reports. Whether the recommendations come from the National Council of Teachers of Mathematics (NCTM), the National Board for Professional Teaching Standards (NBPTS), the National Writing Project (NWP), the National Council for the Social Studies, the American Association for the Advancement of Science (AAAS), the National Council of Teachers of English (NCTE), the National Association for the Education of Young Children (NAEYC), or the International Reading Association (IRA), the fundamental insights into teaching and learning are remarkably congruent. Indeed, on many key issues, the recommendations from these diverse organizations are unanimous. Following on pages 8–9 is a list of these common conclusions—features that begin to define a coherent paradigm of learning and teaching across the whole curriculum.

The latent agreement on these principles is so strong in the various subject fields that it seems fair to call it an *unrecognized consensus*. Although school people are often portrayed as lost and fragmented, the fact is that a remarkably consistent, harmonious vision of "best educational practice" already exists. The coherence of this vision, the remarkable overlap across fields, is quite striking, though even some people in the educational system haven't yet grasped its significance and potential transforming power.

Admittedly, this emerging consensus is not perfectly symmetrical across the different school subjects; some fields are ahead of others. Reading and writing are probably the most advanced in implementing Best Practice instruction, although they were among the slowest to publish official standards. Approaches like Reading/Writing Workshop, Process Writing, Writing Across the Curriculum, Reading as Thinking, and Strategic Reading, which have been solidly in place for years, have been leading the way for practitioners and researchers alike. Although no comparably broad instructional movements yet exist in mathematics, math leaders have made a tremendous contribution with the series of NCTM standards documents published since 1987. These guidelines have shown other fields how learning goals for children can be described in Best Practice terms—progressive, developmentally appropriate, research-based, and eminently teachable. In contrast, while science educators have a decades-long tradition of supporting progressive, hands-on, student-centered instruction, they've had less success with implementation in schools. This relative lack of impact undoubtedly reflects the low priority given to science at all levels of American education: science often gets pushed to the bottom of the curricular agenda, while worries about reading, writing, and math gobble up time, attention, funding, and the energy for staff development.

The social sciences have been especially uneven in embracing progressive practices and disseminating them throughout the profession. At first, this seems surprising, because subjects like history, civics, and geography appear to cry out for collaborative, experiential, student-centered, cognitive approaches—key structures in the emerging Best Practice paradigm. But, as we discuss further in Chapter 6, social studies education has been tangled up in its political baggage. Because this is the one school subject with the explicit duty to inculcate civic values and transmit "necessary" cultural information, it becomes a battleground on which partisans take nonnegotiable stands. The first draft of the national history standards, by some accounts a balanced but warts-and-all version of U.S. and world history, was voted down by the U.S. Senate after right-wing commentators waged a furious media campaign.

For several years, the vociferous and virulent attacks of high-profile critics like E. D. Hirsch and William Bennett intimidated social studies teachers. For some reason, educators rarely pointed out the obvious conflict of interest: Bennett and Hirsch, far from being judicious observers of the educational scene, are both tireless commercial vendors, marketing "cultural literacy" products (e.g., *What Your Second Grader Needs to Know, The Book of Virtues*) to American schools and parents. Finally, after years on the defensive, the National Council for the Social Studies in 1994 issued a set of documents that, along with the revised history and geography standards, staked out a solid progressive position for social science education, despite the continuing fulminations of pundits.

PRINCIPLES OF BEST PRACTICE LEARNING

As the More/Less list on pages 8–9 suggests, there is more afoot here than the congruence of teaching recommendations from traditionally separate fields

Common Recommendations of National Curriculum Reports

- LESS whole-class, teacher-directed instruction (e.g., lecturing)
- LESS student passivity: sitting, listening, receiving, and absorbing information
- LESS presentational, one-way transmission of information from teacher to student
- LESS prizing and rewarding of silence in the classroom
- LESS classroom time devoted to fill-in-the-blank worksheets, dittos, workbooks, and other "seatwork"
- LESS student time spent reading textbooks and basal readers
- LESS attempts by teachers to thinly "cover" large amounts of material in every subject area
- LESS rote memorization of facts and details
- LESS emphasis on the competition and grades in school
- LESS tracking or leveling students into "ability groups"
- LESS use of pull-out special programs
- LESS use of and reliance on standardized tests

- MORE experiential, inductive, hands-on learning
- MORE active learning, with all the attendant noise and movement of students doing, talking, and collaborating
- MORE diverse roles for teachers, including coaching, demonstrating, and modeling
- MORE emphasis on higher-order thinking; learning a field's key concepts and principles
- MORE deep study of a smaller number of topics, so that students internalize the field's way of inquiry
- MORE reading of real texts: whole books, primary sources, and nonfiction materials

- MORE responsibility transferred to students for their work: goal setting, record keeping, monitoring, sharing, exhibiting, and evaluating

- MORE choice for students (e.g., choosing their own books, writing topics, team partners, and research projects)

- MORE enacting and modeling of the principles of democracy in school

- MORE attention to affective needs and varying cognitive styles of individual students

- MORE cooperative, collaborative activity; developing the classroom as an interdependent community

- MORE heterogeneous classrooms where individual needs are met through individualized activities, not segregation of bodies

- MORE delivery of special help to students in regular classrooms

- MORE varied and cooperative roles for teachers, parents, and administrators

- MORE reliance on descriptive evaluations of student growth, including observational/anecdotal records, conference notes, and performance assessment rubrics

SOURCES: American Association for the Advancement of Science 1989, 1997, 1998, 2001; Americans for the Arts 2005; Anderson et al. 1985; Bybee et al. 1989, 1991; California Arts Council 2001; Center for Civic Education 1994; Consortium of National Arts Organizations 1994; Crafton 1996; Critical Links 2002; Dunn and Vigilante 2000; Farstrup and Samuels 2002; Fiske 1998; Geography Education Standards Project 1994; Harste 1989; Hiebert et al. 2003; Hillocks 1986; International Reading Association and National Council of Teachers of English 1996; Joint Committee on National Health Education Standards 1995; National Association for the Education of Young Children 2002; National Board for Professional Teaching Standards 2005; National Center on Education and the Economy 1995; National Center for History in the Schools 1994a, 1994b; National Commission on Reading; National Council for the Social Studies 1994; National Council of Teachers of Mathematics 1989, 1991, 1995, 2000; National Reading Panel 2000; National Research Council 1996, 2000; National Science Teachers Association 1996, 2000; President's Committee on the Arts and the Humanities and Arts Education Partnership 1999; National Staff Development Council 2001; Routman 2003; Saunders and Gilliard 1995; Sierra-Perry 1996; Smagorinsky 1996; U.S. Department of Labor SCANS Report; Wilhelm 1996.

of the American school curriculum. A more general, progressive educational paradigm is emerging across content boundaries and grade levels. This coherent philosophy and spirit is reaching across the curriculum and up through the grades. Whether it is called Best Practice, integrated learning, interdisciplinary studies, or authentic instruction, or some other name or no name at all, this movement is broad and deep and enduring. It is strongly backed by educational research, draws on sound learning theory, and, under other names, has been tested and refined over many years.

What is the nature of this new/old curriculum? What assumptions and theories about learning inform this approach? What is the underlying educational philosophy of this reemergent paradigm? If we study the more/less list systematically, we can identify thirteen interlocking principles, assumptions, or theories that characterize this model of education. These principles are deeply interrelated, each influencing the others. And the list of principles, as you'll see, can be grouped into three main clusters. The first five elements address various aspects of student-centered teaching and learning.

STUDENT-CENTERED: The best starting point for schooling is young people's real interests; all across the curriculum, investigating students' own questions should always take precedence over studying arbitrarily and distantly selected "content."

Experiential: Active, hands-on, concrete experience is the most powerful and natural form of learning. Students should be immersed in the most direct possible experience of the content of every subject.

Holistic: Children learn best when they encounter whole ideas, events, and materials in purposeful contexts, not by studying subparts isolated from actual use.

Authentic: Real, rich, complex ideas and materials are at the heart of the curriculum. Lessons or textbooks that water down, control, or oversimplify content ultimately disempower students.

Challenging: Students learn best when faced with genuine challenges, choices, and responsibility in their own learning.

The next five principles draw our attention to cognitive and developmental aspects of teaching and learning.

COGNITIVE: The most powerful learning comes when children develop true understanding of concepts through higher-order thinking associated with various fields of inquiry and through self-monitoring of their thinking.

Developmental: Children grow through a series of definable but not rigid stages, and schooling should fit its activities to the developmental level of students.

Constructivist: Children do not just receive content; in a very real sense, they recreate and reinvent every cognitive system they encounter, including language, literacy, and mathematics.

Expressive: To fully engage ideas, construct meaning, and remember information, students must regularly employ the whole range of communicative media—speech, writing, drawing, poetry, dance, drama, music, movement, and visual arts.

Reflective: Balancing the immersion in experience must be opportunities for learners to reflect, debrief, and abstract from their experiences what they have felt and thought and learned.

The final three principles remind us to attend to the social and interpersonal aspects of teaching and learning in schools.

SOCIAL: Learning is always socially constructed and often interactive; teachers need to create classroom interactions that "scaffold" learning.

Collaborative: Cooperative learning activities tap the social power of learning better than competitive and individualistic approaches.

Democratic: The classroom is a model community; students learn what they live as citizens of the school.

We can represent these three clusters of principles graphically, as shown in Figure 1.1.

The remainder of this book, as we discuss each subject in the school curriculum, spells out what these key principles really mean in practice. However, to explain why these ideas are so important, we'll elaborate briefly on them now.

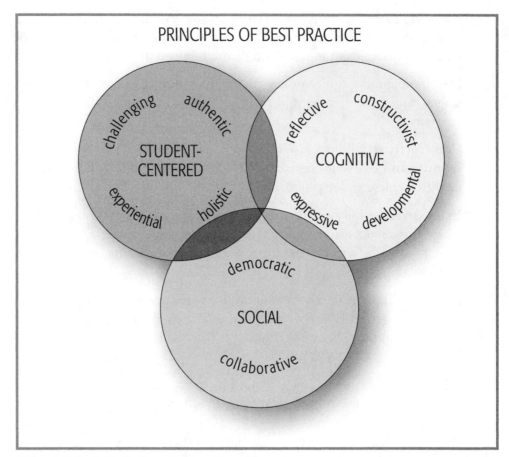

Figure 1.1: Principles of Best Practice

Schooling should be STUDENT-CENTERED, taking its cues from young people's interests, concerns, and questions. Making school student-centered involves building on the natural curiosity children bring with them and asking kids what they want to learn. Teachers help students list their own questions, puzzles, and goals, and then structure for them widening circles of experience and investigation of those topics. Teachers infuse into such kid-driven curricula all the skills, knowledge, and concepts that society mandates—or that the state curriculum guide requires—though always in original sequences and combinations. But student-centered schooling does not mean passive teachers who respond only to students' explicit cues. Teachers also draw on their deep understanding of children's developmental needs and enthusiasms to design experiences that lead students into areas they might not choose, but that they will enjoy and engage in deeply. Teachers also bring their own interests into the classroom to share, at an age-appropriate level, demonstrating how a learner gets involved with ideas. Thus, student-centered education begins by cordially inviting children's whole, real lives into the classroom; it solicits and listens to their questions; and it provides a balance between activities that follow children's lead and ones that lead children.

As often as possible, school should stress learning that is EXPERIENTIAL. Children learn most powerfully from *doing,* not just hearing about, any subject. This simple psychological fact has different implications in different subjects. In writing and reading, it means that students grow more by composing and reading whole, real texts, rather than doing worksheets and exercises. With mathematics, it means working with objects—sorting, counting, and building patterns of number and shape—and carrying out real-world projects that involve collecting data, estimating, calculating, drawing conclusions, and making decisions. In science, it means conducting experiments and taking field trips to investigate natural settings, pollution problems, and labs at nearby factories, universities, or hospitals. For social studies, students can conduct opinion surveys, prepare group reports that teach the rest of the class, and role-play famous events, conflicts, and political debates. In all school subjects, the key is to help students think more deeply, to discover the detailed implications of ideas through direct or simulated immersion in them.

Learning in all subjects needs to be HOLISTIC. In the traditional American curriculum, information and ideas are presented to children in small "building blocks." While the teacher may find these subparts meaningful and may know they add up to an eventual understanding of a subject, their purpose and significance aren't always apparent to children. This part-to-whole approach undercuts motivation for learning because children don't perceive why they are doing the work. It also deprives children of an essential condition for learning—encountering material in its full, lifelike context. When the "big picture" is put off until later, later often never comes. We know that children do, in fact, need to acquire skills and abilities such as spelling and multiplying and evaluating good evidence for written arguments. But holistic learning means that children gain these abilities most effectively by going from whole-to-part, when kids read whole books, write whole stories, and carry out whole investigations of natural phenomena. Brief lessons on the use of quotation marks are learned fastest and remembered longest when the class writes scripts for plays they've decided to stage. And, meanwhile, the focus on a rich whole text or inquiry ensures that children are simultaneously making far more mental connections—albeit often unconscious ones—than the teacher ever has time to directly teach within the one or two or three "skills" that she has time to cover.

Learning activities need to be AUTHENTIC. There is a natural tendency in schools to offer simplified materials and activities so children are not overwhelmed with complexity. But too often we underestimate children and oversimplify things, creating materials or situations that are so synthetic as to be unlifelike—and, ironically, educationally worthless. The most notorious examples of this are the linguistically deprived stories appearing in many basal reading texts. We now understand that children routinely handle phenomenal complexity in their own daily lives—indeed, learning the thousands of abstract rules underlying spoken language is proof of kids' ability to sort out the complex tangle of data the real world inevitably presents. What does authenticity mean in the curriculum? In reading, it means that the rich, artful, and complex vocabulary of Grimm's fairy tales is far more educational than dumbed-down "decodable" versions in trendy commercial reading programs. In math, it means that children investigate ways of dividing a pizza or a cake, rather than working the odd-numbered fractions problems at the end of the chapter. Authenticity also means that children are reading and writing and calculating and investigating for purposes that they have chosen, not just because the teacher gave an assignment or because a task appears in a textbook. Yes, teachers can and should sometimes give assignments that a whole class works on, to share and compare the resulting ideas they've generated. But if teachers don't also take steps to turn schoolwork into something the children truly own, then the results will be mechanical, more an exercise in dutifully following directions than in real valuing of thought and knowledge.

Following all these principles means that school is CHALLENGING. While some people think that experiential, collaborative, or self-chosen tasks are easier for students, teachers using state-of-the-art practices know that the opposite is true. "Letting" students choose their own topics for writing, for example, makes their task harder, not easier. If the teacher commands: "Imagine you are a butterfly. Write one paragraph with lots of adjectives telling how it feels to land on a flower," the author's job is basically fill-in-the-blanks. The really hard job for young writers is to find their own topics every day—pursuing the promising ones as far as they will go, discarding the clunkers and starting over. When teachers steadily assign writing topics without ever asking students to develop their own subjects as real writers do, they are establishing a pedagogical welfare system and lowering the standard of instruction.

Powerful learning comes from COGNITIVE experiences. Many teachers have moved well beyond believing that memorized definitions constitute real understanding and are reorganizing their classrooms to facilitate higher-order, conceptual learning. Full comprehension and appreciation for concepts such as *tangent, democracy, metaphor,* and *photosynthesis* come from complex, varied experiences that gradually build deep understanding that is increasingly abstract, general, and powerful.

Teachers must help students develop the specific types of thinking that our civilization values, such as analytical reasoning, interpretation, metaphorical thinking, creative design, categorization, hypothesizing, drawing inferences, and synthesis. Students need to experience these kinds of thinking for themselves with appropriate modeling and facilitation from their teachers and others. When they do, language, thinking, and conceptual understanding are intertwined as students *construct* ideas, systems, and processes for themselves.

A particularly important kind of thinking is *metacognition*—that is, becoming aware of one's own thinking and concepts. When teachers end an activity with reflective debriefing and questions such as "What led you to do things that way?" or "How did you come to that conclusion?" students become conscious of their own cognitive processes and learn to monitor their work and thinking. This self-awareness helps students develop more effective strategies for accomplishing tasks, making decisions, and reviewing their work.

It's no accident that in discussing many of these principles, we've used examples of child language acquisition. Indeed, this magical and universal phenomenon has provided educators with one of our most important bodies of knowledge—and most generative of metaphors—about learning. Childhood language development is the most powerful, speedy, and complex learning any of us will ever do in our lives. We learn to speak without being directly "taught" and without conscious intention to learn. It happens in the social settings of families and it becomes internalized through play and crib-talk. Once learned, oral language becomes the main tool for future learning and provides the base for reading and writing. Outer speech gradually becomes inner thought.

Teachers now recognize that the cognitive lessons of language acquisition aren't restricted to preschool children at home. The concept of scaffolding—the special kind of help provided by parents and siblings in a family—can be explicitly built into the classroom. The hypothesis testing and temporary linguistic forms that children use to learn language help us to understand rather than punish children's errors in school. The natural instincts of parents to engage, support, enjoy, and extend their children's utterances encourage us to rethink teacher feedback and evaluation practices. The fact that language is learned tacitly, during socializing and play, suggests that we should make the classroom more playful and interactive. Perhaps above all, the fact that you learn to talk by talking implies that children should be allowed to talk far more than they currently do in school. The antiquated school norm of silent classrooms must be abolished; ironically, when teachers enforce the standard of silence, they are in a very real sense making learning illegal.

Children's learning must be approached as DEVELOPMENTAL. This is one of the most carelessly used words in educational parlance, used to support all sorts of contradictory ideas. To us, *developmental* does not mean labeling or teaching students according to their purported level on a fixed hierarchy of cognitive stages. Nor does it mean lockstep instruction according to some textbook company's scope and sequence chart. Instead, *developmental* simply means that teachers approach classroom groups and individual students with a respect for their emerging capabilities. Developmentalists recognize that kids grow in common patterns but at different rates that usually cannot be accelerated by adult pressure or input. Developmentally oriented teachers know that variance in the school performance of different children often results from differences in general growth. Such variations in the speed but not the direction or the ultimate degree of development should not be grounds for splitting up groups, but rather are diversities to be welcomed and melded into the richness of the classroom.

In developmental schooling, we help children by recognizing and encouraging beginning steps when they occur—whether on schedule or not. We study the research on how children actually advance in math or spelling and build programs around this knowledge, rather than marching through arbitrary word lists or problems. In complex areas like writing, we chart children's progress in many ingredients of composing and understand how some abilities will appear to regress as children challenge themselves with other, more difficult rhetorical tasks. In math, along with review and exploration of this week's topic, we include challenging, enjoyable activities that go beyond the textbook unit so that we find out what various kids are really ready for.

Children's learning always involves CONSTRUCTING ideas and systems. Studies of early language acquisition, science learning in school, reading processes, mathematical cognition, and many other areas show that human beings never just take in and memorize material. Even when staring at clouds or smoke or trash in an empty lot, we are constantly trying to find meaning in what we see. In a very real sense, people reinvent whatever they encounter, by constantly making and revising mental models of the world. That's exactly how we learn complex systems like mathematics, language, anthropology, or anything else. For example, when two-year-olds invent and use words like *feets* or *goed,* words that they have never heard from anyone, they are demonstrating constructivism. Children don't just imitate the language around them; they use it as raw material to generate hypotheses, to reinvent the language itself. Along the way, they create original, temporary forms that serve until new hypotheses generate new structures. Kids don't merely learn to speak; every one of them, in a profound sense, rebuilds his or her native language.

Constructivist teachers recognize that all children can reinvent math, reading, and writing, no matter how "disadvantaged" their backgrounds, and they are eager to tap into the thinking abilities children bring to school. They know that the keys are experience, immersion, and engagement in a safe, interactive community. Kids need much time to practice reading, writing, doing mathematics, experimenting. They need encouragement to reflect, to share their emerging ideas and hypotheses with others, to have their errors and temporary understandings respected. Constructivist teachers cheerfully accept that their most helpful role isn't one of direct telling and teaching. Indeed, given the fundamentally internal nature of this deep learning, presenting rules, skills, or facts plays only a limited role in students' growth. Instead, teachers create a rich environment in which the children can gradually construct their own understandings. When we create an appropriate, stimulating, healthy setting, children's urge to make sense of their world propels their own learning.

Students need to learn and practice many forms of EXPRESSION to deeply engage ideas. Traditional school has been reception-based; that is, students sit quietly and listen while the teacher talks, presents, tells, shows, and explains—supposedly "filling them up" with the curriculum. We now understand that learning doesn't work this way, and we recognize the sad irony of schools in which teachers do all the expressing. To understand, own, and remember ideas, students need not just to receive, but also to express them. Expressing ideas can mean something as simple as talking in pairs and informal peer groups, or as sophisticated as preparing and presenting a formal public report or creating an artifact that embodies the concepts under study. When a learner can successfully translate an idea from one medium to another—for example, expressing the sixth amendment to the U.S. Constitution in a dramatic skit or a sonnet—we realize that she possesses the information in a solid and flexible way. And, aside from the cognitive benefits of such rich instruction, expression taps into many children's love of performing. Indeed, it is a natural human tendency to find a friendly audience and exercise your strongest medium of expression. A progressive curriculum stresses exhibitions and performances, inviting students to express ideas through the widest possible array of media.

Effective learning is balanced with opportunities for REFLECTION. Too often, school is a process of stimulus-response. The work cycle is: Do it, turn it in, get your grade, forget it, and move on. But learning is greatly strengthened when children have time to look back on what they've learned, to digest and debrief, to recognize broader principles, to appreciate their accomplishments and understand how they overcame obstacles. It is hard to think reflectively in the middle of doing an experiment or revising a draft, but afterwards students can review what happened and apply what they learned to future efforts. Is this reflective process foreign to kids? No—we find evidence of it in their play and family interactions all the time. But kids need time set aside for reflection, and they need to become consciously aware of its power and their ability to use it. Adding reflective thinking to school learning is one of the simplest of all instructional innovations. Many teachers have found that the mere addition of a student learning log for each subject, with time set aside each day for responding to well-structured teacher "prompts," builds reflection into the day and moves students to a new level of thinking.

Teachers should tap into the primal power of SOCIAL relations to promote learning. Much research has shown how social interactions in the family and community support early language learning. This occurs unconsciously and naturally in families and in groups of children playing together. Such spontaneous support is often called "scaffolding," because just as a temporary scaffold allows bricklayers to construct a wall that finally stands on its own, these interactions support young language builders along the way, but ultimately leave the child independent. Children are far from passive in this scaffolding process. They learn not only by imitating grownup behavior, but also by taking an active part, constructing and testing hypotheses and initiating action themselves. Babies learn language swiftly and effectively without being directly "taught" because they are learning words and structures that get their needs met. Following this model, schools can reverse their old counterproductive patterns of isolation and silence, tapping the power of social interaction to promote learning.

Some of the most efficient social learning activities are COLLABORATIVE. When we think of the social side of learning, we most readily envision group discussions, kids listening to one another's work, carrying out projects and writing letters and stories *for* one another. Collaborative learning also promotes children's learning *with and from* one another. The American workplace requires extensive collaboration and group problem solving, not just competitiveness and isolation. Collaborative small-group activity has proven an especially effective mode for school learning—and solid achievement gains have been documented across the curriculum by Johnson and Johnson (1998), Sharan (1999), Slavin (1994), and others.

Collaborative work allows learners to receive much more extensive feedback from fellow students than they can ever get from a single teacher who must spread his time among all students. Of course, group work requires training students and carefully designing meaningful, authentic activities—otherwise, the result can be inefficient and shallow. But cooperation works very well when teachers employ the training techniques that have been refined in recent years. And habitual cooperation pays off both in time better used in the classroom and, later on, as a valuable skill in life.

Classrooms can become more effective and productive when procedures are DEMOCRATIC. It is a classic bit of American hypocrisy that we claim to be a democracy and yet send our children off to profoundly authoritarian schools. But even if we don't choose to democratize schools as a matter of principle, there are instructional reasons for doing so. Democratic processes can make learning more efficient, more widely spread throughout the classroom, and more likely to have lifelong effects. First and most important, children need to exercise *choice*—choice in books they read, topics they write about, and activities they focus on during some parts of the day. This means that teachers must help children learn how to make intelligent choices, not just arbitrary ones or choices of avoidance. When children learn to make good choices, they are not only more committed to their work, they also acquire habits that make them lifelong readers, writers, and learners of math, science, and social issues—and, not inconsequentially, active, critical, involved citizens.

But democracy is not just freedom to choose. In a genuinely democratic classroom, children learn to negotiate conflicts so they work together more effectively and appreciate one another's differences. They learn that they are part of a larger community, that they can gain from it, and that they must also sometimes give to it. They hear about differences in one another's cultures, religions, regional backgrounds, and personal beliefs. Too often, this valuing of community within difference is missing in both rich and poor neighborhoods, and its absence undercuts education in countless ways, leaving us with discipline problems, vandalism, hostility toward school, and low self-esteem among students. Democracy in the classroom is not just a frill or an isolated social studies unit, but an educational necessity.

Even with young children, Best Practice teachers are careful not to inculcate day-long dependency on teacher instructions, directions, and decisions. They see their overriding goal as nurturing children's capacity to run their own brains, conduct their own inquiries, track and evaluate their own efforts. So they expect students to take considerable responsibility—to establish learning goals, monitor their own learning, apply the abilities they've acquired, keep their own records, and elect new projects when they're finished with something, rather than just fill in an extra ditto sheet. As students gradually assume more responsibilities, the teacher provides a safe space for experimenting with newer and more difficult tasks, adding challenges as kids are ready for them. In the rigorous classes where these approaches abound, kids rise to the challenge.

We first identified these thirteen principles in 1993, after analyzing the curriculum standards reports that had been published by that time. The ideas are still vibrant today; the essentials of good teaching and learning have not changed. In fact, more documents have since appeared in the field of cognitive psychology that echo our analysis. In 1997, the American Psychological Association (APA) produced a very Best Practice–friendly set of Learner-Centered Principles arranged into four broad categories that affect learners and learning: cognitive and metacognitive, motivational and affective, developmental and social, and individual difference factors (available at http://www.apa.org/ed/lcp2/lcp14.html). And in 1999, the National Research Council published a landmark book, *How People Learn: Brain, Mind, Experience, and School* (Bransford, Brown, and Cocking). Expanded in 2000, it is a massive compendium of research findings from cognitive science and the psychology of learning, written in a very readable style and highly applicable to everyday classrooms. The book is organized around five themes that have changed people's conception of "learning" in the past thirty years: *early foundations, memory and structure of knowledge, analysis of problem solving* and *reasoning, metacognitive processes and self-regulatory capabilities,* and *cultural experience and community participation.* (The Executive Summary can be found at http://www.nap.edu/html/howpeople1/es.html.)

BUT DOES IT WORK?

Most people find these Best Practice ideas sensible, congenial, and believable on a commonsense level. But the question remains: does this stuff really work? In classrooms where authentic, collaborative, challenging experiences are the norm, do students learn well? Do they understand and remember the content of the curriculum? Can they perform tasks that show us what they know and are able to do? The short answer is *yes.* We have decades of research and thousands of studies showing that progressive teaching practices do "work." Indeed, the content-area curriculum standards we have been discussing here are based upon the current instructional research in each field.

But in recent years, accountability advocates have made "scientific proof" their battle cry, accusing the curriculum reformers of lacking solid evidence that their paradigm is effective. To emphasize this new focus, the federal government even changed the name of its research arm from the Office of Educational Research and Improvement to the Institute of Education Sciences. Now we have constant battles as opposing reformers lob contradictory research studies back and forth, accusing each other of "bad science," flawed research design, and insupportable interpretations.

Look: *everyone* in the school debate has stacks of "scientific research." The question is, what is being researched and how is it measured? If you ask kids to read aloud nonsense words that they have never seen (*florg, berf,* etc.), and they pronounce them "correctly," can they be said to be *reading?* You might be surprised to hear that reading tests favored by some accountability reformers use items just like these. Other tests look at whether children understand and remember what they read, or examine children's reading skills, tastes, and habits over time. Still other assessments examine what kids can write about a story or passage they have read. All these tests can yield numerical outputs, but which provide "scientific proof" of strong reading achievement?

We're not going to fight this battle here, but we will share one important line of research that concerns all of us, no matter what we teach. For two decades, Fred Newmann and his colleagues have been studying "authentic instruction" and its impact on student achievement (Newmann et al., 2001). These researchers explain that *authentic* lessons have three main ingredients:

- Students construct knowledge—interpreting, analyzing, evaluating, and not just reciting information.

- Students draw conclusions, elaborate on their understanding, or make and support arguments.

- Students connect the topic to their own lives or to similar situations in daily life outside school.

Sound familiar? Yes, these are key ingredients of what we're calling Best Practice teaching. Newmann's formula further describes classrooms where there is less lecturing and more interaction, more hands-on, collaborative activity, and fewer worksheets. He calls classroom activities with these Best Practice characteristics "high-quality assignments."

Over a period of years, Newmann has shown that students who are taught this way remember material significantly better, as measured by carefully constructed tests of the subject matter. But the question remains: what about the kind of high-stakes standardized tests now being mandated by the states? Do kids taught the authentic, Best Practice way score well on those measures, too? Looking at a large cross-section of Chicago Public Schools (Newmann 2001; Smith et al. 2001), Fred Newmann, Julia Smith, and their coworkers found that:

- Classrooms with high-quality assignments make gains 20 percent greater than average on the Iowa Test of Basic Skills (ITBS) in reading, over one year.

- Classrooms with low-quality assignments make gains only 70 percent of the average on the ITBS in reading, over one year.

- With high didactic instruction, students gain 3.4 percent *less* than the city average on reading achievement tests, over one year.

- With low didactic instruction, students gain 3.7 percent *more* than the city average on reading, over one year.

- With high use of interactive instruction, students gain 5.2 percent *more* than the city average on reading, over one year.

- With low use of interactive instruction, students gain 4.5 percent *less* than the city average on reading, over one year.

As Newmann and his fellow researchers note, some of these effects may seem modest, but they *multiply* over the years.

Of course, scores on tests like these are not the main goal of education; at the very best they are a limited measure of the broad cognitive development that we aim for in schools. But in a testing world where a one percentage point change can be statistically significant, where school officials pray for the tiniest upward creep of scores, these are quite stunning findings.

WHAT'S NEW?

This family of ideas, the model we now call Best Practice teaching, will be entirely familiar to anyone who worked in American schools during the late 1960s and early 1970s—someone raised on the ideas of Carl Rogers, John Holt, Herbert Kohl, A. S. Neill, Neil Postman, and Charles Weingartner. But then this list doesn't exactly hold any surprises for people who lived through the progressive era of the 1930s or who have studied the work of John Dewey. Yes, today's "new" integrated and holistic educational paradigm can fairly be called a progressive resurgence. *Another* progressive resurgence.

Yes, but . . . what about special education?

Does Best Practice teaching also "work" for students with special needs, with identified learning problems, or with individualized educational plans? Absolutely. In fact, Best Practice teaching is not a *problem* for kids with special needs—it is a very important part of the *solution*. The traditional model of sitting thirty students in rows and then "teaching to the middle of the class" (which usually means *talking*) never worked very well for anyone—but it especially shortchanged kids with learning issues. Best Practice classrooms, on the other hand, are highly decentralized; they emphasize active, experiential learning and offer students real choices and responsibilities. Their fluid structure opens many more pathways for kids who think differently, who need extra support, or who operate on different timetables.

In true Best Practice classrooms, we don't need (or want) to label, track, or level *anyone*. Instead, teachers provide individually appropriate work, materials, and choices for everyone. In a workshop environment (see pages 243–247), teachers address every child's needs by creating a variety of temporary student groups, holding individual conferences, and using assessment tools sensitive to different learning styles. Contrary to the old "sit 'n git" model, sophisticated and adjustable Best Practice classrooms allow true individualization to happen. The climate welcomes a much wider range of learning styles, personality types, and work habits; kids can try multiple entry points into subject matter; and there are many ways for young people to show what they know. Further, the classroom workshop provides a natural setting for "push-in" special educators to work seamlessly with identified kids—and to provide help for other students along the way, too.

We three authors have raised some children with "special needs" ourselves, and we feel pretty passionate on this subject. We've learned much from our colleague Patrick Schwarz, chairman of the Department of Diversity in Learning and Development at National-Louis University. In his work, Patrick is developing a new paradigm of special education called "possibility studies" (Schwarz 2006). This approach begins with a quite different set of assumptions and baseline procedures about students with "disabilities."

Assumptions
- Each of us has, or during our lifespan will develop, a "disability" (e.g., old age).

- Differences are normal.
- Diversity is an asset; we learn more from people who are different from us.
- Every classroom is diverse.
- All teachers are special educators.
- School structures and procedures cause some "disabilities" (e.g., rules requiring absolute silence or stillness).

Practices

- The only acceptable label is a student's name.
- We should "normalize difference" by incorporating students into classroom life instead of sending them away.
- Kids should not have to "earn" their way into a regular education classroom; instead, it should be the home of all students, whenever possible.
- All kids can meet the same educational standards, but not in the same way or at the same time.
- Classrooms should support effort-based learning.
- Community building is key; successful learning requires strong relationships.
- Caring is OK; pity is not.
- All students deserve the dignity of taking risks and doing challenging work.
- No child should ever be moved out of the regular classroom unless there is a written plan to bring her back in.
- Medication should be the last, not the first, resort.

While our book is not expressly aimed at special educators, Best Practice teaching is deeply harmonious with these progressive ideas about working with students with special needs. When you set up a decentralized classroom with high individualization, plenty of hands-on activity, genuine choices for students, and a strongly supportive social climate, then a much broader range of learners can not only feel at home, but thrive and excel.

However, while it is harmonious with and descended from past progressive eras, this new movement is not identical to the open classrooms of the 1960s or the Deweyian schools of the 1930s. Though still rooted in the view of children as fundamentally good, self-regulating, and trustworthy, today's movement is driven by more than an optimistic conception of children's nature. This time around, the philosophical orientation is better balanced with pedagogical pragmatism and insight about cognition. We are blending a positive view of children with our commitment to meaningful curriculum content and our improved understanding of how learning works. In the 1960s, many progressive innovations failed because they were backed with more passion than practical, well-thought-out procedures for implementing them. Now, a generation later, we return to the same basic theories, with the same fundamental understanding of kids' capabilities, but equipped with much better ideas about how adult helpers can make them work.

Yes, many of these ideas are old and familiar. And while this neoprogressive movement does indeed promise a revolution in education, it is the farthest thing from a fad. Although it has reemerged now partly as a result of contemporary forces, it also represents a much older, ongoing, and long-coming shift in the educational philosophy of this nation. This closely related set of ideas has been struggling for acceptance in American culture for many generations, appearing and reappearing in forms that too many educators and citizens have mistaken for meaningless cyclical trends.

Now, past the turn of the millennium, these ideas appear again, this time in a stronger, more coherent form. Perhaps the current cycle of progressive reform will have a more lasting influence on education than the innovations of the 1960s and 1970s, or even the era of John Dewey. While the authors of this book have no doubt that this cyclical tendency will continue into future generations, we also believe in progress. With each cycle, some things change that never change back, and some cycles leave a stronger heritage than others. We believe that today's is potentially the most important, powerful, and enduring phase of progressive educational reform ever to occur in American schools.

HOW TO READ THIS BOOK—AND WHY

Today we enjoy a rich base of research and exemplary practice that points the way to school renewal through curriculum and instructional reform. As teachers are showing in schools around the country, this progressive paradigm is not just a dream anymore, but a real, practical, manageable, available choice. But this new/old model for school renewal enacts learning and teaching in very different ways from those that most contemporary parents, principals, and teachers themselves experienced in school—and, in some ways, it directly contradicts many teachers' professional training. So when teachers, schools, or districts want to move toward this new model, everyone involved in the change needs lots of information and reassurance: they need a chance to construct their own understanding of what the new curriculum means, what research and theory supports it, how it can be implemented, and why it holds so much promise for our children.

That's what this book is for: to help everyone recognize, understand, appreciate, and start exploiting the remarkably coherent models for across-the-curriculum school reform that already have been built. Toward this end, we take several steps in the next few chapters. First, we provide a compact and accurate summary of current Best Practice research in each of six main school teaching fields, drawing on the consensus documents from each subject area. For the very first teaching field—reading—we'll also provide explicit links between the thirteen principles outlined in this chapter and recommended reading methods. In the next five chapters, we'll leave it to the reader to make those theory-to-practice connections. After explaining each subject-area's research base, we include at least one story of exemplary instruction, showing how real teachers are implementing key content and processes in their classrooms.

This pattern of organization, of course, restricts us for several chapters to the traditional subject-area boundaries. While we certainly don't wish to reify the compartmentalization of the curriculum, the fact remains that knowledge about schooling currently is generated and reported mostly within these customary divisions. The key research centers, professional societies, and even most individual researchers are identified with only one subject field each. In Chapter 8, we discuss ways to move beyond the traditional school subject areas; after all, the new educational paradigm doesn't reach its full potential until better practices are used beyond the same old boundaries.

For all of us, the ultimate goal is more coherent, organic, and integrated schooling for American young people. However, creating that kind of experience is not *guaranteed* by rescheduling the school day, abolishing separate subjects, or instituting thematic interdisciplinary units. Vast changes and improvements in teaching can be made within the old subject boundaries. Indeed, we would warn that schools that reorganize their schedule and curriculum into interdisciplinary units without fully understanding the current research on reading, writing, mathematics, science, social studies, and art may merely devise an elaborate new delivery system for the same old superficial kind of education. This problem leads us to the question of change, which is the final topic of the book. In later chapters, we talk frankly—and, we hope, practically—about the tough but definitely not insurmountable problems of change in American schools.

Readers may approach this book in different ways, depending on their needs and interests. After all, according to the research on reading comprehension that we're about to summarize, meaning in any text is profoundly dependent on the knowledge of the reader. We'd be remiss if we didn't learn from our own inquiry, and we've designed the book to take this variability into account.

So if you are an experienced teacher trying to invigorate your science instruction, you may turn directly to the science chapter for guidelines and possibilities, browse several exemplary classroom segments to see how they actually work, study Chapter 8 for the classroom structures that enable new teaching strategies, and then consult Chapter 9, Making the Transition, to consider teacher-development activities for your district. On the other hand, if you are a school administrator searching for policies to improve children's learning throughout your district, you might scan all the subject-area chapters, and then once you see the pattern they reveal, focus most strongly on Chapter 9 to think about the direction of staff development in the district. If you are a school board member trying to imagine how changes in the curriculum might affect your own and your neighbors' children, you may appreciate most the Exemplary Instruction stories that illustrate how new-yet-old ideas already are making many schools the exciting and enriching places they ought to be.

Whatever your purpose as a reader, we urge you to view the recommendations and classroom stories in this book as elements of a process and not as examples of perfection. School districts or individual teachers rarely advance in one single, straight-line jump. None of the teachers whose classrooms are described here consider themselves paragons; all talk about being somewhere in the middle of a long, complex journey. Indeed, it is a defining characteristic of good teachers that they are learners themselves, constantly observing to see what enriches children's experience—and what makes teaching more invigorating and rewarding. Thoughtful readers will find many ways to improve upon and extend the activities described here. In fact, as we've talked with these teachers, we've usually ended up brainstorming additional options and variations that bring even more principles of Best Practice into play. We certainly invite our readers to join in this process of extending and fine-tuning.

And we need to add a warning. It is tempting, as one reads any book about school reform, to be excessively impressed by innovative, highly wrought, teacher-designed activities, implicitly assuming that increased student learning comes mainly from increased teacher doing. But it's not that simple. There must always be a balance in the classroom between teacher-organized activity and children's own initiative and self-directed work. It is during kids' self-sponsored activities that much of the most powerful learning occurs and the effects of good teaching get a chance to bloom. During the buzz and talk that goes on while small groups work, during the jotting and quiet of journal time, during the children's play with math manipulatives or puzzles, while kids sketch out ideas on a piece of butcher paper—so much learning is happening that even when there's a bit of digressing and fooling around, an observer gets dizzy watching it.

As another way of making clear this special kind of artful, balanced teaching, we have created the chart, Indicators of Best Practice, which appears on the inside front cover. This graphic represents how, as teachers move toward the kind of instruction described in this book, the characteristics of their teaching will change and develop in many dimensions. A reproducible version of this chart is also available as an appendix on pages 326–327.

TWO FINAL STORIES

One thing that deeply troubles us about the accountability version of the national standards movement is its heartless and authoritarian way of talking about—and to—children. The prevailing tone is get-tough, no-nonsense, nose-to-the-grindstone, sit-down-and-shut-up. Standards setters are always issuing demands, exhortations, warnings, and "consequences," as if these were the way to a child's heart and mind, and the keys to motivation. No one seems to care whether school is a safe place, a comfortable place, or, God forbid, a place that's *fun*. Indeed, the knuckle-knocking invocations of the test-and-punish reformers make you wonder whether any of these people have any children of their own—or ever were children themselves.

Meanwhile, in New York City, there's a wonderfully rigorous small school that has redefined standards in an especially constructive way. When setting forth their curriculum goals for each grade level, the teachers at the

Our Hopes for Third Graders

Manhattan New School

Does your child:

1. Show an interest in reading?
   - Does he/she choose to read other than when it is required?

2. Read for a sustained period of time?
   - Is there an increase in the amount of time your child reads independently as the year goes on?

3. Respond emotionally to text?
   - Does he/she laugh, sigh, smile, allow himself to be "touched" by what is being read?

4. Choose literature at appropriate and challenging levels?
   - Can your child read the books he/she chooses with minimal difficulty?
   - Does he/she challenge him/herself to read new genres (nonfiction, poetry, mystery, etc.)?

5. Make reasonable predictions about what might happen next in the story?

6. Connect personally to the characters and plot of the story?
   - Does he/she talk about his/her own experiences in life because he/she is reminded of them from the story?

7. Use a variety of word recognition strategies to figure out unknown words? Does he/she:
   - Skip a difficult word and come back to it later?
   - Use picture clues?
   - Attempt to "sound out" the word?
   - Ask someone what a challenging word is?

8. Talk about how a story is written? Does he/she comment on choices the author made in creating leads, endings, language in a story?

9. Make connections between books?
   - "This book reminds me of another one I've read. . . ."
   - "This is like another book by this author. . . ."

10. Use reading for real-life purposes?

11. Show curiosity about bus signs, advertisements, menus in restaurants, grocery store flyers, signs in store windows, etc.?

(courtesy of Joanne Hindley)

Manhattan New School don't issue standards for learning; instead, they share their *hopes for children*. Accordingly, teacher Joanne Hindley and the third-grade team have developed these "hopes" for one part of the curriculum—reading—expressing them as questions for parents to consider.

How different these standards sound from the benchmarks, cutoffs, multiple-choice tests, and consequences of the accountability reformers! These *hopes* speak the same language that parents use when they talk about their children, unashamedly framing educational goals within the human context of love, empathy, flexibility, patience, and perspective.

 Finally, we can look at these hopes through one child's story. When ten-year-old Kate, who really struggled with reading and writing, composed her very first coherent story, it wasn't part of an assigned, teacher-planned activity. Kate was a fifth grader at Washington Irving School, from a poor neighborhood on the West Side of Chicago. She was belligerent much of the time, a nonparticipant in most lessons, and her teacher agonized over Kate's seemingly bleak future. For several weeks the class had been working on inferential reasoning, imagining "the story behind" various objects and events, through reading books, brainstorming, and taking a walk in the neighborhood—all activities structured by the teacher. Now the class was generating a list of questions to ask a fascinating visitor who was coming after lunch—an investigator from the city morgue, located nearby and thus part of the neighborhood study.

The teacher discovered that Kate had been doodling in her journal, next to a drawing she'd made of a trash-littered lot the class encountered on its neighborhood walk. The one ability Kate recognized in herself was that she could draw quite well. Next to the drawing, Kate has began writing a story titled "The Funky Boot," based on a mysterious object she noticed in the vacant lot. She asked in a whisper if she could work on her story right then, using the computer at the back of the room. Kate worked there until lunch-time, paused impatiently for only part of the morgue investigator's talk, returned to the computer, and later asked to skip gym so she could continue writing—the longest continuous attention that she'd ever given to any school task except drawing. The piece was barely coherent, but it was Kate's first attempt at

authorship. While the classroom climate and activities made this break-through possible, the timing and commitment came from Kate.

As much as we value well-structured teaching and creative classroom activities, in this book we hope to show why schools must also make time for kids—creating not just elegant teacher-orchestrated events, but also simple, regular, predictable space for all of our Kates to achieve their own wonderful discoveries.

WORKS CITED

American Association for the Advancement of Science. 1989. *Science for All Americans*. Washington, DC: American Association for the Advancement of Science.

———. 1997. *Resources for Science Literacy Professional Development*. New York: Oxford University Press.

———. 1998. *Blueprints for Reform*. New York: Oxford University Press.

———. 2001. *Atlas of Science Literacy*. Washington, DC: American Association for the Advancement of Science and National Science Teachers Association.

Americans for the Arts. 2005. Arts Education at Americans for the Arts. Washington, DC http://www.artsusa.org/issues/artsed/

Anderson, Richard C., Elfrieda H. Hiebert, Judith A. Scott, and Ian A. G. Wilkinson. 1985. *Becoming a Nation of Readers: The Report of the Commission on Reading*. Washington, DC: National Institute of Education.

Beane, James. 1991. Middle School: The Natural Home of Integrated Curriculum. *Educational Leadership* (October).

Bennett, William. 1993. *The Book of Virtues: A Treasury of Great Moral Stories*. New York: Simon & Schuster.

Bransford, J., A. Brown, and R. R. Cocking. 2000. *How People Learn: Brain, Mind, Experience and School*. Washington, DC: National Academy Press.

Bybee, Roger, et al. 1989. *Science and Technology Education for the Elementary Years: Frameworks for Curriculum and Instruction*. Washington, DC: National Center for Improving Science Education.

———. 1991. *Science and Technology Education for the Middle Years: Frameworks for Curriculum and Instruction*. Washington, DC: National Center for Improving Science Education.

California Arts Council. 2001. *Current Research in Arts Education: An Arts in Education Research Compendium*. Sacramento, CA: California Arts Council.

Center for Civic Education. 1994. *National Standards for Civics and Government*. Calabasas, CA: Center for Civic Education.

Consortium of National Arts Organizations. 1994. *National Standards for Arts Education: What Every Young American Should Know and Be Able to Do*. Reston, VA: Music Educators National Conference.

Crafton, Linda. 1996. *Standards in Practice: Grades K–2*. Urbana, IL: National Council of Teachers of English.

Critical Links: Learning in the Arts and Student Academic and Social Development. 2002. Americans for the Arts. http://www.americansforthearts.org/public _awareness/pac_article.asp?id=834

Dunn, Ross, and David Vigilante. 2000. *Bring History Alive: A Sourcebook for Teaching World History*. Los Angeles: National Center for History in the Schools.

Farstrup, Alan E., and S. Jay Samuels, eds. 2002. *What Research Has to Say About Reading Instruction*. Newark, DE: International Reading Association.

Feller, Ben. U.S. Slips in Education Ratings. *Detroit News*. September 9, 2004: 1.

Fiske, Edward B., ed. 1998. *Champions of Change: The Impact of the Arts on Learning*. Washington, DC: Arts Education Partnership and the President's Committee on the Arts and the Humanities.

Geography Education Standards Project. 1994. *Geography for Life: National Geography Standards*. Washington, DC: National Geographic Research and Exploration.

Harste, Jerome C. 1989. *New Policy Guidelines for Reading: Connecting Research and Practice*. Urbana, IL: National Council of Teachers of English.

Hiebert, J., et al. 2003. *Teaching Mathematics in Seven Countries: Results from the TIMSS 1999 Video Study*. Washington, DC: U.S. Department of Education, National Center for Educational Statistics.

Hillocks, George. 1986. *Research on Written Composition*. Urbana, IL: National Council of Teachers of English.

Hindley, Joanne. 1996. *In the Company of Children*. York, ME: Stenhouse.

Hirsch, E. D. 1996. *The Schools We Need and Why We Don't Have Them*. New York: Doubleday.

———. 1999. *What Your Second-Grader Needs to Know*. New York: Delta.

International Reading Association and National Council of Teachers of English. 1996. *Standards for the English Language Arts*. Urbana, IL, and Newark, DE: International Reading Association and National Council of Teachers of English.

Johnson, David, and Roger Johnson. 1998. *Learning Together and Alone: Cooperative, Competitive and Individualistic Learning* (Fifth Edition). New York: Allyn and Bacon.

Joint Committee on National Health Education Standards. 1995. *National Health Education Standards: Achieving Health Literacy*. Reston, VA: Association for the Advancement of Health Education.

Lee, Valerie, et al. 1999. *Social Support, Academic Press, and Student Achievement: A View from the Middle Grades in Chicago.* Chicago, IL: Consortium on Chicago School Research.

Lyon, Reid. 2002. Quoted in Wilson, Marilyn. "NCLB: Taylor Made for Deskilling Teachers." www.ncte.org/about/issues/slate/117626.htm.

National Association for the Education of Young Children and the National Association of Early Childhood Specialist. 2002. *Early Learning Standards.* Washington, DC: State Department of Education.

———. 2005. http://www.nbpts.org/standards/stds.cfm

National Center on Education and the Economy. 1995. *New Standards: Performance Standards, English Language Arts, Mathematics, Science, Applied Learning.* Washington, DC: National Center on Education and the Economy.

National Center for History in the Schools. 1994a. *National Standards for United States History: Exploring the American Experience.* Los Angeles: National Center for History in the Schools.

———. 1994b. *National Standards for World History: Exploring Paths to the Present.* Los Angeles: National Center for History in the Schools.

National Commission on Excellence in Education. 1985. *A Nation at Risk: The Imperative for Educational Reform.* Washington, DC: National Commission on Excellence in Education.

National Commission on Reading. 1985. *The Report of the Commission on Reading.* Washington, DC: National Institute of Education.

National Council for the Social Studies. 1994. *Expectations of Excellence: Curriculum Standards for the Social Studies.* Washington, DC: National Council for the Social Studies.

National Council of Teachers of Mathematics. 1989. *Curriculum and Evaluation Standards for School Mathematics.* Reston, VA: Commission on Standards for School Mathematics.

———. 1991. *Professional Standards for Teaching Mathematics.* Reston, VA: National Council of Teachers of Mathematics.

———. 1995. *Assessment Standards for School Mathematics.* Reston, VA: National Council of Teachers of Mathematics.

———. 2000. *Principles and Standards for School Mathematics.* Reston, VA: National Council of Teachers of Mathematics.

National Reading Panel. 2000. *Report of the National Reading Panel: Teaching Children to Read.* Washington, DC: National Institute for Child Health and Human Development, Department of Health and Human Services.

National Research Council. 1996. *National Science Education Standards.* Washington, DC: National Academy Press.

———. 2000. *Inquiry and the National Science Education Standards: A Guide for Teaching and Learning.* Washington, DC: National Academy Press.

National Science Teachers Association. 1996. http://www.NSTA/org/standards.

National Staff Development Council. 2001. NSDC Standards for Staff Development. Oxford, OH. http://www.nsdc.org/standards/index.cfm.

Newmann, Fred, et al. 2001. *Authentic Intellectual Work and Standardized Tests: Conflict or Co-Existence?* Chicago, IL: Consortium on Chicago School Research.

President's Committee on the Arts and the Humanities and Arts Education Partnership. 1999. *Gaining the Arts Advantage: Lessons from School Districts That Value Arts Education.* Washington, DC: President's Committee on the Arts and the Humanities.

Ravitch, Diane. 2003. *The Language Police: How Pressure Groups Restrict What Students Learn.* New York: Knopf.

Routman, Regie. 2003. *Reading Essentials: The Specifics You Need to Teach Reading Well.* Portsmouth, NH: Heinemann.

Saunders, P., and J. Gilliard. 1995. *A Framework for Teaching Basic Economic Concepts with Scope and Sequence Guidelines, K–12.* New York: National Council on Economic Education.

Schwarz, Patrick. 2006. (forthcoming) *The Dignity of Risk: Rethinking Special Education.*

Sharan, Shlomo. 1999. *Handbook of Cooperative Learning Methods.* New York: Praeger.

Sierra-Perry, Martha. 1996. *Standards in Practice: Grades 3–5.* Urbana, IL: National Council of Teachers of English.

Slavin, Robert. 1994. *Cooperative Learning: Theory, Research and Practice.* New York: Allyn and Bacon.

Smagorinsky, Peter. 1996. *Standards in Practice: Grades 9–12.* Urbana, IL: National Council of Teachers of English.

Smith, Julia, Valerie Lee, and Fred Newmann. 2001. *Instruction and Achievement in Chicago Elementary Schools.* Chicago, IL: Consortium on Chicago School Research.

U.S. Department of Labor. 1992. *Secretary's Commission on Achieving the Necessary Skills.* http://wdr.doleta.gov/SCANS.

Wilhelm, Jeffrey D. 1996. *Standards in Practice: Grades 6–8.* Urbana, IL: National Council of Teachers of English.

Chapter 2
Best Practice in Reading

READING BY HART

Sara Nordlund and Melissa Woodbury teach fourth grade at Hart Upper Elementary School in northwest Michigan. The town of 2000, known as the Asparagus Capital of America, is set in low rolling hills not far from Lake Michigan. The school draws from a wide rural attendance area; about half the students are children of Mexican migrants who work the area's farms and fields. Many of these kids attend school for only parts of the year as their families follow the crops; many study in Hart until Christmas, move down to Florida or Texas for the winter, and then return in April.

Sara and Melissa teach in two adjacent classrooms, connected by a teachers' office where the coffee pot is always on and kids continuously troop back and forth. Both rooms are decorated in a homey, up-north style; Sara and Melissa call the décor "Great Lakes Adventure." The walls are hung with pictures of white pine trees, old-time fur trappers, lighthouses, shipwrecks, and other Michigan themes. Couches, pillows, and soft, comfy chairs are scattered around the carpeted rooms, mostly in blue and white. The teachers rarely turn on the buzzing bright fluorescents overhead; instead, kids read under floor and table lamps with nautical motifs. Quiet instrumental music plays in the background most of the day. The atmosphere is calm, soothing, and peaceful.

However, there's plenty of activity and energy when the time is right. Like right now, as kids excitedly head off to their "literature circle" meetings, including many who funnel through the teachers' office to find their book club partners in the adjoining room. All the children carry a novel they have chosen to read with a small group of classmates, and a spiral notebook in which they have jotted down topics they want to discuss with their friends. After a few minutes of organizing and pulling desks into tight groups of five, students open their books and journals, lean in, and start talking about their chosen story, using their notes as sources of conversation topics.

As a visitor gets acclimated to the excited buzz in the room, joins a few student groups, and tunes in to the ongoing conversations, the sophisticated quality of these literary discussions becomes apparent. Children are tucked up close to each other, talking with animation, seriousness, and sometimes passion about the novels they have chosen to read. Among the titles being discussed today are *Sarah Plain and Tall* by Patricia MacLachlan, its sequel *Skylark*, *The Train to Midnight* by Janie Lynn Panagopoulos, *The Hundred Dresses* by Eleanor Estes, *Trouble Don't Last* by Shelly Pearsall, and *On My Honor* by Marion Dane Bauer.

The group reading *The Train to Midnight,* a story about the pre–Civil War Underground Railroad, is finding some surprises in the book. Randolf opens the discussion by blurting out: "It isn't really a railroad at all—and it isn't even underground!" The other kids nod, sharing their confusion about when the train is going to show up. They are also horrified by the stories of abuse by slave owners. In today's reading, the two protagonists are hiding in a wagonload of hay, while a paddyroller (slave catcher) repeatedly stabs at the hay with a pitchfork, nearly killing them. As Mrs. Woodbury walks past the group, the kids stop her and clamor to ask: "Did this stuff really happen? Did people really treat slaves like this?"

After answering their question that yes, sadly, these things and worse really did happen to slaves in America, Melissa moves on. It is not her job to conduct this discussion. Unlike other reading activities that put the teacher on stage, in the expert mode, these book clubs are run by the students, who must take full responsibility for making them work. A few years back, Sara and Melissa used to intervene more directly. They would move from group to group, sitting in for five or six minutes each, listening in and jotting some notes about children's participation. But as Sara recalls: "The closer we got to the groups, the worse the discussion was. They were always asking us to suggest a discussion topic, interject something, or settle an argument." Sara and Melissa didn't want to encourage this kind of dependency. So now, as groups meet in their two adjacent classrooms, each teacher simply sits on a desk in the center of one classroom with a clipboard in hand, and turns to observe one group at a time. Melissa says, "We get a very good idea of their comprehension and their social skills from there. When we spot kids who need help or groups that are floundering, then we step in and join the group for a while."

Obviously, these ambitious and autonomous book clubs did not materialize out of thin Michigan air. Back in September, there were many days of thoughtful training, teacher demonstrations, and practice with short pieces of text. Sara and Melissa have worked hard to gather a rich array of book choices, making sure that there are multiple copies of really exciting books at all reading levels, including books in Spanish for newly arrived Mexican kids. During book clubs, students are supposed to be reading at their independent, recreational level—not struggling with tough "instructional level" text, which is tackled at other times of the day. Helping kids form their own groups with just-right books and with harmonious companions takes skillful teacher steering in the early days. And keeping a useful reading journal requires training, too—so Sara and Melissa share their own book journals, show examples from last year's fourth graders, and set up practice sessions where kids see how different kinds of notes can feed into real conversations.

Sara and Melissa have been using and revising literature circles in their classrooms for nine years now. What's changed? "We've found over the years," Sara says, "the more control we gave up, the better the discussions got. The more we dictated how many pages to read, or what roles kids should take, the flatter the discussions were. If we stand back, they come up with their own ideas that are much better than ours." They've also worked to integrate book clubs into the broad thematic units they have designed to shape kids' whole fourth-grade experience. Under the year-long theme of "Paddle to the Past," kids are reading, writing, and investigating extended topics like these:

The Big Chill (geography of Michigan and the Great Lakes)

The Adventure Begins (Michigan's first people, the native Americans)

Nature's Gifts (lumbering and mining)

Traders in Time (fur trapping and trading)

The Quest for Equality (slavery and the Civil War)

Shipping and Shipwrecks of the Great Lakes

Motion and Design (the automobile industry)

With all these rich topics being pursued, Sara and Melissa are constantly building their collection of books and articles for literature circles. They are always looking for nonfiction, maps, and primary sources as well as fiction. They're especially on the lookout for local authors like Janie Lynn Panagopoulos, who writes meticulously researched historical novels for children about regional themes.

Sara and Melissa's literature circles turn traditional reading instruction upside down in almost every dimension. The children, not the teacher, pick the books. Everyone doesn't read the same book at the same time. With fifty kids in these two sections of fourth grade, there are usually ten different five-member groups meeting at once, each reading a different novel. The groups are temporary and are formed on the basis of student interest in a particular book. The readings are not short, linguistically controlled basal stories but real, whole, unabridged books, drawn from the worlds of children's, young adult, and classic literature. Kids are pursuing their own discussion questions, not following the cues of the teacher or textbook study questions. The reading teacher's role has shifted from being a presenter/questioner at the center of attention to that of an unobtrusive, quiet facilitator and documenter. In this activity, the students are the ones making the assignments, raising the questions, doing the talking and working.

Perhaps most different, the kids love this kind of reading class. They lobby Sara and Melissa for extra meeting time and complain noisily whenever school events rearrange the schedule and shortchange their literature circles. At the end of the year, when Sara and Melissa ask their students which classroom activities worked best for them, literature circles usually top the kids' favorites list. As eleven-year-old Cary put it last spring: "Our book clubs really changed the way I look at reading. I didn't enjoy it before. But after I could share books with my friends, I really loved it. It gave me a reason to want to read it—you could be in the story with the other people."

Today, Sara and Melissa are sharing literature circles with other teachers from all around the Midwest. In the middle of a hotel ballroom, they set up a classroom just like the ones back in Hart, with all the same books and lamps and music and up-north tchotchkes. Then they put teachers into book clubs and show them how to read, question, make notes, meet, talk, argue, and laugh. They cheerfully answer a thousand management questions and share all the forms, handouts, and assessment tools they've developed over the years. They explain to colleagues how kid-led book discussion clubs are not just student-centered and fun, but also help meet state and national standards for comprehension instruction. And they show teachers how authentic reading activities like these also prepare students to pass high-stakes tests like the Michigan Educational Assessment Profile (MEAP) test.

STANDARDS FOR BEST PRACTICE IN READING

Reading invariably comes first on everyone's list of basic academic skills, and we certainly endorse that ranking. After all, much of the information that school (and life) offers us is coded in print, and students' ability to unlock and use all this knowledge depends on fluent, skillful, critical, and independent reading. And while reading instruction always has its passionate controversies, the professional consensus about state-of-the-art reading instruction is stronger and clearer than ever today. The act of reading is no longer the "black box" mystery it was thirty years ago. We now understand quite well how reading works, and we agree—well, pretty much—about how to teach it to the vast majority of children.

Several landmark documents have defined Best Practice in reading. An early base for national standards was established by the influential *Becoming a Nation of Readers,* published by the National Institute of Education (Anderson et al. 1985), and *New Policy Guidelines for Reading,* issued by the National Council of Teachers of English (Harste 1989). In 1996, the NCTE and the International Reading Association (IRA) issued the definitive *Standards for the English Language Arts,* and shortly thereafter began issuing a series of books (Crafton 1996; Sierra-Perry 1996; Smagorinsky 1996; Wilhelm 1996) that illustrated the standards in classroom practice. While the material elaborating and applying the IRA/NCTE standards fills many volumes, the standards themselves are simple and direct.

Around the time these standards were being promulgated, some other national groups developed complementary materials of their own. The New Standards Project, a venture of the National Commission on Education and the Economy, outlined a similarly challenging literacy curriculum. Among other things, it called for all students to read twenty-five books per year, effectively mandating far more reading than the majority of U.S. students were then (or now) doing—and underscoring the IRA/NCTE call for genuinely wide reading. The then-fledgling National Board for Professional Teaching Standards (NBPTS), in an attempt to define proficient teaching in language arts classrooms, developed a framework that was highly congruent with the IRA/NCTE documents. To this day, the NBPTS certification process rewards teachers who faithfully enact the IRA/NCTE standards.

IRA/NCTE Standards for the English Language Arts

1. Students read a wide range of print and nonprint texts to build an understanding of texts, of themselves, and of the cultures of the United States and the world; to acquire new information; to respond to the needs and demands of society and the workplace; and for personal fulfillment. Among these texts are fiction and nonfiction, classic and contemporary works.

2. Students read a wide range of literature from many periods in many genres to build an understanding of the many dimensions (e.g., philosophical, ethical, aesthetic) of human experience.

3. Students apply a wide range of strategies to comprehend, interpret, evaluate, and appreciate texts. They draw upon their prior experience, their interactions with other readers and writers, their knowledge of word meaning and of other texts, their word identification strategies, and their understanding of textual features (e.g., sound-letter correspondence, sentence structure, context, graphics).

4. Students adjust their use of spoken, written, and visual language (e.g., conventions, style, vocabulary) to communicate effectively with a variety of audiences and for different purposes.

5. Students employ a wide range of strategies as they write and use different writing process elements appropriately to communicate with different audiences for a variety of purposes.

6. Students apply knowledge of language structure, language conventions (e.g., spelling and punctuation), media techniques, figurative language, and genre to create, critique, and discuss print and nonprint texts.

7. Students conduct research on issues and interests by generating ideas and questions and by posing problems. They gather, evaluate, and synthesize data from a variety of sources (e.g., print and nonprint texts, artifacts, people) to communicate their discoveries in ways that suit their purpose and audience.

8. Students use a variety of technological and informational resources (e.g., libraries, databases, computer networks, video) to gather and synthesize information and to create and communicate knowledge.

(continues)

IRA/NCTE Standards for the English Language Arts *(continued)*

9. Students develop an understanding of and respect for diversity in language use, patterns, and dialects across cultures, ethnic groups, geographic regions, and social roles.
10. Students whose first language is not English make use of their first language to develop competency in the English language arts and to develop understanding of content across the curriculum.
11. Students participate as knowledgeable, reflective, creative, and critical members of a variety of literacy communities.
12. Students use spoken, written, and visual language to accomplish their own purposes (e.g., for learning, enjoyment, persuasion, and the exchange of information).

Strengthening the Standards

The IRA/NCTE standards have now stood for a decade, without official revision from the authoring organizations. They have been adopted, at least as overarching goals, by many state education departments, and have guided much curriculum and materials development. But the IRA/NCTE standards by themselves are quite general. They cover much more than just reading: incorporating writing, speaking, and listening; reaching out to nonprint media and technology; and addressing a wide range of higher-order thinking skills. For more detailed research findings and more explicit classroom guidance about reading, we need to look further. Happily, many important research and practice documents have continued to grow up around the IRA/NCTE standards, fleshing out and reinforcing their recommendations.

The 1996 standards were built on an emerging view of reading as a kind of thinking, a special type of cognitive work. Since then, this reading-as-thinking paradigm has been further investigated and strongly validated. Thanks to researchers like Keene and Zimmerman (1997) and Duke and Pearson (2002), we better understand the repertoire of cognitive strategies that proficient readers use to enter, unlock, comprehend, remember, and use text. Though many different inventories of reading-as-thinking skills have been proposed, mainstream researchers agree that all skillful readers:

- visualize (make mental pictures or sensory images)
- connect (link to their own experience, to events in the world, to other readings)
- question (actively wonder, surface uncertainties, interrogate the text and author)
- infer (predict, hypothesize, interpret, draw conclusions)
- evaluate (determine importance, make judgments, weigh values)
- analyze (notice text structures, author's craft, purpose, theme, point of view)
- recall (retell, summarize, remember information)
- monitor (actively keep track of their thinking, adjust strategies to text at hand)

This list, meant to represent today's consensus among reading researchers and classroom practitioners, is adapted from Harvey and Steve's book *Subjects Matter: Every Teacher's Guide to Content-Area Reading* (2004).

In 2000, the National Reading Panel, a group of researchers commissioned by a U.S. Senate Committee, issued a report called *Teaching Children to Read.* Although its selection of scholars was narrow, some of its recommendations were highly controversial, and it gave disproportionate space to decoding issues, the NRP report strongly affirmed the reading-as-thinking research and reported significant gains in classrooms where the strategic reading approach was being implemented. In 2002, the International Reading Association brought a wider range of researchers together in the report *What Research Has to Say About Reading Instruction* (Farstrup and Samuels 2002), which provided a more detailed accounting of "what works" in reading. In 2003, the respected educator Regie Routman released *Reading Essentials: The Specifics You Need to Teach Reading Well,* which drew upon this whole body of research to describe the specific classroom assumptions, arrangements, and activities that constitute a research-based, Best Practice reading program.

Since the IRA/NCTE standards were first released, the field has amassed more research that confirms the thrust of the 1996 recommendations. Over the same time, literacy educators have been steadily developing classroom structures and activities that put the standards to work. Today, teachers can draw upon research-based models of reading instruction at all grade levels, thanks to developers like Allen (2000), Atwell (1998), Beers (2003), Calkins (2000), Daniels and Zemelman (2004), Fountas and Pinnell (1996, 2001), Harvey and Goudvis (2000), Miller (2002), Taberski (2000, 2002), Tovani (2000, 2004), and Wilhelm (1996, 2001).

QUALITIES OF BEST PRACTICE IN TEACHING READING

Below we explain the basic qualities and characteristics of Best Practice in reading instruction, the approach validated by our most reliable research—and the model toward which Melissa and Sara and thousands of other teachers are moving. In this section, we will be talking about the ingredients of good reading instruction for students of all ages, from kindergarten through high school. Later, we will give separate consideration to the most critical and controversial phase: beginning reading with primary-grade children. As we open this section, it's worth noting that even before the thousands of pages of reading recommendations issued since 1996, some of the clearest and most concise explanations appeared in the 1989 NCTE *New Policy Guidelines* report. Once again, we incorporate some language from those guidelines, with special thanks to Jerome Harste.

Reading means getting meaning from print. Reading is not phonics, vocabulary, syllabification, or other "skills," as useful as these activities may be. The essence of reading is a transaction between the words of an author and the mind of a reader, during which meaning is constructed. This means that the main goal of reading instruction must be comprehension.

Reading is thinking. Reading is a meaning-making process: an active, constructive, creative, higher-order thinking activity that involves distinctive cognitive strategies before, during, and after reading. Students need to learn how skillful, experienced readers actually manage these processes.

Hearing books read aloud is a key to learning to read. Regie Routman writes: "Reading aloud allows children to hear the rich language of stories and texts they cannot yet read on their own or might never have chosen to read. Our students learn vocabulary, grammar, new information, and how stories and written language work, especially when we talk about the background of a piece of writing and encourage active participation and discussion" (2003, 20). This recommendation is not just for the little ones; teachers of all grade levels (including middle and high school) should set aside time each day for reading aloud, selecting good literature or nonfiction of high interest to young people.

Reading is the best practice for learning to read. The quantity of children's reading experience is related directly to their achievement levels (Guthrie, in Farstrup and Samuels 2002). Free, voluntary reading, both in school and out, is strongly associated with gains in reading achievement (Allington 2000; Krashen 2004). Effective teachers provide time for independent silent reading every day, using structures like literature circles and reading workshop, as well as by encouraging at-home reading of a wide variety of materials.

Beginning reading instruction should provide children with many opportunities to interact with print. These include listening to stories, participating in shared book experiences, making language-experience stories and books, composing stories through play, enacting dialogue, and reading and writing predictable books. From the first day of school, books and paper and pens should be in the hands of children. If children do not have extensive book experiences before coming to school, teachers must begin by providing the reading experiences they have missed. But children should never be treated as though they have not had meaningful encounters with print; in fact, even those from the most deprived families have experienced much more interaction with written symbols than most teachers acknowledge (Paratore 2001). Instead, teachers should build from and extend what children already know about language, whether that knowledge begins with fairy tales in parents' laps or from the ample (and educationally underestimated) print appearing on computer or TV screens.

Children learn to read best in a low-risk environment. Reading experiences should allow children to take risks, make inferences, check their conclusions against the text at hand, and be wrong. Reading teachers should help children understand that predicting what will happen next in stories, jumping to conclusions, and confirming or disconfirming their hypotheses are effective and powerful reading strategies rather than errors. For the most part, teachers should avoid questions that require right answers and instead ask questions that encourage a diversity of well-supported responses. Constant penalties for being wrong, as well as an overemphasis on correctness, grades, and being right, undermine the climate of safety that young readers need to take risks and grow.

Young children should have well-structured instruction in phonics. For children just beginning to read—typically in kindergarten and first grade—it is vital to learn the sound-symbol relationships of written language. Indeed, if children do not crack the alphabetic code, reading (i.e., getting meaning from print) is effectively blocked to them. Therefore, skillful teachers provide young children with a variety of high-involvement activities that help them understand, manipulate, and use sound-symbol correspondences. But even as teachers offer this important experience, they also keep in mind that *phonics is not a subject in itself,* but rather a tool, and that the goal of teaching phonics is comprehension. As early-reading researcher Michael Pressley puts it, "skilled decoding is necessary but by no means sufficient for skilled comprehension" (2002, 294). Smart teachers carefully balance the time given to phonics in the early grades with other key beginning reading activities, and group their students carefully (though temporarily) so that those who have already mastered phonics can go on and read, rather than sitting through whole-class phonics lessons they do not need. In any case, such brief, well-designed lessons in phonics normally should be concluded by the end of second grade for all but those who have identified special learning problems.

Basal readers are not enough. Access to a wide and rich array of print and chances to read many interesting and informative books are the base of a successful reading program. Selections should go well beyond the basal reader to include a variety of materials, both narrative and expository, provide experiences with children's literature, and encourage students' self-selection of books. The Best Practice classroom is stocked with a broad assortment of print of all kinds, including poetry, newspapers, and trade books as well as content-area books and magazines. Fiction and nonfiction materials should be selected on the basis of quality and student interest and should represent a wide range of difficulty, not only so kids can experience successful independent reading regardless of their level, but also so they can challenge themselves by moving up in difficulty. Content-area teachers should use multiple textbooks and trade books, and set up environments in which students work on self-selected topics within the required units of study.

Choice is an integral part of literate behavior. Children should be encouraged to choose reading materials, activities, and ways of demonstrating their understanding of the texts they have read. Reading skills and strategies should be presented as options rather than as rules to be universally applied under all reading conditions. Teachers should schedule regular time periods for reading and writing, rather than giving brief, narrow reading and writing assignments. Teacher-directed instruction in which all children in a classroom or reading group are constantly required to make the same response limits rather than empowers young readers.

Kids need easy books. There's a mistaken assumption that students should spend most of their school days reading books they can only understand with a teacher's active support. But studies show that young readers need much more of what adult readers sometimes call "beach books"—easy, predictable, enjoyable, quick reads, books you can zoom through at full speed, with a high rate of comprehension (Allington 2000). Success, not frustration, is what builds reading power and fluency. If you doubt this, interview some highly sophisticated adult readers (maybe even yourself) and you'll usually find that, as children, these folks spent thousands of hours "practicing reading" with Nancy Drew, the Hardy Boys, the Boxcar Kids, the Babysitter's Club, or even, God forbid, comic books or *Mad* magazines.

Teachers should model reading. Teachers should read widely along with their students, sharing their reading lives and talking about how they select books, authors, or genres. It is vital that children get to observe a joyfully literate adult who loves and uses reading in a variety of ways every day. And teachers should do more than talk about books and authors they love; they must *show* their students how they think while they read. Using a powerful teaching strategy called "think-alouds" (Wilhelm 2001), teachers can read aloud unfamiliar selections in front of their students, stopping frequently to "open up their heads" and vocalize their internal thought processes. "Hmmmm . . . Well, I already know most of this stuff about sharks . . . Wait a minute. I never heard of a shark that's not a predator . . . I'm thinking that these whale sharks might not be much like other sharks. . . . I wonder what that word means, *baleen?*" This kind of teacher modeling demonstrates for kids the complex mental processes involved in skillful reading.

Effective teachers help children use reading as a tool for learning. Teachers can demonstrate the usefulness of reading and writing by offering opportunities for children to engage in meaningful reading and writing during content-area instruction. Brainstorming questions before a subject is explored, pursuing library or Internet research projects, integrating reading and writing in content-area learning logs, and classroom activities that engage students in reading and writing in the ways they are used outside of school—all these strategies help kids see reading as a powerful tool for answering real questions.

Teachers should name and teach reading strategies directly. Research tells us that proficient readers actively visualize, question, connect, predict, evaluate, and more. Teachers shouldn't keep these cognitive strategies a secret, even from the youngest children. In a developmentally appropriate way, they should describe each strategy explicitly, model the strategy in action, do it collaboratively with kids, allow guided practice time, and then let kids use it on their own. This combination of explicit teaching and gradual transfer of responsibility from teacher to student is especially critical for struggling readers (Snow in Routman 2003).

Teachers should support readers before, during, and after reading. Assigning reading is not *teaching* reading. Simply saying "read this for Friday" can leave kids alone to struggle with the text. Instead, wise teachers "frontload" instruction (Wilhelm, Baker, and Dube 2001). Before kids read a particular text, teachers help students activate prior knowledge, set purposes for reading, and make predictions. During reading, teachers help students monitor their comprehension and construct meaning. After reading, teachers help students savor, share, and apply meaning, and build connections to further reading and writing.

Kids should have daily opportunities to talk about their reading. What do enthusiastic adult readers do when they finish a great (or disappointing) book? Usually, they look for someone to talk to, to share their views, recount their reactions, and start a conversation. Kids need the same experience. Daily sharing time, book club meetings, written conversations, dialogue journal partners, book buddies, author's chair presentations, peer-tutoring groups, and collaborative research projects are opportunities for kids to practice this kind of literate talk. Observing kids in these conversations also provides teachers with much information for gauging students' progress. As part of these sharing times, the teacher should help children to value the reading strategies they already have, and also continually introduce and invite children to try new ones (Paratore and McCormack 2000).

Students should spend less time completing reading workbooks and skill sheets. There is little evidence that these activities enhance reading achievement, and they often consume precious chunks of classroom time (not to mention book budgets). Effective teachers critically evaluate so-called skill activities before giving them to students and replace them, where appropriate, with authentic, original activities. Once students have internalized the behavioral norms of reading and writing workshops, these structures provide far more valuable and individualized "seatwork" than any prepackaged worksheet.

Writing experiences are provided at all grade levels. As well as being valuable in its own right, writing powerfully promotes ability in reading. Indeed, for our youngest emerging readers, writing in developmental spelling is often their "lead strategy" for deciphering the sound-symbol relationships of written language. At all grade levels, effective teachers provide a balance of different kinds of writing activities, including both individual, self-sponsored writings like those in journals or writing workshops and teacher-guided writing activities that help students try new genres, topics, and forms for writing.

Reading assessment should match classroom practice. Many of the current standardized reading achievement and basal series tests focus on atomized subskills of reading, and do not stress the essence of reading, which is comprehension. The best possible assessment occurs when teachers observe and interact with students as they read authentic texts for genuine purposes, and then keep anecdotal records of students' developing skills, problems, changes, and goals in reading. Regie Routman describes one-to-one assessment conferences in which the teacher leads a child through these steps (2003, 105):

Bring me a book you can read pretty well. Why did you choose this book?

What is the reading level of this book for you?

Tell me what the book is about so far.

Read part of this book for me.

Tell me what you remember about what you just read.

Let's discuss your strengths and what you need to work on.

How different this caring conversation is from a multiple-choice test that children fill out in silence and fear.

We think that the foregoing list of principles and practices is amazingly simple. These recommendations don't require any complex, futuristic innovations; instead, they invite a thoughtful return to some fundamental instructional strategies that amply predate the basal era: reading good literature aloud; having kids read lots of whole, real books; providing much writing practice; encouraging the patient and varied discussion of the ideas in books; and making the teacher a model of literacy.

THE CONTROVERSY OVER BEGINNING READING

The so-called Reading Wars have lasted over fifty years, pitting skills-centered instruction against more holistic approaches. The contrasting paradigms are often expressed as phonics versus literature, or drill versus play, or teacher control versus student autonomy. The opposing sides constantly launch research studies, invective, and accusations at each other, making primary-grade teachers feel even more nervous about whether they are doing the right thing for the beginning readers in their care.

The most recent skirmish in this endless war has erupted around federal No Child Left Behind legislation and its insistence on phonics-centered programs, for which the government has even endorsed specific commercial materials. In its zeal to put phonics activities at the center of the literacy curriculum, the U.S. Department of Education has lately been encouraging schools to adopt reading programs like "Direct Instruction." The developers of DI claim that kids need a synthetic spelling and punctuation system, along with strictly controlled introduction of vocabulary, in order to learn to read. These assumptions lead to "stories" like the one in Figure 2.1, from a DI textbook.

It's easy to see why many teachers (and reading researchers) find "stories" like this highly problematic—and polarizing. Why would we present kids with text in forms (no capitals, strange letters, special markings) that contradict all the "environmental print" they have seen through their first five years of living? Why start youngsters off with a writing system they will have to *unlearn* later on, in order to function in standard English? Why teach kids inaccuracies about how English is spoken (in this case, that the word *the* is always pronounced with a long *e*)?

And, most of all, why would you give kids weird stories like this? "A Girl in a Cave" lacks the believability, predictability, and character development

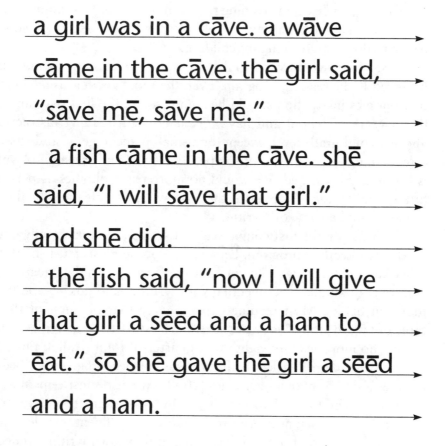

a girl in a cāve

 a girl was in a cāve. a wāve
 cāme in the cāve. thē girl said,
 "sāve mē, sāve mē."
 a fish cāme in the cāve. shē
said, "I will sāve that girl."
and shē did.
 thē fish said, "now I will give
that girl a sēēd and a ham to
ēat." sō shē gave thē girl a sēēd
and a ham.

Figure 2.1: Story from a Direct Instruction textbook

that are hallmarks of effective children's literature. Indeed, the story events
are nonsensical, almost random. Of course, there is a rhyme to this unrea-
son: in such phonics-driven materials, meaning is secondary to the sequenced
appearance of certain sounds and vocabulary. The fact that these materials
are especially marketed to inner-city schools also troubles many educators,
given the infamous claim of DI's original developer, Sigfried Engelmann, that

Black American children do not possess a fully developed human language (Bereiter and Engelmann 1966).

Now you can see why this reading debate is called a *war*, and why the NCTE and the IRA have come down so strongly in favor of the progressive, holistic, literature-based paradigm. We've written elsewhere about this endless wrangle and the dubious kinds of "scientific proof" used to support various partisan and extreme reading programs (Daniels 1996). But here, we just want to offer some perspective on phonics for educators and parents who are trying to do the right thing for children.

First of all, we must remember that phonics is only one ingredient in a balanced K–12 reading program. Even the most vociferous advocates agree that phonics instruction should be completed in the first two (and certainly three) years of school and has little to do with reading instruction much above second-grade level, except for a small percentage of students with specific learning disabilities or other special needs. Once the sound-symbol code is learned, it is learned. We would no more teach phonics as part of, say, a fifth-grade "reading" program than we would teach the alphabet to high schoolers in the name of "writing."

Even during the first couple years of school, phonics is only one part of an effective reading program. Lessons in word analysis must share time with other key activities that help young readers grow, including hearing good literature read aloud, experimenting with writing, and talking about the ideas found in books. Most reading experts agree that phonics, or the broader topic of "word study," is one of several necessary daily activities, and should occupy no more than an eighth to a quarter of total reading time. Even the National Reading Panel, for all its focus on decoding, prescribed just ten minutes a day of phonics activities (2000). We also must remember that the majority of children, 60 to 80 percent by most estimates, can learn all the phonics skills they'll ever need from naturalistic, fluent, ample real reading and (especially) from practicing spelling in their own writing. Indeed, many children crack the alphabetic code at home before ever coming to school. All this puts the role of phonics in perspective: in a responsible and balanced K–12 reading program, phonics amounts to less than 5 percent of the instructional efforts teachers make.

Phonics may be just one ingredient in a properly balanced reading program, but it is a "gateway" skill; if you don't crack the alphabetic code, you can't read. Happily, most kids do break the code and do so early. However, a fraction of children, including a disproportionate number of poor and minority kids, do not acquire their sound-symbol ideas in an embedded, automatic way. But they can learn and use these strategies when they are taught directly. To be certain that we give all children what they need without overteaching phonics for some and underserving others, we must carefully balance time and activities. Below are six key ingredients for a Best Practice first-grade reading program based upon consensus, mainstream research (Braunger and Lewis 1997; Fountas and Pinnell 1996; Routman 2003).

Ingredients of a Balanced First-Grade Reading Program

1. Reading good literature aloud
2. Shared reading (teacher-guided discussions of visual texts, including language-experience stories, "big books," other literature)
3. Independent reading at child's fluency level (wordless books, picture books, chapter books, nonfiction materials)
4. Comprehension instruction through small guided reading groups
5. Phonics and word study (including word sorts, word walls, word families, spelling patterns)
6. Writing (journal keeping, stories, responding to literature; using age-appropriate developmental spelling and drawing)

If a primary teacher allows roughly equal classroom time for each element, we see that explicit, separate instruction in sounds and words might occupy 15 to 20 percent of reading and language arts time—a fractional but important component. Nor are the recommended phonics activities dull, mechanistic drills—rather, they are lively strategies like *word sorts* (when kids arrange words on cards into different kinds of sets), *word walls* (where students cover the classroom walls with huge inventories of words, grouped and regrouped by the way they sound or what they mean), and *personal dictionaries* (in which students record words as they learn how to say, spell, and read them), along with a variety of whole-group choral, singing, and chanting games. Furthermore, sound-symbol relationships get explicit and embedded attention any time children are spelling words in their own writing, as well as when the teacher draws their attention to sounds, letters, or syllables as part of a guided reading lesson.

Once young children are reading fluently (i.e., consistently applying their phonetic knowledge in making meaning from print), phonics instruction should be over. Children will continue to practice their newly acquired phonetic understandings by reading age-appropriate texts and writing using developmental spelling. The portion of the day previously devoted to word analysis in the form of phonics can now be used for vocabulary study. Further phonics instruction may well be needed for a small fraction of children who still need help, and should certainly be offered to them individually or in small groups, but not as whole-class lessons that would steal most classmates' reading time.

DON'T FORGET THE BIG KIDS (THIRD THROUGH TWELFTH GRADE)

The endless controversies over beginning reading often overshadow the reading needs of intermediate, middle, and high school students. And that's a shame, because reading instruction is far from done when kids crack the alphabetic code at six or seven, and start reading fluently. As students move up through the grades, they meet increasingly difficult concepts in mathematics, science, and history, and the kinds of text they encounter pose new challenges. The reading skills learned in the primary grades are no longer enough; kids need to constantly redevelop their repertoire of ways of thinking about text.

Happily, the spotlight seems to be shifting toward older kids' reading. As usual in American education, this renewed attention was initially sparked by disappointing test results. According to the National Assessment of Educational Progress, only 3 percent of American teenagers are "advanced" readers. And according to a recent study by the American College Testing program (ACT), of the 1.2 million students who took its tests last year, only 22 percent were ready for college-level work in English (ACT 2004). International comparisons of student achievement seem to confirm these weaknesses, consistently putting America's teenage readers in the middle of the pack. Even more worrisome, in states that have initiated high-stakes graduation assessments, arbitrary cutoff scores are labeling hundreds of thousands of teenagers as failing readers, and have prevented many from receiving a high school diploma. We also know that our country has 60 million "adult illiterates," so there's clearly room for improvement in the reading skills of young adults.

The reading research and standards documents we have been discussing have just as many applications for older students as they do for primary children. In our own recent book, we argue that intermediate and adolescent readers need three things: a balanced diet of good books, an expanding repertoire of cognitive strategies, and the social skills to interact productively with classmates around books and ideas (Daniels and Zemelman 2004).

For generations, America's young readers have been hamstrung by our system's overdependence on textbooks, and the concomitant neglect of important shorter texts, fiction and nonfiction trade books, primary sources, and more recently, hypertext. But things are changing. To both engage and strengthen young readers, teachers are moving toward a more balanced mix of real-world material in a variety of genres. They use textbooks more selectively, helping students to dig deeper into a smaller number of topics. They supplement textbooks with an array of other sources—especially ones with alternative interpretations, contrary views, or competing hypotheses. They also value and create time for free voluntary reading, not just in English but across the curriculum. In science, social studies, and even math classes, teachers are building classroom libraries where kids immerse themselves in biographies, historical novels, journals, magazines, and current trade books related to the field. And as they create these collections, teachers recognize that *all kids need books they can read,* which means gathering reading materials at a wide range of reading levels, from comics to encyclopedias.

The reading-as-thinking approach of the IRA/NCTE standards takes on added significance as kids move up through the grades, encountering new genres, tougher, more technical text, and more challenging writing styles. Students continue to need teacher demonstrations, think-alouds, and strategy lessons that help them tackle ever more difficult materials. Lately, a number of authors have offered workable models and materials that help students understand and remember subject-matter material, while stressing enjoyment, engagement, and positive reading attitudes (Beers 2003; Daniels and Zemelman 2004; Robb 2003; Tovani 2004). And big kids still need to study *words;* at this age level, with phonics long since mastered, word study can focus on vocabulary. But this doesn't have to mean word-list drudgery: authors like Blachowicz and Fisher (2001) and Allen (1999) offer lively, playful approaches that help words really stick with kids.

Talking about books is a definitive trait of lifelong readers. So, because they value literate conversation, teachers make their classrooms into collaborative communities where kids can work effectively in pairs, teams, inquiry groups, book clubs, and other peer-led groupings. This kind of decentralized, cooperative literacy work runs counter to traditional, teacher-centered school culture, and may require "reprogramming" kids at the start of the school year. Nancy Steineke (2002) has shown how teenagers can interact successfully around books in school by developing the skills of friendliness, active listening, face-to-face interaction, mutual interdependence, reflective debriefing, and individual self-assessment.

CONNECTING WITH PROGRESSIVE PRINCIPLES

It is important to recognize how the many recommendations in this chapter reflect the thirteen principles of Best Practice outlined in Chapter 1 (pp. 10–21). While we'll leave it to the reader to recognize these connections in later chapters, we want to offer here at least one "guided tour"—showing that, in the field of reading, those thirteen principles are not just *pro forma* abstractions, but powerful guides to both general policy making and practical teaching. Later, in Chapter 8, we return to the principles to reflect on ways they are commonly applied in all of the major school subjects.

Perhaps the most fundamental theoretical construct in Best Practice reading instruction is its *cognitive,* psycholinguistic orientation, which simply says: children learn to read the way they learn to talk, and school ought to operate accordingly. When young children are learning to speak, adults do not try to teach them the subskills of talking or put them through speaking drills. Mostly, what they do is surround kids with real, natural language, talking to them and around them all day long. Young children listen and vocalize, playing and pretending with sounds and words, creating successively better approximations of talking. Parents treat all of the child's utterances, no matter how fragmentary or idiosyncratic, as meaningful. If a nine-month-old infant murmurs "ta," nearby parents are likely to rush to the cribside exclaiming, "She said 'Daddy'!" Parents intuitively offer heaps of immediate feedback and indiscriminate encouragement for any communicative effort. By the time children are five, they have mastered more than 90 percent of the structures of adult language, not through direct teaching or correction but through immersion, demonstration, and experimentation.

In the same way, children learn to read experientially, by being immersed in real texts and real literacy events from an early age. No one needs to break down written language into segments or sequences for kids; they learn best holistically, when they are exposed to complete, real texts that exist in their world, including books, menus, signs, and packages. They learn to read by playing at reading, by making closer and closer approximations of reading behavior. A familiar example of this is when young children memorize a book that has been read to them repeatedly, until they can recite it while the pages turn. Parents sometimes worry that this is not "real reading" because the child has "only memorized" the words—but teachers recognize such approximations as vital steps toward literacy.

Children who are learning to read are not just receiving and absorbing a system that exists outside of them, but rather they are *constructing* that system anew, for themselves. In oral language, we recognize this phenomenon in kids' use of unheard forms like *goed* or *foots*. The existence of these invented but entirely logical word forms shows that the kids are not merely absorbing an adult system, but are creating new intermediate language systems, using rules that they originate. In literacy, we see this constructivism clearly in the phenomenon of invented spelling, where children who are first trying to spell the short vowel sounds will substitute from their existing inventory of long vowel sounds the one with the most similar manner of articulation in the mouth. And, of course, all this literacy learning is individually *developmental*—that is, it proceeds through a number of predictable and well-defined stages. Although the sequence is roughly the same for all kids, the age and rate of change will differ significantly from child to child.

Children learn to read best when the materials they read are *authentic* and *challenging.* The old textbooks and the latest "decodable-text" products all are designed to offer near-perfect materials for beginning readers by limiting length and controlling vocabulary, but this intention usually backfires. Synthetic stories of the "seed and ham" variety are often harder for kids to read than seemingly more complex and uncontrolled literature. This is because logic or playfulness or simple interest are often sacrificed in the effort to control linguistic features, thus rendering the story unreadable. In other words, fake easy stuff can be harder to read than hard real stuff. Of course, there's nothing new or shocking about this—it always has been somewhat peculiar for adults to "control reading vocabulary" for six-year-olds who know and routinely use words like *pterodactyl, tyrannosaurus,* and *Jurassic.* We must not belittle the powers of emerging readers any more than we patronize young speakers. If we respect what kids can do with language, they'll not only tell us a lot, they'll also choose whole, real books for themselves.

Wise reading teachers are *student-centered,* encouraging kids to follow their interests and choose their own books regularly. One of the insights from family literacy research is that in the ideal parent-child bedtime episode, the child, not the parent, picks the book and sets the pace for reading and talking. Learning to read, like learning anything else, is driven by curiosity and interest on the part of the learner; if these elements are missing, the motive for learning is absent. In school, when teachers always and only choose the stories or books to be read, motivation is sacrificed for most students most of the time.

Literacy is *socially* constructed and socially rooted. While there are obviously some solitary moments in the reading and writing process when the reader or writer bends her head over a page, the beginning motive and ending payoff for most literacy work is still profoundly social. In the "real" world, people read and write for some social purpose, to get or give information from or to someone else, for some real reason. The traditional school approach to literacy has cut kids off from this social connection and purpose for literacy, rendering too many reading activities into lonely, alienating exercises. Instead, children grow better amid rich and regular interaction, in classrooms where *expression* and *collaboration* are the norm, where there are many chances to read and write and talk with other readers.

Of course, classroom reading instruction itself is a complex social enterprise with powerful relationships and meanings. For just one example, consider how students traditionally have been grouped in three levels for reading by some measure of "ability," past reading achievement, or intelligence. We now recognize that this practice is unnecessary and often destructive: the research on such tracking shows that it invariably harms the achievement and attitudes of the children assigned to the middle and low groups, while proving little or no benefit for even the highest-ranked group. Today we seek a more heterogeneous classroom, not just for the *democratic* model it offers, but also for the genuine richness and stimulation that a diverse class of readers provides. Teachers are perfecting classroom structures and strategies—like Sara and Melissa's literature circles—that make tracking irrelevant and unnecessary. Such activities are inherently individualized; when kids group themselves, flexibly and temporarily, no one needs to be classified and segregated. Everyone benefits and everyone can work in the same room.

Finally, not only do growing readers need to develop a repertoire of cognitive strategies for predicting, monitoring, and evaluating texts, they also need to practice metacognition. Kids need to become *reflective,* actively examining the meanings they construct from what they read as well as noticing their own reading processes and strategies. This is one reason why journal keeping and portfolios are both such important tools in Best Practice classrooms. Both of these structures invite students to reflect regularly—keeping track of what one reads and writes, jotting down responses and plans, reviewing one's own history and accomplishments as a reader, and pondering the nature of one's own thinking processes.

We realize that this simple, innocent segment of the public school curriculum called *reading* is perennially afflicted with pseudoscientific claims, transient fads, instant cures, political vendettas, and professional posturing. Nor, unfortunately, does this tangled state of affairs seem likely to change in the immediate future. This leaves all of us raising or educating children to find our own way through the adamant claims, counterclaims, and conflicting research. But the human beings called teachers matter most of all. As Regie Routman reminds us: "Without devoted teachers to individualize instruction for the students in their classroom, any program—even a scientifically proven one—will be, at best, minimally effective. Art and science must always work together" (2003, 10). In the end, wise teachers and responsible school districts will ground their reading instruction in a deep understanding of children and in the recommendations of reputable, enduring professional organizations that are guided by the preponderance of responsible research, educators and experts who have shown that they have children's best interests at heart.

HOW PARENTS CAN HELP

The crucial role of home experience in the development of effective readers is well documented and has been widely publicized. When children grow up in print-rich homes, where literacy is a tool of day-to-day family life, where stories and words are treasured, where reading aloud is a bedtime ritual, good readers usually emerge. The International Reading Association web-based brochures offer commonsense advice to parents of children from preschool to teenage years (http://www.reading.org). The IRA materials are realistic, and acknowledge that many effective young readers also watch a lot of TV, but emphasize that even poor families who don't own many books can create rich print experience with newspapers and library books.

Nevertheless, some parents are so stressed, distracted, or exhausted by their own lives that there's no energy left for reading at home; obviously, this problem especially afflicts poor, single-parent families, and it is their kids who disproportionately fail at reading. So schools in turn can support parents.

■ Without becoming intrusive missionaries, teachers can show parents how to integrate simple and natural literacy-building experiences into the family routine. In Lynn Cherkasky-Davis' kindergarten class in Chicago, each week begins with children reporting about the stories their parents read to them. Lynn requires that some adult—a grandparent or sibling or neighbor if parents aren't available—does the job. At the start of the year, when Lynn meets parents for the first time she tells them about the importance of reading to their children, and instructs them that their kids must come prepared each week having been read to. Saying no just isn't a viable option. Once each week, when Lynn's five-year-olds go home, each child has identified a book to read that evening with someone. They leave the classroom carrying a plastic-handled bag with a book inside, withdrawn overnight from Lynn's large classroom library. These books are always treated with care and respect, and returned on time.

■ In Milwaukee, Jim Vopat runs a Parents' Literacy Project where inner-city parents meet one night a week to build confidence in their own reading and writing as well as their ability to help their children. They hear stories read aloud, they write or draw in response to these stories, they keep journals, they interview each other, they learn how to use their public library, and they learn exactly what's happening in their children's schoolrooms from their kids' teachers. During each weekly meeting, parents try one new literacy experience within the deepening familiarity of the workshop; then, every week, they return to their own families to try out a variation of this experience with their own children. Everything the parents do in the workshop underscores and supports what teachers are doing with their children.

■ But for those kids whose parents and families, for whatever reason, currently fail to nurture literacy it must be substituted, provided in some analogous form, at school. Every child needs to go through the "lap stage" of reading development, ideally at the ages of two, three, and four, with a parent. But if this doesn't happen, then echoing the intimate, one-to-one reading relationship is exactly what special tutoring programs like Reading Recovery are all about. School must be ready, not to *be* the parent, but to fill in analogous adult-child literacy experiences that were missed at home.

WHAT PRINCIPALS CAN DO

- Be a reader and a writer. Visit classrooms and read aloud or discuss books with children. Write and share your writing in the school community.

- Be an audience for students. Read kids' work on the walls and in classrooms. Let the authors know you've read and appreciated their words. Have a principal's mailbox, and enter into active correspondence with kids.

- Make sure classrooms have all the supplies and materials needed to create a true reading workshop atmosphere; above all, this means *books*. Help teachers tap the right budget lines to buy books, encourage parents to raise money for more books, hold bake sales if necessary to get more books into classrooms.

- Celebrate literacy in your school. Incorporate reading and writing into special school events and programs. Create space and occasions for displaying and sharing written work noncompetitively. Everyone needs an audience, not a contest with few winners and many losers. Contests that stress only quantity of reading or writing degrade literacy and invite cheating.

- Help teachers communicate with parents *proactively* by letting them know how reading and writing are being taught and why the school has embraced its model of literacy education, and *reactively,* by stepping in and supporting the teachers when uninformed or skeptical parents question their book choices or activities.

- Use your role as instructional leader, supervisor, and evaluator. Let teachers know it's good to use language arts/reading time to read aloud, do storytelling, conduct a daily reading or writing workshop, share dialogue journals, or adopt other promising practices. In your classroom visitations, evaluate congruently: if teachers are using a process approach, you'll see non-presentational, highly individualized, student-centered workshop activities in which the teacher mostly takes a facilitator/coach role.

- Work at the district level to align the curriculum guide, textbook adoptions, and the standardized testing program with good reading instruction. It may be necessary to work for the *dis*adoption of basals, skill-and-drill workbooks, certain standardized tests, or other materials if they undermine a balanced reading curriculum. Talk to fellow administrators and help them understand and buy into the new paradigm.

■ Ask teachers what kind of professional development activities they would value and then provide them. If requested, bring in teacher-consultants, the local writing project, or other genuinely facilitative experts to help your teachers explore the research, standards, and classroom practices of good reading instruction. After the workshop phase, provide the necessary follow-up and support to help teachers "install" new practices in their classrooms.

■ Nurture continuing growth and emerging peer leadership among your staff by sending volunteer teachers to workshops, courses, summer institutes, or teachers-training-teachers events. Starting a "teacher book club" that meets once or twice a month (at school or at different colleagues' homes) has been a powerful change strategy in many schools. Support your outstanding and committed teachers by giving them a chance to lead, to share with colleagues.

■ Even though you don't have time, read the research, scan the journals, and pass along ideas and articles to your teachers. Order books that teachers request for their own growth—from Heinemann, Stenhouse, Richard Owen, the NCTE, IRA, Teachers College Press, Boynton/Cook, Christopher-Gordon, and others.

■ Help teachers find *time* to talk about teaching together, exchange ideas, work on joint projects, think and grow as a faculty.

A Feast of Books in First Grade

PAT BARRETT DRAGAN
Martin Elementary School, South San Francisco, California

The more passionate I am about children's literature and sharing it with my students, the more success I have in creating readers—children who love books, take them home each night, and talk about them as if they are old friends. This approach works for my English learners as well as the rest of my first-grade class. Of course, I include many other types instruction in literature, writing, and phonics in my reading program, but the heart of it all is the time I read aloud to the children.

Sometimes I get an almost electric tingling up my spine as I am reading a book aloud. When I get this same sort of silent "electric hum" coming from the children as well, then I *know* the book is reaching all of us! This happened recently when I read the kids David Shannon's picture book, *A Bad Case of Stripes*. Children had much to say as they worked to uncover meaning in this imaginative tale.

Shannon's book is the story of Camilla, who wakes up covered with stripes. The stripes turn into other patterns throughout the story. Ultimately we find out what causes these odd happenings, and how Camilla solves her problem. Crucial to the plot is the fact that she is craving lima beans, but doesn't think she should eat them because her friends don't like them. Here are some brief samplings of the children's thoughts about what is causing Camilla's spots, stripes, and other difficulties:

"I know! It's bacteria!"

"Ohhh! Camilla didn't wash her hands."

"She should wash her hands all the time."

"If somebody says something, she changes into it."

"Or she changes into the color of it."

"If somebody said, 'Make Camilla turn normal,' she'd turn normal. But nobody said it."

"The lima beans are magic."

"Maybe she ate too many lima beans when she was little."

There is much discussion over whether doctors should give Camilla worms, jellybeans, magic beans, medicine, or lima beans to turn her back into herself. There is a lot of use of the word *normal*.

"Maybe there's regular, normal lima beans and magic lima beans. Is that what you're thinking about, buddy?" (One child said this to another, to help his friend sort out his thoughts.)

"This story is like *Imogene's Antlers!*

"It's like *I Wish That I Had Duck Feet.*"

"Camilla wanted lima beans SOOOOOOO bad!"

"She's not eating what her body wanted."

"If she ate lima beans and changed back into normal she should eat lima beans every day. I solved the case!"

"You know how you say, 'I got a frog in my throat?'" (This child grabs his throat, so I'll "get it.") "She mighta said, 'I got a chameleon!' Get it? You know, Camilla, chameleon?"

"And now she has a bow with a rainbow color."

"And now she eats lima beans always."

I was astonished at the children's spontaneous comments and discussion as they made meaning together and built on each other's thoughts and ideas. They were *thinking* as they talked and listened to the story. These six-year-olds were doing just the kind of thinking done by smart readers of any age: mulling over visual connections, making inferences and predictions, determining what is important in the unfolding story, and evaluating the events and the story solution.

This momentous discussion was spontaneous. I was just trying to read the story—but the children were trying to figure it out. I quickly came to my senses and moved out of their way. I continued reading the story, but paused for kids' comments before and after reading each page. As different children spoke, I jotted down their thoughts. Even as I read their words now, I am reminded that sometimes my first graders know what they need even sooner than I do.

STARTING OUR DAY

Let's go back to the beginning of the morning and I'll tell you how we use our reading time. After coats and lunches have been put away and I have taken attendance, I look to see who has returned "overnight books." These are the choice treasures selected by the children to take home to read and have read to them. Students put books and homework at their seating places, so I can easily see if a book or paper is missing. I make little marks on a grid to remind myself who is missing an item. "B" means missing book, "H" means no homework. I remind children if a book was not returned, and usually it comes back the next day.

And now the fun begins. Children return books to special bookcases in the front of the room, team by team, and choose another book to take home "for overnight." There is a lot of competition to get popular books, and students are quick about making selections. Each table team has an assigned day of the week to choose first. There is great joy in getting to take a special book home. Esmeralda hugged her reading choice one morning, on the eleventh day of school, and said, "I've been waiting *forever* for this book!"

I have already read these books aloud, so children are familiar with them. This particularly helps our English learners. They have heard me read the story, have seen the pictures, and have spent time with a partner who speaks their language, looking at the book and retelling the story. There are paired copies of some books, one in English, one in another language. Children may take one or both home. I try to make sure that there are some books for all the home languages represented in our class. I keep just a few more books available for overnight than there are students. This makes it easier for children to focus on the reading material they *really* want to spend time with. Each child prints the title and reads it to me, getting help from classmates if needed. I write the title on my weekly grid. Now they are all free to read.

FREE CHOICE READING TIME—HOORAY!

Independent reading time is one of the most crucial and valuable parts of our day. This special time for books helps turn children into avid, lifelong readers, but it doesn't have to be long. Sometimes the period is as short as seven to ten minutes, while other times it lasts twenty or thirty minutes. And long rainy-day recesses can be wonderful!

Any book or magazine in the classroom is available to students, and they may read wherever and with whomever they wish. Many children want to read in our "book nook"—a cozy classroom area with over a hundred books placed "covers out" on rain gutters on the wall. Stuffed animals lurk there, waiting for children to read to them. The nook has a racecar rug to sit on and some special pillows (one in the form of a giant frog), as well as additional tubs and tubs of books. Only four or five children fit comfortably in this special space, so we take turns by "table teams." Other children read on the carpet in the library area, while some hole up under tables, at desks, or in little clusters in other places in the classroom, alone, in pairs, or in little groups.

There's nothing like sharing a good book with friends. "Look," says Brenda, with great excitement: "A mouse lemur!" She is reading an issue of *Ranger Rick* magazine with Irvin and Edgard. All three children are thrilled to learn about the mouse lemur. I'm pretty thrilled too. I didn't know there was any such kind of lemur. I mention this to the children so they will see my enthusiasm, and will realize that I am a learner too. I'm also delighted that Brenda is able to figure out the information about this animal. Edgard, who is fluent in both English and Spanish, explains all about lemurs to Irvin, who is just beginning to learn English. The *Ranger Rick* magazine article has wonderful photographs, and these visuals help all three children access the text.

Several children are sitting on the floor surrounded by open books and reading about reptiles together. Maria and Obdulia are choral reading *Sheep in a Jeep* by Nancy Shaw. Other children are comparing editions of *Come Along Daisy* by Jane Simmons in English and Arabic. And Jesús, Ariel, and Cesar are folding paper airplanes and hovering over a large book full of different kinds of planes to make (and fly after school or occasionally during a brief afternoon break). Believe me, I thought long and hard about making this paper airplane book and copy paper available to children during free choice independent reading time!

I love to watch children make reading and browsing choices based on their own intense interests in specific topics. Throughout the year Andrea has chosen several picture books and nonfiction books about animals. One spring day I comment to her that she is so lucky to know some things she is interested in already, such as her fascination with wild animals. Later, at recess, Andrea sidles up to me and confides that she really wants to be a zookeeper when she grows up. She has many questions about this job, so I help her write an email to the education department at the San Francisco Zoo.

One of Andrea's main questions is whether she needs to be a veterinarian to work at the zoo. She also wants to know how to tell when animals are sick, and whether part of her job would be to "wake up the baby animals in the morning." We are all thrilled when Andrea gets a helpful email back from the education office at the zoo.

 Dear Andrea,

The best way to become a zookeeper is to volunteer in your local zoo. As a good volunteer, you are in the front line when any jobs open up. The more science classes you have, the better; such subjects as biology, zoology, chemistry, etc., although a degree is not required.

Generally, the keepers are assigned to various animals to care for. For example, one keeper might work with primates, another might work with carnivores, still another might work with marsupials. When a keeper starts out in a job, they usually are rotated through all the animals so that they can care for any one of them. You do not have to be a veterinarian to work as a keeper.

Animals can't tell you when they are sick, so keepers are very observant. They look for how much the animal is eating, how much it is pooping, and the animal's activity level. If any of these things change, the keeper will notify the veterinarian to check the animal. I hope this helps. Thank you for your interest in the San Francisco Zoo.

Cindy Cameron
Docent Coordinator, Education Department
San Francisco Zoo

Reassured by this helpful message, Andrea continues reading books about animals. On our next visit to the school library, Andrea asks me to help her find a book about working at the zoo. These nonfiction titles are shelved too high for first graders to reach, so I hand down to Andrea a book with many large photos of wild animals. She peruses it and literally sticks her head into it. I hear her saying something over and over, right into the book. I lean in and whisper in her ear, asking what she is saying. "Too scary! Too scary!" she says. I hand her a different book and a little while later she tells me, "You are so incredible to find me just the book I need to be a zookeeper!"

During free choice reading time in my classroom, many of the students excitedly peruse large reference books they can't really read, but they learn a lot from the captions, photographs, and pictures. The children's intense interest in specific topics carries them past the difficulties of the text. They just take in whatever information they can and use the "group brain" to figure things out. At the beginning of the year, when we are just beginning to develop special relationships with books and reading, I do a lot of pretending and acting "as if." I just act "as if" the children are real readers, passionate about books and learning. And pretty soon I find that this really is the case. Most of my students are English learners and may not have access to books or reading material at home. They *desperately* need this time to connect with books (and to watch me model my own excitement as I read).

THE CHILDREN HAVE *GOT* TO HAVE IT ALL!

Now we put independent books away and join up at the class meeting area for the flag salute, some music, and of course, more stories. I am obligated to teach a basal reading series and I do so during this part of the day. The basal includes organized lessons that encompass phonemic awareness, phonics, a story to read, comprehension activities, and other literacy skills that relate to the text we read. Because phonics makes more sense to children in the context of the story, we "scavenger hunt" in our basal readers for the words that go with the phonics part of the lesson. This helps reinforce these skills. While I prefer more authentic activities with literature, the basal teachers' manual and student books give a useful structure to this part of our reading period. I adapt this basal series to the needs of my group of children, and I make sure that I also leave plenty of time for shared reading, guided reading, and other important elements of my reading program.

At the beginning of the year, the basal stories are frequently too difficult for my children. So I modify the lessons by "enlarging" story pages on the copy machine and reading the story to students as a homemade "big book." This activity helps children transition to using the actual basal reading books. It also provides a way for our English learners to participate with us, even getting the gist of the story by just looking at the pictures. Sometimes I make transparencies of stories and we read them together on the overhead projector. These transparencies are a great resource for children to use during center time, especially since they love to use the overhead projector.

This week the basal has a story for children to listen to and visualize as the teacher reads the text. But there are no pictures. Because the majority of my students are second language learners, it is imperative that I modify this lesson. No one will get anything out of an auditory activity without any props, realia, illustrations, or clues about the text. I decide to turn the story into a "drawing tale," and I draw pictures of characters and events as I read. These are not great drawings, but they give some meaning to the text, and my class is fascinated watching pictures appear on the whiteboard.

At the end of the story we form a circle, sit down, and choose characters to enact the tale, "creative dramatics" style. I "feed" characters the lines, but they can say them however they wish and are free to make up their own dialogue. Children act out the story, without props—we just imagine them. The class is enthusiastic about the drama, and our follow-up discussion indicates that children have understood the story. At the end of the lesson, Betsy, a child with an emerging command of English, comes up to me with her arms folded, hands across her heart. She is all eyes. "That was a lovely story," she says.

I believe that children have got to have it *all*—many different types of reading instruction—phonics, shared and guided reading and writing, literature books, big books and basals, fiction and nonfiction, large- and small-group instruction. Who knows what specific lessons will help all the pieces fall into place for a child? I believe that children learn lots of phonics and vocabulary through many activities woven throughout our day. As I described in my book *Literacy from Day One* (2001), we play word games with our overnight book titles. We do many phonics and language activities in the context of our reading lessons in both basal readers and leveled books, and also as we read and recite poetry and songs. Reading and writing their own stories also reinforces children's phonics skills, and many other skills as well.

SMALL-GROUP INSTRUCTION—GUIDED READING

After recess, children go to small guided reading groups with me. Guided reading is not round-robin reading, where children take turns orally reading parts of a story on command. And it is not whole-group instruction with a lengthy skills-based introduction and twenty to thirty children reading the same story. Guided reading is where I teach a small number of children, usually four to six, to read books at their *instructional* reading levels. I determine these levels by taking a "running record" for each child. When children are reading at their instructional levels (92 to 97 percent accuracy), they have to struggle just a bit but can read the material with a short introduction and a little personal help from the teacher. In my guided reading groups, children are spending their time engaged in the learning activity that will help them the most in their efforts to become literate: actual *reading*.

And what, pray tell, is the *rest* of the class doing during this time? In the past, I always provided centers during the guided reading time period, when I meet with two or three groups a day for about ten to fifteen minutes each. I finally realized that even though I spent hours getting centers ready, sometimes I saw minimal learning going on. I still provide center time for my group, but we do it later in the day. Now during guided reading, children who are not reading with me meet in their leveled reading groups to hone their reading skills.

During this time on their own, children gather in their groups around tubs of leveled books. These materials, many with multiple copies, are books children have previously read in guided reading, and can now reread and enjoy socially as well as intellectually. As they practice reading together, kids can also read the little "retelling booklets" we have made earlier in our guided reading groups. To create these, children retell the story we just read together, and I print out their words so they can use their own retelling to practice reading and illustrating. While I teach a guided reading group, I sneak little peeks at the rest of the class; I enjoy watching the interactions as students help and energize each other, build fluency and comprehension as they read and reread, talk about the stories, illustrate, and take charge of their own learning.

HELPING ENGLISH LEARNERS PRACTICE READING

While I am busy with guided reading groups, one little independent group reads together at the listening center. They have organized stacks of four or five leveled books in front of them, coordinated with a cassette tape they helped make. They create these tapes with me, with all of us reading in unison, after we read the books in the guided reading group. These children speak little English yet, but they are able to read book after book, following along as they listen to these taped stories. The stories are comprehensible because of simple pictures and our prior activities and discussions.

Students are successful at all the reading activities because they have already had small-group lessons with these materials. The books selected for this independent practice are at their specific learning levels, and children are relaxed and in charge. As they connect with text and life and each other, there is an atmosphere of play. I think that is what the children are doing: playing. They are using spontaneous expression and gaining fluency as they work to say the words, read with understanding, and make the books come to life. And they are having a great time doing it.

There are many background scaffolds or supports for these reading practice sessions. Children experience written text in many ways: by listening to real literature read aloud, through "big book" shared readings, and by reading trade books and basal texts together, often on an overhead projector "shared-reading style." They take part in guided reading lessons in small groups with leveled texts. They read and create poetry charts, act out books they love, and have many writing experiences—with mini-lessons, classroom interviews, and writing their own poems, memoirs, and stories. There is an emphasis on oral language and on connecting language with visuals to help language learners understand what is being said.

More than anything else, my students are gaining a language to depend on. Reading aloud to children gives them vocabulary, concepts, and language structures they need and helps them "own all of it." They listen to stories they love, read aloud over and over again. Many of these are "participation books," with catchy repeating phrases and sentences. Children begin to speak the language of these stories, play with the words, and try them out in their own lives. As the great children's author Bill Martin, Jr., said: "Students will only learn to read when they have language inside of themselves."

Hearing and reading glorious works of children's literature fills the children up with heaping helpings of language and story. And my kids seem to understand the importance of the work we are doing with literature and with each other. As one of my children, Sabine, told me, "Reading is for getting smart."

WORKS CITED

Allen, Janet. 1999. *Words, Words, Words: Teaching Vocabulary in Grades 4–12.* Portland, ME: Stenhouse.

———. 2000. *Yellow Brick Roads: Shared and Guided Paths to Independent Reading, 4–12.* Portland, ME: Stenhouse.

Allington, Richard, 2000. *What Really Matters for Struggling Readers.* New York: Allyn and Bacon.

American College Testing Program. 2004. Most High School Grads Not Ready for College or Work. www.act.org/news/releases/2004/10-14-04.html.

Anderson, Richard C., Elfrieda H. Hiebert, Judith A. Scott, and Ian A. G. Wilkinson. 1985. *Becoming a Nation of Readers: The Report of the Commission on Reading.* Washington, DC: National Institute of Education.

Atwell, Nancie. 1998. *In the Middle: Writing, Reading, and Learning with Adolescents* (Second Edition). Portsmouth, NH: Boynton/Cook.

Beers, Kylene. 2003. *When Kids Can't Read, What Teachers Can Do.* Portsmouth, NH: Heinemann.

Bereiter, Carl, and Sigfried Engelmann. 1966. *Teaching Disadvantaged Children in the Preschool.* Englewood Cliffs, NJ: Prentice-Hall.

Blachowicz, Camille, and Peter Fisher. 2001. *Teaching Vocabulary in All Classrooms.* Englewood Cliffs, NJ: Merrill.

Braunger, Janet, and Jan Lewis. 1997. *Building a Knowledge Base in Reading.* Portland, OR: Northwest Regional Educational Laboratory.

Calkins, Lucy McCormick. 2000. *The Art of Teaching Reading.* New York: Allyn and Bacon.

Crafton, Linda. 1996. *Standards in Practice, K–2.* Urbana, IL: National Council of Teachers of English.

Daniels, Harvey. 1996. Whole Language: What's the Fuss? *Rethinking Schools* (Fall).

Daniels, Harvey, and Steven Zemelman. 2004. *Subjects Matter: Every Teacher's Guide to Content-Area Reading.* Portsmouth, NH: Heinemann.

Dragan, Patricia. 2001. *Literacy from Day One.* Portsmouth, NH: Heinemann

Duke, Nell, and P. David Pearson. 2002. Effective Practices for Developing Reading Comprehension. In Farstrup, Alan E., and S. Jay Samuels, eds. *What Research*

Has to Say About Reading Instruction. Newark, DE: International Reading Association.

Engelmann, Sigfried, and Elaine C. Bruner. 1995. *Reading Mastery I: Storybook I.* Columbus, OH: SRA/McGraw-Hill.

Farstrup, Alan E., and S. Jay Samuels, eds. 2002. *What Research Has to Say About Reading Instruction.* Newark, DE: International Reading Association.

Fountas, Irene, and Gay Su Pinnell. 1996. *Guided Reading: Good First Reading for All Children.* Portsmouth, NH: Heinemann.

———. 2001. *Guiding Readers and Writers (Grades 3–6): Teaching Comprehension, Genre and Content Literacy.* Portsmouth, NH: Heinemann.

Harste, Jerome C. 1989. *New Policy Guidelines for Reading: Connecting Research and Practice.* Urbana, IL: National Council of Teachers of English.

Harvey, Stephanie, and Anne Goudvis. 2001. *Strategies That Work: Teaching Comprehension to Enhance Understanding.* York, ME: Stenhouse.

International Reading Association and National Council of Teachers of English. 1996. *Standards for the English Language Arts.* Urbana, IL, and Newark, DE: International Reading Association and National Council of Teachers of English.

Keene, Ellin Oliver, and Susan Zimmermann. 1997. *Mosaic of Thought: Teaching Reading Comprehension in a Reader's Workshop.* Portsmouth, NH: Heinemann.

Krashen, Stephen. 2004. *The Power of Reading: Insights from the Research.* Portsmouth, NH: Heinemann.

Miller, Debbie. 2002. *Reading with Meaning: Teaching Comprehension in the Primary Grades.* Portland, ME: Stenhouse.

National Center on Education and the Economy. 1995. *New Standards: Performance Standards, English Language Arts, Mathematics, Science, Applied Learning.* Washington, DC: National Center on Education and the Economy.

National Reading Panel. 2000. *Report of the National Reading Panel: Teaching Children to Read.* Washington, DC: National Institute for Child Health and Human Development, Department of Health and Human Services.

Paratore, Jeanne R. 2001. *Opening Doors, Opening Opportunities: Family Literacy in an Urban Community.* New York: Allyn and Bacon.

Paratore, Jeanne R., and Rachel L. McCormack, eds. 2000. *Peer Talk in the Classroom: Learning from Research.* Newark, DE: International Reading Association.

Pressley, Michael. 2002. Metacognition and Self-Regulated Comprehension. In Farstrup, Alan, and Jay Samuels, eds. *What Research Has to Say About Reading Instruction.* Newark, DE: International Reading Association.

Robb, Laura. 2003. *Teaching Reading in Social Studies, Science and Mathematics.* Jefferson City, MO: Scholastic.

Routman, Regie. 2003. *Reading Essentials: The Specifics You Need to Teach Reading Well.* Portsmouth, NH: Heinemann.

Sierra-Perry, Martha. 1996. *Standards in Practice, 3–5.* Urbana, IL: National Council of Teachers of English.

Smagorinsky, Peter. 1996. *Standards in Practice, 9–12.* Urbana, IL: National Council of Teachers of English.

Steineke, Nancy. 2002. *Reading and Writing Together: Collaborative Literacy in Action.* Portsmouth, NH: Heinemann.

Study of College Readiness Finds No Progress in Decade. *The New York Times.* October 14, 2004.

Taberski, Sharon. 2000. *On Solid Ground: Strategies for Teaching Reading K–3.* Portsmouth, NH: Heinemann.

———. 2002. *Reading with Meaning: Teaching Comprehension in the Primary Grades.* Portland, ME: Stenhouse.

Tovani, Cris. 2000. *I Read It, But I Don't Get It: Comprehension Strategies for Adolescent Readers.* Portland, ME: Stenhouse.

———. 2004. *Do I Really Have to Teach Reading?* York, ME: Stenhouse.

Wilhelm, Jeffrey D. 1996. *Standards in Practice, 6–8.* Urbana, IL: National Council of Teachers of English.

———. 2001. *Improving Comprehension with Think-Aloud Strategies.* New York: Scholastic.

Wilhelm, Jeffrey D., Tanya N. Baker, and Julie Dube. 2001. *Strategic Reading.* Portsmouth, NH: Heinemann.

SUGGESTED FURTHER READINGS

Allen, Janet. 2000. *Yellow Brick Roads: Shared and Guided Paths to Independent Reading, 4–12.* Portland, ME: Stenhouse.

Allington, Richard L. 2001. *What Really Matters for Struggling Readers: Designing Research-Based Programs.* New York: Addison Wesley Longman.

Atwell, Nancie. 1998. *In the Middle: Writing, Reading, and Learning with Adolescents* (Second Edition). Portsmouth, NH: Boynton/Cook.

Beers, Kylene. 2003. *When Kids Can't Read, What Teachers Can Do.* Portsmouth, NH: Heinemann.

Blachowicz, Camille, and Donna Ogle. 2001. *Reading Comprehension: Strategies for Independent Learners.* New York: Guilford Press.

Burke, Jim. 2000. *Reading Reminders: Tools, Tips and Techniques.* Portsmouth, NH: Boynton/Cook Heinemann.

Calkins, Lucy McCormick. 2000. *The Art of Teaching Reading.* New York: Allyn and Bacon.

Clay, Marie. 1993. *Reading Recovery: A Guidebook for Teachers in Training.* Portsmouth, NH: Heinemann.

Daniels, Harvey. 2002. *Literature Circles: Voice and Choice in Book Clubs and Reading Groups.* York, ME: Stenhouse.

Daniels, Harvey and Nancy Steineke. 2004. *Mini-lessons for Literature Circles.* Portsmouth, NH: Heinemann.

Dragan, Patricia. 2001. *Literacy from Day One.* Portsmouth, NH: Heinemann.

Fay, Kathleen, and Suzanne Whaley. 2004. *Becoming One Community: Reading and Writing with English Language Learners.* York, ME: Stenhouse.

Hindley, Joanne. 1996. *In the Company of Children.* York, ME: Stenhouse.

Miller, Debbie. 2002. *Reading with Meaning: Teaching Comprehension in the Primary Grades.* Portland, ME: Stenhouse.

Reynolds, Marilyn. 2004. *I Won't Read and You Can't Make Me: Reaching Reluctant Teen Readers.* Portsmouth, NH: Heinemann.

Sibberson, Franki, and Karen Szymusiak. 2003. *Still Learning to Read: Teaching Students in Grades 3–6.* York, ME: Stenhouse.

Smith, Michael, and Jeffrey Wilhelm. 2002. *Reading Don't Fix No Chevys: Literacy Lives of Young Men.* Portsmouth, NH: Heinemann.

READING RESOURCES ON THE INTERNET

The International Reading Association is the largest and most influential reading society and co-creator of our national literacy standards. For association news, research bulletins, publications, and conference announcements, visit http://www.ira.org.

Although a K–12 organization, the membership of the NCTE is predominantly middle and high school teachers, and NCTE is the top source of information on reading, literature, and writing for secondary students. Visit http://www.ncte.org.

The NCTE and IRA recently partnered with the MarcoPolo Education Foundation to create a highly teacher-friendly website that offers lesson plans and student materials in the spirit of the IRA/NCTE standards at http://www.readwritethink.org.

National Research Center on English Learning and Achievement (CELA) at the State University of New York at Albany is a clearinghouse for research and information about reading instruction, and features promising classroom practices for young readers. Visit http://cela.albany.edu.

Accomplished teachers who are ready to seek national certification can learn about the rigorous one-year process, find out the benefits of a successful review in their own state, and find a support group at the website of the National Board for Professional Teaching Standards at http://www.nbpts.org.

Literature teachers of all grade levels, and especially teachers facing censorship issues, rely on the American Library Association at http://www.ala.org.

RECOMMENDATIONS ON TEACHING READING

Increase	Decrease
Teacher reading good literature aloud to students	Students compelled to read aloud to whole class or reading group, being corrected and marked down for errors
Time for independent reading	Exclusive emphasis on whole-class or reading-group activities
Children's choice of their own reading materials	Teacher selection of all reading materials for individuals and groups
Balance of easy and hard books	Exclusively difficult "instructional level" books
Exposing children to a wide and rich range of literature	Relying on selections in basal reader
Teacher modeling and discussing his/her own reading processes	Teacher keeping his/her own reading tastes and habits private
Primary instructional emphasis on comprehension	Primary instructional emphasis on reading subskills such as phonics, word analysis, syllabication
Teaching reading as a process: • Use strategies that activate prior knowledge • Help students make and test predictions • Structure help during reading • Provide after-reading applications	Teaching reading as a single, one-step act
Social, collaborative activities with much discussion and interaction	Solitary seatwork
Grouping by interests or book choices	Grouping by reading level
Silent reading followed by discussion	Round-robin oral reading
Teaching skills in the context of whole and meaningful literature	Teaching isolated skills in phonics workbooks or drills
Writing before and after reading	Little or no chance to write
Encouraging invented spelling in children's early writings	Punishing preconventional spelling in students' early writings
Use of reading in content fields (e.g., historical novels in social studies)	Segregation of reading to reading time
Evaluation focused on holistic, higher-order thinking processes	Evaluation focused on individual, low-level subskills
Measuring success of reading program by students' reading habits, attitudes, and comprehension	Measuring success of reading program only by test scores

Best Practice, Third Edition by Zemelman, Daniels, and Hyde (Heinemann: Portsmouth, NH); © 2005

Chapter 3
Best Practice in Writing

HOW WRITING WAS

Steve recalls his own education in writing: "In third grade, for a geography project, I chose Canada. I went home, pulled out the *World Book Encyclopedia* my father had bought, and marked the passages I would use. I meticulously traced a map of Canada—the kind with those tiny corn plants and coal cars showing the products of various regions—and drafted my mother to type passages from the encyclopedia. 'Are you *sure* this is how you're supposed to do this?' she queried. I reassured her and began designing the cover. I received the expected "E" for excellent. We were shown no model of a good report, had no audience for our work, generated no questions we wanted to answer, received no help getting started.

"On another occasion, we wrote about a family event. I innocently described the exhilaration I felt when my father drove at high speeds on family trips. The teacher, shocked at this celebration of recklessness, humiliated me before the class with a lecture about disrespect for the law.

"And oh, yes: all the boring routines—endless worksheets and sentences copied fifty times off the board, using writing as punishment. The purpose of book reports was simply to prove that you read the book, so even if the reading was enjoyable (*Winnie the Pooh* and *Wind in the Willows* were my favorites), the reports were merely mechanical. Otherwise, writing meant 'spelling quizzes.' I was good at those. And 'handwriting.' As a lefty, I was regularly told I held my pencil wrong, and my script was hopeless. I really don't know why I didn't come to hate writing as most of the other kids did."

WRITING THE NEW WAY

Located a few blocks west of the Dan Ryan Expressway in Chicago, near the Robert Taylor public housing projects, Hendricks School serves an all–

African American student body, 98 percent at poverty level. Writing consultant Barbara Morris and teacher Tina Archuleta created a third-grade writing project centered around Cinderella stories that shows what good writing instruction can achieve. Here's how Barbara tells their story:

I suggested that Tina read to the children several versions of the same fairy tale to prime the pump. While the long-range goal was a more "pure" writing workshop where kids would choose their own topics, we felt safer beginning with a carefully staged activity that picked up on Tina's and the children's love of literature. Over two and a half weeks, Tina read aloud several versions of the Cinderella story. She started with the original, followed by Frances Minter's *Cinder-Elly*. After hearing the first two versions, the students in groups of four discussed the elements of stories and created notes they could refer to as the reading continued. They identified similarities, differences, and the parts they liked best. To get past kids' hesitancy, Tina created a crown for herself and told her students they could make their own to wear during the read-aloud time. The kids made tall ones and small ones, decorated with everything from sparkles to torn paper. This was the spark they needed. Now there was a gathering of kings and queens for each day's read-aloud.

One day, Tina read two poems instead of another book: "In Search of Cinderella" by Shel Silverstein and "Glass Slipper" by Judith Viorst. The boys really connected with Silverstein's last line, "I've started hating feet." They chanted this phrase at the girls, who indignantly responded with Viorst's closing line, "He's not nearly as attractive as he seemed the other night. So I think I'll just pretend that this glass slipper feels too tight." This spontaneous call-and-response battle of the sexes added pep and movement. Kids strutted around to the rhythms and asked for the poems to be read daily.

Over the next three weeks, Tina shared many more Cinderella stories from around the world, including:

Cinderella, retold by Amy Ehrlich

The Golden Slipper: A Vietnamese Legend, retold by Darrell Lum

Mufaro's Beautiful Daughters, by John Steptoe

The Egyptian Cinderella, by Shirley Climo

Cinder Edna, by Ellen Jackson

Princess Furball, by Charlotte Huck

Soot Face: An Ojibwa Cinderella Story, retold by Robert D. San Souci

Yeh Shen: Cinderella Story from China, retold by Ai-Ling Louie

The Korean Cinderella, by Shirley Climo

Princess Cinders, by Babette Cole.

Tina integrated geography with these stories. With each book we located its geographical source, and the kids put star stickers on the appropriate spots on their own maps. We organized a "radio read"—a readers' theater activity—for the Frances Minter book, giving reading parts to as many kids as possible. The kids then taped their performance for future classes to hear (a great way to increase reading fluency, along with motivation). And children began bringing in other Cinderella-type stories, so we filled a box with them. Of course, Tina read aloud as many as she could.

We also worked on vocabulary as she read. She asked the kids to stop her whenever they heard a new or confusing word, or a word they really liked. We created a Cinderella "word wall," with class-developed definitions, on chart paper. Kids used these words in their own writing, and the practice spread to the rest of our reading throughout the year. It was great that children weren't afraid to speak up about a word they didn't know—so they were able to learn more.

By now, the children had been immersed in literature for two and a half weeks, and it was almost time to write their own stories. But to be sure they would take the writing process seriously, Tina read the picture book *What Real Authors Do* by Eileen Christelow, about two children's authors who have different styles and interests but use the same writing strategies. The terms—*draft, edit, proofread, revise, publish*—both described the writing process and became the children's spelling words for the week. Tina taught a mini-lesson for each step, creating a model that hung on the bulletin board.

Finally, the children brainstormed some of the elements they might use in their stories. The kids listed choices for characters, settings, opening lines, problems, solutions, shoes (instead of glass slippers), and vehicles (instead of pumpkin carriages). Tina wrote their suggestions on chart paper that she left up for reference. Among the children's possibilities:

Shoes

Penny loafers	gym shoes	glass slipper
Hush Puppies	K Swiss	Nike Lugz
high heels		

Transportation

bike	convertible	BMW	broom
car	motorcycle	cab	snowmobile
CTA	Land Cruiser	carriage	garbage can
parade	horse	train	Cadillac
limo	dog	horse	Firebird

Now the children's mouths were watering at the idea of writing their own versions of Cinderella. When Tina finally said, "Now you can write!" all you could hear was, "Yes, yes, yes!" They wrote and wrote and revised and rewrote and published their stories. I was so excited to see those students I had known since first grade writing with such energy. Many of them rushed up to me, pleading to read their story. Is writing supposed to be this much fun? The children certainly thought it should be.

Tina taught a number of mini-lessons to help the children revise. She introduced descriptive adjectives using a "think-quick" activity, writing a word like *cake* on the board with a blank line before it and then asking, "Think quick! What kind of cake?" Kids would call out, "Chocolate!" or "Birthday!" We read books composed around adjectives—*A Is for Angry, Many Luscious Lollipops,* and *Feely Bugs.* She gave students five small Post-it notes each and asked them to find five good places to add adjectives to their writing.

A mini-lesson on punctuation developed around the poem "Call the Periods, Call the Commas," by Kalli Dakos, which playfully focuses on its own total lack of punctuation. Kids had a great time trying to read the whole thing without taking a breath—we were priming the pump with literature! Then we worked on a sample paragraph and noticed where the voice pauses or an idea comes to an end.

As their drafts developed, students worked in peer-editing groups, using an evaluation sheet for content and a checklist for mechanics. Through modeling, Tina taught the kids to question each other: "What was interesting? What was confusing? What parts did you like?" Tina held a conference with each child after the second draft. The conferences were long, but the students had written much more than Tina anticipated; the rest of the kids worked productively while she conferenced. After final corrections, Tina guided them to decorate their covers and design title pages. Finally, they eagerly signed up to debut their books at "Author's Chair" sharing sessions. Before the first books were read, though, Tina talked about ways that a helpful audience responds to stories. As I looked at their faces during the sharing, I realized these were truly happy children deeply pleased with what they had accomplished.

The start of third-grader Milton Dockins' story shows how all this work came together in one student's writing:

Long, long ago there lived a girl named Selly. She had two cruel stepsisters named Kelly, and Velly. Selly had one brother named Relly. He was nice and never treated Selly badly. Selly always wore an old and dirty dress. She worked almost all day doing things like washing dishes and cleaning her sister's dresses. Selly never got that much sleep when she had to do a lot of chores. One day Selly didn't feel like doing her chores. When the stepsisters saw that their dresses weren't clean, they went and said to the stepmother "Selly didn't clean our dresses." They started to yell at Selly. Selly ran, and ran, and ran. Selly stopped. Selly sat under a big, big apple tree and started sobbing. Out of no where, out came Angel. Angel was Selly's Fairy Godmother. . . .

Milton's story was typical of the whole class. Every child's work was well-structured, elaborate, detailed, full of personal voice, carefully edited, and reverberating with the structures and conventions of fairy tales. As a consultant who visits schools throughout the region, I knew that these pieces compared favorably with the writing of third graders anywhere.

What made it possible for these children—for whom many people hold such low expectations—to write so well? Above all, Tina gave children extensive prewriting experience, immersing them deeply in rich literature so that they would have plenty of content and models for writing. She reversed the traditional pattern of writing assignments where the teacher issues marching orders and then leaves children alone to gather and shape material. Tina showed kids a clear, staged process of composition, and provided help at every step. She left children plenty of room for originality within her careful guidance. She made the process social, collaborative, energizing, and fun, inviting kids to meld their own interests and culture with the fairy-tale world. The "Cinderella Workshop" was a demanding unit, but these kids enjoyed the challenge and took pride in their efforts. As Brittany put it: "We worked hard but the stories are sooooo good!" And Tina admitted, "I veered from the required curriculum to do all this. But think what the kids learned!"

A LOOK AT THE STANDARDS DOCUMENTS AND STATE STANDARDS

The blossoming over the past thirty years of research and pedagogical experiments on writing has created a clear picture of effective writing programs. George Hillocks summarized the early work of this period in *Research on Written Composition* (1986). More recently, these ideas were affirmed in *Standards for the English Language Arts*, by the IRA and the NCTE (1996), the twelve main principles of which appear in Chapter 2 on pages 41–42. For writing, the principles emphasize real audiences, students' own authentic purposes for writing, and the need for students to learn a wide range of writing strategies. These practices were elaborated in the NCTE's *Standards in Practice* series, four volumes that took readers into primary, intermediate, middle school, and high school classrooms where writing was part of an integrated approach to literacy education (Crafton 1996; Sierra-Perry 1996; Smagorinsky 1996; Wilhelm 1996). These principles have been applied and elaborated by Nancie Atwell (2003), Lucy Calkins (2003), JoAnn Portalupi and Ralph Fletcher (2004), Regie Routman (2005), and others.

Most states have, of course, established standards for teaching and learning composition, along with statewide tests of writing skills. A look at Ohio's standards and tests for writing provides a good example of the strengths and weaknesses of a typical state effort (Joint Council of the State Board of Education and the Ohio Board of Regents, 2001). We'll focus on tenth grade to get a snapshot. The Ohio standards document divides writing into four elements: (1) writing process, (2) writing applications (focused on a mixture of modes, genres, and purposes for writing), (3) writing conventions, and

(4) research. Benchmarks are outlined for each of these, at five grade levels: end of K–2, 3–4, 5–7, 8–10, and 11–12.

Typical writing process benchmarks at the end of grade ten include "Formulate writing ideas and identify a topic appropriate to the purpose and audience" and "Use revision strategies to improve the style, variety of sentence structure, clarity of the controlling idea, logic, effectiveness of word choice, and transitions between paragraphs, passages, or ideas." These goals and statements embody widely accepted concepts of the writing process. It's mystifying, however, that some valuable items for earlier grades disappear by the tenth-grade list. Fourth graders, for example, are expected to "Determine audience and purpose for self-selected and assigned writing tasks," but this deeper thinking, though it is a vital step, is absent from the high school outline lists. Other expectations and types of writing come and go at different grade levels, disappear from the general benchmarks, but reappear in the more detailed sections of the document.

The Applications benchmarks prove to be just lists of types of writing that students should master, and at tenth grade these combine literary essays with writing in fairly traditional school genres—fictional narrative, business letters, persuasive pieces, research papers. Rather quirkily, a number of more interesting kinds of writing emerge in eleventh and twelfth grade, including "reflective writings," and "functional documents," but not at grades eight through ten. Surely these kinds of writing would be highly motivating for younger writers who are just gaining confidence and need maximum connection with their own lives and with real-world purposes. In Ohio these seem to be treats reserved only for the most mature students.

Sometimes the listing of elements just seems arbitrary and confusing. The detailed tenth-grade benchmarks for Writing Applications reintroduce some forms missing from the outline version, including "informal writings (e.g., journals, notes, and poems) for various purposes." Does this mean that informal writing is somehow less important and thus doesn't rate a place in the up-front summary benchmarks? And we weren't aware that poetry was an "informal" kind of writing.

Finally, the English Language Arts Standards document ends with a series of assertions about the importance of connecting English with other disciplines, real-world issues, and technology—all valuable points. And while these connections do indeed show up in the other Ohio standards and tests on reading, science, and math, they are simply missing from the writing test itself.

Our overall judgment of these standards, then, at least for tenth grade: they combine some thoughtful attention to the research and development of Best Practice in teaching writing, but with much quirky arbitrariness and occasional reliance on traditional school-style advice about writing that does not reflect what good writers in the real world actually do.

When we turned to the tests, tenth grade meant looking at the Ohio Graduation Tests, which are mandatory high-stakes tests as of 2005. The writing test includes two writing samples, to be holistically scored, one short-answer question, and ten multiple-choice questions on writing process. Of the prompts for the fall 2004 practice test for ninth graders (Ohio Department of Education 2004), one—on whether drug testing should be required for participants in school sports—was potentially engaging. The other, on the writer's favorite season of the year, seemed like an invitation to generate fluff and filler. Most of the multiple-choice questions were about conventions or organizational structure. Disturbingly, to an experienced, published writer, a number of answer choices seemed equally acceptable, so it is likely that many competent adults would not score well. And the sample paragraphs upon which questions were based ranged from innocuous (I wasn't chosen for the basketball team even though I practiced hard!) to inane (Camping is hard work!).

While the Ohio writing test may appear mediocre, it actually compares well to those given by some other states. The 2004 Massachusetts MCAS writing test, for example, asked tenth-grade students to recall a work of literature of his or her choice that includes a heroic character and explain the nature of his or her heroism. While English teachers might argue that this involves an important literary skill they wish to validate, it presents some serious problems from a test designer's point of view, for it combines writing skills with literary analysis in a single question. A student might easily have strengths in one of these two areas but not the other, and the assessment would simply fail to reflect this fact.

At the other extreme, however, Ohio's writing tests don't have nearly the strength shown by the writing portfolios used in Kentucky, just across the Ohio river. In that state, all fourth, seventh, and twelfth graders are required to assemble portfolios of five writing pieces done in school over a period of years, and at least two of the samples must come from subjects other than English. Students also write an "on demand" piece during state tests, though the portfolio counts for much more of the overall writing score. Researchers report a dramatic increase in the amount and quality of student writing across the state. It must be added, however, that Kentucky accompanies its testing with a strong system of regional consultants to help schools where test results have been weak.

So the Ohio state standards and even the tests for writing are probably better than those of many other states. They are, however, a pale reflection of the inspired writing that kids in schools pour out on paper every day. Best Practice invites us as teachers to live up to our students' wonderful expressive abilities.

QUALITIES OF BEST PRACTICE IN TEACHING WRITING

All children can and should write. A preschooler recites a story from her "pretend" writing and later repeats it nearly word-for-word, as her parents admire her "cute" behavior. But recognizing constancy of meaning in written symbols shows that this child is already practicing literacy. Most children write long before they reach kindergarten. They make meaningful marks on paper, starting with drawings and moving through imitation writing to more conventional messages.

Children of all backgrounds bring to school extensive involvement in literacy, though the cultural patterns of language use can vary widely—not just in grammar or pronunciation, but also in purposes and occasions for talk. Teachers must build on children's strengths and then help widen their repertoires. It is vital to listen to children and learn their particular language abilities and needs, rather than assume that the teachers' own language styles and customs are universal.

Writing should not wait for reading or grammar to develop first; experimenting with written language is one of children's prime paths to reading achievement. So kids need sufficient time to complete and reflect on communicative tasks. However, these can be incorporated readily as tools for learning various subjects, rather than competing for time during the day.

Teachers must help students find real purposes to write and real audiences to reach.

 In Pat Bearden's third-grade classroom, David reads a piece about why certain kids make him angry, ticking off insults and conflicts out on the playground. The children listen solemnly and debate the justice of each charge. David is writing for himself, to the class. Later, Cherisse is

found upset at the back of the room. Her journal reveals captioned cartoon squares with a stick-animal in each. "These are my pets," she says. "They've all died." The teacher, briefly at a loss as to how to respond, finally observes, "It's hard being a child, isn't it?" Cherisse nods gravely.

When the topic matters, children work hard and invest time and effort in crafting their work. The best language learning occurs when students attempt actual communication and see how real listeners/readers react. Meaningful writing tasks bridge the cognitive demands of school and the issues of students' cultures and personalities. If the writer has no real commitment to the topic or audience, she cannot interpret feedback to learn how words communicate. Further, arbitrarily assigned topics with no opportunity for choice deprive students of practice in a most crucial step of writing—making the first decision about what to write.

Publication of writing is vital for fulfilling these purposes: making bound books, cataloging student works in the school library, and displaying products in classrooms, school hallways, local libraries, neighborhood stores, and dentists' waiting rooms. When the teacher is the only audience, students are robbed of the rich and diverse response from audiences that is needed to nurture a writer's skills and motivation.

Students need to take ownership and responsibility. The more choices teachers make, the fewer the responsibilities left for students. For a significant percentage of writing activities, students should choose their own topics. Students can look critically at their work, decide which pieces are worth continued effort, and then set their own goals.

Effective writing programs involve the complete writing process. Many children never see skillful writers at work and are unaware that writing is a staged, craftlike process that competent authors typically break into manageable steps. Teachers must help children enact and internalize such steps as the following:

- selecting or becoming involved in a topic, finding a purpose for writing, and clarifying the audience
- prewriting—considering an approach, gathering thoughts or information, mapping plans, free-writing ideas

- drafting—organizing material and getting words down
- revising—further developing ideas and clarifying their expression
- editing—polishing meaning and proofreading for publication

Teachers can help children recognize that the process varies between individuals and between writing tasks. However, just as with other crafts, not all pieces are worth carrying through all stages, and children can learn by focusing on just one or two stages for a given piece of writing. If they revise and edit just their best pieces, the work will be meaningful and likely to reflect real effort.

Yes, but . . . does this mean that teachers don't teach writing? Many students don't have the skills they need!

When students take ownership of their writing, there's actually much more teaching than before, and it's focused on higher-level thinking. Good teaching means helping students learn these authoring processes. Teaching techniques to promote real authorship and decision making include:

- modeling topic choosing and self-evaluation processes using the teacher's own writing
- brief one-to-one conferences between teacher and student (effective, however, only if the teacher asks real questions about the student's thinking process and ideas, rather than just telling the student what to fix or posing "read-my-mind" queries)
- small-group collaborative work and peer evaluation (which requires training students to work together constructively and meaningfully)

Teachers can help students get started. Support begins from the very start. Children can be helped to develop abundant ideas about self-chosen or teacher-assigned topics. Lists of topics and questions, in students' folders or on wall charts, can help kids get started on successive writing tasks on their own. Skillful teachers conduct many kinds of prewriting activities:

- memory searches
- listing, charting, webbing, and clustering of raw ideas

- drawing and sketching
- group brainstorming
- free-writing (a specific process for free probing of thoughts)
- discussion in pairs, small groups, and the whole class
- reading and research on questions students generate

Teachers help students draft and revise. "Is this your first draft or did you revise it already?" Lakesha asks her partner. For these children, revising writing is a regular activity. They've learned to ask lots of questions to discover the stage the writing is at and the needs the writer perceives *before* discussing a piece.

Successive stages in the writing process often are ignored in traditional approaches. Children can learn that good writing usually is not created in one quick shot, and they need instruction in how to revise. By using role-plays, modeling, and group problem-solving activities, teachers can explore various revision processes:

- reviewing one's work and comparing what one has said to the intended meaning
- seeing the words from the point of view of a reader, who may not know all that the writer knows about the topic
- becoming aware of styles and strategies by seeing examples from other writers
- generating multiple options for expressing an idea and choosing the one that works best

Revision is about thinking and communication, not just fixing mechanical details. Simply telling how to fix an essay may achieve a better piece of writing, but doesn't teach the child the process of revising.

Teachers must help students learn the craft of writing. While children absorb a great deal about language through listening, talking, and reading, most also need to focus conscious awareness on particular strategies for expressing ideas, ranging from ways to begin and end, to options for organizing a piece, to identifying vivid details that bring ideas to life, to composing sentences clearly and with standard English conventions.

The craft of writing is most effectively taught through brief mini-lessons focused on skills appropriate to particular writing tasks students are tackling, so the skills can be practiced immediately in meaningful settings. Effective teaching strategies for mini-lessons include modeling by the teacher on an overhead, having students compare various ways of expressing an idea, noticing good strategies in reading that the class is doing, and asking students to brainstorm a solution to a particular problem in a sample piece. Good mini-lessons also include brief sessions for practicing the new strategy, either as a whole group or individually. Then the teacher can follow up with one-on-one conferences.

Grammar and mechanics are best learned in the context of actual writing. Grammar should be integrated into later stages of the writing process and connected with writing in which students are invested. When work that writers care about is going public, they want it to look good and to succeed. Research has shown for decades (see George Hillocks' classic *Research on Written Composition,* 1986) that isolated skill-and-drill grammar lessons do not transfer to writing performance. Beginning writers in primary grades can use invented spelling, so they'll develop fluency and not waste half the period waiting for the teacher to provide the correct spelling of a word.

Students need a classroom context of shared learning.

 A teacher and three middle school writers listen to a fourth read her narrative about recuperating from a broken back. The student author asks for help with the ending and everyone makes weak suggestions. Finally, asked for more about the experience, she declares, "I was never so happy as the day I came back to school." The group cheers that she's found her ending—not through directives or criticism, but through supportive talk and listening.

Building a supportive context for working collaboratively is perhaps the most important step a teacher can take to promote writing growth (Nancy Steineke's *Reading and Writing Together: Collaborative Literacy in Action,* 2002, provides excellent strategies for this). In fact, if students don't find their classroom a safe place to try new approaches and to say what they really believe, then even the most up-to-date techniques will likely fall flat. On the other hand, when students hear one another's work in a positive setting, they're eager to try new topics and learn new strategies. Listening to each other's compositions, students discover, by examining their own reactions, what makes writing strong.

Teachers build this interactive learning context through lessons about listening and respecting other people's ideas, and through guided practice on working responsibly in small groups. The teacher must model respect and supportive questioning in her own conferences with children as well. Then children readily learn to help each other critique themselves and figure out their own improvements. This approach yields much more learning than does direct advice about how to "fix" a piece because the writer experiences the actual problem solving. Writing acquires greater value because it serves to promote learning and friendship and itself strengthens classroom community.

 Yes, but . . . don't we owe it to children to help them succeed in our culture by teaching correctness?

As with other aspects of writing, a shift in philosophy does not mean that the teacher abandons this vital concern. Rather, the aim is to make teaching efficient and effective, something that most teachers agree traditional grammar instruction has not achieved. Focus lessons can be conducted during editing, when correctness is more likely to matter to the writer (if, that is, the writing has a communicative purpose and destination) and doesn't interfere with motivation or the development of ideas. Specific grammar and mechanics lessons can then cover items appropriate to the present task or needs that the teacher has observed.

Grammar actually needs less reteaching than we think. When young children get a lot of practice reading and writing, spelling gradually moves toward conventional forms, even without direct lessons. However, teachers must promote student responsibility. Students can keep lists in their writing folders of the elements of grammar and mechanics they've mastered, as reminders to proofread rather than wait for a teacher's complaints.

Writing should extend throughout the curriculum. Students value writing and use it more when it supports many learning activities. Writing is, in fact, one of the best tools for learning any material because it activates thinking. Brief, ungraded writing activities can activate prior knowledge, elicit questions, build comprehension, promote discussion, and help students reflect on ideas covered.

Writing in various subjects need not absorb large amounts of time or create an impossible paper load. Brief exploratory efforts that make learning more engaging and efficient include these techniques:

- First Thoughts: Two- to three-minute free-writes at the start of a unit to surface students' knowledge about it
- KWL Charts: What students **K**now about a topic, what they **W**ant to know (questions or wonderings), and later, what they've **L**earned
- Admit Slips and Exit Slips: A few sentences on a notecard handed in at the *start* of class, summarizing the previous day's work or reading; or a statement of something learned (or not understood) submitted at the *end* of class
- Dialogue Journals: In reaction to material studied, students write letters discussing ideas, along with responses to them, in pairs or between student and teacher
- Stop-N-Write: Brief pauses during teacher presentations or reading periods when students jot questions, responses to ideas, or predictions about what is coming next

Teachers can read through student responses to these activities quickly to learn whether concepts are understood or not. Students receive a "check" to monitor the work or, better yet, an informal written response from the teacher. (For more about these writing-to-learn activities and artistic alternatives, see Chapter 8, pp. 234–239.)

Use evaluation constructively and efficiently. Masses of red marks on a page discourage children and don't teach revising or proofreading. Research indicates that writers grow more by praise than by criticism. (Again, George Hillocks' review of research made this clear many years ago.) Better strategies for evaluation include:

- focusing on one or two kinds of errors at a time
- brief oral conferences at various stages of the work

- portfolios or folder systems for evaluating cumulatively
- student involvement in goal setting, evaluation, and written reflection
- official grading only of selected, fully revised pieces

 Yes, but . . . won't all this writing, revising, and conferencing take more time than a teacher can possibly give?

Students need to write a lot, so much that teachers couldn't possibly mark every error in every paper. Research strongly shows that traditional intensive marking of papers doesn't promote improvement. Instead, a brief conference, or marking a sample paragraph for just one type of problem, results in more real learning. The child then takes responsibility for making the improvements in the rest of the paper. Students can periodically submit their best revised pieces for in-depth evaluation. Thus, different types of evaluation—brief/informal versus extensive/formal—are employed to suit particular purposes. Good teachers aim for learning *within the child,* not just achieving a correct manuscript.

Along with more selective marking, a sheet in each child's folder can list skills and processes the child has learned, plus brief notes on broader aspects of growth. Such records enable individualization, help children reflect on their progress, focus on actual learning rather than just the written product, and yet maintain clear accountability for both students and teachers. Growth in writing means trying something new and probably making mistakes in the process. Students must feel trust in order to take that risk, and evaluation practices should support this necessary condition for learning.

HOW PARENTS CAN HELP

- Encourage writing at home. Children's most efficient and powerful language learning—learning to speak as babies—occurs at home with complete naturalness. So continue this as kids grow.

■ Writing done at school or at home should be celebrated, just as families celebrate children's first words, clever remarks, stories, and other achievements. Playful notes can be exchanged on the refrigerator, slipped under a bedroom door, or included in the child's lunchbox.

■ Parents should respond first not to a grade, but to the content of what the child writes for school assignments.

■ Use writing at home for real purposes—chores completed, birthday-present lists, grocery lists, vacation itineraries, labels in family photo albums, invitations, letters to grandparents (encourage them to write back so children get a response), requests to companies for free information and brochures.

■ Parents can *model* this practical literacy for their children. A letter to Grandma can include one sheet from the child and one from an adult in the house.

■ Reading stories aloud at bedtime immerses children in the language of good writers, and it's pleasurable, increasing motivation for both reading and writing.

■ Parents can make literacy regular and *predictable*. A special corner with writing implements and a convenient flat surface, regular times for writing and/or reading, ritualized note-leaving and word-game times all make literacy a stable part of children's life that becomes a treasured memory as they grow older.

■ Develop family terminology to talk over the activities associated with writing and publishing: book, author, character, ending, illustration, chapter, layout, caption, and headline.

■ Parents should let children take the lead, reversing parent-child roles. Children can make decisions about what to read and write, how long to work on a project, whether to display it—and will take more ownership of writing when they have this control.

■ Parents should urge that writing receive high priority throughout their child's schooling, and should look for the kinds of teaching described in this chapter. When possible, parents should help their children's classes with publishing projects or serve as writing coaches and audiences. Good teachers will organize as much of this involvement as possible.

WHAT PRINCIPALS CAN DO

- Principals should encourage state-of-the-art teaching of composition, letting teachers know it's valuable to use language arts/reading time to conduct a daily writing workshop, journal writing, and other effective practices.

- In classroom visitations, principals should evaluate congruently: if teachers use a process approach, one will see nonpresentational, individualized activities in which the teacher mostly takes a facilitator role.

- Principals must organize time for teachers to talk about writing together, exchange ideas, work on joint projects, and think and grow as a faculty.

- More immediately, principals can make sure classrooms have the supplies needed for a writing workshop: plenty of paper, pens, folders, notepads, scissors, blank books, computers, printers, scanners, and software to make kid-written books.

- The principal should be a writer, sharing his or her own writing in the school community. He or she can be an audience for students, read kids' work on the walls and in classrooms, and let authors know their words have been appreciated. A principal's mailbox invites active correspondence with the kids.

- The principal can make certain that writing is incorporated into special school events and programs. Space and occasions can be created for displaying and sharing written work noncompetitively. Identify outlets for publishing writing beyond the school building, find community sponsors for writing projects, support kids' efforts to print a magazine, and even buy postage stamps for pen pal projects.

- Principals can communicate with parents proactively, letting them know writing is valued and how it is being taught. When necessary, principals can address parental concerns by explaining the goals of the program and the research supporting it.

- Principals can work at the district level to align the curriculum guide and standardized tests with a state-of-the-art approach (i.e., get kids' noses out of dusty grammar drills and into creating whole, original, polished texts).

- And even though there's never enough time, principals should read the research, scan the journals, pass along articles to teachers, and order books that teachers request for their own growth.

Writing Workshop in High School

DIANE CLARK AND REBECCA MUELLER

Lake Forest High School, Lake Forest, Illinois

Clumps of teenagers gather in pockets of intent conversation. The room pulses with chatter, punctuated with laughter and argument over voice and tone—sounds of writers at work. Next door, three office-style cubicles attempt to contain the spill-over sounds of teachers and students, head-to-head in dialogue. Two boys fidget in the outer area, sheaves of paper in hand, pencils tapping, as they watch the clock and wait. A third student pops her head into a cubicle for feedback on a poem she submitted to the literary magazine. The period ends and harried but exhilarated teachers gather notes and papers, mentally shifting gears for the next class.

This scenario is typical throughout the day at Lake Forest High School, where students and teachers are carving new roads of insight into reading, writing, and learning. Our work has changed the learning environment in English classes and the writing culture of the school at large. At the core are kids who care about writing, who have learned that real writing comes from the heart, and who have discovered how an informed listener can help shape the impact of their message. They have discovered the connection between process and product, the rhythm of roles between writer and reader.

Things were not always so. Ours was a traditional, literature-based curriculum, enhanced by a carefully sequenced analytic writing program. Students were highly successful readers of assigned literature and writers of in-depth analysis. But a key element was absent: authenticity. Students' reading was guided by teachers' interests, not learners'. Compelled by recent research, we investigated avenues into the student experience, ways to bring literature and writing into the hearts and minds of our kids.

So the English Department proposed an integration of our traditional program with a student-centered workshop in reading and writing. Guided by Nancie Atwell's principles of *ownership*, *time*, and *response* (1998), we proposed several basic elements. First and most critical was the revision of the teacher's classload to accommodate the increased demands of student-centered instruction. Instead of five classes, teachers would have four, with the fifth devoted to individual conferences. Class size would be limited to twenty for all reading-writing workshop classes in English I, II, and III and the writing-centered senior electives.

Students would still study the required literature—four to five significant works and a sampling of poetry and short stories—and would continue their analytic writing. However, within each semester, for fourteen in-class workshop days students would read self-selected books, and another fourteen would involve writing on topics and in genres of their choosing. Teacher-student conferences, both in class and during the conference period, would afford in-depth exploration of students' work. The focus of conference and workshop instruction would be writing craft and reading strategies. Students would be expected to complete at least three to five polished pieces of writing during writing workshop, to make significant progress as readers, to reflect extensively on their growth, and to complete portfolios as a culminating demonstration of learning. Based on findings of published research and results of our own pilot program, the Board of Education endorsed the proposal and granted us a three-year trial implementation. Our real work had just begun (though we've continued with great success and support ever since).

For twenty-eight days of the semester, then, our classes took on a dramatic new spin. Half those days, students entered the classroom and grabbed a floor pillow or curled up in a corner with their latest book, suggested by a friend, parent, or Barnes and Noble bookstore clerk. Following a "status report" on their progress, they zeroed in on their books, silently engrossed until jolted from their absorption when it was time to go. At planned intervals and unplanned moments, they shared their observations in letters to teachers and conversed with classmates about reading, their book-talk often overflowing into the hallways on the way out the door. This was reading workshop.

For the other half of the workshop days, students wrote. Following a status report similar to that in reading workshop, the teacher typically presented a brief mini-lesson, often on a writing strategy such as "show-don't-tell" or sharpening focus, or offered a student model of writing for discussion. The rest of the period was theirs to perform the multiple tasks of real writers. Some paired up for peer conferences or joined their writing group of three or four to discuss their latest revisions. A handful went to the computer lab or to the library for research. Others sat at desks and drafted, brainstormed, searched for topics, edited, or paged through literary magazines for inspiration. The teacher circled the room, checking drafts, answering questions, hearing parts of stories, making suggestions, and keeping the noise to a productive level.

A few students completed teacher-student conferences during the class period, while others signed up to confer during lunch or study hall. If the sign-up sheet was jammed, a before- or after-school conference became the only other option. Near the end of the year, the pace only quickened as portfolios neared completion and the words *revision, reflection, selection,* and *editing* became the background music. This was writing workshop.

Some years and a number of minor modifications later, it is gratifying to report not just the success of our experiment, but a revolution in our practices as teachers and learners that has demonstrated the power of student-centered learning. Foremost is the caring students exhibit about their writing. Before, the writers who really cared were the few seniors taking creative writing or producing the literary magazine; now they are regular freshmen and sophomores who come early and stay late for conferences before a piece is due. Early in the program, one conference per piece was required. Now that students realize the value of the teacher's individual attention, they seek out conferences themselves. Before, most students cared mainly about semester grades. Now, they accept that writing workshop pieces are frequently ungraded, pencil-graded (an interim grade), or graded only as components of the portfolio. Yet they complete multiple drafts to create pieces that impact the reader. In fact, most students would probably be upset if their efforts were reduced to a simple grade. They value the teacher's response because it is authentic and personal.

Caring about writing is created by several factors. The first is the freedom of expression that writing workshop offers. When initially given free rein in choice of topics, freshmen often compose John Grisham or Tom Clancy look-alikes, with predictable plots and clichéd characters. With experience and ongoing instruction in strategies such as Lucy Calkins' writer's notebook (1994) or Donald Murray's writing territories (1996), students learn that good writing is experiential, coming from the heart. An atmosphere of trust in the classroom encourages students to explore subjects in which they are emotionally invested. As writing brings them closer to the point of truth, the sense of risk increases. Yet so, too, does their understanding of the impact of honest words. Students wrestle with the dilemma of sharing their most effective pieces—those with personal significance and authentic voice.

Today, risk taking and publication are at all-time highs at Lake Forest. The annual writing contest of the Illinois Association of Teachers of English (IATE) always produced a handful of Lake Forest winners. In a typical year before our new program, five authors won awards. Nowadays we see twenty-five or more award-winning pieces per year. Once upon a time the literary magazine staff consisted of ten to fifteen dedicated souls; today it numbers more than eighty, and submissions have more than tripled. Our *Young Idea* magazine has won a series of first-place awards: from Merlyn's Pen, the Golden Pen Award; from Columbia University, the Gold Crown Award; and from the NCTE, its highest recognition. Interest in writing has spilled into the school's popular culture in the form of a poetry rap group. Managed totally by students, "Prozac and Cornflakes" boasts lively, well-attended weekly sessions. The writing culture of LFHS indeed reflects growing participation by kids who care.

This emotional commitment to writing evolves through immersion in the writing process. The student becomes less the viewer of a completed painting and more an artist giving line, shape, form, and color to the details of the picture. The process of composing, as well as the writing workshop structure that immerses the student in that process, creates student-centered learning. This happens gradually. Exploring the murky waters of experience in a writer's notebook, a student delves to find a chest filled with memories, thoughts, and ideas. Sometimes the chest is intact and sometimes the contents are spread across the water's floor. Examining the treasures engages the writer in questions, talk with peers and teachers, new insights, and continual writing, all supported by the workshop structure. A topic emerges with a sharper focus, sometimes through threading together bits and pieces, sometimes through study of a single item. In recreating this discovery for others, the writer moves from experience to language—the craft of writing. The student surfaces not only with a sense of accomplishment, but also with more treasures—the collection of learning experiences, expertise, and confidence that fortifies his next writing adventure. The process becomes a method he applies to all writing, academic or otherwise, in English class and outside of it.

This immersion leads to improved craftsmanship and a deepening sense of pride. In the third and fourth years, teachers observe growing sophistication of the writing and adapt instruction to meet the students' needs. In earlier stages, mini-lessons tend to focus on such subjects as vivid description, effective use of dialogue, or engaging introductions. Instruction in the junior and senior years turns to focus, voice, compression of poetic language, manipulation of structure to reinforce meaning, and the use of transitions as conceptual connecting devices. Individual teacher-student conferences during four years of workshop offer many teachable moments where writing strategies are modeled, discussed, and added to the writer's growing repertoire of techniques. And as students listen to the work of their peers, they cultivate the discerning ear of student-as-critic.

Students gain an understanding of how a writer grows. One wrote: "It allows me to sort out and make sense of things in my life . . . It has given me the confidence to explore as a writer and has shown me that I can write if I work hard at it." Freedom to explore personal experiences gives student writing a power previously unknown to them: "Writing workshop is important, not only as a tool in developing writing, but it's really the only creative outlet for emotions or ideas you've got during the school day. I realize that perhaps the key issue is to become a better or more rounded writer, but it's also a place to step back and get a grip on what's going on around you. If good writing comes out, that's all the better." For many, writing workshop touches personal truth: "I've learned that writing too can serve as a way to cope . . . Poetry has been a safe way for me to say those things that are too terror-filled for verbal communication. It has saved me." For others, the approach takes down social barriers: "Writing workshop makes a classroom more comfortable. You are on a more personal level with your peers, a level I like." Saying it best is the girl who moved to Lake Forest from a traditional high school in California: "Kids here don't know what they have. Writing at most schools is a chore. Here at Lake Forest, it's a sport."

Students are not the only ones feeling the impact. The classroom role of the teacher has changed from center stage to backstage, or at least to the wings. Teachers see themselves as advisors, valued for their expertise and objective point of view. The interaction between student and teacher is dynamic, lesson plans are fluid, and the learning of both student and teacher is ongoing. As one teacher said, "That's what happens in the conferences. You know the students and you push them, and you can see in their eyes that they are moved by what they have done." Such interactions dramatically heighten the community and mutual respect within the classroom. Observed another committed teacher: "Conferences knock down walls. The relationships I create with my students individually intensify our rapport as a class." This new teaching relationship is invigorating, challenging, and most important, renewing. A third colleague explained, "Despite the drain on my time and energies, I'd feel oddly refreshed. My teaching changes from moment to moment to meet the needs of students—it's forever interesting." But most of all, the authenticity of the student-centered approach is what strikes us to the quick. As our faculty agrees: Real kids. Real writing. Real teaching.

WORKS CITED

Atwell, Nancie. 1998. *In the Middle: Writing, Reading, and Learning with Adolescents* (Second Edition). Portsmouth, NH: Heinemann.

———. 2003. *Lessons That Change Writers: A Yearlong Writing Workshop Curriculum for Grades 5–9*. Portsmouth, NH: Heinemann.

Calkins, Lucy McCormick. 1994. *The Art of Teaching Writing* (Second Edition). Portsmouth, NH: Heinemann.

———. 2003. *Units of Study for Primary Writing: A Yearlong Curriculum*. Portsmouth, NH: Heinemann.

Crafton, Linda. 1996. *Standards in Practice: Grades K–2*. Urbana, IL: National Council of Teachers of English.

Hillocks, George. 1986. *Research on Written Composition: New Directions for Teaching*. Urbana, IL: National Council of Teachers of English.

International Reading Association and National Council of Teachers of English. 1996. *Standards for the English Language Arts*. Urbana, IL, and Newark, DE: International Reading Association and National Council of Teachers of English.

Joint Council of the State Board of Education and the Ohio Board of Regents. 2001. *Academic Content Standards, K–12 English Language Arts*. Columbus, OH: Joint Council of the State Board of Education and the Ohio Board of Regents.

Murray, Donald. 1996. *Crafting a Life in Essay, Story, Poem*. Portsmouth, NH: Boynton/Cook.

Ohio Department of Education. 2004. *Ohio Graduation Tests: Writing Practice Test for Ninth Graders*. Columbus, OH: Ohio Department of Education.

Portalupi, JoAnn, and Ralph Fletcher. 2004. *Teaching the Qualities of Writing*. Portsmouth, NH: Heinemann.

Routman, Regie. 2005. *Writing Essentials: Raising Expectations and Results While Simplifying Teaching*. Portsmouth, NH: Heinemann.

Sierra-Perry, Martha. 1996. *Standards in Practice: Grades 3–5*. Urbana, IL: National Council of Teachers of English.

Smagorinsky, Peter. 1996. *Standards in Practice: Grades 9–12*. Urbana, IL: National Council of Teachers of English.

Steineke, Nancy. 2002. *Reading and Writing Together: Collaborative Literacy in Action*. Portsmouth, NH: Hienemann.

Wilhelm, Jeffrey D. 1996. *Standards in Practice: Grades 6–8*. Urbana, IL: National Council of Teachers of English.

SUGGESTED FURTHER READINGS

Allen, Janet. 1999. *Words, Words, Words: Teaching Vocabulary in Grades 4–12*. York, ME: Stenhouse.

Allen, Janet, and Kyle Gonzalez. 1998. *There's Room for Me Here: Literacy Workshop in the Middle School*. York, ME: Stenhouse.

Anderson, Carl. 2000. *How's It Going? A Practical Guide to Conferring with Student Writers*. Portsmouth, NH: Heinemann.

Anson, Chris, and Richard Beach. 1995. *Journals in the Classroom: Writing to Learn*. Norwood, MA: Christopher-Gordon.

Avery, Carol. 2002. *And with a Light Touch: Learning About Reading, Writing, and Teaching with First Graders* (Second Edition). Portsmouth, NH: Heinemann.

Burke, Jim. 2003. *Writing Reminders: Tools, Tips, and Techniques*. Portsmouth, NH: Boynton/Cook.

Fay, Kathleen, and Suzanne Whaley. 2004. *Becoming One Community: Reading and Writing with English Language Learners*. York, ME: Stenhouse.

Fletcher, Ralph. 1993. *What a Writer Needs*. Portsmouth, NH: Heinemann.

Fletcher, Ralph, and JoAnn Portalupi. 1998. *Craft Lessons: Teaching Writing K–8*. York, ME: Stenhouse.

———. 2001. *Writing Workshop: The Essential Guide*. Portsmouth, NH: Heinemann.

Graves, Donald. 1994. *A Fresh Look at Writing*. Portsmouth, NH: Heinemann.

Harwayne, Shelley. 2001. *Writing Through Childhood: Rethinking Process and Product*. Portsmouth, NH: Heinemann.

Heard, Georgia. 1998. *Awakening the Heart: Exploring Poetry in Elementary and Middle School*. Portsmouth, NH: Heinemann.

———. 2002. *The Revision Toolbox: Teaching Techniques That Work*. Portsmouth, NH: Heinemann.

Hill, Bonnie Campbell, Cynthia Ruptic, and Lisa Norwick. 1998. *Classroom-Based Assessment*. Norwood, MA: Christopher Gordon.

Hindley, Joanne. 1996. *In the Company of Children*. York, ME: Stenhouse.

Kirby, Dan, Dawn Kirby, and Tom Liner. 2003. *Inside Out: Strategies for Teaching Writing* (Third Edition). Portsmouth, NH: Heinemann.

Lane, Barry. 1993. *After the End: Teaching and Learning Creative Revision*. Portsmouth, NH: Heinemann.

Macrorie, Ken. 1988. *The I-Search Paper.* Portsmouth, NH: Boynton/Cook.

Moeller, Dave. 2002. *Computers in the Writing Classroom.* Urbana, IL: NCTE.

Porter, Carol, and Jannell Cleland. 1995. *The Portfolio as a Learning Strategy.* Portsmouth, NH: Boynton/Cook.

Ray, Katie Wood. 2002. *What You Know by Heart: How to Develop Curriculum for Your Writing Workshop.* Portsmouth, NH: Heinemann.

Rhodes, Lynn K., and Curt Dudley-Marling. 1996. *Readers and Writers with a Difference: A Holistic Approach to Teaching Learning Disabled and Remedial Students* (Second Edition). Portsmouth, NH: Heinemann.

Short, Kathy, Jerome Harste, and Carolyn Burke. 1996. *Creating Classrooms for Authors and Inquirers* (Second Edition). Portsmouth, NH: Heinemann.

Snowball, Diane, and Faye Bolton. 1999. *Spelling K–8.* York, ME: Stenhouse.

Zemelman, Steven and Harvey Daniels. 1987. *A Community of Writers.* Portsmouth, NH: Heinemann.

WRITING RESOURCES ON THE INTERNET

The National Council of Teachers of English offers information on the teaching of writing. For association news, research bulletins, publications, and conference announcements, visit http://www.ncte.org.

The only truly national staff development effort in any subject area, the National Writing Project shares reports of outstanding practice, research bulletins, and a wide range of publications. Visit http://www.writingproject.org.

The International Reading Association and the National Council of Teachers of English together sponsor a website at http://www.readwritethink.org that provides a wide variety of classroom lessons, along with standards and lists of related Internet sources. While the majority of the lessons focus on reading and literature, some good writing activities can be found as well.

A valuable resource, especially for teachers of poetry and creative writing, is the Teachers and Writers Collaborative at http://www.twc.org. See particularly the section of their site called WriteNet.

The Yale–New Haven Teachers Institute has for twenty-five years catalogued interesting classroom lessons on a variety of topics. Several lesson groups focus on writing. Visit http://www.yale.edu/ynhti/curriculum/units/.

Accomplished teachers who are ready to seek national certification can learn about the rigorous one-year process, find out the benefits of a successful review in their own state, and find a support group at the website of the National Board for Professional Teaching Standards at http://www.nbpts.org.

RECOMMENDATIONS ON TEACHING WRITING

Increase	*Decrease*
Student ownership and responsibility by: • helping students choose their own topics and goals for improvement • using brief teacher-student conferences • teaching students to review their own progress	Teacher control of decision making by: • deciding all writing topics • dictating improvements without student problem-solving • setting learning objectives without student input • providing instruction only through whole-class activity
Class time on writing whole, original pieces through: • real purposes and audiences for writing • instruction and support for all stages of writing • prewriting, drafting, revising, editing	Time spent on isolated drills on "subskills" of grammar, vocabulary, spelling, etc. Writing assignments given briefly, with no context or purpose, completed in one step
Writing for real audiences, publishing for the class and wider communities	Finished pieces read only by teacher
Teacher modeling writing • drafting, revising, sharing • as a fellow author and as demonstration of processes	Teacher talks about writing but never writes or shares own work
Learning grammar and mechanics in context, at the editing stage, and as items are needed	Isolated grammar lessons, given in order determined by textbook, before writing is begun
Making the classroom a supportive setting, using: • active exchange and valuing of students' ideas • collaborative small-group work • conferences and peer critiquing that give responsibility to authors	Devaluation of students' ideas: • students viewed as lacking knowledge and language abilities • sense of class as competing individuals • cooperation among students viewed as cheating, disruptive
Writing across the curriculum as a tool for learning	Writing taught only during "language arts" period
Constructive and efficient evaluation that involves: • brief informal oral responses as students work • focus on a few errors at a time • thorough grading of just a few of student-selected, polished pieces • cumulative view of growth and self-evaluation • encouragement of risk taking and honest expression	Evaluation as negative burden for teacher and student by: • marking all papers heavily for all errors, making teacher a bottleneck • editing by teacher, and only after paper completed, rather than student making improvements • grading punitively, focused on errors, not growth

Best Practice, Third Edition by Zemelman, Daniels, and Hyde (Heinemann: Portsmouth, NH); © 2005

Chapter 4
Best Practice in Mathematics

THE WAY IT USED TO BE

We often ask adults to write their math autobiographies, and their stories would make a grown man cry. They struggled through a labyrinth of incomprehensible symbols and rules, memorizing facts and procedures. They remember their panic when called upon to go to the chalkboard to compute $2\frac{1}{2}$ divided by $\frac{5}{12}$. "Ours is not to reason why; we just invert and multiply." Many of these adults are now parents, and they not-so-subtly send a message to their children: "Math is hard. I never could understand it. Gee whiz, I can't even balance my checkbook."

Is mathematics so inherently difficult that only a few who are "wired" for math can understand it? Unfortunately, most people in the United States would say yes. This erroneous view of mathematics has been prevalent for decades. Many come to believe that they are incapable of doing math. As they progress through the grades, fewer and fewer students understand and enjoy math, leaving only a handful to continue with capability and confidence. Most high school students take the minimum number of math classes needed to graduate. By college, only a small percentage of our nation's students elect to major in mathematics. Others take only the minimum courses required, despite the fact that many careers depend upon mathematical knowledge.

It does not have to be this way. We know more than ever before about human cognition and how to help students understand mathematics. Here is how one middle school teacher, Katie George, used "Chocolate Algebra," an activity from Arthur's course on teaching algebra, and implemented it in her classroom at Daniel Wright Junior High School in Lincolnshire, Illinois.

TEACHING MATHEMATICS A BETTER WAY: CHOCOLATE ALGEBRA

Armed with a giant bar of chocolate and a king-sized box of Tootsie Rolls, I prepared my initial attack on linear equations with my seventh-grade students. My objective for the day was simple: introduce linear relationships, one of the cornerstones for beginning algebra students. From the several times I'd done this activity, I was keenly aware that Chocolate Algebra hinges on careful pacing and precise questioning. I planned two 44-minute class periods for this activity.

I began by posing a problem to my class: "If you have $10 to spend on $2 Hershey Bars and $1 Tootsie Rolls, how many ways can you spend your money without receiving change? All chocolate, no change—tax included." I had determined in advance the items to purchase and the dollar amounts to spend so that the tables and graphs would reveal patterns readily. Bringing in props such as large candy bars was very motivating for the students and provided concrete representations.

The students quickly began generating solutions. As expected, most randomly jotted down any combination that popped into their minds. As they shared solutions, it became apparent that we needed an organizational system. With scheming intent, I suggested they each make a simple two-column table (or T-chart) to keep the combinations in order. We decided as a class to label the left-hand column "Number of Hershey Bars" and the right-hand column "Number of Tootsie Rolls."

The combinations elicited from the class were not arranged in any particular order. I asked them, "Did you find all the possible combinations?" To make it easier to answer, we agreed to purchase the most $2 Hershey Bars that we could as a place to start ("the most of the bigger item") and decrease the number of Hershey Bars one at a time. The first row of our table showed that 5 Hershey Bars and 0 Tootsie Rolls were purchased. The second row had 4 Hershey Bars and 2 Tootsie Rolls. The class quickly saw patterns and the table was complete in a matter of minutes.

We spent a lot of time talking about patterns in the tables. By using a different color pen to highlight one pattern, I asked the class to explain to me how the numbers changed in the table. "The left side goes down by one and the right side goes up by two," one student exclaimed. "Why?" I asked. Another student asked, "Will the left side always go down and the right side always go up?" Yet a different student asked, "Will the numbers at the top always make the pattern?" I countered, "Where does the pattern come from?" Many students volunteered that because the Hershey Bar was twice as expensive, there would be a 2:1 relationship. "Oh, the Hershey Bar is exchanged for two Tootsie Rolls!" one student said as a big light bulb appeared over her head. As I expected, the vast majority of the students now understood the tables and could recognize the patterns.

To extend the concept, I had them try to buy $1 Tootsie Rolls and $5 Toblerone Bars with $27 dollars and, finally, $5 Toblerones and $2 Hershey Bars with $37. Again, they made tables and discussed the patterns they saw. These students had worked with equations having one variable but this would be their first classroom experience with two, so I wanted to tread very carefully. I ended by asking, "Is there another way to represent this situation?"

To start the second day, we pulled out our tables again and reviewed the situation from the previous class. Out to the side of the table on the board, I wrote each solution as a coordinate point with parentheses and a comma. "Does this format remind you of anything you have seen before?" I inquired. "Yes, it is for graphing," several students replied. I spent a couple of minutes reviewing the basics of graphing for those who needed a reminder. "Let's see what happens if we use our table as a collection of coordinate points and put them on a graph," I said. They each graphed the points but seemed thoroughly unimpressed. I could see "so what?" written all over their faces.

"Take your pencil and put it on the point (0, 10). Let's say we want to go from this point to (1, 8), the next point down, but our pencil has to stay on the lines like in a video game. Can someone tell me how to move my pen so that it will be on the point (1, 8)?" I prodded. "Move down," someone called out. "How far should I move?" I responded. "Move down two and over one," a student directed. Almost instantaneously, most of them realized what was going on. "That's the pattern in the table! Cool!" As if I had performed a magic trick, my pre-algebra classes delighted in watching the pattern from the table reappear in the graphs. We moved down two and over one until our pencils were on the point (5, 0). "But our table said up two and down one. It is backward," Jackie whined. "What happens if we go in the other direction? Can we go back to point (0, 10) using a different path?" I inquired, knowing that they were not quite ready for slope but hoping that this would lay a nice foundation for them.

After playing around with the graph and the table for a few minutes, the class had a good initial understanding of the connection between the table and the graph. In fact, they could see that there was a relationship between the number of Hershey Bars and the number of Tootsie Rolls. The word *cool* was completely overused in my classroom over the course of those two days.

Looking at the tables, I hinted that perhaps we could make an equation from this information. Given the look on their faces, I knew that my suggestion had been a huge leap from a candy-purchasing example to the mysterious world of mathematics. How could we bridge the expanse? "Let's look at our first table. There is a lot going on here. What numbers are always staying the same?" Without much hesitation, the kids recognized that the price of the candy ($2 and $1) and our budget ($10) always stayed the same. On the board, I wrote down those numbers ($2 $1 $10) with space between them for the symbols and variables that I was hoping they would produce.

"Let's look at the table again. What is changing? What is different in every row or every situation?" I asked. A bit more hesitation than the first question, but they recognized that the number we were buying was changing. "What can we do to show that a number is changing or that we don't know what the number will be?" I inquired. "Use a variable," Sunny said. "*X*," Jackie contributed.

"Think about the relationship between the price of the candy, the quantity that we purchased, and our total budget. How can we add variables to the numbers I wrote down to show that the amounts change?" I asked. Most of the students wanted to use H for the number of Hershey Bars and T for the number of Tootsie Rolls.

"Where should we put the H and the T?" I pushed. The students decided on the variables and their placement to come up with the following equation: $\$2 H + \$1 T = \$10$. "How do we know that this will work? Let's look back at the table," I directed. Derek explained that as we made the table we had multiplied the number of Hershey Bars by 2 and the number of Tootsie Rolls by 1 and we had to be certain that these two amounts added up to 10. He explained that we got our equation right from the table.

At the end of the lesson, I asked them to think about what we had done and what they had learned. Many mentioned the use of a table and "the most of the bigger." Others noticed that we were using variables but not solving for them the way that we had in the past. A few students thought we were just buying candy. A few were not sure how we got our equation. This was an introductory activity, requiring follow-up and extensions. For homework, the kids needed to come up with their own problem with a budget and two items to buy. They should make a table, a graph, and try to write an equation. Most students delighted in creating their own problem and created a table with ease. Quite a few were able to make a graph to go along with their table, but the biggest challenge was in writing an equation. As this is the most abstract part of the activity, it did not come as a surprise that equation writing was the biggest challenge.

Chocolate Algebra has many, many layers, easily extended or modified; I just change the objects and their costs. It is a fabulous springboard for a unit on linear equations. It can be used in various formats throughout a school year as a way to expand on concepts over time. All my students, regardless of their level, had a revelation at some point.

A LOOK AT THE STANDARDS DOCUMENTS

In 1989 the National Council of Teachers of Mathematics (NCTM) released their landmark document *Curriculum and Evaluation Standards for School Mathematics*. It was followed by *Professional Standards for Teaching Mathematics* (1991), *Assessment Standards for School Mathematics* (1995), and twenty-two addenda booklets that addressed mathematical topics at various grade levels. Taken collectively, the NCTM standards and their related materials offer a significantly broadened view of the nature of mathematics, what it means to know mathematics, how students can learn mathematics, and what kinds of teaching practices best foster this learning.

The influence of the original standards has been substantial. The National Science Foundation (NSF) funded the development of a dozen new curriculum programs that embodied the standards. Most commercial publishers of mathematics textbooks in various ways incorporated these standards in their programs. However, the NCTM standards also stimulated a backlash, dubbed by the media the Math Wars, not unlike the Reading Wars we talked about in Chapter 2. When planning to revise the standards, the NCTM solicited input from a wide range of sources, including many of its most vocal critics. The council published a revision of the standards that integrated the three previous documents into one, *Principles and Standards for School Mathematics* (2000). It did not entirely satisfy the critics.

The *2000 NCTM Standards* offer a vision for mathematics based on six major principles

1. **Equity** (maintaining high expectations and support for *all* students).

2. **Curriculum** (articulating coherent, important mathematics across the grades).

3. **Teaching** (challenging and supporting students in building new knowledge).

4. **Learning** (helping students build an understanding of mathematics by actively creating meaning by connecting new knowledge with their prior knowledge).

5. **Assessment** (supporting the learning of important mathematics through formative and summative assessment of what students actually understand).

6. **Technology** (expanding the mathematics that can be taught and enhancing student learning).

In *NCTM 2000* these principles are applied to the **ten standards** for grades K-12. Five **content** standards address the familiar branches of mathematics, and five **process** standards describe the interrelated aspects of cognition that build understanding of concepts.

The ten standards are explained in a global fashion for grades pre-K–12. Then each standard is examined in detail in four grade-level bands (pre-K–2, 3–5, 6–8, and 9–12). **Expectations** of what students should understand, know, and be able to do for each of the five content standards for each grade level are provided in a ten-page appendix. These expectations are a great resource to those developing curriculum frameworks.

Content Standards	Process Standards
Number and Operations	Problem Solving
Algebra	Reasoning and Proof
Geometry	Communication
Measurement	Connections
Data Analysis and Probability	Representations

NCTM 2000 presents additional concepts in the five content standards that were not in the curriculum of prior generations. Also, many concepts are represented and connected in new and exciting ways. The five process standards are drawn from extensive research on human cognition and mathematics. It is our job as teachers to help students learn how to use these processes appropriately to develop the mathematical knowledge described in the content standards.

QUALITIES OF BEST PRACTICE IN TEACHING MATHEMATICS

Teachers should help *all* students understand that mathematics is a dynamic, coherent, interconnected set of ideas. Unfortunately, few teachers, let alone students, have experienced mathematics this way. Most students and adults see mathematics as a collection of unrelated topics, theorems, procedures, and facts. Study after study for the past twenty-five years has found the mathematics curriculum of the United States to be narrowly focused on procedures and facts, not concepts, and highly repetitive, with significant overlap and review from year to year—sometimes covering a topic in the same superficial manner for four or five years in a row.

In order to see mathematics as a coherent whole, one must realize that although numbers and computation are an important part of mathematics, they are only one part. *Mathematics is the science of patterns.* Mathematical concepts describe patterns and relationships. A concept is an abstract idea that explains and organizes information. Mathematicians look for relationships among ideas and try to see patterns in these relationships. Every branch of mathematics (e.g., geometry, probability) has its own patterns. Expert mathematicians use abstract, symbolic notation to describe the patterns they conceive.

The *2000 NCTM Standards* call for the creation of a mathematics curriculum for all students that includes familiar strands but also addresses big ideas, such as patterns, dimension, quantity, uncertainty, shape, and change. These big ideas anchor the important concepts of mathematics as well as terminology, definitions, notation, and skills. Teachers can promote coherence by emphasizing big ideas and helping students see the connections among concepts.

Yes, but . . . is this kind of mathematics teaching really possible?

Sure. Many other countries do mathematics this way. Comparisons of U.S. mathematics curricula with the five top-scoring countries (respectively, Singapore, Korea, Chinese Taipei, Hong Kong, and Japan) in the Third International Mathematics and Science Study (TIMSS) revealed that they focused more on reasoning and understanding concepts, while the U.S. schools stuck more to procedures and facts. The curricula of high-scoring countries had more in-depth study of fewer topics each year (e.g., ten in Japan) compared to the U.S., which had superficial coverage of thirty to thirty-five topics. These high-scoring countries included significant amounts of algebra and geometry in grades six through eight, with the expectation that all students would learn these topics. This expectation contrasted sharply with the finding that 80 percent of U.S. eighth graders study almost exclusively arithmetic topics, with little coverage of algebra and virtually no geometry. The TIMSS authors said the U.S. mathematics and science curricula are "a mile wide and an inch deep" (Schmidt, McKnight, and Raizen 1998, 1).

The goal of teaching mathematics is to help all students understand concepts and use them powerfully. Students should develop true understanding of mathematical concepts and procedures. They must come to see and believe that mathematics makes sense, that it is understandable and useful to them. They can become more confident in their own use of mathematics. Teachers and students must come to recognize that mathematical thinking is part of everyone's mental ability, and not confined to just a gifted few.

Research in cognitive psychology over the past twenty-five years has consistently shown that understanding increases the ability to learn, remember, and use mathematics (Bransford, Brown, and Cocking 2000). When students learn with understanding, they are able to use their new knowledge flexibly, making connections to new situations. Furthermore, developing a deep, connected understanding of mathematics promotes the learning of computational skills.

Yes, but . . . do you really believe that all or even most students can understand math?

Many more students are capable of learning and understanding more mathematics than previous generations ever thought possible. Conceptual understanding does not come from a teacher *telling* students what a concept is. Concepts are *built* by each person; understanding is created. Students have to explore many examples and talk about what they see and think, as well as hear explanations from the teacher.

In Japan, teachers' primary concern is helping students understand mathematical concepts. The additional time gained by in-depth attention to fewer ideas allows the teachers to help students examine mathematical relationships in depth. The TIMSS research found that in Japan more than half (54 percent) of the problems that students worked on emphasized making connections among many mathematical concepts, versus an anemic 17 percent in the United States. What were American teachers doing? More than two-thirds of their problems emphasized procedural skills. When challenging problems were addressed, the Japanese teachers *required* students to discuss solutions to make connections; *none* of the American teachers in the study did so. In fact, a third of time the teachers *just gave the answer.* It is not surprising to find that the average amount of time spent on a problem was fifteen minutes in Japan and five minutes in the United States (Hiebert et al. 2003).

Teachers in Japan focused on developing new concepts and solving problems that reveal concepts; they spent 60 percent of class time on new content (compared to less than 25 percent by the Americans). Instead of working with new content, the American teachers spent over half the class time on review (versus less than one-fourth of the time by the Japanese). An astonishing 28 percent of U.S. classes were devoted *entirely* to review (versus only 5 percent of Japanese classes). American teachers focused much more heavily on memorizing, although interviews revealed that many American teachers thought they were teaching for understanding. American students were practicing skills while Asian students were thinking. Clearly, the Japanese teachers believed their students could understand, and they did. In contrast, American traditionalists want us to go "back to basics." *We never left.*

Five intertwined processes build mathematical understanding. Teaching for conceptual understanding means helping students build a web of interconnected ideas. Teachers provide experiences for students in which they actively engage in these key processes:

- making connections
- using reasoning and developing proofs
- problem solving
- creating representations
- communicating ideas

Teachers help students *make connections* to their prior mathematical knowledge, between related mathematical concepts, and between concepts and procedures. They help students build bridges between situations or contexts that may appear different but are examples of the same concept. They help students realize the connections between different representations of a problem, which is especially important in moving from concrete to more abstract representations.

A skillful teacher is always juggling examples and explanations. For students to see patterns or to develop true conceptual understanding, they will need many more examples than are provided in the textbook. Presentation of an explanation, no matter how brilliantly worded, will not connect ideas unless students have had ample opportunities to wrestle with examples. An explanation must have something to which it connects.

Making connections requires *reasoning*. Teachers should provide experiences so that students can make and investigate mathematical conjectures, select and use various types of reasoning (inductive pattern finding, deductive logic), and develop and evaluate mathematical arguments and proofs. Reasoning mathematically is essentially a habit; it is developed by use in a variety of contexts. When students believe that mathematics is supposed to make sense, that patterns can be uncovered, and that they can justify the results of their investigations, they are more willing to develop the habit of reasoning.

Problem solving is an excellent vehicle for developing understanding. Traditionally, problem solving has been seen as an application of skills *after* mastery. But the *2000 NCTM Standards* show that problem solving is a means to build mathematical knowledge. Teachers should choose worthwhile mathematical problems or tasks for students to work on. How to solve these problems should not be obvious; students should have to think. The best problems are authentic, challenging, intriguing, mathematically rich, and perhaps counterintuitive. With help from the teacher to apply and adapt good problem-solving strategies, the students can attack problems and develop understanding. Teachers need to help students develop *metacognition*—being aware of their own problem-solving processes, monitoring their progress, and reflecting on their own thinking.

Teachers need to ensure that students gain experience with a variety of strategies and are able to decide when to use each one. With the most powerful strategies, students *create their own representations*. The common strategies of looking for a pattern and using logical reasoning are overarching and are essential to doing mathematics. Students must be encouraged to look for patterns and to use logical reasoning in *every* problem. But at a more specific level, students should develop capability with five critical strategies that are based on creating representations:

- Discuss the problem in small groups (language representations).
- Use manipulatives (concrete, physical representations and tactile sense).
- Act it out (representations of sequential actions and bodily kinesthetic sense).
- Draw a picture, diagram, or graph (visual, pictorial representations).
- Make a list or table (symbolic representations).

These representations build understanding of the problem (and often find a solution) because in creating them, students are developing different *mental models* of the problem or phenomena. In worthwhile tasks, students may use several of these representations, moving from one to another to figure out more about the problem. Later they might draw on supplementary strategies (e.g., guess and check; work backwards, simplify problem), but these cannot be used effectively unless one understands the problem. As students become more mathematically sophisticated, they are able to use more abstract and symbolic strategies (e.g., use proportional reasoning, apply a formula).

Students often need help from the teacher to move back and forth between representations, seeing how they are related and how each reveals something different. Recall how Katie George asked questions designed to help students see the connections between the actual chocolate items and the numbers in the table, between a row in the table and a point on the coordinate graph, and between the symbols "(4, 2)" and the situation in real life. Flexibility of translating between representations and realizing the value of each are good indicators of true understanding.

In mathematics, students should be encouraged and helped to *communicate* their ideas by using a full range of language representations—speaking, writing, reading, and listening. Communication and reflection go hand in hand. Even though symbols are used to represent the most abstract aspects of mathematics, the symbols represent ideas that are developed and expressed through language. Oral language—discussing, verbalizing thoughts, "talking mathematics" for most students, most of the time, greatly facilitates their understanding. Of course, teachers must build a safe environment in their classroom where students believe they can freely express their ideas without negative consequences for mistakes.

Math journals provide another opportunity for students to use language to express and justify their reasoning and ideas. They can describe how they solved a problem, why they used a particular approach or strategy, what assumptions they made, and so forth. When they have to explain a mathematics concept in their own words, students have to think and rethink what is really important. With feedback from the teacher, they begin to move from the specifics of each activity to more general and abstract conceptions, expressed more precisely in mathematical language. Eventually, children's mathematical language, oral and written, becomes a powerful tool for thinking, helping them create *models*—mental maps used to organize their world, solve problems, and explore relationships.

All students should understand and be able to use number concepts, operations, and computational procedures. *NCTM 2000* defines the term *computational fluency* as "having and using efficient and accurate methods for computing" (NCTM 2000, 32). "Developing fluency requires a balance and connection between conceptual understanding and computational proficiency. . . . [S]tudents must become fluent in arithmetic computation—they must have efficient and accurate methods that are supported by an understanding of numbers and operations" (NCTM 2000, 35). Five critically important processes that lead to understanding, proficiency, and fluency need to be developed in many different contexts to gain generalized understanding. They are explained on page 119. When students have many successful experiences using five processes, remembering math facts becomes a simple matter.

Yes, but . . . aren't these ideas controversial?

There is definitely a controversy. Groups of parents, along with a number of mathematicians and scientists, formed a group called Mathematically Correct (MC), and they have spoken out against the NCTM standards. With the help of the Internet, they organized opposition across the United States. In letters to the editor and over the Web, they have posted horror stories of bad math teaching, attributed to the standards. Their website has a hundred "papers"—an amazing collection of half-truths, misconceptions, and rhetoric. The MC folks refer to themselves as traditionalists and criticize NCTM for:

- having students derive math facts and rely on calculators instead of memorizing basic math facts
- having students invent procedures instead of learning traditional algorithms
- focusing on problem solving; cooperative, small groups; and discovery instead of direct instruction
- promoting a curriculum that is "soft and fuzzy" and dumbed-down, with too much fun and games in place of "rigor"

The MC supporters are saying the same things that traditionalists have said for most of this century. From the MC website we read: "'Understanding' is a complex, poorly understood process that involves linking multiple stored 'chunks' of knowledge. We have no idea how this magical process occurs."

This quote would be news to the phalanx of cognitive psychologists whose illumination of human "understanding" is described in Bransford, Brown, and Cocking (2000). The MC traditionalists appear to be unaware of the research on cognition showing how concepts are more easily developed, reflected upon, and understood from rich experiences than from facts and procedures that are memorized, but not understood.

This controversy has a long history. "Drill does not develop meaning. Repetition does not lead to understanding," wrote William Brownell in 1935 (10). "[Algebra] presents mechanical processes and therefore forces the student to rely on memorization rather than understanding. . . . On the whole, the traditional curriculum does not pay much attention to understanding," wrote mathematician Morris Kline in 1973 (4–5). A group called Mathematically Sane has launched a website to counter the traditionalist critics; visit http://www.mathematicallysane.com to see a more comprehensive rebuttal.

Counting: Building one-to-one correspondence and number sense. A serious problem with traditional basic skills is going directly from counting to memorizing computation facts.

Number relations: Decomposing and recomposing quantities to see relationships among the numbers (e.g., 10 objects is 1 less than 11 and 1 more than 9; 10 objects can be separated into 2 piles many ways, such as 7 and 3; 10 can be 5 groups of 2). These activities develop models of number relationships and a generalized concept of equivalence. Though skipped by traditionalists, it is absolutely essential for students to invest great amounts of time investigating and playing with these relationships. If done well, this practice facilitates other processes immensely.

Place value: Creating sets of ten with objects and beginning to understand the base ten, positional notation (e.g., the 1 in 15 means 1 group of 10 and the 5 means a group of 5 more). Traditionalists briefly explain place value, but do not show how these processes are related.

The meaning of the operations: Creating models (mental maps) of different situations and realizing that operations have multiple meanings (e.g., subtraction does not always mean "take away"; it could mean the difference in comparing two quantities). This step is often skipped by traditionalists.

Fact strategies: Thinking strategies for learning the facts for the operations. If students have done extensive work with number relations, they can group the facts into patterns for meaningful understanding, derivation, and recall. This is very different from the rote memorization advocated by traditionalists.

It is important to distinguish between memorization and automaticity. Memorizing basic math facts has meant the students must focus directly on committing to memory the results of unrelated computation so they don't have to think about what they are doing. These isolated bits of information are practiced with no regard to their relationships. In contrast, automaticity depends on students thinking about these relationships.

If a student needs to know the sum of $9 + 7$ and quickly responds 16 because he has thought, that is the same as $10 + 6 \ldots 16$, has he learned the fact? And what about the student who, presented with 9×6, quickly reasons that it would be 54 because $10 \times 6 = 60$, and this would be 6 less? Remembering basic math facts is not a struggle when all the pieces of the puzzle (from counting and number relations through fact strategies) are in place. These facts should and eventually can be remembered. The question is, which process does one use: memorization or developing automaticity through understanding?

Analogous reasoning applies to algorithms for computing with multiple digits. For nearly two decades, studies have described how children become much more capable at doing mathematics when, instead of memorizing traditional algorithms that they don't understand, they are encouraged to use their knowledge of simple computation to construct ways of accomplishing more complex computation. Students do not merely "discover" these non-traditional algorithms; they construct them based on their understanding of number relationships, from dialogue with peers, and from the questioning and guidance of the teacher. Students explore a variety of procedures, including traditional algorithms. The 1998 NCTM yearbook has thirty-two articles devoted to examining the nature and role of algorithms (Morrow 1998).

Some mathematics educators and researchers have asserted that memorizing traditional algorithms in grades K–4 can be *harmful*. Kamii and Dominick (1998) give two reasons for this claim: (1) Children abandon ways of thinking about quantity that make sense to them and instead try to work with memorized procedures they do not understand; (2) traditional algorithms "unteach" place value. At the very time when they should be solidifying their understanding of place value, the traditional algorithms demand they stop thinking about the meaning of the positions of the numbers and treat them *not as quantities,* but as single digits. "Write down the two; carry the one!"

All students must have opportunities to do algebra and reason algebraically, throughout their K–12 school years. Algebra is a way of thinking with various representations that become increasingly more symbolic and abstract. In the United States, algebra historically has been a "gatekeeper course" consisting of generalized arithmetic; a relatively narrow range of paper-and-pencil skills for transforming, simplifying, and solving equations; and "problems" that might have been real-life contexts a hundred years ago, but are barely imaginable today. This model should not be mandated for all students. When districts moved the traditional, symbolic Algebra I course from ninth grade to eighth grade, as a required course, the students' failure rates skyrocketed.

Instead, NCTM has advocated the creation of a K–12 algebra strand in the mathematics curriculum that engages all students in context-based problems, using tables, graphs, and equations (especially functions). With full understanding, students should be able to flexibly move back and forth between these different representations. They must understand that each one is a different way to represent the same thing, but each allows one to perceive different aspects of the phenomenon. Recall the multiple representations in Katie George's algebra class.

Such activities can help students build an understanding of the big ideas of algebra, such as *change, variable, equality/equation, function, rate of change,* and *linearity.* They need to understand how to use these ideas and related tools to describe patterns in the real-world contexts around them. They do have to learn how to represent and model using equations. In the process, they can learn the rules of the game of balancing equations, simplifying radicals, rationalizing denominators, factoring polynomials, and so forth. But these symbol manipulation skills are best learned when they are embedded within in a meaningful context that gives students a good reason for learning these skills—to find the answers to real problems.

Geometry and measurement concepts are best learned through real-world experiences and problems. The big ideas of *shape* and *dimension* appear in these overlapping content standards. Some geometric concepts we do not measure (e.g., symmetry, similarity, spatial visualization); other concepts we might call geometric measurement (i.e., angles, length, area, volume, which correspond to dimensions 1, 2, and 3). Then there are attributes we measure that are not geometric (e.g., capacity, mass/weight, temperature, time, money). We ask students to develop a deep understanding of the attributes being measured (e.g., compare and contrast volume and capacity, both conceptually and procedurally). However, traditional geometry and measurement chapters in textbooks have been a game of memorizing definitions, plugging in values for variables in formulas, and memorizing conversions between units.

In contrast, NCTM wants students to understand geometric concepts, characteristics and properties of two- and three-dimensional shapes, coordinate geometry to represent relationships, and units of measure. Such understanding can be accomplished only through *hands-on manipulation of concrete materials.* All students must have extensive experience handling real three-dimensional objects, comparing and measuring their attributes. They must work with individual attributes to build understanding before working with rates and derived measures that require understanding the relationship between two measures. These real-world experiences must precede the more abstract work with symbols and formulas.

 Yes, but . . . why do students in Asia do so well in mathematics? Don't their teachers use a rigorous, traditional approach?

The Mathematically Correct website has trumpeted Liping Ma's book comparing Chinese and U.S. elementary school teachers in their knowledge of mathematics (especially arithmetic) and the ways that they teach (Ma 1999). Her research showed some serious gaps in the U.S. teachers' conceptual and procedural knowledge. The Mathematically Correct website claims that Ma's research shows that U.S. teachers are failing to correctly teach "traditional mathematics" as the Asians do. They charge that Americans have substituted "the gospel of discovery learning" for "rigor." This is a red herring; in fact, it's a school of red herrings.

Ma describes how the Chinese teach computational algorithms much more conceptually than American teachers. Using the students' knowledge of number relations and deep understanding of place value, equivalence, and expanded notation, the Chinese teachers help them understand procedures and underlying concepts and procedures of computation. How did the young Chinese students acquire this foundational knowledge on which the teachers could build? That is the real story.

Asian languages are structured very differently from English (and other Indo-European languages). For instance, English speakers will count "ten, eleven, twelve . . . twenty"; whereas Asian speakers will count "ten, ten-one, ten-two, . . . two-tens." Asian languages introduce and support base ten, place value thinking from a child's very first oral counting experience *before even coming to school*. This language feature greatly facilitates regrouping and renaming in computation. Chinese teachers build on this base-ten language in using different thinking strategies than Americans do to help students learn the basic facts (Sun and Zhang 2001). Furthermore, in Asian languages the concept of fractional parts is inherent in the words used. "One-third"in English would be spoken in Japanese as *"san bun no ichi"*—literally, "of three parts, one" (Miura 2001).

These language differences probably give Asian children a two- to three-year advantage over English-speaking students in computation and a much stronger foundation in counting, number sense, number relations, place value, and fractions. United States elementary teachers need to provide their young students with a wealth of experiences that young Asian students have already had before entering school.

On their website, the Mathematically Correct traditionalists criticize NCTM for a lack of rigor, encouraging discovery learning and teaching "special cases, an emphasis on problem solving, and connections to real-world uses of mathematics, such as applications." The ironies abound. These practices are what one can clearly see on the TIMSS videotapes of Japanese classrooms, where three-fourths of the problems involved applications (versus only one-fourth in the United States). In fact, NCTM is *not* proposing discovery learning where the teacher is prohibited from explaining ideas to students; the standards clearly describe the necessity for teachers and students to engage in discourse and dialogue.

Mathematician Morris Kline introduces his mammoth book on "the calculus" by saying: "The **rigorous** presentation is difficult to grasp and obscures understanding . . . [It] should be reserved for a course in advanced calculus for mathematicians." Instead he wrote a calculus book where the "justification for the theorems and techniques is [based on] . . . geometrical, physical, and heuristic arguments and generalizations from concrete cases" (1998, vii). "One should always try to understand new concepts and theorems in an intuitive manner before studying a formal and rigorous presentation of them" (1998, 6).

One would expect calculus courses to be exactly the place where the rigor advocated by traditionalists would apply. However, many mathematicians, like Kline, have realized that because the goal is the development of mathematical understanding, students of all ages need to construct meaning, even those taking their first calculus course.

Concepts from statistics, data, chance, and probability thrive on real-world applications. One definition of data is "numbers with a context." The NCTM standard on data analysis and probability urges teachers to provide challenging tasks in which students formulate questions and design their own studies that can be addressed with data that they collect, organize, and analyze. They need to understand a variety of statistical methods and when to use them. Some of them fit hand in glove with algebraic concepts such as variables, tables, and graphs and creating mathematical models. We are now seeing a strong interest in data modeling in mathematics and science for students K–12. This work is always embedded in real contexts of authentic inquiry. Students are highly motivated to argue for their inferences from data-based evidence.

Probability has a host of slippery concepts that should be addressed inductively via probability experiments. We should exercise caution in pushing theoretical probability too soon. When the ideas are grounded in extensive data collection to build understanding, theoretical ideas can take hold. The language of probability helps us; even in kindergarten questions often have

 Yes, but . . . what if the mathematics textbooks in my district don't support these Best Practices?

Although virtually all publishers of mathematics texts have attempted to move toward the standards, there is no program or textbook series that *comprehensively* incorporates NCTM recommendations. Teachers will have to supplement whatever main "program" or series is bought by the district. However, the textbook or adopted program should not *define* the curriculum. Instead, each teacher should know what concepts and thinking will be addressed during the year, how they fit together, how they build on the previous year, and how they will form the foundation for the subsequent year.

Even the NSF-funded programs that have mathematically rich activities will need to be supplemented with extensions for differentiation. Textbook-based programs usually must be supplemented with manipulatives and activities. But copious additional help is available on the Internet, as we note at the end of this chapter.

answers such as "maybe," "perhaps," and "probably," appropriately dealing with the big idea of *uncertainty*.

Assessment should help teachers better understand what students know and make meaningful decisions about teaching and learning activities. A variety of assessment methods should be used to assess individual students, including written, oral, and demonstration formats, all of which must fit with the curriculum. All aspects of mathematical knowledge and its connections should be assessed and used to help the teacher organize teaching and learning activities. Excellent resources are available to help teachers and districts, such as Exemplars and Balanced Assessment. (See resource list.) Standardized tests are better suited to evaluating programs rather than assessing individual students.

HOW PARENTS CAN HELP

- Parents can help by seizing every opportunity to involve their children in talking and thinking about the meaningful mathematics they encounter each day.

- Parents and children can figure out answers *together*. For instance, "How many days until my birthday?" is an opportunity to look at the calendar together.

- Parents should encourage the use of manipulatives, concrete materials, and various objects for counting, sorting, arranging, and grouping.

- Parents should encourage children to look for patterns in the world around them—in floor tiles and wallpaper; in paintings and sculpture; in coins, paper money, and change; in combination pizzas.

- Parents should encourage their children to measure heights, weights, objects, ingredients in recipes, and so forth.

- Parents can purchase educational/mathematical toys, games, and puzzles and play them with their children.

- Parents can nurture the spatial sense of these future architects and engineers with blocks and other three-dimensional building toys.

- Parents should always send the clear message through words and actions that mathematics is all around us, is a vital part of our lives, and is understandable with some effort: "Let's do it together; it can be fun."

WHAT PRINCIPALS CAN DO

- First, principals should become knowledgeable about the changes occurring in mathematics education by reading the NCTM reports and other related publications, going to workshops to learn about them, and visiting classrooms where they are happening.

- As the spokesperson for the school, its teachers, and its programs to the community and parents, the principal can actively promote Best Practice mathematics.

- The principal can explain new methods and materials, counter misconceptions, and help build support at home for this new vision of mathematics.

- The principal can hold Parents' Nights where teachers present new mathematics ideas, methods, and materials to parents and can make videotapes of these presentations for parents who did not attend.

- The principal can arrange for programs on evenings or Saturdays at which teachers engage parents in mathematical activities they can do with their children (e.g., the very successful Family Math program with dozens of activities for parents. See resource list.).

- The principal should validate dynamic activity (discussion, movement, and noise) in the classrooms as an essential part of doing mathematics.

- The principal should set budget priorities to support teachers doing staff development in the new approaches to mathematics and in purchasing materials.

- The principal can rearrange available time within the school calendar for teachers to collaborate on trying these new practices, planning, sharing ideas and materials, visiting each other's classrooms, and helping one another.

■ The principal can promote alternatives to standardized achievement tests as the sole method of assessment for grouping and placement of individual students and for evaluating schools and programs. The principal can validate for teachers and parents the legitimacy of performance assessments (e.g., Balanced Assessment, Exemplars), math journals, and open-response written formats as well as demonstrations and oral formats through which students can show their understanding.

Math Stations in a First- and Second-Grade Loop

MARY FENCL
Beye School, Oak Park, Illinois

As a student, I hit the wall with math at about seventh or eighth grade. When I first began teaching, I really didn't enjoy math. I had been a special education teacher before having a regular classroom at Beye School, and I really wanted to find something that would work for all children. The traditional approaches to math clearly did not. I specifically chose as one of my own evaluation goals to develop the math stations approach, to force myself to make it work. And math became my favorite subject! Over the past fifteen years, I have designed and redesigned many different hands-on activities for my students in mathematics.

I teach a first- and second-grade loop, having the same children for two straight years. I believe strongly in ideas and structures that will support connections for learning across disciplines and into real life. It can be a struggle to find time for rich and purposeful activities within district curriculum requirements. But I believe if students are given a framework for strategizing and the tools for exploration, they will be highly motivated to solve problems in creative and varied ways.

Over the years, my math stations have changed somewhat, and I use many variations of them throughout the school year. Some resemble workshop settings; others are more like projects. I do attempt to integrate math with other areas of the curriculum, so that all areas of our learning will benefit from cooperative learning, real-life connections, problem-solving strategies, and the use of manipulatives. My math stations continue to involve small-group work as well as individual challenges. A variety of strands (number work, measurement, geometry, etc.) are present within every cycle of stations.

On the days that we do math stations, there are usually four to six stations in the room with groups of four or five children working at each one.

We tend to have math stations two days a week, so after three weeks everyone has had a turn at every station. While I make sure that several of the stations allow the children to continue to build on concepts they've studied earlier, others offer the challenge of new explorations and several are laying the groundwork for future topics.

During the other three days of the week, my students participate in the district-adopted math program. Hands-on activities and math labs are built into that program. However, the children seem to especially enjoy the more unexpected activities on future topics or ones related to other curricular areas. I discover which explanations the children will need, where they will have difficulties, and which concepts they are ready to tackle. The children pick up the ideas through experience at the stations, which allows them to easily make connections when I later formally introduce the concept in the district program.

Each day of stations begins with clear instructions and questions to be answered. Students who have already completed the tasks often become the instructors of students new to the activity. When a round of stations is completed, I model for everyone how we write about them in our math journals. As a class, we decide on language that best describes what we did in the clearest terms. We ask ourselves, "What did this activity have to do with math? What did we learn or discover? What strategies helped us solve the problem or task?" Each student is encouraged to write about how he or she felt. First graders may start the year drawing a happy face describing an activity and may end it writing the words "I saw a pattern" or "It was hard, but I liked it." The thoughts of second graders often make connections to previous activities and to their learning process.

Each day that math stations are scheduled, I begin by going over the activities at the stations so the children remember what to do. This preparation also serves as an efficient review lesson, and by the end of the cycle for a set of stations, I ask children to do most of the re-explaining. Those who already have been to a table can readily describe it for those who haven't. A typical three-week period in a second-grade class might include the following stations:

1. *Board games.* Children can play a game using a die whose sides have geographical directions (N, S, E, W). The object is to see how many rolls it takes for each player to move from the center of the board to the edge, "out of the city." The children add and work with directionality, a topic in social studies as well as in math.

2. *Tangrams.* Tangrams are seven polygons that can be arranged into many different shapes. Children use the concept of similarity to make new shapes with larger, similar cut-out polygons that they then display in the hall.

3. *Categorizing and Venn diagrams.* Children think up their own categories for grouping cut-out figures of fish from a large and varied boxful. Then they lay two large wire loops on the floor with an overlapping area and sort fish by categories that allow for some fish to fall into the mutually inclusive overlap (e.g., fish with spots, fish with big fins, and some fish that have both).

4. *Averaging.* The children carry out various timed activities—signing their names in cursive (which they are starting to learn), jumping rope in the hall, dropping clothespins in a bottle, adding numbers on flashcards. The kids count the number of times they each complete a given activity within a three- or four-minute period. Then they use a variety of ways to figure out the "average" for the group for each activity. This is a challenging concept for second graders, but I like to see how far they can go with it.

5. *Generating arrangements.* Children work with three recipes—an ice cream sundae with three ingredients, a four-layer cake, and a pizza with five ingredients. Colored-paper layers and cut-outs represent the various ingredients. The object is to see how many different ways they can arrange the ingredients to make each food. The pizza combination activity starts with a cardboard base of sauce and cheese and cut-out paper toppings of onions, mushrooms, green pepper, pepperoni, and black olives. They manipulate the pieces and then color a picture of each pizza made. A pizza can have one, two, three, four, or five toppings. They need to write out or draw each combination to see for themselves.

6. *Lunch menus.* Each child gets $20 of play money and a copy of a restaurant menu. On a blank chart, the child writes his or her name and the names of the others in the group, and decides what will be ordered for each. The child uses a calculator to add up the subtotals for main dishes, side orders, drinks, and desserts. Finally, the child must tally the total bill, which cannot be more than $20 for the whole group of diners.

Many of the activities are connected with other subjects the class is studying or interests the children share. The fish come from the Lake Michigan unit the class has been exploring in science. The food combinations led to making pizza on another day (using English muffins). And the class is planning to go to a restaurant to celebrate the end of the school year, so each group will actually have to decide on their final choices for lunch.

As we discuss the stations before each session, I urge the children to use a *system* for approaching each one. I might ask: "Who used adding to figure out your restaurant bill as you went along? Did anyone use subtracting? How would you do that?" I try to help them see many kinds of connections. When they get to categorizing, I ask them about comparisons they've been making with two books they've read. Some elements are unique to one book, some to the other, and some are common to both. They use a Venn diagram concept to show this relationship.

While some of the stations require cooperative work, others are individually focused. The Venn diagrams and combinations are done cooperatively; the lunch menus and Tangrams are done individually; and the averaging and the directions game are actually done somewhat competitively.

It is important to start with group work immediately, at the beginning of the year. The children choose where they want to sit on the first day, and the groups that form around the tables become permanent. The children quite naturally form groups with mixed ability levels and during the year only a few changes are needed to solve behavior problems or achieve a better ability mix. The children love the variety and challenge of the math stations, so it doesn't take much warning for them to get back on track if they've strayed.

Sometimes math stations will have a workshop or project approach, allowing for greater integration of the curriculum. For example, our celebration project in first grade relies greatly on cooperative work and an understanding of patterns and relationships, with an emphasis on math problem solving while connecting math, writing, and computer work.

First, students work in teams of four to agree upon an event worthy of a celebration and then collectively write a persuasive paper that states their reasons for the celebration. The events chosen to be celebrated include the arrival of spring, the principal's birthday, and kindness to others.

Second, the team chooses a menu for the celebration within a planned budget, using pictures of food items from newspaper ads. They create coin combinations for payment of each item with an organized list and create a cash record of the various amounts with clip art coin pictures. Teams of four often break into teams of two here: one team creates the organized coin combinations list and the other makes the coin pictures on the computer.

The third aspect of the celebration is designing a seating arrangement that could accommodate the whole class. How many tables of each shape would they need to seat the entire class? Each team has choices of square, rectangular, triangular, hexagonal, and circular tables for seating. When one team has used a particular table plan, it cannot be repeated by another team. There is often a race among teams to be the first to "claim" a plan. Students make a cut-and-paste replica of their seating arrangement.

Writing an expository essay about a gift that would be appropriate for a particular celebration is the fourth step. These essays are written individually, in contrast with the cooperative persuasive writing effort. Among the gifts students have chosen are kites and jump ropes for a spring celebration, books and picture frames for the principal's birthday, and medals and trophies for kindness awards.

The final, fifth part of the project is creating gift-wrap combinations for the chosen presents. Each team has samples of three kinds of wrapping paper (pig paper, duck paper, and ice cream cone paper); three colors of bows (red, blue, and green); and three kinds of gift tags (cherry, tree, and flower pictures). They color a template to reflect the combinations they have created and to provide a visual record. Each student finishes with a booklet that includes artifacts from each step of the project. The project takes about three weeks, generally the same amount of time needed for the six-station cycle of activities.

Even though we may use one or two math periods every week for math stations, workshops, or projects and only three on the prescribed curriculum, the class is able to keep pace with other first- and second-grade classes using the district program. The combination of textbook and activities is handy, because the book organizes the topics and I can work gradually on expanding the hands-on activities. The children like the variety and the connections to things in their lives. I am always thrilled when one of them shouts, "I see the pattern!" By second grade, they expect to see patterns in math and they get really excited when they find one. Isn't that what mathematics is all about?

WORKS CITED

Bransford, J., A. Brown, and R. R. Cocking. 2000. *How People Learn: Brain, Mind, Experience, and School.* Washington, DC: National Academy Press.

Brownell, William A. 1935. *Psychological Considerations in the Learning and the Teaching of Arithmetic,* 1935 Yearbook of National Council of Teachers of Mathematics. Reston, VA: National Council of Teachers of Mathematics.

Hiebert, J., et al. 2003. *Teaching Mathematics in Seven Countries: Results from the TIMSS 1999 Video Study.* Washington, DC: U.S. Department of Education, National Center for Educational Statistics.

Kamii, C., and A. Dominick. 1998. The Harmful Effects of Algorithms in Grades 1–4. In *The Teaching and Learning of Algorithms in School Mathematics,* 1998 Yearbook of National Council of Teachers of Mathematics, edited by L. J. Morrow. Reston, VA: National Council of Teachers of Mathematics.

Kline, M. 1973. *Why Johnny Can't Add: The Failure of the New Math.* New York: St. Martin's Press.

———. 1998. *Calculus: An Intuitive and Physical Approach.* Mineola, NY: Dover Publications.

Ma, L. 1999. *Knowing and Teaching Elementary Mathematics: Teachers' Understanding of Fundamental Mathematics in China and the United States.* Mahwah, NJ: Lawrence Erlbaum.

Miura, I. 2001. The Influence of Language on Mathematical Representations. In *The Role of Representation in School Mathematics,* 2001 Yearbook of National Council of Teachers of Mathematics, edited by A. A. Cuoco. Reston, VA: National Council of Teachers of Mathematics.

Morrow, L. J., ed. 1998. *The Teaching and Learning of Algorithms in School Mathematics,* 1998 Yearbook of National Council of Teachers of Mathematics. Reston, VA: National Council of Teachers of Mathematics.

National Council of Teachers of Mathematics. 1989. *Curriculum and Evaluation Standards for School Mathematics.* Reston, VA: National Council of Teachers of Mathematics.

———. 1991. *Professional Standards for Teaching Mathematics.* Reston, VA: National Council of Teachers of Mathematics.

———. 1995. *Assessment Standards for School Mathematics.* Reston, VA: National Council of Teachers of Mathematics.

———. 2000. *Principles and Standards for School Mathematics.* Reston, VA: National Council of Teachers of Mathematics.

Schmidt, W. H., C. C. McKnight, and S. A. Raizen. 1998. *A Splintered Vision: An Investigation of U.S. Science and Mathematics Education.* Hingham, MA: Kluwer Academic Publishers.

Sun, W., and J. Y. Zhang. 2001. Teaching Addition and Subtraction Facts: A Chinese Perspective. *Teaching Children Mathematics* 7(2): 28–31.

SUGGESTED FURTHER READING

Carpenter, T. P., and T. A. Romberg. 2004. *Powerful Practices in Mathematics and Science.* Madison, WI: National Center for Improving Student Learning and Achievement in Mathematics and Science.

Devlin, K. 1997. *Mathematics: The Science of Patterns.* New York: Scientific American Library.

Fosnot, C. T., and M. Dolk. 2001a. *Young Mathematicians at Work: Constructing Number Sense, Addition, and Subtraction.* Portsmouth, NH: Heinemann.

———. 2001b. *Young Mathematicians at Work: Constructing Multiplication and Division.* Portsmouth, NH: Heinemann.

———. 2002. *Young Mathematicians at Work: Constructing Fractions, Decimals, and Percents.* Portsmouth, NH: Heinemann.

Hiebert, J., et al. 1997. *Making Sense: Teaching and Learning Mathematics with Understanding.* Portsmouth, NH: Heinemann.

Hyde, A. A., and P. R. Hyde. 1991. *Mathwise: Teaching Mathematical Thinking and Problem Solving.* Portsmouth, NH: Heinemann.

Kamii, C. 1985. *Young Children Reinvent Arithmetic.* New York: Teachers College Press.

———. 1989. *Young Children Continue to Reinvent Arithmetic: 2nd Grade.* New York: Teachers College Press.

———. 1994. *Young Children Continue to Reinvent Arithmetic: 3rd Grade.* New York: Teachers College Press.

Lehrer, R., and L. Schauble, eds. 2002. *Investigating Real Data in the Classroom: Expanding Children's Understanding of Math and Science.* New York: Teachers College Press.

Van de Walle, J. A. 2003. *Elementary and Middle School Mathematics: Teaching Developmentally.* New York: Longman.

MATHEMATICS RESOURCES ON THE INTERNET

The National Council of Teachers of Mathematics is the premier source of mathematics education materials for teachers of grades K–12. NCTM offers the standards and a wide range of supporting books, journals, electronic materials, and activity books. Of particular interest should be their *Navigation* series, activity books keyed to strands and grades (e.g., probability for grades 3 through 5). The place to start is their website: http://www.nctm.org.

We believe it is valuable to know what your critics are saying. See the California MC folks at http://www.mathematicallycorrect.com/ and be sure to read the rebuttals at http://www.mathematicallysane.com/.

Two excellent sources of performance assessments and open-ended problems by grade levels with specific rubrics are http://balancedassessment.concord.org/ and http://www.exemplars.com/.

The National Science Foundation (NSF) offers a variety of printable mathematics curricula at http://www2.edc.org/mcc/images/currsum6.pdf. The NSF has funded three national Implementation Centers, and their websites have information about the extensive NSF-funded curricula programs. After looking at their overviews, use their sites to link to the websites of the individual programs. The three implementation sites are the ARC Center (http://www.arccenter.comap.com/), which handles three elementary programs; the Show-Me Center (http://showmecenter.missouri.edu/), which reviews four middle grades programs; and COMPASS (http://www.ithaca.edu/compass/), which addresses five high school programs.

The CSMC (http://www.mathcurriculumcenter.org/) does scholarly inquiry and professional development around issues concerning the K–12 mathematics curriculum.

Family Math at http://www.lhs.berkeley.edu/equals/FMnetwork.htm is a program developed by the Lawrence Hall of Science (LHS) at the University of California, Berkeley, to bring parents and their children together to do math problem solving. Activities using inexpensive materials of all kinds (e.g., beans, blocks, bottle caps, toothpicks, coins), are described in several very readable books for parents.

Accomplished teachers who are ready to seek national certification can learn about the rigorous one-year process, find out the benefits of a successful review in their own state, and find a support group at the website of the National Board for Professional Teaching Standards at http://www.nbpts.org.

There are hundreds of websites for supplementary mathematics activities, problems, and materials. Some are mediocre and some are excellent. A short list of the very best would have to include:

Cynthia Lanius' Math Projects at http://math.rice.edu/~lanius/Lessons/
Ask Dr. Math and the Math Forum at http://mathforum.org/dr.math/dr-math.html and http://mathforum.org/

Aunty Math at http://www.dupagechildrensmuseum.org/aunty/index.html

Mega Math at http://www.c3.lanl.gov/mega-math/workbk/contents.html

Shodor Educational Foundation at http://www.shodor.org/curriculum/index.php

National Library of Virtual Manipulatives at http://matti.usu.edu/nlvm/nav/vlibrary.html

RECOMMENDATIONS ON TEACHING MATHEMATICS

Increase	*Decrease*
TEACHING PRACTICES	TEACHING PRACTICES
Use of manipulative materials	Rote practice
Cooperative group work	Rote memorization of rules and formulas
Discussion of mathematics	Teaching by telling
Questioning and making conjectures	Single answers and single methods to find answers
Justification of thinking	Stressing memorization instead of understanding
Writing about mathematics	Repetitive written practice
Problem-solving approach to instruction	Use of drill worksheets
Content integration	Teaching computation out of context
Use of calculators and computers	Reliance on paper and pencil calculations
Being a facilitator of learning	Being the dispenser of knowledge
Assessing learning as an integral part of instruction	Testing for grades only
PROBLEM SOLVING	PROBLEM SOLVING
Word problems with a variety of structures and solution paths	Use of cue words to determine operation to be used
Everyday problems and applications	
Problem-solving strategies (especially representational strategies)	Practicing problems categorized by type
Open-ended problems and extended problem-solving projects	Practicing routine, one-step problems
Investigating and formulating questions from problem situations	
CREATING REPRESENTATIONS	CREATING REPRESENTATIONS
Creating one's own representations that make sense	Copying conventional representations without understanding
Creating multiple representations of the same problem or situation	Reliance on a few representations
Translating between representations of the same problem or situation	
Representations using electronic technology	
Using representations to make the abstract ideas more concrete	Premature introduction of highly abstract representations
Using representations to build understanding of concepts through reflection	Forms of representations as an end product or goal
Sharing representations to communicate ideas	

(continues)

Best Practice, Third Edition by Zemelman, Daniels, and Hyde (Heinemann: Portsmouth, NH); © 2005

Increase	Decrease
COMMUNICATING MATH IDEAS	**COMMUNICATING MATH IDEAS**
Discussing mathematics	Doing fill-in-the-blank worksheets
Reading mathematics	Answering questions that need only yes or no responses
Writing mathematics	
Listening to mathematical ideas	Answering questions that need only numerical responses
REASONING AND PROOF	**REASONING AND PROOF**
Drawing logical conclusions	Relying on authorities (teacher, answer key)
Justifying answers and solution processes	
Reasoning inductively and deductively	
MAKING CONNECTIONS	**MAKING CONNECTIONS**
Connecting mathematics to other subjects and to the real world	Learning isolated topics
	Developing skills out of context
Connecting topics within mathematics	
Applying mathematics	
NUMBERS/OPERATIONS/COMPUTATION	**NUMBERS/OPERATIONS/COMPUTATION**
Developing number and operation sense	Early use of symbolic notation
Understanding the meaning of key concepts such as place value, fractions, decimals, ratios, proportions, and percents	Memorizing rules and procedures without understanding
Various estimation strategies	
Thinking strategies for basic facts	
Using calculators for complex calculations	Complex and tedious paper-and-pencil computations
GEOMETRY/MEASUREMENT	**GEOMETRY/MEASUREMENT**
Developing spatial sense	Memorizing facts and relationships
Actual measuring and exploring the concepts related to units of measure	Memorizing equivalencies between units of measure
	Memorizing geometric formulas
Using geometry in problem solving	
STATISTICS/PROBABILITY	**STATISTICS/PROBABILITY**
Collecting and organizing data	Memorizing formulas
Using statistical methods to describe, analyze, evaluate, and make decisions	

(continues)

Best Practice, Third Edition by Zemelman, Daniels, and Hyde (Heinemann: Portsmouth, NH); © 2005

Increase	Decrease
ALGEBRA	ALGEBRA
Recognizing and describing patterns	Manipulating symbols
Identifying and using functional relationships	Memorizing procedures
Developing and using tables, graphs, and rules to describe situations	
Using variables to express relationships	
ASSESSMENT	ASSESSMENT
Making assessment an integral part of teaching	Having assessment be simply counting correct answers on tests for the sole purpose of assigning grades
Focusing on a broad range of mathematical tasks and taking a holistic view of mathematics	Focusing on a large number of specific and isolated skills
Developing problem situations that require applications of a number of mathematical ideas	Using exercises or word problems requiring only one or two skills
Using multiple assessment techniques, including written, oral, and demonstration formats	Using only written tests

Best Practice, Third Edition by Zemelman, Daniels, and Hyde (Heinemann: Portsmouth, NH); © 2005

Chapter 5
Best Practice in Science

In the suburbs of Chicago, Naperville School District 203 has the distinction of scoring above every country in the world on the TIMSS-R science test—even above Singapore, Korea, and Japan. Two Naperville teachers, one from high school, the other fourth grade, show how they teach science with both excitement and understanding.

WASH YOUR HANDS, PLEASE!

At the start of each school year at Naperville North High School, Jim Effinger uses an activity that illustrates how a scientific inquiry approach can excite students about biology. He brings donuts to class and asks what sorts of things people might do before they eat their donuts. Possibilities include choosing and inspecting a donut, saying a prayer, and sooner or later someone mentions washing hands. "Why do that?" Jim asks. The students decide that *getting rid of germs* is the main purpose.

"How could we test to see if washing really does the job?" Jim asks. The kids agree to give this a try, and Jim brings out Petri dishes, soap, and pans of water. Each student touches one Petri dish, then washes up, and touches a second one. They inspect the dishes the next day to see what has grown. Invariably, these are the results:

- 60 to 70 percent of the dishes show more bacteria after washing than before.
- 10 to 15 percent are the same before and after.
- 15 to 30 percent have fewer bacteria after washing.

The students are surprised and confused, and begin to hypothesize about the cause of these results—old versus new bars of soap, drying or leaving hands wet. They redesign more experiments following rules they've decided on to both standardize their efforts and maximize cleaning, and try again—only to get the same results!

The kids are now hooked, eager to discover what factor influences the difference in the number of bacteria on their hands. But Jim tells them the experiment is taking too much class time. If they really want to continue, they'll have to come after school. They do, of course, and after trying out many variables (quick-thinking groups organize into cooperative teams so they can try a number of factors at the same time), they finally discover the secret: *time*. A short scrub just loosens the bacteria, so that more end up on the dish. A long, eight-minute scrub (as doctors use) indeed does the job. But far more important than just finding an answer, the students have learned many important aspects of scientific thinking: to consider many possible causes for a phenomenon, to design ways to look for these causes, to plan and control their experiments so that additional variables are not introduced, and most important, to expect that their everyday beliefs and guesses may not always be correct.

LIFT THAT WEIGHT

Maureen Nolan, a fourth-grade teacher at Mill Street Elementary School, tells her own story.

I had been teaching the Simple Machines unit for a few years. I knew what ideas were important. The teacher's guide to the unit was basically a good one, but I felt that the guide did not give the children enough ownership for their own learning. So I put the guide aside this time.

The part of the unit on levers went very well. I was very familiar with the content and the concepts the kids needed to understand. The students learned about the fulcrum by balancing two potatoes on each side of a meter stick. Their questions led to the introduction of force units and the spring scale. The children were interested, and had lots of insight while working through inquiry questions. Some of the questions were theirs; some were mine. Using lever explorations, the children learned much about force, load, fulcrum, and mechanical advantage.

But the pulley part of the unit was where the children really took over. They had learned about advantages of machines and the advantage of position with the *lever,* but the idea didn't seem to carry over to pulleys. They first had to lift a weight directly from the floor with a force gauge attached (a spring scale). Then they had to lift the weight by pulling down on a rope through a single fixed pulley (hung from the ceiling) and connected to the weight via the spring scale. I asked, "Does this wheel and rope give us an advantage?" The children tried lifting the weight with the fixed pulley and learned that although pulling down on the pulley rope seemed easier than merely lifting the weight by hand, the spring scale readings showed the same force in both cases.

The students tried to manipulate the pulley and the rope over and over. Then some kids hooked a movable pulley to the weight on the floor, looped the rope around the pulley, tied one end of the rope to a dowel sticking out from a table, and pulled up on the other end. They discovered that it actually did produce a force advantage (it took less effort to lift the weight), but they couldn't figure out why.

Another group of children who were working with the fixed pulley on the ceiling accidentally discovered something interesting. One of them had detached the weight, and another who had been pulling down happened to let go of the end of the rope. The spring scale was still attached to the pulley rope and came tumbling down on the other side of the pulley. One member of the group exclaimed, "I've got it! The weight of the scale is pulling on the rope. If you lift, you're not using your own weight to help pull down." The investigation continued out in the playground where I let the students use makeshift pulleys (ropes flung over the playground equipment) to lift each other up by pulling down. Another child, instead of continuing to work with the actual pulley, had gone to the Internet and come back armed with similar conclusions—and a lot more. He shared information about pulleys called *winches* and said that we could use more than one pulley in our systems. The excitement was contagious.

All the children wanted to build systems with more than one pulley or build winch systems from pictures. It was all I could do to keep up with requests for more pulleys, longer rope, and places to hang them. They used up more rope than I have ever used to "teach" pulley systems. The children found that more pulleys strategically placed used less force. They created their own versions of winches, block and tackle, and some arrangements I doubt anyone has ever tried. The children tried many different pulley systems, some efficient, some not, but along the way they "invented" *all* the pulley systems that I was supposed to teach. The difference was that this time the concept was attained by the children's own investigations. They realized that the ideas of physics were possible to discover for themselves.

Later that year, I remembered the Simple Machines unit when we did an investigation of weather. On a day when the weather was pretty dynamic, I asked the class, "What would we have to know and test if we wanted to have a classroom weather station?" And later, "How could we build these instruments?" Armed with a pile of books from the library, computers, the Internet, cardboard, junk, and the children's natural curiosity, they were off and running again.

A LOOK AT THE STANDARDS DOCUMENTS

In 1985 when Halley's comet reappeared, the American Association for the Advancement of Science (AAAS) began a long-term initiative to reform K–12 science education in the United States. In Project 2061, named for the year Halley's comet will reappear, scientists set out to identify the basic knowledge and skills needed by U.S. students in the sciences, mathematics, and technology. Their landmark document, *Science for All Americans: A Project 2061 Report on Literacy Goals in Science, Mathematics, and Technology,* came out in 1989 and signaled that significant transformations were needed in science curricula and teaching. *Science for All Americans* set an important tone in calling for students to experience science as an intriguing, exciting, active search for meaning and understanding of their world rather than the passive accumulation of information from lectures or the memorization of unconnected facts and definitions.

The vision of science literacy inherent in Project 2061 included developing a comprehensive map of science content. *Science for All Americans* gave teachers and schools a narrative account of the knowledge and abilities that make up science literacy. *Benchmarks for Science Literacy* (AAAS 1993) listed ideas and skills as the goals for student learning in four grade bands. Although lacking the vitality of *Science for All Americans,* the benchmarks provided a necessary step in developing the *Atlas of Science Literacy* (AAAS 2001). The *Atlas* took the benchmarks and wove more than half of them into a rich tapestry of interconnected ideas to be developed over time. The *Atlas* illustrates these connections through forty-eight "strand maps," graphical representations of the development of students' understandings of both concepts and thinking skills. The *Atlas* does not prescribe a particular curriculum, but its strand maps do give a framework for designing a curriculum. In a forthcoming edition of the *Atlas,* the remaining maps will be provided. The chapters of the *Atlas* are major topics of science and tend to follow those used in *Science for All Americans* and *Benchmarks.* Each chapter includes "clusters" of closely related maps.

The National Research Council (NRC), in collaboration with the National Science Teachers Association (NSTA), AAAS, and other organizations, created the *National Science Education Standards* (1996), a far-reaching document outlining standards in four areas of science education: *teaching, professional development of teachers, assessment,* and *science content knowledge.* This document amplified the vibrant portrayal of teaching and learning begun in *Science for All Americans.* These new standards made it clear that the content of science should no longer be studying disciplines (physical, life, earth, and space sciences) simply for their own sake. Rather, our concern must be for learning these disciplines in the context of inquiry, technology, personal and social perspectives, and the history and nature of science, via a few fundamental, unifying science concepts.

During this time, two high-profile studies appeared: the Third International Mathematics and Science Study (TIMSS) in 1995 and its follow-up study, TIMSS-R, in 1998. Results showed that although the U.S. fourth-grade students were above the international average, the eighth graders slipped below and twelfth graders considerably below international averages. Significant fuel was added to the fires of reform of the U.S. science curriculum, teaching, and learning (Schmidt, McKnight, and Raizen 1998; Martin et al. 2000).

The NRC followed its exciting description of teaching and learning in the 1996 *National Science Education Standards* (henceforth, referred to as *The Science Standards*) with the very impressive *Inquiry and the National Science Education Standards: A Guide for Teaching and Learning* (NRC 2000), which will be referred to as *Inquiry.* The authors of *Inquiry* drew heavily upon Bransford, Brown, and Cocking (1999, the expanded edition was available in 2000) for cognitive science research that supported its recommended practices. *Inquiry* presents a remarkably full and clear description of what teachers can do in their classrooms to help students understand science concepts through the process of inquiry. Taken together, *National Science Education Standards* (NRC 1996), *Inquiry and the National Science Standards: A Guide for Teaching and Learning* (NRC 2000), and *Atlas of Science Literacy* (AAAS 2001) provide a solid basis for the principles of Best Practice in science that follow.

QUALITIES OF BEST PRACTICE IN TEACHING SCIENCE

Teachers should build on students' curiosity about the natural forces of the world to stimulate scientific inquiry. The science standards about teaching encourage teachers to provide their students with inquiry-based science that emphasizes not only the knowledge and skills of scientific inquiry but also its attitudes and values—especially intellectual curiosity. Inquiry is natural for young children; they are in a state of perpetual inquisitiveness. They ask anyone who will listen a dazzling array of questions. Why is the sky blue? Where do the squirrels go at night? How did the snow get up in the sky? They try to make sense of their world, to *construct* for themselves their own explanations of what they observe and experience. It is a sad commentary on our schools that we too often dampen this fire (NRC 2000, xii).

In science, with its countless amazing phenomena, teachers can harness this innate curiosity of children and encourage a passion for exploring mysteries. The extent to which students experience the awe and wonder of confronting natural phenomena determines their future willingness to seek out those moments of profound insight into life's mysteries. When teachers of science exude a passion for knowing why and invite students to share the power and beauty of scientific understanding, they can nourish that wonder already present in the minds of their students (NRC 1996, 37).

Not all will choose to become scientists, but the science standards ask teachers to foster in *all* students the awareness of science as a dynamic, creative interplay of questions and evidence, data and ideas, predictions and explanations. We must enable all students to experience the exhilaration of the search for answers and the satisfaction of putting together the pieces of a great puzzle. We have seen that the excitement of these experiences will sustain them through the hard work of sifting through mounds of information, trying to make sense of it. If they have never experienced the power and joy of playing scientist, they have no way of knowing that the time spent in tedium is worth it. When taught well, science has enormous power to attract and motivate.

For students to build deep knowledge of sciences, they must do more than merely cover the topics. They must immerse themselves in doing science, conducting systematic inquiry. There is a broad consensus about how people learn and develop true understanding of concepts. Research from child development, cognitive psychology, and educational practice strongly supports science inquiry and hands-on science. Conversely, direct instruction dominated by science lectures, front-of-the-class demonstrations, and rote memorization of isolated facts, definitions, or explanations does not build deep or enduring conceptual understanding (Bransford, Brown and Cocking 2000; Ruby 1999).

In all the science standards documents, "inquiry" is conceived in two ways. First, inquiry is a content standard—understanding what inquiry is and developing the abilities needed to conduct it. Second, inquiry is a way to learn science, a method by which teachers help students build understanding of science concepts and theories through investigations. These are the important features of student inquiry:

- Teachers help students learn how to ask scientifically oriented questions.

- Learners attempt to answer these questions through many types of hands-on investigations. As appropriate, they analyze and interpret data, synthesize their ideas, make inferences and predictions, build models, and actively create, modify, and discard some explanations or answers. Students work together to compare results and discuss what evidence is the best. (Notice how closely these kinds of scientific thinking resemble the mental strategies of proficient *readers* on page 43.)

- Learners communicate and justify their proposed explanations to classmates and teachers by presenting their reasoning and evidence.

- Learners evaluate their explanations in light of alternative explanations, particularly those reflecting scientific understanding. They clarify concepts and explanations with teachers and other expert sources of scientific knowledge.

- Learners extend their new understanding and abilities and apply what they have learned to new situations.

- Learners, with the teacher, review and assess what they have learned and how they have learned it (NRC 2000, 24–35).

For true inquiry to occur, the teacher must ensure that students try to answer a scientific question with good evidence. To inquire means to have a *question* and to try to answer it with the best *evidence* one can find. Unfortunately, much of what happens in science classes in schools does not meet those two criteria. No provocative question, no examining evidence; just a lecture or a textbook with information, devoid of a spark that might ignite interest. This is the opposite of the NRC recommendation: "Inquiry into authentic questions generated from student experiences is the central strategy for teaching science" (NRC 1996, 31).

This concern for a scientific question and good evidence is not just for older or more capable students; it is for all students. Obviously, younger students will require more guidance from the teacher. But even at grades K–4, the standards are emphatic: students must learn how to evaluate evidence and determine the quality of the data used to make explanations. They begin this process in their early years and become increasingly sophisticated over time.

Students can and should engage in systematic inquiry in a variety of ways; there is not just one scientific method. A common misconception is that the scientific method is the same as experimentation and is the only way to "do science." Actually, scientists engage in many different activities, not all of which fit the stereotype of experimentation, and some of which are extremely creative, nonlinear, and messy (NRC 1996, 123).

The *Science Standards* acknowledge that there are many kinds of investigations. Some science educators have identified eight types that differ in purpose. Each is a form of systematic inquiry, appropriate for students in grades K–12. They are listed here from the least to the most sophisticated in terms of thinking:

- Trial and error (arbitrary search for solutions)
- Documenting (making and recording observations)
- Prediction testing (making and testing predictions)
- Product testing (identifying and using criteria)
- Experimenting (identifying and controlling variables)
- Reflecting (contemplating ideas)
- Generating models (creating constructs)
- Inventing (selecting and combining ideas/objects)
  (Bentley, Ebert, and Ebert 2000, 145–175)

The teacher gives more guidance and direction in the early grades and students assume more responsibility for the inquiry in later grades. In middle school and high school, student investigations should be far more flexible than the rigid, lock-step procedures of the familiar lab manual. They should require imagination, inquisitiveness, and inventiveness, especially in creating models, which may be physical but are just as likely to be visual, mathematical, or conceptual.

Even in grades K–4, the standards for inquiry expect students to formulate and revise scientific explanations and models. Science educators are encouraging teachers to help their students conduct model-based inquiry and engage in the key practices of modeling, generalizing, and justifying (Carpenter and Romberg 2004). An emphasis on modeling can help teaching be more like the authentic inquiry of scientists. Modeling with real data, where students use increasingly sophisticated mathematics in describing natural phenomena, is probably the most authentic inquiry (Lehrer and Schauble 2002).

Inventing may seem like a pretty tall order for students, especially in the early grades. Yet this is a wonderful way for students to consider the similarities and differences between science and technology. Technology addresses problems of human adaptation in the environment, while science attempts to answer questions about the natural world. And each, of course, influences the other. *The Science Standards* urge that we give students opportunities to engage in "technological design" (sometimes called *design science*). In Maureen Nolan's description of fourth graders studying force via pulleys, we saw her students designing their own apparatus with multiple pulleys. At the end of this chapter, we'll read how Ben Warner's high school classes designed a variety of "devices"—a hang glider, a wind pump, a ballista, and a hot-air balloon—to learn physics principles.

Scientific inquiry and hands-on science are not synonymous; many teachers do hands-on science, but not inquiry. Since 1957, when the Soviets put Sputnik into space and shocked the U.S. policy makers into science education reform, we have seen a variety of hands-on science programs attempt to balance the traditional direct instruction method of teachers *telling* students *about* science. Many hands-on activities are relatively easy for teachers to implement in a regular classroom, but students are not necessarily doing inquiry.

Five different approaches to science teaching have used hands-on activities, and one of them is inquiry (Ruby 1999). The others are demonstration, discovery, exploration, and process skills. In a *demonstration*, the phenomenon is described in a lecture or in the textbook, and the students then carry out a well-specified (by the teacher or lab manual) demonstration that allows them to see the phenomenon. The teacher then follows up with direct instruction. The demonstration is useful to make an abstract concept concrete. However, students are following a recipe without having to use their own abilities to understand what should happen.

The *discovery* approach provides students with materials, but little direct guidance on what they should do or what they might find. It is assumed that

Yes, but . . . does this mean that inquiry occurs only when students generate and pursue their *own* questions?

In most U.S. science classrooms students rarely get an opportunity to ask and pursue their own questions. If students are to develop the ability to ask questions, they must practice doing so. Classroom inquiry will vary in the amount of direction from the teacher and the self-direction of the students. Each of the features of classroom inquiry may be guided by the teacher quite directly, especially in students' early years of learning about inquiry. *Inquiry* (NRC 2000, 29) describes the continuum from teacher-directed to student self-directed. For instance, initially students are learning what "scientifically oriented" means. Therefore, the teacher supplies a question that will engage them. The students learn to sharpen or clarify the question provided by the teacher. In the most self-directed form, the students pose their own questions. Many teachers have found that the end of one inquiry can be the springboard for another based on *authentic questions* that have arisen. Students are highly motivated to pursue these new questions. However, teachers do not have to pursue every question that students ask, nor are they prohibited from providing answers their questions. How to respond to students' questions depends on the teacher's goal and the context of the classroom. There are definite occasions when the teacher can effectively build students' knowledge by answering their questions with developmentally appropriate explanations of phenomena. Likewise, not every question students might pose is suitable for investigation through inquiry. Some questions may be ill formed, others too costly, and some too far removed from the curriculum to be addressed. However, to avoid causing students to feel disenfranchised or crushing their zeal, the teacher can ask the student and the class to "play" with the question, to reword or reformulate it, and to use it as a creative springboard to a more feasible inquiry.

students will experience how science is actually done and will discover concepts on their own. In practice, pure discovery has proven too difficult for students. The approach is usually modified to be *guided discovery,* in which the teacher gives much more direction, generally through questions and dialogue. However, a great many science concepts cannot be encountered through discovery, given the limits of school settings.

In *exploration,* students are given materials to handle with little guidance and few expectations. The goal is to make them comfortable with the topic, stimulate their interest, and encourage them to raise questions. Following the exploration phase, they often receive direct instruction in the topic. They may identify issues and questions that can be addressed later.

The *process skills* approach attempts to teach individual processes used in science (e.g., observation, measurement) very explicitly and directly using hands-on activities. There are three basic problems with a pure process approach: teachers focus on the process and ignore the science concept and its context; students cannot readily transfer process skills from one context or problem to another; and the individually taught skills do not readily add up to a coherent whole.

In practice, these four approaches to hands-on science are not always so distinct and are often combined. For instance, many teachers use the "learning cycle" model of science, which originally had three phases but is now often seen with four (Bentley, Ebert, and Ebert 2000, 181–183). In the *introduction* phase, the teacher attempts to motivate students' interest by using their personal experiences and natural inquisitiveness. During *exploration,* students explore materials that stimulate them to ask questions. There may also be a strong element of *guided discovery* of the concept by the teacher. In the *concept development* phase, students share their findings about the concept. In the *application* phase, students use their understanding of the concept in a new, but related context. This phase often becomes a new investigation as students generate more new questions. Still, this learning cycle does not necessarily add up to true inquiry.

We have noted that the *inquiry* approach requires a scientifically oriented question that is answered with evidence. Inquiry expects that students will learn specific concepts and develop the capability to carry out inquiries on their own. Inquiry differs from the process skills approach in that it tries to teach an overall method that incorporates process skills rather than addressing them separately. The NRC's *Inquiry* states that the cognitive abilities required in inquiry go beyond process skills:

Inquiry abilities require students to mesh these processes with scientific knowledge as they use scientific reasoning and critical thinking to develop their understanding of science. The basis for moving away from the traditional process approach is to encourage students to participate in the evaluation of scientific knowledge. (NRC 2000, 18)

During student inquiry, the teacher should keep the focus on understanding. Research on "transfer of learning" has determined that students' understanding greatly enhances their ability to apply their knowledge to new and different (novel) situations. Students must attain an initial "threshold of knowledge," apply that knowledge in various contexts, and then receive feedback from others. If these experiences have helped them grasp the underlying principles, then they are more likely to be able to apply what they know to novel situations. They need time to wrestle with particular information, to explore underlying principles, and to make connections between new and existing knowledge. Tasks should be challenging but not frustrating. Students need to talk about the new knowledge with others to gauge its usefulness and their reactions. These factors are not present in the passive learning students get by listening to lectures (NRC 2000, 119–120; Bransford, Brown, and Cocking 2000, 235–237).

 Yes, but . . . doesn't a teacher have to use direct instruction and explain science concepts so that students can understand them?

Explanations by the teacher are not the same thing as direct instruction. During inquiry investigations, the teacher is continually interacting with the students. The teacher and students are talking about the things being studied, about data and evidence, about explanations, and about expert resources. As the inquiry concludes, the teacher may offer a good explanation to help students crystallize their understanding. Numerous research findings confirm that the cognitive process used in inquiry produces understanding (NRC 2000, 116–117; Bransford, Brown, and Cocking 2000, 11, 16–17, 185–187). This dynamic interaction contrasts sharply with direct instruction, in which there is precious little dialogue. Monologues by the teacher do not require students to use the cognitive process that produces significant conceptual understanding and scientific knowledge.

Learning science requires "conceptual change" in students; teachers must address students' existing beliefs and knowledge and directly confront misconceptions and naïve theories. Students create new knowledge by modifying and refining their existing ideas and by adding new ideas to what they already know (NRC 2000, 115). Most often new information requires some kind of cognitive reorganization. However, many learners' preconceptions are inconsistent with accepted, existing scientific knowledge. Students often hold tenaciously to these ideas, and their preconceptions can be amazingly resistant to change. Simply *telling* students what the accurate scientific conception is will not dislodge misconceptions.

The research on students' conceptions of science principles is substantial, addressing a wide range of scientific areas (Bransford, Brown, and Cocking 2000, 68–73). Students' misconceptions can dramatically interfere with understanding. Following are some common misconceptions among children:

- A worm is not an animal.
- Shadows are made of matter.
- Styrofoam is weightless.
- Cold causes rust.
- The light of a candle goes farther at night than in the day.

- Sugar ceases to exist when put in water.
- Gravity requires the presence of air.
- Heavier objects fall faster than light ones.
- Soil, water, and fertilizer are food for plants.

It is not only children who hold such misconceptions. In the marvelous video *A Private Universe,* interviews with graduates and faculty of Harvard University—including science majors—reveal startling misconceptions about earth's seasons and planetary motion. The title suggests how each of us creates our own personal, private set of conceptions about reality. This video is available for purchase; see science resources on the internet at the end of this chapter.

Some teachers and policy makers assume that *presenting* students with evidence and sound scientific reasoning will *give* them new knowledge. However, what students accept as explanations depends on their beliefs. When students think of science as a collection of facts to be memorized and explanations as reports of isolated events, they are less likely to actively seek evidence for different explanations, to think about why one set of evidence is stronger than another, and to make good decisions about which explanation has the most support. Thus, their misconceptions may not be changed by even sound scientific reasoning (Bransford, Brown, and Cocking 2000, 70, 176–179).

Research on conceptual change has found that students change their ideas only under certain conditions: (1) They attain a minimal *threshold* level of understanding of the scientific explanation; (2) they become *dissatisfied* with their current conception because it does not explain an event; (3) they think the scientific explanation is *plausible,* more *useful* in explaining other phenomena than their current misconception, and can be used to *predict* (Strike and Posner 1985).

A powerful way to dispel misconceptions is for the teacher to increase students' dissatisfaction with their current belief by means of a "discrepant event," a phenomenon that is puzzling, intriguing, and even disconcerting. For example, about 70 percent of the students in Jim Effinger's class showed more bacteria grown in the Petri dish after washing their hands than before. That's counterintuitive! These situations have the potential to create cognitive conflict in the learners and provoke in them a desire or a need to resolve the conflict—a motivation and openness to learn more (Stepans 1996; Liem 1987). A good science teacher helps students to be aware of their current conceptions and make predictions about the outcome of an event. The teacher encourages kids to publicly share their beliefs, predictions, and conceptions with the class. Then the teacher can guide them through an investigation in which they confront their belief through testing and discussion. Students work toward resolving conflict by accommodating the new concept (Posner et al., 1982; Bentley, Ebert, and Ebert 2000, 75).

Students' science learning is enhanced by collaborative group work. Saying that learners construct their own knowledge does not mean they do so alone. Research indicates that learners benefit from opportunities to express their ideas to others, challenge each other's ideas, and, in doing so, reconstruct their ideas.

Real-world scientists frequently work in groups, and science educators stress the importance of group work in school. Discussion promotes thinking and problem solving by leading students to compare alternative ideas and solutions. When differences of opinion occur in a group, the students are naturally forced to elaborate their explanations and reasoning, making them more explicit and testing them against opposing arguments. From this process, students think through scientific explanations instead of just memorizing them. They are motivated to seek answers from the text or the teacher because they desire to settle the passionate arguments that develop. As a result, they also remember a lot more of what they've studied. Group work need not be confined to lab periods. Students can work together throughout entire units, having each group investigate a different question under the same theme or topic and then report its findings to the class.

Teachers should help their students become increasingly self-directed in their learning. Especially in the classroom inquiry they conduct, teachers should help students become less dependent on them for guidance and increasingly self-reliant during the school year and over many years. Students need to become more *metacognitive,* more able to monitor their own processes of doing inquiry. They must learn how to recognize when they do not understand and should seek more information. They need to realize when they should ask questions, such as, "What evidence would convince me that these explanations are probably true?" Research underscores the value of student self-assessment in developing their understanding of science concepts as well as their abilities to reason and think critically (Bransford, Brown, and Cocking 2000, 140; NRC 2000, 119).

Teachers of science should select content and adapt curricula to meet the interests, understanding, and experiences of students. Both the NRC *Science Standards* (1996) and the *Atlas* (AAAS 2001) give us a wonderful picture of what science content ought to be and how content and process are related. These documents do not constitute a curriculum; rather, they present a framework for thinking about how science knowledge and inquiry can fit together. Although they are not grade-level specific, they do arrange the content in grade-level bands: K–3, 4–8, and 9–12 for the *Science Standards*; K–2, 3–5, 6–8, and 9–12 for the *Atlas*. They can guide teachers to select content appropriate for the developmental levels of their students. The *Atlas* has a special advantage because it makes very explicit connections among content knowledge and skills across its maps. Teachers and curriculum developers can readily use the maps of the *Atlas* as a set of evaluative criteria when selecting curricular programs. Also, the maps can help highlight gaps in the program so they know where to supplement.

In selecting and adapting curricula, teachers of science should be guided by a few fundamental concepts that students explore in depth, rather than a bunch of disconnected topics "covered" superficially. For many years, science educators have stressed in-depth inquiry of a few "big ideas" instead of wide coverage of science topics. The TIMSS researchers noted that in the top-performing countries in the world, teachers worked with fewer topics and thus could go into more depth than U.S. teachers with their broad and superficial curriculum (Schmidt, McKnight, and Raizen 1998).

The *Science Standards* state:

> Emphasizing active science learning means shifting emphasis away from teachers presenting information and covering science topics. The perceived need to include all the topics, vocabulary, and information in textbooks is in direct conflict with the central goal of having students learn scientific knowledge with understanding. (NRC 1996, 20–21)

Science curricula too often focus on discrete topics and present a maze of information, facts, and definitions without providing a coherent structure of the ideas to help students organize the information. Simply using direct instruction to tell students about theories, principles, and macro-concepts will not produce the needed understanding of the structure of those ideas. Each student must *construct* that structure herself, with the teacher providing scaffolding.

Teaching can be organized around broad unifying themes, concepts, and kinds of thinking. The *Science Standards* provide five groups of unifying concepts (NRC 1996, 104). The common themes of the *Atlas* (shown in parentheses) are quite similar and intended for the same purposes:

- Systems, order, and organization (systems)
- Evidence, models, and explanation (models)
- Evolution and equilibrium
- Form and function (scale)
- Change, constancy, and measurement (constancy and change, also addressing stability, conservation, equilibrium, steady state, and symmetry)

The common themes of the *Atlas* are more elaborate than their counterparts in the *Science Standards* because of the special mission of the *Atlas*. The strand maps provide connections among traditional scientific disciplines that are fundamental, comprehensive, understandable, and usable. The themes (underlying concepts and processes) can be expressed and experienced in a developmentally appropriate way across the K–12 grade levels.

Meaningful assessment of students' learning in science must promote, not undermine, the objectives of a good science curriculum. Since assessment influences curriculum, if we don't test the *doing* of science, our schools won't teach it. Testing in science classrooms often focuses on the body of knowledge in science, rather than the thinking and investigative processes or attitudes a student should acquire. If teachers are to promote experiential work and thinking skills in science, then assessment should stress these as well. Otherwise, teachers and students are being asked to do one thing while being held accountable for another. The *Science Standards* provide an entire set of guidelines just for assessment, highlighting the need to bring it more in line with inquiry-based science teaching. They couldn't put the need more strongly:

> Rather than checking whether students have memorized certain items of information, assessments need to probe for students' understanding, reasoning, and ability to use knowledge. Assessment and learning are so closely related that if all the outcomes are not assessed, teachers and students likely will redefine their expectations for learning science only to the outcomes that are assessed. (NRC 1996, 82)

The *Science Standards* also affirm the value of authentic assessments such as portfolios, interviews, performance tasks, and self-assessment. While it is difficult for formal pencil-and-paper tests to assess attitudes and thinking skills, informal but structured assessment based on teacher monitoring of group investigations can do this job very well. Teachers can use checklists to guide their observations, have students fill out self-evaluation forms, and in brief conferences, ask questions about why individuals or groups are proceeding in a particular way. Even written tests can be designed so that they focus on the *process* of finding an answer, rather than just the answer itself. Some questions can be designed so that they have more than one right answer, so as to recognize creative thinking and problem solving.

To firmly establish these Best Practices in schools, extensive, comprehensive professional development must be sustained over time. Fortunately, we have many more resources and tools for helping teachers implement new teaching methods than in the past. Professional development takes time and should be considered more like cultural change than mere technical training. Especially among elementary school teachers, science literacy is desperately needed. A marvelous resource for improving science teaching is Susan Loucks-Horsley et al. (2003), which describes in detail fifteen strategies for professional development, including immersion in inquiry, immersion in the world of the scientist, action research, study groups, and examining student work/student thinking and scoring assessments.

Yes, but . . . what about the state competency tests? Don't the students need to cover a large number of science topics to do well on these?

When tests focus almost entirely on memorized facts and definitions, the study of science can become a game of trivial pursuits. Many science educators have fervently argued against high-stakes testing of this nature. Policy makers and administrators tend to react to the presence of these tests by pressuring teachers to increase *direct instruction*. This reaction is ironic since this type of teaching has produced low test scores in the past. Unfortunately, proponents of this form of testing have little or no knowledge of cognition and what it means for students to understand a science concept. One of the major functions of a concept is to organize and explain a collection of facts at a somewhat greater level of abstraction. Similarly, unifying principles and common themes help students to grasp and organize the concepts of science. With greater understanding of a core principles, they will be better able to understand their related concepts. And understanding concepts will help them understand and remember facts. All of these understandings are best built through student inquiry, not by teachers telling students about underlying principles.

Unfortunately, many state departments of education have translated the marvelous ideas in Project 2061 and the *Science Standards* and *Inquiry* into tests of narrowly focused skills and science facts. For instance, in Virginia the state *Standards of Learning* for science contain goals with many of the lofty ideas of inquiry and understanding unifying principles. (See science resources on the internet.) These state standards were then transformed into a grade-level curriculum framework that has eviscerated the spirit of the national documents. They do not draw on the *Atlas of Science Literacy*, which was designed to assist in creating frameworks. They cite the unifying principles, but then boldly state that they are going to use something else because there is no consensus for them. Each section of the framework spells out the detailed factual knowledge and skills expected of children. While they espouse inquiry in some sections, they ignore the way the two NRC documents explain inquiry and how to do it. Instead, they opt for a list of process skills narrowly and tediously defined, exactly what the national standards are trying to move science teachers away from. Is it any wonder that the state test consists of forty multiple-choice questions focused with laserlike intensity on specific factual knowledge?

Nevertheless, while we fight for the better assessment practices urged by the 1996 *Science Standards,* we should not hesitate to implement Best Practices in teaching and learning in our schools and classrooms. The inquiry-based science teaching described in the documents will foster the development of students who love and understand science. These students will understand more science, take more science courses, and develop more well-structured science knowledge. There is also research evidence that these students will score well on any *reasonable* science achievement test (Bransford, Brown, and Cocking 2000, 11).

HOW PARENTS CAN HELP

Parents don't need to be science experts to help stir the interest and imagination of their children. Kids are questioners, and the world around them can stimulate their natural curiosity. Parents need only be supportive. Here are some ways they can help.

- Encourage children's questioning, as this is the real basis for scientific learning. Questions are an opportunity to reinforce kids' natural desires to learn and to gain some control over the complex world around them.

- Read aloud from the steady stream of newspaper reports on science discoveries and technological problems and advances.

- Read aloud and encourage the children to read independently from the many children's nonfiction books about nature, health, and technology; biographies of scientists (male and female); and children's literature (where natural forces play a key role).

- At gift-giving time, choose some of the excellent nonfiction books (e.g., Ruth Heller's books on wildlife, David Macauley's splendid architecturally illustrated books on how things work, and Alfred A. Knopf's Discovery series, which covers everything from diamonds to dinosaurs).

- Plan family activities that promote an interest in science—observing the habits of pet hamsters or guinea pigs; vacationing at the beach or in the mountains; visiting zoos, museums, and special exhibits.

- Ask teachers and principals how science is taught in their schools. Are there in-depth, hands-on study units? Are the kids encouraged to ask questions, develop hypotheses, and interpret the data, or is the process primarily lecture, workbook pages, and cookbook experiments? What kinds of learning do the tests emphasize?

WHAT PRINCIPALS CAN DO

The leadership demonstrated by the principal may be critical to the successful implementation of Best Practice in science. It may also ensure that science is not relegated to the back burner, taught infrequently and ineffectively. Here are some ways the principal can demonstrate support for good science teaching.

- Read as much as possible of the documents cited here. Get copies for the faculty and take part in faculty meetings to discuss key ideas. Ask teachers to rotate as discussion leaders for a day.

- Ensure teachers get effective professional development for meaningful, conceptually and experientially rich science explorations.

- Lobby for excellent hands-on, inquiry-based materials and programs.

- Help the faculty think through the logistics of doing hands-on inquiry—how to set up the materials for investigations, clean up, store materials, etc.

- Model an inquiring, problem-solving spirit in the school. When unusual natural or biological events occur—violent storms, mold infestations, measles outbreaks—classes can be invited to investigate them and prepare explanatory displays.

- Arrange for sufficient planning time for teachers to incorporate new ideas into their teaching plans.

- Get resources for after-school and summer curriculum design time for teams of teachers.

- Build community understanding and support of real scientific inquiries by having students share their inquiry projects with parents on Back-to-School night.

- Encourage neighboring hospitals, industries, universities, botanical gardens, zoos, and other facilities to provide visiting experts and data sources for inquiring kids.

- Ensure that the school library has books for independent nonfiction reading.

- Seek help from community businesses and parents to obtain the simpler supplies that can support many excellent classroom experiments.

- Encourage the district to adopt assessment practices that reflect the goals advocated by the science standards.

Design Science in Physics: A Collaborative Adventure

BEN WARNER
Federal Hocking High School, Stewart, Ohio

Seven years ago I stood on the front steps of Federal Hocking High School in southeastern Ohio and took in the view of the woods and pastures that surrounded the school on all sides. I thought, what a beautiful place, and how very rural. I had come to the school to interview for a science teaching position and was impressed with the staff and students. It was the only place I interviewed that involved students in the selection process.

When I was offered the position I readily accepted, but I knew that I would be facing some big changes. I was moving from a fairly well-to-do school district that seldom had difficulty in providing whatever materials a teacher would need in the classroom. I knew from the start that funds would be limited and that I would need to be creative to provide a good science experience for my students.

Like most science teachers, I wanted to have a great deal of hands-on, project-based learning in my classroom. I love doing big, complex projects that take a while to complete. These kinds of projects are daunting to the students at first, but as they get into them, they realize that if they establish a logical, step-by-step process, looking at individual components instead of at the entire project, they can do some amazing things. I wanted my physics students to build siege engines and flying machines and cool laboratory gizmos that would get them as excited about science as I am. So I jumped in with both feet my first year and tried a "big idea" project with my very first physics class.

I started with the intention of building a full-scale working hang glider. The students had suggested the idea and were very excited to begin. We had a block schedule with a double period, two to three times a week. About half the time of each session was spent on the project and about half on the formal curriculum, which included a textbook that they read, lab activities, and discussions about physics concepts. The formal curriculum did have some hands-on work, such as determining different amounts of force with various levers. We also studied the physics of roller coasters. I always tried to connect the concepts from the physics text and our formal curriculum to the key concepts in the "big idea" projects.

The students were excited about the glider project and held fund-raising activities to earn money for supplies and materials. They researched, they designed, and they constructed. In the end, we had a full-scale working hang glider that flew (like a kite, unmanned, and with an added weight). The students learned a great deal about the physics of flight and, all in all, the project was a success.

However, a number of problems arose during the process. I discovered that even if the project was large and complex, sometimes there was not enough work to keep the entire class occupied. I had several frustrating days in which many students were not working and progress was slow. I also found that some students who were confident in the research and design aspect balked at the idea of building something, and vice-versa. They seemed to go through a sequence, starting with frustration at not knowing how to get started or what steps to take; then they would begin to make progress but would become impatient, wanting to test out their device immediately. Finally, when the device was operational and all the testing and modifying was complete, they were very satisfied with their success. They were proud of their tangible accomplishment.

Each year I tried something a little different to make the experience more effective. I would initially explain the design process to students, but I found that instead of jumping right in to their chosen devices, they needed to experience a shorter, modified version of the design/build/test process. So I asked kids to practice by building a Rube Goldberg–type machine. I gave a few suggestions and answered their questions, and the students worked in small groups to produce some pretty unusual machines.

Along the way, I continually asked myself, "How can the students do large-scale, whole-class projects that engage all of them, all of the time?" I struggled with this problem for two more years, trying different organizational approaches to the projects, but I continued to have problems with the consistency of student work. The end products were always great. For instance, one year a group of students created a small replica of a *trebuchet*, a medieval siege machine—essentially a very powerful catapult. The real-life trebuchets could hurl a four-hundred-pound stone hundreds of feet in an arc and with tremendous force, enough to smash holes in eight-foot-thick castle walls. The students were initially surprised that when their model trebuchet was in a fixed position on the ground, it did not launch its payload even half as far as when it was on wheels. From their readings and our class discussions, they realized that when the trebuchet was on wheels, all the energy from the catapult and its counterweight remained in the device itself. But when it was stationary, fixed to the ground, significant energy was transferred into the ground and did not contribute to the launch. The students were learning so much from these projects that I really didn't want to give up on the idea, but I needed a way to distribute the labor so that everyone was being productive through the entire process.

I thought about doing several projects at the same time, but felt that this didn't fit with what I wanted in terms of a whole-class scenario. Too many separate projects going at the same time seemed disjointed and were difficult to manage. I also believed that I needed a multiple-intelligence approach to be able to keep the whole class interested and on task.

When I considered those two characteristics together, the solution came to me. The production of each of the physics projects is inherently a multiple-intelligence process. The process of developing a device can be broken down into several steps that use different intelligences and that can be accomplished by different teams. I imagined a research and design team that would:

- research the history and variable designs of the chosen device
- bring the historical design concepts together to create their own design of a device
- produce scale drawings and exploded drawings to help construct the device

A materials acquisition team would:

- acquire the monies and materials necessary to construct the device

Finally, an engineering team would:

- construct the device from the drawings of the design team
- test the device and make modifications

I realized that three or four projects could be run at the same time with each individual student working on each device, but as a member of a different team for each one. Each student could then be responsible for different tasks on the various projects. By taking this approach, students had the opportunity to shine in one or more aspects of a project and also to expand their horizons by being involved in project responsibilities that were new to them.

The first year that I tried this jigsawed team approach, the students chose three projects to build: a ballista (a medieval siege weapon that looks like a giant crossbow), a hot-air balloon, and a wind-generated pump. I explained to them how they would have a role in the development of each of the projects and how each project would have three teams. Here is an example of how one student experienced this process.

For one project, Susan worked with two other students as a research and design team; they first researched the historical background of the hot-air balloon and then developed their own plans for making a smaller-scale hot-air balloon for the class. Once they had decided on a design, Susan and her team members made detailed drawings of the balloon and all of its components. They then presented their idea to the rest of the class, who acted as consultants to offer other ideas and opinions for the successful design of the hot-air balloon. The other design teams presented their plans for a ballista and a wind-powered pump the same day. The design teams then incorporated any changes that they agreed on during this consultation phase and passed the plans off to the materials acquisition teams.

Susan then joined a new group of students who were the materials acquisition team for a wind-generated pump. The class decided to hold a servant-for-a-day auction to raise money for the projects and had raised enough to purchase the majority of the materials needed for all three projects. Some of the students brought materials from home. Susan was given the task of picking up the wood needed to build the frame and the blades for the pump. Any time some of the materials proved harder to obtain than was first thought, the acquisition teams met with the design teams to look at some alternatives.

Once the materials were obtained, Susan joined her third project group, the engineering team responsible for building a ballista. Before the engineering team began building, they met with the design team and materials acquisition team to ensure that all of the plans were understood and that all of the materials were available. Susan had not built anything before and was concerned as to how well she would do. Her engineering teammates had built things before and, along with me, showed her how to use different tools and how different parts of the ballista would fit together.

I have learned through several years that the research and design teams create projects that vary enormously in complexity. On occasion, the designs were too complex for the engineering teams to build. Sometimes the engineers discovered that plans on paper don't necessarily translate well to making the real thing, especially if the designers didn't clearly think through every step. In both these cases, the engineering teams met again with the design teams to rethink particular aspects of the design. Occasionally I had to work with them to help with the feasibility. Mostly, I asked questions such as, "What do you think is going to happen if you do that?'

At the end of the group's first semester, I was thrilled with the outcome. Throughout the process all of the students had worked consistently, produced three fine products, and learned an amazing amount of physics about how they worked. They were all able to explain the principles of physics that applied to each of the devices because, unlike most projects, they had worked on each device.

I have since used this collaborative team process with several other classes and have achieved consistent success with whole-class projects. The class numbers have varied, but with a little manipulation of group numbers and tasks, the process has continued to engage the kids and their teacher.

WORKS CITED

American Association for the Advancement of Science. 1989. *Science for All Americans: A Project 2061 Report on Literacy Goals in Science, Mathematics, and Technology.* Washington, DC: American Association for the Advancement of Science.

———. 1993. *Benchmarks for Science Literacy.* New York: Oxford University Press.

———. 1997. *Resources for Science Literacy: Professional Development.* New York: Oxford University Press.

———. 1998. *Blueprints for Reform.* New York: Oxford University Press.

———. 2001. *Atlas of Science Literacy.* Washington, DC: American Association for the Advancement of Science and National Science Teachers Association.

Bentley, M., C. Ebert, and E. S. Ebert. 2000. *The Natural Investigator: A Constructivist Approach to Teaching Elementary and Middle School Science.* Belmont, CA: Wadsworth/Thomson Learning.

Bransford, J., A. Brown, and R. R. Cocking. 2000. *How People Learn: Brain, Mind, Experience and School* (Expanded Edition). Washington, DC: National Academy Press.

Carpenter, T. P., and T. A. Romberg. 2004. *Powerful Practices in Mathematics and Science.* Madison, WI: National Center for Improving Student Learning and Achievement in Mathematics and Science.

Lehrer, R., and L. Schauble, eds. 2002. *Investigating Real Data in the Classroom.* New York: Teachers College Press.

Liem, T. 1987. *Invitations to Science Inquiry.* Lexington, MA: Ginn Press.

Loucks-Horsley, S. et al. 2003. *Designing Professional Development for Teachers of Science and Mathematics* (Second Edition). Thousand Oaks, CA: Corwin.

Martin, M. O., et al. 2000. *TIMSS 1999: International Science Report.* Boston, MA: International Study Center, Boston College.

National Research Council. 1996. *National Science Education Standards.* Washington, DC: National Academy Press.

———. 2000. *Inquiry and the National Science Education Standards: A Guide for Teaching and Learning.* Washington, DC: National Academy Press.

Posner, G., K. Strike, P. Hewson, and W. Gertzog. 1982. Accommodation of a Scientific Conception: Toward a Theory of Conceptual Plan. *Science Education* 66 (2), 211–227.

Ruby, A. 1999. Hands-on Science and Student Achievement. Report RGSD-159. Santa Monica, CA: Rand Corporation.

Schmidt, W. H., C. C. McKnight, and S. A. Raizen. 1998. *A Splintered Vision: An Investigation of U.S. Science and Mathematics Education.* Hingham, MA: Kluwer Academic Publishers.

Stepans, J., 1996. *Targeting Students' Science Misconceptions: Physical Science Concepts Using the Conceptual Change Model.* Riverview FL: The Idea Factory.

Strike, K., and G. Posner. 1985. A Conceptual Change View of Learning and Understanding. In L. West and A. Pines, eds. *Cognitive Structure and Conceptual Change.* Orlando FL: Academic Press.

SCIENCE RESOURCES ON THE INTERNET

The website of Project 2061 of the American Association for the Advancement of Science features the Center for Curriculum Materials in Science, professional development workshops, books, and online tools. Visit http://www.project 2061.org.

The Annenberg Foundation has excellent curriculum materials and many videos for students and teachers, including *A Private Universe,* at http://www.Annenberg .org and http://www.learner.org.

The Exploratorium Institute for Inquiry provides elementary science educators with excellent experiences with inquiry through workshops, online resources, follow-up opportunities, and networking at http://www.exploratorium.edu/IFI /resources/websites.html.

Lawrence Hall of Science at the University of California, Berkeley, is probably the premier source of science resources. It offers programs, workshops, publications, and excellent K–8 curricula—GEMS (Great Explorations in Math and Science) and FOSS (Full Option Science System)—at http://www .lawrencehallofscience.org/.

Massachusetts Institute of Technology includes on its website a section with an incredible amount of information on inventions and discoveries; see http: //web.mit.edu/invent.

National Science Teachers Association offers teachers excellent professional development programs, tons of resources for all grade levels, books, materials, guides, and even a science store at http://www.nsta.org.

NOVA Online is a great resource for science activities and video resources; see http: //www.pbs.org/wgbh/nova/teachers/resources/subject.html.

Science NetLinks provides lesson plans and reviewed Internet resources for K–12 science educators at http://www.sciencenetlinks.com.

Accomplished teachers who are ready to seek national certification can learn about the rigorous one-year process, find out the benefits of a successful review in their own state, and find a support group at the website of the National Board for Professional Teaching Standards at http://www.nbpts.org.

The state of Virginia's Science Standards of Learning Curriculum Framework (2003) are available at http://www.pen.k12.va.us/VDOE/Instruction/Science /sciCF.html

RECOMMENDATIONS ON TEACHING SCIENCE

Increase	*Decrease*
ADAPTING THE CURRICULUM	
Selecting and adapting curriculum	Rigidly following curriculum
Curriculum with a variety of components emphasizing active and extended scientific inquiry	Curriculum dominated by presentations of scientific knowledge through lecture, text, and demonstration
Learning disciplines (physical, life, earth sciences) in the context of inquiry, technology, personal and social perspectives, history and nature of science	Studying disciplines (physical, life, earth sciences) for their own sake
Curriculum that includes natural phenomena and science-related social issues that students encounter in everyday life	Broad coverage of unconnected factual information
Studying a few fundamental, unifying science concepts	Covering many disconnected science topics
Understanding scientific concepts and developing abilities of inquiry	Memorizing scientific facts and information
Integrating all aspects of science	Separating science knowledge and science process
Connecting science to other school subjects	Treating science as a subject isolated from other school subjects
BUILDING UNDERSTANDING	
Providing challenging opportunities for all students to learn science	Providing science learning opportunities that favor one group of students
Focusing on student understanding and use of scientific knowledge, ideas, and inquiry processes	Focusing on student acquisition of information
Building on students' prior knowledge to foster conceptual change	Providing direct instruction irrespective of prior knowledge
Sharing responsibility for learning with students	Teacher maintaining responsibility and authority
Supporting a classroom community with cooperation, shared responsibility, and respect	Supporting competition
Providing opportunities for scientific discussion and debate among students	Asking for recitation of acquired knowledge
Understanding and responding to individual student's interests, strengths, experiences, and needs	Treating all students alike and responding to the group as a whole

(continues)

Best Practice, Third Edition by Zemelman, Daniels, and Hyde (Heinemann: Portsmouth, NH); © 2005

Increase	*Decrease*
PROMOTING INQUIRY	
Implementing inquiry as instructional strategies, abilities, and ideas to bea learned	Implementing inquiry as a set of processes
Activities that investigate and analyze science questions over extended periods of time	Activities that demonstrate and verify science content and investigations confined to one class period
Emphasizing multiple process skills (manipulation, cognitive, procedural) in context	Emphasizing individual process skills (e.g., observation or inference) out of context
Using evidence and strategies for developing or revising an explanation	Getting an answer
Science as argument and explanation	Science as exploration without purpose and experiment based on recipes
Communicating science explanations	Providing answers to questions about science content
Student collaborative groups defending conclusions, analyzing and synthesizing data	Individuals and groups of students analyzing and synthesizing data without defending a conclusion
Doing more investigations in order to develop understanding, ability, values of inquiry, and knowledge of science content	Doing few investigations in order to leave time to cover large amounts of content
Applying the results of experiments to scientific arguments and explanations	Concluding inquiries with the result of the experiment
Public communication of student ideas and work to classmates	Private communication of student ideas and conclusions to teacher
ASSESSING SCIENCE LITERACY	
Continuously assessing student understanding with students engaged in ongoing assessment of their work	Testing students for factual information at the end of the unit, chapter, or term
Assessing to learn what students do understand	Assessing to learn what students do not know
Assessing what is most highly valued: rich, well-structured knowledge as well as scientific reasoning and conceptual change	Assessing what is easily measured: discrete, scientific knowledge

Best Practice, Third Edition by Zemelman, Daniels, and Hyde (Heinemann: Portsmouth, NH); © 2005

Chapter 6
Best Practice in Social Studies

POSTHOLES IN HISTORY

When Wayne Mraz' U.S. history class at Stagg High School (in Palos Hills, Illinois) heads to the library to prepare group reports on the 1960s and the Vietnam War, some groups are clear about their topics and immediately begin looking for books and articles. Others struggle to understand what they're after. One pair, Greg and Jim, has chosen the phrase "guns versus butter," the 1960s debate over spending money for war or for domestic social needs. Wayne confers with them: What have they learned about the Vietnam War? "My father was there," Jim muses. "He says it was just a huge waste. It didn't do any good for anyone, and a lot of his friends got killed." The boys decide to focus on the "guns" side of the equation. "So how do you relate the war to the weapons?" Wayne asks. They list some issues—the cost of military equipment, situational advantages held by the Viet Cong, limitations on what the military was permitted to do, the problematic nature of the most powerful unused weapon, The Bomb—all mentioned only sketchily in the textbook. On a scrap of paper, the students draw a cluster to see how the issues are connected, and Wayne moves on.

Wayne calls his course "Postholes." Instead of a myriad of dates, names, and events, he wants students to grasp a limited, carefully chosen set of major issues and turning points in U.S. history. An example would be the progressivism of the 1890s, which occurred simultaneously with the rise of a middle class in this country—in other words, the postholes aren't exactly themes, but more like important historical moments that draw numerous issues and developments together. With these postholes, students can dig deeply and make connections, building the rest of the structure, the "rails," themselves. Wayne rarely lectures. Instead, key concepts are explored in two-week units, each centered around reports by collaborative groups. By the time the students reach the 1960s, they're well practiced at using clustering or time lines as visual guides, and teaching and learning with one another.

For several days, Wayne begins the unit by exploring the period and topics to investigate. He starts with an "admit slip." Responding to sections on the sixties and the Vietnam war in their textbook, students must identify ten key words or phrases on a slip of paper to get in the classroom door. At first, some end up sitting on the hallway floor to fill out their admit slips, but by now everyone follows the routine. Wayne checks the slips for highlights to share with the class and reviews possible report topics, some of which were mentioned in the kids' admit slips:

- Guns vs. butter—the Great Society
- The 1968 Democratic National Convention
- The civil rights movement
- The U.S. military doctrine of "flexible response"
- Tensions between domestic and foreign policy
- The return of Richard Nixon

Students add other topics, such as "music of the sixties" and "films about Vietnam."

The next day, everyone brings in a summary of an article from the library about the sixties, or of an original document if they can get to the Internet or the microfilm collection at the nearby community college. Again, highlights are shared. In groups of three, students chart what they know about the period and their questions. These lists give direction to their reading and often influence choices of report topics.

Students now watch portions of a video, *Homefront During the Vietnam War*. Wayne doesn't let kids snooze while the VCR runs, however. He repeatedly pauses the tape to pose a question or make a connection with an idea he has introduced. Finally, the groups fill out a form to reflect on the work so far.

For a few minutes of day three, introductory activities continue. Students arrive to hear a Simon and Garfunkel tape bringing them sounds of the sixties. They complete short summaries of articles of their choice from a collection Wayne has handed out, and then watch and discuss a few more minutes of the videotape begun the day before. Then it's off to the library to begin researching possible report topics. Wayne circulates, observing which groups have found topics and which need help. By the end of the period, all the groups have usually decided. One more class period is then spent in the library.

A few groups are ready to give reports on Friday, while the rest finish on the weekend. Monday and Tuesday are devoted to the balance of the presentations. One might wonder how the students draft reports so quickly, and whether this allows for sufficient thought and learning. But Wayne has done much to ensure that the reports are productive. The entire first week of the year is spent on thinking strategies and logical problem solving. Then there's the regular practice. By the time the class reaches the 1960s, everyone has completed at least a dozen reports. In addition, he finds that students' frequent use of visuals—clusters, time lines, flowcharts—develops habits of organized thinking. While teachers worry about coverage of mandated curriculum, Wayne estimates that 85 percent of the topics he would have discussed in lectures emerge in the reports. And students remember the material more permanently because the reports are their own.

Wednesday is test day. Each group has prepared one essay question and five multiple-choice questions on their topic. Wayne circulates, helping the groups craft fair and interesting questions. For the test, each group draws an essay question out of a hat. Everyone answers all the multiple-choice questions, plus one or two items Wayne adds. The group that originated a given essay question also grades it. As homework, each student must evaluate the essay of one other and provide a written rationale for the grade awarded. Wayne adjudicates discrepancies and complaints, and finally the evaluating students meet with the corresponding essay writers to discuss the evaluations.

This approach to testing results in a great deal of learning. Students listen carefully to the reports since they will have to answer questions on one of them. Much thinking goes into the question drafting, evaluation, and rationale writing. Students who find it hard to accept a teacher's evaluation give much more credulity to their peers' observations about a problem. Sometimes it takes several periods just to talk through these evaluations.

Wayne is constantly rethinking and enriching these units. For his government class, he has built in connections to the world beyond the classroom. For example, each student must bring in a newspaper political cartoon every Monday, with a brief explanation of its topic, its main point, and the student's response. Students must watch *Washington Week in Review* on television every Friday night (and he tapes it so no one can offer excuses). By the following Wednesday, students must submit a report on a topic from the previous show, connecting it with some specific item in the textbook. In addition, they must discuss their topic with a parent—and Wayne serves as the "parent" for students whose parents struggle with English or are unavailable.

Wayne has also devised a strategy to connect each day's work to the "postholes" of the course. He's painted a hopscotch outline on the floor at his room's entrance, with a phrase for one of the big concepts in each square. At the period's end, every student must hop on the squares that connect with the day's topics to get out of the room. The kids moan about this "dorky" ritual—but they do it and watch each other land on the squares. They learn the important ideas and continually connect separate pieces of information with them. "I'm getting old," Wayne tells the kids. "Just humor me." And they do.

A LOOK AT THE STANDARDS DOCUMENTS AND STATE STANDARDS

As in other major school subjects, national education organizations have drawn up recommendations for high-quality teaching and learning in the social studies. The National Council for the Social Studies (NCSS) published *Expectations of Excellence: Curriculum Standards for Social Studies* in 1994 and followed up with *National Standards for Social Studies Teachers* in 1997. The NCSS approach is highly conceptual, emphasizing ten thematic strands:

- Culture
- Time, Continuity, and Change
- People, Places, and Environments
- Individual Development and Identity
- Individuals, Groups, and Institutions
- Power, Authority, and Governance
- Production, Distribution, and Consumption
- Science, Technology, and Society
- Global Connections
- Civic Ideals and Practices

The document outlines four perspectives for approaching these themes: personal, academic, pluralist, and global. Four learning skills are called for: (1) acquiring information and manipulating data; (2) developing and presenting policies, arguments, and stories; (3) constructing new knowledge; and

(4) participating in groups. The authors then list principles for teaching and learning intended to make social studies meaningful, integrative, value-based, challenging, and active. Clearly, the NCSS aims to make social studies engaging for students, central to the development of citizenship, and focused on higher-level thinking to the greatet extent possible.

What happens, then, when a state develops its own standards, course guidelines, and tests in this area of learning? How do these documents measure up? And how can teachers pursue excellent teaching and learning while fulfilling the accountability requirements that a state sets out? We offer the social studies standards for the state of California as an instructive example.

The California standards in social studies consist of three components published by the California Department of Education: (1) a document called *History–Social Science Framework for California Public Schools, Kindergarten Through Grade Twelve* (updated 2001); (2) *History–Social Science Content Standards* (2001), which lists the expectations for each grade; and (3) the social science portions of the California Standards Tests, which are intended to measure students' learning as outlined in the first two publications. Let's look at samples of each of these.

The *Framework* is an extremely ambitious document that presents broad principles and outlines coursework for each grade level. It begins with a set of seventeen principles that set very high, laudable aims for content knowledge, development of citizenship, active application of learning, and in-depth thinking. Many sound similar to those provided by the NCSS, though the *Framework* is so sharply centered on the chronological study of history that other social studies areas are pushed to the side. The principles, briefly:

1. The *Framework* is centered on the chronological study of history.
2. Teaching should use both an integrated and a correlated approach to the teaching of history–social science.
3. History should be viewed "as a story well told."
4. The study of history should be enriched with literature, "both literature *of* the period and literature *about* the period."
5. A richer and broader curriculum is needed for the early grades (K–3).
6. Major historical events and periods should be studied "in depth as opposed to superficial skimming of enormous amounts of material."

7. Curriculum should be sequential, "with knowledge and understanding built up in a systematic fashion from kindergarten through grade twelve."

8. A multicultural perspective should be incorporated throughout.

9. Coverage of world history should increase to three years (grades six, seven, and ten).

10. "Ethical understanding and civic virtue" should guide thinking about public affairs.

11. Civic and democratic values should be developed "as an integral element of good citizenship."

12. Students should frequently study and discuss "the fundamental principles embodied in the U.S. Constitution and Bill of Rights."

13. Teachers should "present controversial issues honestly and accurately within their historical or contemporary context."

14. Social studies should acknowledge "the importance of religion in human history."

15. Critical thinking skills should "be included at every grade level."

16. A variety of content-appropriate teaching methods must be supported to "engage students actively in the learning process."

17. Students should participate "in school and community service programs and activities." (*Framework*, 4–8)

For the most part, a noble and impressive list! How do the standards and teaching recommendations give expression to this list? Let's consider sixth grade as an example. These standards, we quickly discover, are composed entirely of lists of historic events, people, and social developments for each of seven periods or cultural groups: prehistoric development, Egypt and Mesopotamia, ancient Hebrews, ancient Greece, ancient India, early Chinese civilization, and ancient Rome. Considering that the start and end of the year, plus December holiday preoccupations and spring testing, all eat up time, that comes to about one month per topic—exceedingly tight. It's just barely enough to dip into each one with no breathing room, verging on the "forced march across many centuries and continents" that the *Framework* specifically warns against. In contrast, students at one high-performing school we know of spend three months studying the history and culture of Japan, covering many of the *Framework's* seventeen principles in the process.

The California curriculum for sixth grade does meet some of the larger standards that the *Framework* sets out. It's certainly multicultural. It allows for integrating social sciences other than history—archaeology, geography, political science, comparative religion. The curriculum is open to critical thinking and a variety of teaching methods, though it doesn't allow much time or specifically invite them. But it doesn't address students' active participation in school or community service, or real-world application of democratic values. A creative teacher might help students compare earlier societies to our present American scene. But because the California social science curriculum is so exclusively chronological across the entire twelve grades, involvement of students in contemporary issues doesn't occur until senior year. Thus a number of the major principles of the *Framework* can't be addressed until then, unless the teacher devotes time to topics not in his or her grade-level standards.

Things get still more troubling when we look at the tests (California Department of Education 2004). Social science is not tested in California until eighth grade. The eighth-grade test, however, covers material from sixth through eighth grades. And the questions are almost entirely focused on factual recall. Questions released from the 2003 history–social science test ask about the topic of a speech by Horace Greeley, the source through which papermaking was introduced to Europe, and the geographic center of Incan civilization. Some questions can be answered by logical guessing. But thinking skills, citizenship, exploration of controversial issues? Gone. Caring "deeply about the quality of life in their community, their nation, and their world"? Unfortunately, not a hint.

What can good teachers do? Must they simply stuff kids' heads with as many factoids as possible? In fact, brushing lightly over thousands of bits of information is highly unlikely to make many of them stick. Mentioning something is not teaching it.

We need to recognize that the broader standards outlined in the introduction to the California *Framework,* just like those in the NCSS thematic strands, are mostly standards for good teaching and learning, standards aimed at increasing students' opportunities to learn things important to them and to our society. The wide range of possible questions on the test can be best dealt with not through mind-numbing memorization, but by having students read widely and deeply. And in-depth inquiry activities will help them to make meaning from the information they encounter. That way, they'll remember the material because it's part of something larger, something important. It's easy to panic when you see the long list of content "standards" that are just topics to cover, or when you look at the parade of factual test questions from previous years. But good teachers know that the principles in the introduction to the California *Framework* are good ones, and if we stick to them, our kids will do just fine on the tests. California teachers needn't let a weak standards design derail them from good teaching. And we find similar stories when we look at other state standards across the country.

QUALITIES OF BEST PRACTICE IN TEACHING SOCIAL STUDIES

Students of social studies need regular opportunities to investigate topics in depth. Complete "coverage" in social studies inevitably results in superficial and unengaging teaching, like painting a room—covering plenty of square feet but only one-thousandth of an inch thick. All the national reports and even some state standards recognize that real learning involves in-depth understanding of the complexities of human existence. *National Standards for History* urges "the use of more than a single source: of history books other than textbooks and of a rich variety of historical documents and artifacts that present alternative voices, accounts, and interpretations or perspectives on the past" (NCHS 1996, "Standards in Historical Thinking," Standard 3, Internet version). *Expectations of Excellence: Curriculum Standards for Social Studies* also highlights this need:

> Instruction emphasizes depth of development of important ideas within appropriate breadth of topic coverage and focuses on teaching these important ideas for understanding, appreciation, and life application. . . . The most effective teachers . . . select for emphasis the most useful landmark locations, the most representative case studies, the most inspiring models, the truly precedent-setting events, and the concepts and principles that their students must know and be able to apply in lives outside of school. (NCSS 1994, 163)

Yet with so many social studies fields—history, geography, sociology, anthropology, psychology—each including many topics, teachers have no choice but to accept that under *either* approach—thin coverage on everything or depth for a few areas—students won't learn it all in twelve years of school. Covering less in more depth, however, not only ensures better understanding but increases the likelihood that students will pursue further inquiry on their own.

Students need opportunities to exercise choice and responsibility by choosing their own topics for inquiry. Particularly because social studies is meant to prepare students for *democratic* citizenship, student initiative is necessary in the classroom. Student choice need not mean chaos or avoidance of important content. Good teachers like Wayne Mraz provide lists of significant topics, give mini-lessons on thoughtfully choosing what to study, and conduct brief conferences to help students focus their work. This not only increases students' engagement, but teaches an important academic skill needed for research projects in the upper grades and college—how to judiciously choose topics for reports and papers.

Social studies teaching should involve exploration of open questions that challenge students' thinking. Just about any study of human social existence brings up meaningful and often controversial questions—the pull between community and individual freedoms, scarcity of resources, particularity of local regions versus interrelatedness in a larger world. Reports and panels have recommended the use of large essential questions for many years, but abstract and brief prescriptions are not enough to help teachers change—just as they aren't enough to help students learn. Teachers need to ask questions that invite discussion, rather than merely check for memorized facts or seek confirmation of the teacher's own conclusions. And then, teachers must help students to examine both problematic and positive historical events honestly, and to analyze their meaning.

This open approach requires effective management of small-group learning. Teachers can assign brief learning-log entries and small-group tasks to prepare students to contribute to class discussion. Climate-setting activities are also essential, helping students respect one another's opinions and trust that their ideas will not be ridiculed. After a good discussion, students' follow-up reports and wall charts—or at the very least, end-of-class reflections—solidify learning so ideas do not evaporate when class is over.

To make concepts real, social studies must involve active participation in the classroom and the wider community. Real-world involvement is crucial for imparting the values of civic involvement and responsibility in our society. *Expectations of Excellence* goes to considerable length to describe the possibilities, including field trips, collaborative learning, and increased individual responsibility for learning. In spite of our overstuffed district curriculum guides, the task need not be overwhelming. Concepts in sociology, economics, and politics are often embodied right in the school building. Children of most ages can debate an issue, draft letters and proposals, seek changes in school procedures, or set up committees to accomplish some new goal. Student participation in these matters will, as an additional benefit, contribute to the social health of the school (Apple and Beane 1995). Active involvement can easily reach outside the school walls as well. Representatives of many social and governmental organizations happily visit classrooms. Parents who work in relevant fields make willing resource people. Genuine responses from community leaders to students' letters, proposals on community projects, and real advocacy are long remembered by students.

Yes, but . . . how can a teacher find time to prepare such projects if individuals or groups of students are working on different issues and there's no textbook for any of them?

Increasingly, fascinating and useful units and inquiry projects are available on the Internet. "History Lab" at http://hlab.tielab.org, for example (run by the Technology in Education Laboratory), features thirty-three projects using primary sources, which are themselves viewable on the Web. A thematic approach, as outlined in Tarry Lindquist's *Seeing the Whole Through Social Studies* (2002), makes student participation easier to include in the curriculum. Many strategies are described in Janet Alleman and Jere Brophy's *Social Studies Excursions, K–3* (2003), Stephanie Steffey and Wendy Hood's *If This Is Social Studies, Why Isn't It Boring?* (1994), and David Kobrin's *Beyond the Textbook: Teaching History Using Documents and Primary Sources* (1996). When teachers take a thematic approach to the subject, they find that many of the items listed in their social studies curriculum guides are automatically covered.

Social studies should involve students in both independent inquiry and cooperative learning in order to build skills and habits needed for lifelong, responsible learning. Social studies classes can easily use cooperative learning. Inexperienced kids will need training, but this in itself is an important skill throughout students' schooling as well as their adult lives. Then, it is wise to balance individual and group work. Students differ in their learning styles. A "classroom workshop" structure, in which students research topics of their own choosing while the teacher holds brief one-to-one conferences, is a highly efficient way of immersing children in individual study. These two organizational structures—cooperative groups and classroom workshop—are also essential tools for making a nontracked, heterogeneous classroom work (see Chapter 8 for descriptions of these strategies).

Social studies reading should include engaging real-world documents and not just textbooks. Textbooks present many limitations for effective learning. They are difficult to read because they are stuffed with facts, and yet nothing is explored in depth. Students find them boring. And especially problematic, they generally present just one view of events, compared with the many intense and engaging controversies that surround so many social studies topics. Primary sources, in contrast, bring history to life. Articles from newspapers, magazines, and the Internet abound. An excellent example is *Making Freedom: African Americans in U.S. History* (2004), a five-volume set of primary documents and materials. To ensure that kids become lifelong readers, able to evaluate many points of view on topics important to their lives, we must help them get well into the habit of reading widely in school.

Social studies should involve students in writing, observing, discussing, and debating to ensure their active participation in learning. Reports and studies all recommend active learning, but teachers often picture writing, discussion, or group work as time-consuming add-ons. They imagine essays that take days for kids to write and nights for teachers to grade. But activities can be brief and informal—taking only moments to help students focus, consider a problem, or reflect on the material. Students can write for two minutes at the beginning of the period to recollect main points covered the day before. They can stop in the middle of the class to talk for five minutes in pairs or threes about possible solutions to a problem. At the end of class, they can reflect on a notecard about what they've learned or don't understand.

Modes other than lecturing and quizzes are important tools to advance learning of the subject matter. To review concepts in a unit, for example,

Diane Deacy has her sixth graders at Washington Irving School in Chicago make what she calls ABC charts. Each student develops her own alphabet chart using words she identifies from the unit (grouping X, Y, and Z together, since words beginning with these letters are rare). On butcher paper, each student creates her chart with twenty-four squares, drawing a representation and writing a brief explanation in each square. Students naturally review the material they've studied while admiring each other's charts.

Writing, drawing, and other forms of expression help students create new understandings for themselves. As *Expectations of Excellence* puts it:

> Students . . . do not passively receive or copy curriculum content; rather, they actively process it by relating it to what they already know (or think they know) about the topic. Instead of relying on rote learning methods, they strive to make sense of what they are learning by developing a network of connections that link the new content to preexisting knowledge and beliefs anchored in their prior experience. (NCSS 1994, 169)

Social studies learning should build on students' prior knowledge of their lives and communities, rather than assuming they know nothing about the subject. It is usual media practice to bash education by recounting the geography or history bloopers kids may write for quizzes. Yet children listen far more closely to adult conversation than we like to acknowledge, and they sense issues and paradoxes in their community, school, and families much more sharply than we realize. When we do take notice, many of us find this phenomenon alternately cute and threatening.

We do far better to find out just how much children *do* know about the world around them and build our teaching on that. By drawing out and building on this prior knowledge, we show how social studies concepts are relevant to children's lives, and not just abstract words.

Of course, children grasp more complexities as they move up the grades and grow more aware of the wider world and social interactions around them. Traditional social studies curricula have followed an "expanding environments" formula for elementary grades, starting with the family and working outward. More recently, however, educators have developed ways to introduce young children to history, geography, and other topics in forms they can grasp. *Doing History: Investigating with Children in Elementary and Middle Schools,* by Linda Levstik and Keith Barton (2000), provides detailed guidance along with vignettes of elementary school teachers involving children in active historical inquiry.

Social studies should explore the full variety of cultures found in America, including students' own backgrounds and other cultures' approaches to various social studies concepts. The acrimonious debate over "our common heritage" versus study of individual ethnic groups has sadly obscured much of the real meaning in both these options. First, minority children are not the only ones who have been cut off from their own history. Most students in any age group or social stratum know little of the historical and political developments that affected their families and forebears. History, politics, economics, culture, folklore—all become more meaningful to students through interviews with parents, grandparents, neighbors, and other adults. Children of minority backgrounds especially tend to see school as disconnected from their own lives. However, once the connection is made, study of other cultural groups creates an understanding of the common struggles and aspirations of various groups, and an appreciation of their rich particularity. Far from engendering divisiveness, this approach helps eradicate it.

What is crucial is *how* these things are studied. We've observed children endure profound boredom as a teacher demanded memorization of the principal grain crops of various African countries. Such methods do not reconnect children with history but further alienate them. In contrast, when students make choices, discover facts that they find significant in their own family backgrounds, and share them with mutual respect, they not only feel pride in their own heritages, they also become more excited about history and geography and culture in general—and perhaps even learn to critique and evaluate aspects of their own past, as well as to honor them.

Social studies should avoid tracking of students because it deprives various groups of the knowledge essential to their citizenship. The *National Standards for History* is eloquent on this matter:

> Standards in and of themselves cannot ensure remediation of the pervasive inequalities in the educational opportunities currently available to students. The roots of these problems are deep and widely manifested in gross inequities in school financing, in resource allocations, and in practices of discriminatory "lower tracks" and "dumbed-down" curricula that continue to deny large sectors of the nation's children equal educational opportunity. . . . Every child is entitled to and must have equal access to excellence in the goals their teachers strive to help them achieve and in the

instructional resources and opportunities required to reach those ends. Nothing less is acceptable in a democratic society. (NCHS 1996, "Three Policy Issues," Internet version)

As more educators contemplate the social and racial implications of tracking, they realize they must find alternatives. Research indicates that tracked classes do not even benefit high-track students as much as once claimed, but they do systematically discourage the lower-achieving ones. Particularly in social studies, students of various backgrounds can benefit by hearing from one another (Wynne and Malcolm 1999).

Social studies evaluation must reflect the importance of students' thinking and help prepare students to be responsible citizens, rather than rewarding memorization of decontextualized facts. In the history class described at the beginning of this chapter, Wayne Mraz has each small group of students compose a test question, evaluate the answers written by individual students from another group, and then review answers with the test takers. This may take longer than a traditional quiz, but it ensures a tremendous amount of learning. Evaluation in Mraz' classes is not just time spent checking on students or tallying bubbles on a score sheet; it's another occasion for learning.

Because the goal of social studies education in the national reports and many state standards documents is not just acquisition of information, but preparation for democratic citizenship, it's obvious that evaluation in social studies should serve that goal. Thus, perhaps more than in any other subject, evaluation in social studies must involve reflective *dialogue* between teacher and student. Yes, we can ask students to show they have specific knowledge of a subject. But every evaluation should also include larger questions; for example, in the student's view, what constitutes a good historian (or history book, or observer of folk traditions)? We should ask *how* students have learned about families or governments or economic systems. Students should analyze the significance, implications, and human issues within the material studied. Then the answers should be valued by extending discussion out from them, rather than leaving tests to be simply graded and forgotten.

However, for students to feel free to speak their minds, we must have many occasions when their ideas are *not* evaluated. Students should be able to select essays and products they will submit for evaluation, out of a larger portfolio, to maintain a zone of safety for expression that is risky, tentative, or unresolved.

Yes, but . . . how can a teacher simultaneously meet the needs of students with differing achievement levels, particularly in the upper grades?

The answer is found in how the classroom is organized. Traditional lectures and quizzes are least adaptable to heterogeneous grouping, offering only one version of the material for everyone. Small-group work, mixing children of differing levels in each group, is much more successful, as long as children are trained to take an active role. When kids talk through and argue over ideas, more learning happens. The teaching that stronger students provide for the less prepared benefits them both—the old saw being quite true, that the teacher of a subject often learns more than her students. When clusters of students need particular kinds of support, the teacher can form temporary, ad hoc groups, but needn't employ permanent divisions that label and segregate kids.

The other effective structure for a part of each day or week in a nontracked setting is the classroom workshop. As we describe in Chapter 8, in a classroom workshop, students use individual and group brainstorming to list topics they are interested in reading and/or writing about. They work independently while the teacher circulates for *brief* one-to-one sessions where, rather than giving answers, the teacher leads the student to solve problems. In brief mini-lessons at the beginning or end of class, concepts or processes are taught, based on what the class may need. Near the end of the period, one or two individuals share something they've done, and every few weeks everyone turns in a written product.

This structure requires training, for both teachers and kids. But it uses time very efficiently, allows students to work at their own levels and to make choices according to their interests, and teaches responsibility, something surprisingly missing from traditional classrooms. Teachers at all grade levels, in every socioeconomic setting, have found classroom workshop highly effective.

Finally, to mirror the democracy for which we are preparing them, students can participate in setting the standards by talking together about what makes a good paper/answer/project and how to evaluate it. In fact, the issue of meaningful evaluation of students' education is a worthy social studies topic in itself.

HOW PARENTS CAN HELP

- Model social involvement. When parents participate in community activity, children learn its importance. They pick up on how groups work and what issues matter. Also valuable are trips to museums, historical societies, ethnic fairs, interesting neighborhoods, and historically or culturally significant sites in the surrounding regions.

- Subscribe to or bring home newspapers and news magazines. For awareness of politics, social issues, and history, parents and kids can read articles together and discuss them, with the children talking first so adult opinions don't overpower them. History teacher Wayne Mraz requires government students to discuss with a parent or other adult at least one issue on TV news each week. Students report briefly, and parents sign off that the discussion took place.

- Share family history, memories, and customs to help children value their heritage and realize how the family's experiences are a part of the surrounding world. Visits to other places family members live or grew up expand students' world.

- Share the satisfactions, problems, and issues involved in work lives. Discussing our own work makes the economic world more understandable to children. Of course, sharing these matters also helps make a family more close-knit and mutually supportive.

- Parents can visit classes to discuss with students the work they do and the community efforts they are involved in. The impact of politics and economics on our lives illustrates for students the reality of the material they are studying. While at the school, parents can also let administrators know they support the concept of mixed ability levels in social studies (and other areas too). Educators often worry that the public won't understand if the school adopts a more equitable approach to learning.

WHAT PRINCIPALS CAN DO

- Encourage focus on just a few of the many topics in the social studies curriculum. Some topics can become themes for grade-level or schoolwide units, alleviating the pressure for wide but shallow coverage in areas like history and geography.

- Help the community value children's honest thinking about real social concerns. Teachers need confidence that people truly support such inquiry. At Stagg High School, the social studies department publishes an annual journal of student writings on history and government, and distributes it throughout the community, with the principal's support. The school has also held public forums on occasions such as the fiftieth anniversary of *Brown v. Board of Education*.

- Work to develop the school as a community. If students learn about democracy in the classroom but find it missing from their surroundings, then the learning seems a mere exercise. The school can become a model community where students participate in making decisions, developing norms and expectations, and planning schoolwide learning activities. Kids can then reflect on what takes place and find connections with topics they've studied.

- Adopt programs that help social and ethnic groups relate positively. This includes peer mediation, by which students arbitrate conflicts or deal with tensions that may arise between individuals or groups.

- Use your influence to help move a school or district away from tracking. Ability grouping separates social groups and deprives some students of learning. Change requires not just working on policy, but staff development on differentiated instruction, classroom workshop, and collaborative work so that learning flourishes for all students.

Getting to Know You Culturally

YOLANDA SIMMONS
School of the Arts, South Shore High School, Chicago, Illinois
PATRICIA BEARDEN
Executive Director, American Family History Institute, Chicago, Illinois

Sisters Pat Bearden and Yolanda Simmons have taught in Chicago schools at many different grade levels. They've designed similar cross-disciplinary family history projects for three different audiences—elementary school kids, high schoolers, and teachers and parents in in-service programs—and described this work in *History Comes Home: Family Stories Across the Curriculum* (Zemelman et al. 1999). The biggest difference between the three groups is simply the time allotment—high schoolers work longer than either younger kids or adults. We'll describe the activity as it plays out in a middle school classroom.

Day One. Yolanda introduces family history by discussing with students various types of families, making sure that those in alternative situations—living with grandparents or adopted families, for example—are included. The class charts the numbers of students living in various situations. Everyone considers, "What is family, and what does it mean?" Yolanda shares her own family history using baby books and photo albums. She also passes around copies of naming books and kids enthusiastically thumb through to see what their names mean. Students head home excited to research their own families, carrying letters explaining the project along with an agreement to be signed by parents, to avoid misunderstandings later. The letter outlines project objectives:

- Learning in social studies, particularly history and geography
- Connecting family to public history
- Teaching core democratic values
- Learning in language arts, including writing narrative and learning research skills

A set of questions goes home as well to help students begin their inquiries:

1. What is your full name?
2. Whom are you named after?
3. What is the meaning of your name?
4. Describe your favorite childhood memory.
5. Where were you born?
6. If you lived in other places before coming to this city, where did you live and when did you come here?
7. Where were your parents and grandparents born?
8. Where did your ancestors originate from, within the United States or outside this country?
9. Does your family have reunions or other gatherings where you can meet and learn about them?
10. Has anyone in your family recorded your family's history?

Day Two. (Day two is actually several days later, to allow for return of agreement forms and gathering of information.) Yolanda begins by reading a passage from literature or a high-quality picture book such as *Grandfather's Journey* (by Allen Say) or *The Great Migration* (by Jacob Lawrence)—books that speak as powerfully to teenagers and adults as to younger children. While students conduct interviews with partners, sharing information they've gathered, Yolanda circulates around the room, snapping a Polaroid picture of each kid. She also makes sure she has information of her own about at least one student. Students then take a minute to select data from their notes for oral presentations.

Next, each student introduces his or her partner "culturally." Simmons models the first introduction:

This is John. He was born here in Chicago on the South Side, and he was named after his great uncle. His family comes from Macon, Georgia, where he used to visit every summer when he was small. He loved his grandmother's cooking, but hated the farm work he had to do. He hasn't yet discovered where his family came from before that, but he wishes he did. Mee-ee-eet John Coleman!

Everyone applauds. As introductions proceed, Yolanda records the place-of-family-origin information in two columns—inside and outside the United States—using newsprint on the wall.

Day Three. Students begin bringing in family data. The sharing usually proceeds over several days while the next activities simultaneously unfold. This way, quicker-responding students encourage the more hesitant to get their stories in. Then, working in small groups, the students tally information from the interviews to develop a class profile, each group focusing on one question. The groups chart their results, using percentages and visual representations, and report briefly to the class. Students go home with a sheet for obtaining more detail on their families' stories. They are encouraged to call or e-mail grandparents who live out of town.

Day Four. Students now have enough data to create a time line for their family histories. They brainstorm stepping-stones—important events in their own lives and the lives of their families—and when the time lines are completed, Yolanda circulates time lines for Chicago and recent U.S. history. The students begin to identify connections between larger public events and their own families' activities.

Day Five. Students are now prepared to share their learning with the class, and they spend much of the period on this. At the end of the hour, they jot in journals and debrief on what they're learning—similarities and differences among family experiences, and connections between these experiences and larger world developments, such as wars, migrations, economic cycles, and political events.

Days Six and Seven. Students now draft personal biographies that include family history as well as connections with local and world events. Yolanda helps the students create a rubric for an effective biographical essay, using examples from previous years so the kids see what it takes to make their biographies strong.

Days Eight and Nine. Students take turns sharing biographical essays in small groups and with the whole class.

Day Ten. At the end—and at points all along—the students debrief their research in short discussion and writing sessions. Yolanda asks, "How did you feel when you were doing _____? Why do you think we included that step?" Students find the latter question especially thought-provoking. They feel ownership of the curriculum because they are asked to evaluate it. Reflection also highlights processes that have helped them learn.

For a culminating evening, parents, grandparents, and other family members come to the school to view the students' work at stations around the classroom. Response sheets at each station allow family members to enter additional information and comments.

Clearly, this unit starts students thinking about multicultural issues, but it does much more, integrating many school subjects and applying them to topics of real interest in students' lives. It employs interviewing, writing, researching, working individually, in pairs, and in small groups, and giving oral reports. It honors students' own knowledge and backgrounds, but also unearths much that they did not know about their own past, and connects it with academically traditional geography and history. It builds community and a level of intergroup understanding sorely needed in many locales. It requires an extended span of time—two weeks—but provides a powerful springboard to many other social studies topics, both in traditional areas and farther afield.

WORKS CITED

Alleman, Janet, and Jere Brophy. 2003. *Social Studies Excursions, K–3*. Portsmouth, NH: Heinemann.

Apple, Michael W., and James A. Beane. 1995. *Democratic Schools*. Alexandria, VA: Association for Supervision and Curriculum Development.

California Department of Education. 2001. *History–Social Science Content Standards*. Sacramento, CA: California Department of Education. Available online at http://www.cde.ca.gov/be/st/ss/hstmain.asp.

———. 2004. Standardized Testing and Reporting, 2003 and 2004 CST Released Test Questions. Sacramento, CA: California Department of Education. Available online at http://www.cde.ca.gov/ta/tg/sr/css05rtq.asp.

History–Social Science Curriculum Framework and Criteria Committee. 2001. *History–Social Science Framework for California Public Schools, Kindergarten Through Grade Twelve*. Sacramento, CA: California Department of Education.

Kobrin, David. 1996. *Beyond the Textbook: Teaching History Using Documents and Primary Sources.* Portsmouth, NH: Heinemann.

Levstik, Linda, and Keith Barton. 2000. *Doing History: Investigating with Children in Elementary and Middle Schools* (Second Edition). Mahwah, NJ: Lawrence Erlbaum.

Lindquist, Tarry. 2002. *Seeing the Whole Through Social Studies* (Second Edition). Portsmouth, NH: Heinemann.

National Center for History in the Schools. 1996. *National Standards for History Basic Edition* (Revised). Los Angeles: National Center for History in the Schools.

National Council for the Social Studies. 1994. *Expectations of Excellence: Curriculum Standards for Social Studies.* Washington, DC: National Council for the Social Studies.

———. 1997. *National Standards for Social Studies Teachers.* Washington, DC: National Commission on Social Studies in the Schools.

Primary Source, Inc. 2004. *Making Freedom: African Americans in U.S. History.* Portsmouth, NH: Heinemann.

Steffey, Stephanie, and Wendy Hood. 1994. *If This Is Social Studies, Why Isn't It Boring?* York, ME: Stenhouse Publishers.

Technology in Education Laboratory. The History Lab. http://hlab.tielab.org.

Wynne, Harlan, and Heather Malcolm. 1999. *Setting and Streaming: A Research Review* (Revised Edition). Edinburgh: Scottish Council for Research in Education.

Zemelman, Steven, Patricia Bearden, Yolanda Simmons, and Pete Leki. 2000. *History Comes Home: Family Stories Across the Curriculum.* York, ME: Stenhouse.

SUGGESTED FURTHER READINGS

Ankeney, Kirk, ed. 1996. *Bring History Alive: A Sourcebook for Teaching U.S. History.* Los Angeles: National Center for History in the Schools.

Banks, James A., and Cherry McGee Banks. 2003. *Multicultural Education: Issues and Perspectives* (Fifth Edition). Indianapolis: Wiley.

Brown, Cynthia. 1992. *Like It Was: A Complete Guide to Writing Oral History.* New York: Teachers and Writers Collaborative.

Daniels, Harvey, and Marilyn Bizar. 2004. *Teaching the Best Practice Way: Methods That Matter, K–12.* York, ME: Stenhouse.

Dunn, Ross, and David Vigilante. 2000. *Bring History Alive: A Sourcebook for Teaching World History.* Los Angeles: National Center for History in the Schools.

Edinger, Monica. 2000. *Seeking History: Teaching with Primary Sources in Grades 4–6*. Portsmouth, NH: Heinemann.

Geography Education Standards Project. 1994. *Geography for Life: National Geography Standards*. Washington, DC: Geography Education Standards Project.

Lindquist, Tarry, and Douglas Selwyn. 2000. *Social Studies at the Center: Integrating Kids, Content, and Literacy*. Portsmouth, NH: Heinemann.

Loewen, James. 1996. *Lies My Teacher Told Me: Everything Your American History Textbook Got Wrong*. New York: Simon & Schuster.

National Council on Economic Education. 1997. *Voluntary National Content Standards in Economics*. New York: National Council on Economic Education.

———. *Choices and Changes: In Life, School, and Work* (four-volume series covering various grade levels). New York: National Council on Economic Education.

Percoco, James. 1998. *A Passion for the Past: Creative Teaching of U.S. History*. Portsmouth, NH: Heinemann.

Selwyn, Douglas, and Jan Maher. 2003. *History in the Present Tense: Engaging Students Through Inquiry and Action*. Portsmouth, NH: Heinemann.

Short, Kathy, et al. 1996. *Learning Together Through Inquiry: From Columbus to Integrated Curriculum*. York, ME: Stenhouse.

Tunnell, Michael O., and Richard Ammon. 1993. *The Story of Ourselves: Teaching History Through Children's Literature*. Portsmouth, NH: Heinemann.

Zinn, Howard. 2001. *A People's History of the United States, 1492 to Present* (Revised). New York: Perennial Books, Ltd.

SOCIAL STUDIES RESOURCES ON THE INTERNET

The McREL (Mid-continent Research for Education and Learning) website lists the standards created by the Geography Education Standards Project, along with very (perhaps overly) specific content-knowledge benchmarks. It also provides lesson plans, many of which are interactive and thoughtful. Visit http://www.mcrel.org/lesson-plans/index.asp.

The National Center for History in the Schools developed the current national history standards, and lists for purchase dozens of study units on U.S. and world history. Several sample units are downloadable from the website: http://www.sscnet.ucla.edu/nchs.

The National Council on Economic Education website provides a large collection of 432 quite interactive lessons on economic concepts, organized by grade level, concept, and standards covered: http://www.ncee.net/resources/lessons.php.

The National Council for the Social Studies offers association news, research bulletins, publications, and conference information at http://www.ncss.org.

The National Geographic Society has an elaborate website that features a variety of lesson and unit plans for teachers on topics like ecology, resources, and wildlife: http://nationalgeographic.com/xpeditions/standards/matrix.html.

The Smithsonian Institution offers materials on a wide variety of social studies topics, from archaeology to economics to studies of war, and more. Some sections offer virtual tours of museum exhibits, while others feature articles, links to online copies of primary sources, and detailed lesson plans. Visit http://www.si.edu.

Accomplished teachers who are ready to seek national certification can learn about the rigorous one-year process, find out the benefits of a successful review in their own state, and find a support group at the website of the National Board for Professional Teaching Standards at http://www.nbpts.org.

RECOMMENDATIONS ON TEACHING SOCIAL STUDIES

Increase	Decrease
In-depth study of topics in each social studies field, in which students make choices about what to study	Cursory coverage of a lockstep curriculum that includes everything but allows no time for deeper understanding of topics
Activities that engage students in inquiry and problem solving about significant human issues	Memorization of isolated facts in textbooks
Student decision making and participation in wider community affairs, to build a sense of responsibility for their school and community	Isolation from the actual exercise of responsible citizenship; emphasis only on reading about such topics
Participation in interactive and cooperative classroom study processes that bring together students of all ability levels	Lecture classes in which students sit passively; classes in which lower-achieving students are deprived of knowledge and opportunities to learn
Integration of social studies with other areas of the curriculum; use of real-world reading	Narrowing social studies activity to include only textbook reading and test taking
Richer content in elementary grades, using children's prior knowledge, from psychology, sociology, economics, and political science, as well as history and geography; younger students' experience can relate to social institutions and problems of everyday living	Assumption that students are ignorant about or uninterested in issues raised in social studies
	Postponement of significant curriculum until secondary grades
Students' sense of connection with American and global history, diverse social groups, and the environment that surrounds them	Use of curriculum restricted to only one dominant cultural heritage
Inquiry about students' cultural groups and others in their school and community, thus building ownership in the curriculum	Use of curriculum that leaves students disconnected from and unexcited about social studies topics
Use of evaluation that involves further learning and that promotes responsible citizenship and open expression of ideas	Assessments only at the end of a unit or grading period; assessments that test only factual knowledge or memorization

Best Practice, Third Edition by Zemelman, Daniels, and Hyde (Heinemann: Portsmouth, NH); © 2005

Chapter 7
Best Practice in Visual Art, Music, Dance, and Theater

As elsewhere in America, the hallways of many Chicago elementary schools tell a sad story. Rows of identical children's artworks stretch down the corridors, neatly hung in class sets: thirty matching pink valentines on white doilies, thirty cute cutout Thanksgiving turkeys, thirty leaping leprechauns with the same yellow pipes puffing the same grey smoke. Usually the only thing that distinguishes one of these products from the next is the signature at the bottom (often done with a flourish that hints at much greater possibilities) and the degree to which each child can stay inside the lines. Often, these clone galleries originate with seasonal art projects offered up by teachers' magazines, complete with photocopy masters and instructions for the students: "Attach cotton ball here." "Now, color the beak yellow."

Meanwhile, across town, Linda Voss' third graders nervously climb off the school bus at Clinton School, in an unfamiliar Chicago neighborhood far from their own homes. They have come to meet Eleanor Nayvelt's students, who until now have been unseen cross-city pen pals. Linda and Eleanor have embarked on a family history project that will bring together these children—recent Russian immigrants from Clinton and African American and Hispanic children from Washington Irving—to explore their own stories of movement and change and to link these stories with U.S. and world history. In addition to meeting local curriculum mandates, Linda and Eleanor hope their students will confront, explore, and perhaps overcome the worrisome stereotypes that they've already begun to express about other races and cultures as they live in their separate communities and attend ethnically segregated schools.

The young visitors troop quietly up the stairwell to the Clinton library, where Eleanor's students are waiting in a big circle of chairs, an empty seat next to each child. With some hesitation, the Irving kids filter into the room, taking the alternating seats and carefully not staring at the Russian children beside them. After a few welcoming comments, the teachers introduce Cynthia Weiss, a mosaicist and painter who works with the Chicago Arts Partnerships in Education (CAPE). Cynthia gently explains that she is there to help everyone get acquainted with their pen pal. She passes out black construction paper and pastel markers to everyone, inviting students to doodle a bit to get the feel of the medium. For practice, she asks the kids to try to blend a color that exactly matches their own skin tone.

Then Cynthia asks pen pals to pair up, one from Irving and one from Clinton, and to carefully, patiently look at each other. Suddenly, the thing that everyone was avoiding a minute ago (but really wanted to do) has become the assignment. Cynthia talks a few minutes about different approaches to portraits, and then turns the children loose to portray each other in pastels. The kids look each other over, many shyly, and slowly begin to draw. Thus begins a study of immigration, ethnic history, and U.S. and Chicago history, with pairs of children of vastly different heritages facing and drawing each other.

Twenty minutes later, an extraordinary set of pair portraits has been created, signed, and hung around the room: "Vasily by Rebecca," "Rebecca by Vasily." As artwork, the quality of many portraits is astounding: faces are vibrant, lively, colorful. Many of the children could be picked out of a lineup by these accurate renderings. On the other hand, even after Cynthia's skin-tone demonstration, some children of color have depicted their Caucasian pen pals as stark ice-white, while some of the Russian kids have drawn their African American partners with outsized lips and pitch-black skin. The preexisting images that children carried with them to this meeting are manifest in the artwork. Linda, Eleanor, and Cynthia know they were right to start this project; everyone has much to learn.

On and off over the next couple of months, the children work in their own classrooms, and also meet several more times, using art to explore and connect their heritages and to relate that heritage to the wider stories of immigration to and within the United States. They choreograph dances to express key events, creating performances that combine traditional cultural elements with of-the-moment hip-hop favorites. These dances occur in front of stage sets designed and painted by the children. They write and publish stories, poems, and nonfiction pieces about their family and community history. As a culminating project, each student makes a large collage of his or her home, using colored construction paper and a snapshot of himself or herself, to be trimmed and placed somewhere in the collage. Some kids perch themselves on the roof of their apartment building; a few peer through windows; others wave from the stoop.

Finally, the Clinton and Irving kids get back together to see what they've got. Looking at the rows of colorful houses, one student suggests, "Let's make a neighborhood." Everyone puzzles over how to form all these homes into a community. The teachers carefully try to stand back, letting students find their own direction. After some discussion, the kids decide to create a huge square, with everyone's house around it. But what to put in the middle? The Russian kids want to put the ocean in the center to represent their journey to their new home in America. "But what about us?" the African American kids ask. "Our people came from Mississippi and Alabama." Within moments, the village square takes shape: on the right, a wavy ocean filled with ships and planes; on the left, a railroad track, connecting Chicago to the American South.

Linda and Eleanor's students have come a long way. Starting with sweet but stereotypical portraits of each other, they have now created a symbolic integrated community that honors everyone's individual and group story. It has been quite a journey. They may not have learned every name and date in U.S. history, and they are probably not permanently vaccinated against prejudice. But this hasn't been about leapin' leprechauns or identical turkeys either. These children have had the kind of learning experience that only real arts can provide: they've encountered and grappled with serious ideas in ways that are deep, personal, and transformative. They and their teachers will never be quite the same.

THE ARTS IN SCHOOL AND SOCIETY

The arts have long led a marginal existence in American schools. Historically, visual art, music, drama, and movement have been looked upon as frills, extras, or add-ons. In the workaday parlance of many elementary schools, the arts are "specials"—those intervals during the week when the *real* teachers get a well-earned break while someone else takes the kids off their hands. In the words of arts educator Arnold Aprill, this is "art as recess, not resource." In this typical model, the building's one or two arts specialists see each class of children once or twice a week for half an hour, and rarely does that instruction have a chance to achieve intensity or continuity. In secondary schools, the arts rarely are considered part of the core curriculum at all, and usually can be taken only as electives. In Illinois, most high schools require four years of English, three years each of math, science, and social studies, and only one year each of music and art. For students in upper-track college preparatory programs, the exclusion of the arts can be even more pronounced: counselors recommend taking more "challenging" courses, and tracked grading systems award fewer GPA points for A's in music and art than in more academic subjects.

The arts are marginalized in the wider culture as well, so their limited role in public schools merely parallels the lack of esteem the arts are accorded in American society. Our country offers mild and inconstant support for the arts. Philanthropy in support of arts institutions is sometimes lavish, sometimes sporadic and niggardly. Censorship constantly looms, and seems to drive the most conspicuous public discussions about art. A handful of well-funded major arts institutions uphold the high-culture art forms—opera, painting, and ballet—but the main activity they support is *viewing*. Community arts organizations, which explore more experimental or popular art forms, involve more everyday people and working artists, and support *doing* as well as viewing, struggle perennially at the brink of extinction. We are simply a country that is ambivalent about the arts; we show a mild reverence for certified fine art, but don't put much importance on everyday art making by our citizens, young or old.

But then, the unstable place of art in our culture is not so unusual. Art and artists have always been independent and somehow apart. Although throughout human history and across diverse cultures some art has always been harnessed to glorify the existing culture, many artists have been critics, renegades, and reformers. These artists both preserve traditions and transgress them—holding up various kinds of mirrors to society, culture, and art itself. Often, they paint quite unpretty pictures. One job of such artists is to redirect the path of a culture, not to revere it.

So while we grieve the undersupport of the arts in our educational system, we would never want its reformist power to be tamed or muted by its incorporation into public education. We want to bring art to children in its full-strength formulas: robust, powerful, idiosyncratic, critical, and more than a little bit dangerous. If we have to leave these attributes outside the classroom door, we would do better to leave art out of the curriculum altogether.

A LOOK AT THE STANDARDS DOCUMENTS

While arts educators have lost many battles over school staffing and budgets, they have also been spared some of the entropic wrangles that afflict the "basic" school subjects. Until lately, art, music, theater, and dance teachers were largely unaffected by clarion calls for more standards, benchmarks, targets, assessments, accountability measures, standardized tests, and international achievement comparisons. The arts have been a break for everyone. For the kids, they offer an occasional hiatus from the relentless passivity of "real" subjects, a rare invitation to learn by playing, a chance to actually *do* something or make something tangible. And arts teachers are somewhat compensated for their heavy loads and low academic clout: they get to have some fun with kids, are exempt from micromanagement via state mandates, and don't have to march students toward unjust screening tests.

When the push for national standards in the 1990s belatedly offered arts educators a chance to make their case, the results were rough and imperfect. The first major document, *National Standards for Arts Education: What Every Young American Should Know and Be Able to Do,* was created by a shotgun marriage of professional associations in visual art, music, dance, and theater (Consortium of National Arts Education Associations 1994). In spite of some problems we'll address shortly, *National Standards* provides an adequate base for describing Best Practice in the arts. It makes a strong case for the inherent value of the arts in public education, in the growth of well-educated people, and in the building and improvement of a culture. It defends the value of the arts as disciplines, while asserting that hearing about, studying, or appreciating art is not enough. Students also need to draw, paint, make, choreograph, design, play, sing, act, and direct real artworks throughout their schooling. By high school graduation, the report recommends, young people should be able to communicate at a basic level in all four art forms, and should develop significant proficiency in at least one chosen medium.

The document also has some shortcomings. Each of the four coauthoring professional organizations used the occasion to lobby for more time and money for their own subject area in schools, and for more work and better working conditions for their members. Tired of their ancillary place in school curricula, the groups pleaded for more teachers of art, music, drama, and dance; more contact hours with students; and more equipment and materials. Unfortunately, the authors elected to buttress their case by making art sound just like any other school subject, depicting it largely as a fixed body of content that could be transmitted to students in comfortably academic ways. Fourth graders are expected to "accurately answer questions about dance in a particular culture and time period (for example, 'In Colonial America, why and in what settings did people dance? What did the dances look like?')" (25). In middle schools, students are expected to "read whole, half, quarter, eighth, sixteenth, and dotted notes and rests in 2/4, 3/4, 4/4, 6/8, 3/8, and alla breve meter signatures." High school students are to "create and answer twenty-five questions about dance and dancers prior to the twentieth century" (57). In these low moments, the *National Standards* document inadvertently endorsed content it wouldn't even take a skilled artist or musician to teach; mere lectures and textbooks could have transmitted these mundane cultural subskills.

So the 1994 *National Standards* document fell short by not being visionary enough. But a second wave of arts standards documents has since closed the gap, enunciating a much more ambitious and more carefully researched agenda. In 1998, the Arts Education Partnership and The President's Committee on the Arts and the Humanities issued *Gaining the Arts Advantage: Lessons from School Districts That Value Arts Education,* which documented positive effects on student achievement in schools that used the arts as a tool of learning across the curriculum, featuring project-based learning and interdisciplinary teacher teaming. The following year, the General Electric Fund and the MacArthur Foundation commissioned seven teams of the nation's most prominent arts researchers to provide a definitive report on "what works" in arts education. The final report, entitled *Champions of Change,* documented a range of positive effects for students with high arts involvement in their schools:

- The arts reach students who are not otherwise being reached.
- The arts reach students in ways that they are not otherwise being reached.
- The arts connect students to themselves and to each other.
- The arts transform the environment for learning.
- The arts provide learning opportunities for adults in the lives of young people.
- The arts provide new challenges for those students already considered successful.
- The arts connect learning experiences to the world of work. (1998a)

This body of evidence grew even further with *Current Research in Arts Education* (California Arts Council 2001), a book-length compendium of studies published by the California Arts Council, and *Critical Links: Learning in the Arts and Students' Academic and Social Development* (2002), published by the Arts Education Partnership.

Together, all these documents did more than confirm that music, drama, dance, and the visual arts are worthy of study for their own sake. They pointed toward the arts as a tool of engagement and learning across the curriculum. The documents showed that art makes kids "smarter," draws them deeper into academic work, helps them achieve more, and may even improve their scores on high-stakes tests. They reported positive impact on everything from SAT scores to dropout rates when kids have intensive and regular arts experiences in their schools.

One of the most noteworthy findings across these reports was that *arts experiences level the playing field* for minority and special education children. When New York's Educational Priorities Panel studied a group of struggling inner-city elementary schools that raised their standardized test scores dramatically and got off the city's academic "probation" list, panel researchers made a surprising discovery. Even though probation status focused urgent attention on the basic reading and math content appearing on achievement tests, many of the schools that got off the list had actually *increased* their arts programming (Connell 1996). These successful schools, the report said, were distinguished by "a strong arts program that was infused through the instructional program and that included most of the students in the school." These schools used art as a lever to enhance student learning across the curriculum, and included media as disparate as opera, rap, and fabric art. "In all eight schools," the report concluded, "these programs were not add-ons or treated merely as classes to be held so as to give regular teachers their forty-five minutes of preparation time . . . the arts, at least in these schools, were a strategy for improving learning" (Connell 1996, 13). Given that increased basic-skills test scores were the sole criterion for getting off the New York City probation list, this story has implications for schools around the country.

So why would students' academic performance improve as a result of arts involvement? At the most basic level, arts activities make school more motivating and attractive. The Educational Priorities Panel was not afraid to invoke the F-word in explaining this phenomenon—because art is *fun*, they reasoned, students attend school more regularly and are more engaged and attentive. Logically enough, when students come to school and pay attention, they learn more across the whole day and across all subjects. Further, many arts activities involve tactile, active learning that can connect with the many children for whom the old, sit-in-your-seat-and-listen style of teaching is ineffective. We now have an ample body of research and documentation of multiple learning styles and intelligences (Gardner 1983, 2000) that explains why kids would score higher in basic skills, and why whole schools might even get off the probation list, with the help of more intensive arts programming. Indeed, the failure of schools to teach in such multiple modalities, to offer invitations to students of different cognitive styles, actually deprives many children of their right to learn basic academic skills.

In secondary schools, the arts seem to have the same capacity to enhance academic skills, engaging students and integrating the curriculum. A University of California at Los Angeles study of twenty-five thousand middle and high school students shows strong correlations between the arts and a number of important outcomes (Catterall 1997). Students with more intensive arts involvement during their adolescent years have significantly better school grades; achieve higher standardized test scores in reading, writing, and mathematics; have higher levels of persistence in school; report less boredom in school; are more likely to be involved in community service work and rate it as important; have greater self-esteem and confidence; and make time for their artistic and community interests by watching less TV than their classmates.

These correlations hold up strongly for urban students, even though they are currently far less likely to have arts-rich childhoods. While many education pundits believe that poor kids in low-achieving schools should get extra doses of knuckle-knocking "basics" and fewer "frills" such as art, this report counsels just the opposite. As the study's author concludes: "The arts do matter—not only as worthwhile experiences in their own right for reasons not addressed here, but also as instruments of cognitive growth and development and as agents of motivation for school success. In this light, unfair access to the arts for our children brings consequences of major importance to our society" (Connell 1996).

So the case for the arts is well documented and conclusive, across age levels and subject areas. Clearly, students need far more arts experience than they are getting. But there's a danger here—a theoretical and practical trap that the National Consortium fell into in 1994. Lobbying for more instructional time for separate arts discipline instruction in schools is not the only answer. At a practical level, we cannot allow the national movement for standards, in art or any other subject, to be simply additive. Reform does not mean larger and larger time allocations for any subject that can make a case for itself: more time for math, more time for art, more time for drivers' education. Instead of waging these craven turf wars, educators should be using time in new, more powerful ways. We need synergy, overlap, integration.

That's why key national arts organizations like the Arts Education Partnership and its 140 affiliated groups take a different approach. Instead of politicking to shoehorn more art classes into school schedules, the partnerships ask: How can art experiences leverage the exisiting curriculum? How can art be a tool of learning instead of just another disconnected school subject? A key book about this kind of art education, *Renaissance in the Classroom* (Burnaford, Aprill, and Weiss 2001), shows how the Chicago Arts Partnerships in Education (CAPE) has transformed learning in scores of city schools and documented growth in both student achievement and teacher morale. CAPE was the partner for the project described at the beginning of this chapter, in which Linda Voss and Eleanor Nayvelt's students used music, dance, visual art, and drama to learn history. That story showed the integrating role that the arts can take in our schools. We don't have to steal time away from reading, math, or science to do art; instead, art helps us to do science, math, and reading—to explore them, express them, and connect them. Indeed, the arts are the prototypical "integratable" subjects; music, dance, visual art, and drama have a rightful place in every field of human inquiry. The story coming up at the end of this chapter is also from a CAPE school, and shows how one art form—in this case, the Mexican *retablo*—can anchor a ten-week, team-taught, cross-curricular middle school unit in language arts and history.

QUALITIES OF BEST PRACTICE IN TEACHING THE ARTS

Now that we have looked at the development of arts standards over the past two decades, we can draw on all the key reports to talk more specifically about "what works" in school art programs.

Students should do art, not just view art. From the earliest preschool years, children have a powerful urge to make art. We don't have to "assign" children to draw with markers, chant jump-rope rhymes, share dramatic monologues, make theatrical faces, or dance. Artistic expression seems to be wired into children's genes. Therefore, the first job of teachers and other adults is to get out of the way and let kids express and experiment. We need to provide tools, materials, equipment, models, examples, coaching, and plenty of time. Grown-ups don't have much trouble taking this role until about third or fourth grade, when they start thinking maybe they should make the kids put away the songs and crayons and get serious. While it is probably OK to "get serious" about math or science for part of the school day, it is most definitely not OK to put away art or the exploratory, playful spirit that drives it. As kids get older and the curriculum gets more overstuffed with content-area mandates, smart teachers incorporate art activities into integrated curriculum units. Students who are reading a novel can show their understanding by illustrating critical scenes, acting them out, translating them into movement and dance, or creating background music for them. In every subject, doing the arts can provide new ways of exploring and expressing ideas about practically anything—the Civil War, triangles, photosynthesis, or *To Kill a Mockingbird*.

The arts should be integrated across the curriculum as well as taught as separate disciplines. The arts have value both in themselves and as useful tools of thought and connection throughout life. That means schools with exemplary arts programs will have a balance of arts discipline teaching and arts integration across the curriculum. There are infinite opportunities for weaving artistic thinking and expression into the rest of the curriculum. Ideally, the arts take a central place in broad, interdisciplinary inquiry projects that teachers and students plan together and that extend over long chunks of time. After all, life is integrated, not divided into separate-subject events. Real-life projects and problems tend to be interdisciplinary, and the arts can be a lever for understanding, connecting, or sharing inquiries into them. School should be organized in the same way, preparing students for that real, complex world.

Children need to exercise genuine choice, control, and responsibility in their art making. This chapter's opening image, of hallways decorated with identical children's art, symbolizes the way schools too often turn art from a creative process into an obedience ritual. Indeed, why would any child care about "art" after a few years of mandatory matching leprechauns, especially if she is also being graded on the caliber of her copying? Choice is an integral part of artistic thinking. Real artists choose their own subjects, materials, media, and audiences. They decide how to begin, when something is valuable, when something should be abandoned, when something is ready for an audience. In school, students should be helped to learn how to exercise the same kinds of choices.

This means that there should be plenty of "free" art time, when students have authority for deciding what kind of art or music or drama or dance they want to make, and responsibility for carrying out their choices, under careful teacher guidance. In some school subjects, like reading and writing, we call this student-directed segment of the day "workshop," and it alternates with equally important teacher-guided lessons. Elsewhere during the daily or weekly schedule, whole classes can pursue more focused, teacher-guided art activities. For example, after reading a short story, everyone can make a torn-paper collage that represents an interpretation of one of the characters. As long as students have real choices within such assignments, deciding within the teacher's parameters what to represent and how to represent it, this kind of art making provides an excellent balance for open-ended workshop time.

Students should be helped to nurture their special talents and to find their strongest art form. Every student's education should assist in the lifelong quest to discover and develop one's strongest, most powerful modes of expression. If we take seriously the theory of multiple intelligences (or even if we simply go back to the American educational platitude about developing each child's full potential), we realize that people have different strengths, gifts, and talents. If there are indeed eight intelligences, as Howard Gardner claims, then arts clearly tap into many of them. This means schools must not just tolerate, but celebrate and extend children's various talents, inviting them to explore a wide range, make selections, and gain lots of practice in their areas of greatest strength and highest potential. A straightforward approach to this is taken by the Key School in Indianapolis. During the morning, every student pursues what looks like a normal elementary or middle school program. Then, after lunch, everyone goes off to study their chosen, usually strongest, intelligence. The musical kids get out their horns and blow, the writers make poetry, the kinesthetic kids refine their physical skills, the artists paint and sculpt. This is one school—one of very few schools—that organizes itself so that all children actually do find success and develop their talents.

The arts should be used as a tool of thinking. While students need plenty of chances to create final, polished artworks, the arts should also regularly be employed as tools for the exploration of ideas, without being pushed to final, edited, or exhibited forms. These informal, tentative, exploratory applications of the arts can help kids engage and grapple with ideas in any subject area. For example, teachers often ask students to keep a learning log in which they write notes about their learning. Instead, teachers can have students keep a sketchbook, where they can still jot words—*or* sketch pictures, make diagrams, map ideas, or create unique combinations of words and graphic elements in response to class activities. Another example is the strategy called "say something," in which students are asked to give an immediate verbal response after hearing a presentation, reading a story, or conducting an experiment (Short et al. 1996). Adding the artistic choices, students can "draw something," "dance something," "sing something," or "act something" after any content lesson. These kinds of expression are not refined, formal artworks; rather, they are spontaneous, along-the-way uses of art as a tool of thinking. But when teachers add these different media to the instructional mix, many more students' learning styles are engaged, and more students can comprehend and remember what they study.

Students should experience a wide variety of art forms. Music, drama, visual art, and dance should be included throughout students' schooling. To begin with, all children will naturally participate in certain art forms in their own homes and communities, and they can be invited to bring these into school. These should be welcomed, honored, and studied, whatever they are: folk dance, cartooning, teen 'zines, hip-hop music, jump-rope chants, or "playing the dozens," the dueling insults game. Teachers and schools should be careful not to judge or disvalue children's enjoyment of art forms considered "lowbrow." Any of these popular or childhood art forms could be the base upon which a lifelong artistic involvement is built.

But it is also the job of teachers and schools to widen the range, to introduce children to the wondrous variety of arts from around the world and back through time. This certainly includes traditional "high culture" art, which can be encountered more than just reverentially. It is worth remembering that Shakespearean drama was popular entertainment in its day, that Oscar Wilde toured English coal-mining towns giving boisterously received readings, that Mozart's wind ensemble pieces were written as dinner party entertainment, and that in the nineteenth century, American symphony orchestras often played parties and weddings. School should also expose children to arts from a wider range of cultural and ethnic groups, and arts that represent people around the world. And "experience" does not just mean observing these diverse forms, but trying one's own hand at them. Kids should try a Polish folk dance, make a portrait after the style of Frida Kahlo, perform a scene from Shakespeare, memorize and recite a set of haiku. As a result of this wide exposure and experimentation, students will gain an informed acquaintance with many exemplary artworks, not as arbitrary ingredients on a list of "cultural literacy," but as a natural byproduct of becoming artistic thinkers and students of cultural history.

Students should have opportunities to share their work. Young artists should be provided safe and encouraging venues to perform, exhibit, or publish their work, both what they create during the study of specific arts disciplines and the products completed within wider interdisciplinary inquiries. During each step in the process of creating such artworks, there should be routine, informal, noncritical collaboration among student pairs, teams, and groups, paralleling the way that cooperative groups work to gradually create objects or events in many "real" art forms. When works move toward a more final, potentially public form, teachers can help students set up exhibitions or performances that reach a wider audience of other students, parents, and community members. These occasions are not provided mainly for competition, ranking, or scoring students against each other, and certainly not for putting a few students on stage and silencing others. In the adult world of professional art, there may be a place for competition; in public schools, the fundamental job of teachers is to ensure that all children have chances to advance successfully through whole cycles of art making, over and over throughout their school years, and to provide real, supportive audiences.

This means that when teachers help students publish class magazines, everyone's best story is included; when plays are produced, everybody gets a part; when dances are created, there are roles for all; when collages are hung, every one goes on the wall. Schools may periodically sponsor selective, competitive programs, but the main work of arts education is helping everyone grow, not encouraging a fraction and prematurely excluding others. For everyone, these culminating experiences provide a natural and realistic kind of pressure to do one's best: to prepare carefully, to practice, to polish, to refine. And the main purpose of this sharing is the same for students as for grown-up artists: to connect with and learn from an audience.

Children should attend a variety of professional arts events. Schools should take students to performances and exhibitions, as well as bring artists and performers to school. Especially in poorer communities, children's exposure to the arts may well depend on the school's taking this kind of action. But the annual bus trip to the symphony is not enough. A school's schedule of arts performances should be continuous and varied, and should include not just "downtown" institutions, but local community arts organizations, musicians, galleries, and dance and theater companies as well. These visits and performances should not be disconnected inoculations of culture or random treats; instead, they should be integrated into the ongoing curriculum of the school. Events should be chosen either because they fit an existing school theme or focus, or because an academic theme will be built around them. Making the most of any performance means starting well before the event, with students and teachers learning background information, reading, doing artwork, getting ready to actively engage the performance. Afterward, it is important for students to respond, debrief, and critique, to connect the event to their ongoing studies. A valuable experience, where possible, is for artists to talk with students after a performance or during an exhibit, sharing candidly how they work and think. Even more valuable is conversation with artists *before* they perform, when they open up their own planning and preparation process, sharing their real creative struggles with students.

Artists should be present in schools and classrooms. There's something special and different about people who make their livelihoods as musicians, videomakers, dancers, actors, sculptors, artists, poets, Web game designers, storytellers, or painters. They can make special, sometimes magical, connections with young people and provide knowledge, motivation, and inspiration to growing artists. Therefore, children need chances to meet, observe, and work with adult artists in their school. While one-shot performances and traditional residencies are helpful, even better are genuine long-term partnerships between the school and community arts organizations, providing sustained, intensive arts experiences for children, coplanned with the regular teachers and integrated into the school's overall curriculum. This model transforms the artist from a transient celebrity to a long-term consultant and deeply involves the classroom teacher as a coartist, as well.

All teachers, not just arts specialists, should be artists in their classroom. If we expect students to take risks and grow artistically, teachers must be willing to do the same, demonstrating how a grown-up grows. This is no different from the demand that teachers read with their students, explore science with them, be a fellow writer with them. Still, this requirement frightens many working teachers whose own artistic explorations may have been shut off in childhood, and who don't feel the least bit like artists in any medium or genre. The fact that our culture tends to label artists as "gifted," rather than credit them as largely self-made practitioners who studied long and hard to develop their "gift," adds to this feeling among teachers and other citizens that they are not worthy to participate. We do not ask regular classroom teachers to be professional-caliber artists, but simply to act as ordinary citizens who use the tools of the arts to explore ideas and express themselves. Like students, teachers will probably be on a quest to find and develop their strongest and most preferred arts discipline, as well as trying to grow in others.

HOW PARENTS CAN HELP

A good arts education begins when loving parents respond to their infant's earliest expressions—gurgling, smiling, babbling—with delight, amazement, and the predisposition to see it all as meaningful. The sometimes comical tendency of parents to dote on their children's earliest utterances, however meaningless they sound to outsiders, is an important factor in child development. A natural extension of this phenomenon is the refrigerator door, where parents proudly post their young children's first attempts at visual art. The adults don't mark them up with red pens, critique them. Instead, they look at the three-legged blue horse, get a tear in their eye, hug the kid, and get out the Scotch tape.

- Parents should immerse their offspring in the arts. Recent brain research pointing to the importance of early and diverse stimulation of young minds only adds validation to the wisdom of providing children an arts-rich childhood. Parents and kids can draw, paint, and sing together at home. Parents can involve children as they pursue their own artistic activities—practicing piano, sewing, painting, reading novels.

- Although TV viewing is condemned by many educators and child-development experts, it is an inevitable part of the landscape, and parents may mitigate its banality and passivity by watching with their children; guiding them to better choices; renting tapes of quality children's films; and helping kids to discuss, understand, and evaluate what they are watching. Even better, parents and children can produce simple videos together.

■ In taking children to arts events and activities outside of home, parents should follow their own tastes and passions. If it is blues music you love, sneak the kid into a club and keep him up late. If you are going to fall asleep in your seat at the opera, don't drag yourself or your children there. (But do send them with a friend or relative who really loves opera.) What is most important is for the child to see the adult engaged, involved, and moved by an art form, and to be in conversation with him during and after the event.

■ Probably the most powerful family arts experience is when parents and children make art together. Among Harvey Daniels' most treasured memories are playing punk-rock guitar with his son and serving in his daughter's Motown backup band, mostly down in the family basement, and a couple of precious times on stage.

■ Even as we expose children to a wide range of art forms, it is important that we help them to be empowered, not awed, audiences. On the way home from the movie, play, or concert, parents should invite kids' response and critique: what they liked, what they didn't, and especially, *why* they felt a given element did or didn't work. Children learn from these conversations the implicit criteria of successful performance in different art forms, and grow toward becoming active consumers of the arts who have developed their own taste and judgment.

■ To the extent that budgets allow, parents should buy art supplies and materials, from markers to leotards to instruments to graphics software programs. Parents should mainly follow their children's interests or their own predictions of what might be welcome. Making a list and shopping for art supplies together makes a wonderful family outing, whether the destination is a fabric store, an art supply house, a music store, or an office-supply warehouse.

■ As children show particular interests and abilities, out-of-school lessons or classes can extend their exploration of arts—if the child is ready and eager for them. While private instruction is one option, many community centers and park districts also offer free or inexpensive classes of high quality.

■ All children are artists and performers to some extent, and these recommendations apply to all young people. But what if a child shows special talent in the arts? We caution against overweening parental arts mentoring. Many young artists have been permanently bruised by forced dance lessons, pressure to win awards, or premature public performances. The arts work powerfully for kids because they are fun, and a lot of that fun comes from making your own choices and finding your own voice. It's not much fun to live out someone else's artistic agenda or to be dragooned into unpleasant or ill-timed commitments. Let the child lead, and when he or she evinces an interest, offer every opportunity you can: lessons, materials, visits, coaching, and audiences.

WHAT PRINCIPALS CAN DO

The starting point for principals is to feel and act like artists themselves, modeling for the students in their building how one highly visible adult does art, thinks about art, responds to art, uses art. But this is a tall order. Most American school principals, like most teachers, scarcely think of themselves as artists. On the contrary, they often feel artistically incompetent, intimidated, and self-conscious. They are full of self-deprecating excuses. "I can't draw," we've heard more than one principal say. "But I can hardly carry a tune," others moan. However, no one expects school principals to be professional-level musicians or sculptors. Instead, the task is simply to be an everyday, arts-involved adult who is willing to open up his or her artistic thinking for kids.

■ Find your own strongest art mediums and share them with children. Visit classrooms and read your poems or someone else's poems, show your cartoons or pictures, play the piano. Talk about the paintings or music or films you love. Lead a field trip to your favorite gallery or theater company, and talk about your involvement. If you are a graphic artist, pour some of that artistry into the school newsletter.

■ Help your teachers become artists. Many teachers are art-phobic too, and they need chances to heal the shamed and silenced artist inside. There's one main way teachers can accomplish this rebirth: making art alongside a patient and generous artist who can help them recover their curiosity and confidence. Some of the most powerful, transformative staff development experiences we have ever attended are teacher workshops led by the phenomenal artists of the Chicago Arts Partnerships in Education, who help damaged grown-ups become arts-loving, arts-doing teachers. In your school, arrange and fund staff development that lets teachers rediscover their own joy in art.

- Be an audience for students. View kids' work on the walls and in classrooms. As teachers schedule culminating performances and exhibitions, attend as many as you can. Being a fully engaged audience, simply being a witness in the moment, is a powerful demonstration that the students' work is being taken seriously. Give children constructive feedback as they are ready for it, bearing in mind that you are viewing "first drafts," and that for young artists, fluency and productivity are more important than perfection. Far better than prizes or awards are individual handwritten notes, delivered to kids in their classrooms, telling them how you responded to pieces of art or performances you viewed.

- Make sure classrooms have all the supplies and materials needed to support the arts. Because art supplies can be costly, your legerdemain with budgets may determine what kids can do. Along with arts specialist teachers, classroom teachers require serious inventories of art materials as well. You can also encourage teachers to visit local scrounging sites, recycled materials centers, or other sources of cheap art stuff. Professional performances and long-term artists-in-the-school programs may require special central-office or external grant funding, which you can apply for and expedite.

- Space is another resource that many arts require: space with the right kind of light, with the necessary sinks, with enough room to move, with room for an audience, and so forth. Because space is often at a premium in chronically underfunded public schools, you may even need to connect with neighborhood partners who can offer performance or studio space.

- Celebrate the arts in your school, building special events around them, and incorporating them into other school programs. Invite professional and community artists to perform or exhibit at the school. If possible, make the school a gallery, a studio, a rehearsal space. Create many occasions for displaying and sharing student work noncompetitively. Everyone needs an audience, not a contest with few winners and many losers.

■ Involve parents and families in school arts programs. Obviously, they are natural audiences for all kinds of school art events. Parents can also teach or perform when their skills match the curriculum; they can bring in their saxophone, brushes, or tap shoes and give demonstrations. When younger children need lots of help with complex or messy art projects, a few extra parent hands can be a real blessing.

■ Rethink the role of the arts specialists in your building. If art or music teachers are seeing hundreds of children a week, maybe a new model is in order. Invite the specialists to partner with some teachers—the second-grade team, the middle school faculty—to design and teach long-range integrated curriculum projects together. Instead of trying to teach overwhelming loads of students in not nearly enough time, let specialists infuse the arts into studies of ecology, history, or literature. If this seems like too big a commitment to make, try a two-week pilot arts-integration program and see what happens.

■ Use your role as instructional leader, supervisor, and evaluator to let teachers know that the arts matter. In your classroom visitations, evaluate congruently: if teachers are incorporating the arts, let them know they are on the right track. When they are not, make suggestions, offer resources, link them up with teachers who are farther along.

■ Work at the district level to support arts programming across the curriculum. In most school systems, the arts are in a constant battle to maintain their funding and their place in the curriculum, so it is vital that principals be arts advocates. If you can testify about the impact of the arts in your school, do so. If you can pass along articles documenting the academic value of the arts, copy away. If you can refer a fellow principal to an artist who works well with students, great.

Born to Do Art!

PAT BARRETT DRAGAN
Martin Elementary School, South San Francisco, California

When children know it's time for art, they are excited and raring to go. They need this daily opportunity for self-expression, experimentation, and play, and for connecting their art experiences both to their lives and to other curriculum areas. When kids have the opportunity to draw, paint, arrange, tear, and construct, they internalize lessons that cannot be learned through other experiences. They have a great chance to joyfully express the things that matter to them.

Now, it is early in the school year, and my first graders have been excitedly looking at some art study prints and talking about things they notice. The large photos depict many different media—painting, sculpture, frescoes, and more—art throughout time and across many cultures. I mention to the children that what is so special is that *people* create art and have done so for thousands of years. Ricky is particularly inspired by this thought. He stands up, flings an arm up in the air as he speaks, and says in a voice full of emotion: "I was *born* to do art!"

The children and I are caught up in this moment, and for just a heartbeat time seems to stop . . . then other voices join in: "I was *born* to *learn!*" "I was *born* to *make stuff!*" "I was *born* to *read!*" "I was *born* to *color!*" "I was *born* to *play soccer!*" "I was *born* to *go to school!*" "I was *born* to be *teached* by the teacher!"

The children are fired up and eloquent. I quickly type up a "sentence frame" using some of Ricky's words: "I was born to _____," and run off copies for everyone. Now I invite the children to personalize this sentence by drawing their own ideas and by spelling words "their way." Or, if they prefer, they may dictate their words for me to write.

The "born-to" project was not a planned assignment, nor did I make it required work. Students were free to work on other art or writing during this time. But I find that when a class member comes up with a great idea like this one, most of the kids want to be part of it. I always do my own illustrations and writing so I can be involved, too. Of course, I don't share my own endeavors until the end of our work period, when we meet to look at our masterpieces. I want to support children's efforts, but I don't want to interfere with their *own* thoughts and creations by giving a teacher model they may feel obligated to follow.

ART IS ANOTHER WAY OF SEEING AND KNOWING

On a different day, children look at an art print and talk about "line" and "color" and how these are used to create city and neighborhood scenes. They notice the most minuscule things—some of which I never would have seen. Next, we savor the illustrations in some great city-related picture books like *Madlenka* by Peter Sis (2000); *My New York: New Anniversary Edition* by Kathy Jakobsen (2003); and *The City by the Bay: A Magical Journey Around San Francisco* by Tricia Brown and the Junior League of San Francisco (1981). After hearing and viewing one of these picture books, children go to their tables to create their own neighborhood drawings using marking pens and oil pastels.

My students are involved in their neighborhood drawings at different degrees of intensity, but no one else is working at the feverish pace of Beatríz. Perhaps this is because she speaks almost no English, and her level of speech development in Spanish makes it difficult to understand her. But Beatríz is gifted in communicating in other ways. Through pens, oil pastels, crayons, paint, and torn paper, she works fervently to make herself understood, to "make her mark." We all marvel at the rich and detailed world she creates. Art is another language for Beatríz, and she speaks to us eloquently through this medium.

I like to use one or two art prints or transparencies at the beginning of each art lesson. They help children "zero in" on what I'm teaching: different art styles, elements of art, or thematic ideas for their own creations. This activity helps them to "see" and to get revved up to create. It also teaches vocabulary in a context that makes sense. Discussing artworks fits right in with children's natural love of talking about themselves. As students look at these images they talk about things they notice, and relate things to their own lives. Making connections like this is very powerful: it helps us all make sense of our personal experiences as well as facilitates learning in many curriculum areas.

ART LESSONS IN FIRST GRADE

In our first-grade classroom, we use art in many ways. Some lessons are mainly for teaching kids how to use specific materials or media. Others use art to support our study of science, math, or social studies. I believe students need both kinds of learning experiences. Here are some examples:

- "how-to" art lessons on the use of specific materials, such as glue and scissors
- "how-to" art lessons to teach specific skills: how to tear paper, make rubbings, do crayon resist, and so on
- lessons focused on learning to use specific media, such as block printing, watercolor paints, or plaster of Paris
- lessons that connect with cultural themes: *papel picado* (cut-paper Mexican banners), Mexican bark paintings, Italian *impasto* paintings, Russian fairy tale boxes, Kwanzaa weavings, Chinese New Year dragons, Black History Month portraits, and so on
- lessons connected to holidays and seasons: leaf prints, scarecrows, jack-o'-lanterns, dreidels, elves and Santa, snowmen, spring flowers, Mother's Day gifts, Fourth of July
- lessons that link to and integrate other curricula, such as music, dance, drama, math, social studies, science, language arts, children's literature, and physical education
- art history lessons about specific artists, periods in art, or art movements

In planning my art curriculum I frequently refer to the State of California Standards for the Visual and Performing Arts. I also use the Sequential Art Media Program created by Dick Sperisen, Art Coordinator Emeritus at the San Mateo County Office of Education in Redwood City, California. Working with a committee of teachers, Dick put together a sequence of art techniques that teaches children a repertoire of ways to proceed in art. Once they know how to manipulate materials and have learned some simple basics, children can use this knowledge to create art in many media, across all curriculum areas.

This Sequential Art Media Program begins with bold activities that work on large motor skills and then introduces techniques that foster small motor development. Following this format and teaching techniques in a loose sequential order gives children the skills they need to express themselves through art. These are some of the activities I teach students in my first-grade class.

Bold Media Activities

- Torn-paper collage; cut-paper collage.
- Crayon rubbings (also called rub-overs). Place a paper over a torn or cut paper image. Rub with crayon. Add details with other media, such as torn paper scraps.
- Drawing with hunks of paraffin (canning wax). Paint over the drawing with watercolors. A variation of this technique, called "crayon resist," is to draw with crayons, coloring heavily, and then paint over the image.
- Glue-line drawing. Draw on newspaper or construction paper with white glue and let it dry overnight. Make rubbings by placing paper over dried glue lines. Rub with a crayon; add tissue, crayon, paint, or torn paper. Or add color to the dry glue-line drawing with crayons, pens, paper scraps, oil pastels, or watercolor.
- Tempera painting washes. Paint over crayon with a "wash" of diluted tempera paint.
- Tempera painting with sponges. Cut sponges into small pieces. After painting, let them dry in cardboard soft-drink trays and use them again. There is no need to wash the sponges. The remaining paint adds interesting effects to the next paintings they are used to create.

More Detailed Media Activities

- Double-pencil drawings made with two pencils taped or rubber-banded together; single-line pencil drawings.
- Double-crayon drawings made with two crayons rubber-banded together; crayon sketching.
- Double–marking pen drawings.
- Watercolor and paintbrush experiences.
- Tempera and brush experiences.

The double pencil, crayon, or pen activities force students to draw "large." Many lines are created at a time. Students may then use a darker color to go over the lines they want to emphasize. All these techniques free children to experiment and create.

UPSIDE-DOWN ART

Around the time my children were "getting to know" Van Gogh, Gaugin, Manet, and other Impressionist artists, we spent some time learning about Matisse. I focused on teaching about his paper cuts. Children particularly loved the transparencies of his "Circus" cut-paper collage series. After looking at some prints, talking about and practicing cutting flowing shapes, students created their own individual paper cuts "in the style of Matisse." They then moved into creating some incredible class murals. I placed three different colored six-by-eight-foot pieces of fadeless paper on the carpet, and provided scissors and all colors of construction paper. I also set out our wonderful scrap box full of paper remnants from other lessons.

My group decided on their own themes: "playground games" and "kites." Children cut incredible paper shapes, then took turns placing the cutout shapes on the colored background sheets. In table teams and large group meetings we "played" with the paper placements and moved things around. Sometimes we even switched cutouts from one background piece to another of a different color. Language flourished, and children learned about shape, color, design, and composition as they internalized the work of one of history's greatest artists.

Later, a few children took turns gluing things in place by carefully lifting (but *not* moving) the corner of a shape, putting small drops of glue underneath and pressing the cut paper piece down. In this way our original creations were not disturbed while they were being made permanent.

A few days later, on a field trip to a local art gallery and nearby science museum, we passed through a public building. There, by coincidence, hung a large framed Matisse print. Children gathered around, excited to see a work of art they knew. But they were dismayed by something they noticed. "It's upside down!" several of the kids cried out. The rest of the class gathered to look, and agreed. Passersby and people who worked in the building smiled indulgently. I heard one receptionist say to another, with a smirk and a laugh, "As if *they* would know!"

But the children *did* know. The print *was* upside down! I was insulted for the kids. But *they* were insulted for Matisse, a beloved fellow artist.

Honoring Our Ancestors in Retablo

AMY VECCHIONE

Thomas J. Waters Elementary School, Chicago, Illinois

In Mexican culture, *retablos* are paintings on tin panels that document a miraculous occurrence in a person's life. They serve as reminders and celebrations of unexpected good fortune. They function as portable shrines of acknowledgment and grateful appreciation of the perseverance of an individual over the difficulties of everyday life throughout the world. They symbolize vision and grace.

Room 301 embraced this ancient tradition in their ten-week bookmaking project, *Honoring Our Ancestors in Retablo*. These seventh graders at Thomas J. Waters Elementary School created monuments to their ancestors that rivaled the charm, reverence, and devotion of any nineteenth-century retablo found in Oaxaca, Mexico, or in the early twentieth-century border towns of the Rio Grande. These retablos are powerful. They are spiritual yet secular. They are personal representations of days gone by, preserved by the tradition of oral history. They are also the braiding of state language arts standards and goals, homeroom curriculum, and fine arts integration found at Waters School, where we honor student culture and family experience while nurturing the hard work and talents of our children.

At the beginning of this art project, students immersed themselves in a six-week writing workshop, focusing on family history stories. These students didn't complain or assert, "This is art class . . . why do we have to write?" as my students first did when I began teaching art two years ago. They knew my philosophy—authentic art is not an isolated experience but a way to express the world around you. Diane Gebhardt, their homeroom teacher, agreed. She opened her classroom to this project, shared personal anecdotes, and became a true team teacher with shared responsibility, because she believes in authentic instruction and project-based learning. Students brought me their narratives each week as they composed their stories, and I would laugh and weep as I read them. I would end up writing, "Tell me more!" After three edits, peer review, and a final author sign-off, the students, Ms. Gebhardt, and I had an enormous investment in the text of this bookmaking project. Now it was time for the next step.

As a class, we read aloud Harriet Rohmer's *Honoring Our Ancestors* and discussed the similarities and differences between narrative writing and narrative painting before we created a sketch. Students talked about what they had learned about each of the honored ancestors in Rohmer's text and compared the written descriptions to the visual imagery on the adjacent page of the book. Students made judgments about the value of written words and the power of pictures. *Do the words tell the same story as the pictures? What did we learn in the written story that the artwork doesn't say?* The students were constantly making critical and creative distinctions as they deconstructed our reference text.

Each student was asked to think about the family member they would honor in a retablo and get ready to interview that person. To sharpen our interviewing skills, we learned about the Socratic method and practiced careful questioning before we ever drew a picture. After trying out interviewing techniques on one another, students went home to ask their honored ancestor about personal stories, cultural myths, immigration experiences, historical events, and life lessons. Parents, grandparents, uncles, aunts, brothers, and sisters became oral historians right along with our students.

We also reviewed students' narratives from the six-week writing workshop project. After working so hard at creating images with written words, we were excited to begin the study of traditional retablo art. We viewed photos of numerous retablos painted in Mexico throughout the ages. We talked about the need for retablos to be portable as people migrated. We learned how the art of retablo painting itself migrated from Spain to Mexico and then to the United States. We viewed the secular retablos of Frida Kahlo and the Jimenez family as alternative interpretations of retablo painting today. Meanwhile, students had their personal stories and the historical perspective of the art form under their belt as they began the final step of the bookmaking project: visual documentation of the miraculous person in their lives.

The painting sessions were full of energy and determination. Students explored the use of metal awls and acrylic paints as new methods and tools to make art, scratching out contour drawings and adding color to transform sheets of flimsy tin into stories. Enthusiastically, students used a combination of personal iconography, bits of poems, family adages, and a lot of creativity to render the significance of their honored ancestor into *one* image. Students painted parents cooking *flautas*, brothers playing guitars, sisters swimming by the sea, grandmothers watering flowers, fathers in superhero costumes, and much more. Each narrative painting was a reinterpretation of student narrative writing but somehow seemed imbued with the simplicity of spirit of retablo artists of long ago. Each one was striking in its own way. With a couple of paragraphs and one image, students were able to create individual yet interdependent "pictures" that reconnected family members to their everyday lives, recaptured personal experience to document history, and empowered their ancestors in an age-old, yet fresh way.

This project became a sixty-five-page classroom book. When we sent the text to the printer, students worked on making the front and back covers of the books out of black foamcore. The front cover of each book was the student's personal retablo. The retablo was mounted onto a student-created frame in the style of Mexican folk painting—bright reds, greens, pinks, and yellows enhanced by paper cutouts, yarn, and sequins. The back cover of each book had an easel that served to turn the book into a freestanding shrine that mimicked traditional retablos' portability, unlike artwork to be hung on museum walls. Students pored over the books when they returned from the printer, reading each other's stories, and dived into them again at our book-signing/publication party.

As the culminating activity to the project, students facilitated a presentation that was somewhere between a gallery opening, a poetry reading, a seminar on retablo history, and a family party. A makeshift Mexican flag was created out of red, green, and white butcher paper and hung as a backdrop. Small color copies of traditional retablos were hung in its center. A folding table was in the front of the room with all of the students' retablos standing as testaments to each honored ancestor. More than fifty fellow seventh graders, family members, former teachers, community members, and administrators were a rapt audience of witnesses as students told their family members' stories.

Ms. Gebhardt and I melted into the audience and the students ran the show. Lluvia welcomed everyone and introduced the project both in English and Spanish. Adrian explained the significance of retablo painting throughout history and the world. Mary Lou delineated the bookmaking process with humor and precision. She also read aloud her favorite story from *Honoring Our Ancestors*. Each student was then invited to share his or her retablo story. I was amazed at the courage and pride of these students. More than half the class got up and shared their personal oral histories. Some read quietly and with sadness. Some evoked laughter from the audience. Some read with their honored ancestor standing beside them. Silvia honored her five-year-old twin brother and sister because "[they] have taught me life can be full of surprises." Yonathon honored his older brothers, who worked to help his mother pay rent after his father died. Amanda honored her mom and dad, who encourage her to be a writer. Alberto honored his father, who worked long hours to bring his whole family to America while fighting kidney disease. José honored his uncle, who inspired him to be an artist and who gave him his most prized possession, his paintbox, at the age of nine. Patricia and Diana honored their grandmothers, who raised them when they were little in Mexico. David honored his mom, who told him to "lie to the world but not to me." Jonathon honored his father, who taught him Mexican riddles when he was little and is his best friend. The room was charged with emotion, grace, and dignity. At the close of the presentation, students became teachers of the project as their peers, using teacher-prepared exit slips, interviewed them. Later, I used these exit interviews as a final assessment of the overall project. At the end of the event, each student kept his or her retablo book as a way to preserve the students' collective past and as a reminder of a job well done.

Room 301's retablos are an example of project-based learning that was only possible through the collaboration of teachers who were nurtured by a school culture that celebrates innovative ideas and values meaningful education. This project was empowering for everyone—the students, the families, and the school as a whole. *Honoring Our Ancestors in Retablo* was truly miraculous. Why? Everyone had ownership of this project. Everyone was invested. That's what Best Practice instruction means—sharing authentic experience whereby everyone comes away enriched and better for the endeavor. We all grow in this form of teaching and learning. It's attempting to do what is possible, because it should be done.

WORKS CITED

Arts Education Partnership. 2002. *Critical Links: Learning in the Arts and Students' Academic and Social Development.* Washington, DC: Arts Education Partnership.

Arts Education Partnership and the President's Committee on the Arts and the Humanities. 1998a. *Champions of Change: The Impact of the Arts on Learning.*

Washington, DC: Arts Education Partnership and the President's Committee on the Arts and the Humanities.

———. 1998b. *Gaining the Arts Advantage: Lessons from School Districts That Value Arts Education.* Washington, DC: Arts Education Partnership and the President's Committee on the Arts and the Humanities.

Brown, Tricia, and the Junior League of San Francisco. 1981. *The City by the Bay: A Magical Journey Around San Francisco.* San Francisco: Chronicle Books.

Burnaford, Gail F., Arnold Aprill, and Cynthia Weiss, eds. 2001. *Renaissance in the Classroom: Arts Integration and Meaningful Learning.* Mahwah, NJ: Erlbaum.

California Arts Council. 2001. *Current Research in Arts Education: An Arts in Education Research Compendium.* Sacramento, CA: California Arts Council.

Catterall, James. 1997. *Involvement in the Arts and Success in Secondary School.* Los Angeles: The UCLA Imagination Project.

Connell, Noreen. 1996. *Getting Off the List: School Improvement in New York City.* New York: Educational Priorities Panel.

Consortium of National Arts Education Associations. 1994. *National Standards for Arts Education: What Every Young American Should Know and Be Able to Do.* Reston, VA: Music Educators National Conference.

Gardner, Howard. 1983. *Frames of Mind: The Theory of Multiple Intelligences.* New York: Basic Books.

———. 2000. *Intelligence Reframed: Multiple Intelligences for the 21st Century.* New York. Basic Books.

Jakobsen, Kathy. 2003. *My New York: New Anniversary Edition.* New York: Megan Tingley.

Rohmer, Harriet. 1999. *Honoring Our Ancestors: Stories and Pictures by 14 Artists.* San Francisco, CA: Childrens Book Press.

Short, Kathy, Jerome Harste, and Carolyn Burke. 1996. *Creating Classrooms for Authors and Inquirers.* Portsmouth, NH: Heinemann.

Sis, Peter. 2000. *Madlenka.* New York: Farrar, Straus and Giroux.

SUGGESTED FURTHER READINGS

Blecher, Sharon, and Kathy Jaffee. 1998. *Weaving in the Arts: Widening the Learning Circle.* Portsmouth, NH: Heinemann.

Brandt, Elizabeth Feldman. 1996. *Power in Practice: The Arts Education Development Project.* Philadelphia: Pew Charitable Trusts.

Cohen, Elaine Pear, and Ruth Strauss Gainer. 1995. *Art: Another Language for Learning.* Portsmouth, NH: Heinemann.

Ehrenworth, Mary. 2003. *Looking to Write: Students Writing Through the Visual Arts.* Portsmouth, NH: Heinemann.

Fowler, Charles. 1996. *Strong Arts, Strong Schools: The Promising Potential and Shortsighted Disregard of the Arts in American Schooling.* New York: Oxford University Press.

Galligan, Anne. 2001. *Creativity, Culture, Education, and the Workforce.* Washington DC: Center for Arts and Culture.

Gee, Karolynne. 1999. *Visual Arts as a Way of Knowing.* York, ME: Stenhouse.

Gilmore, Barry. 1999. *Creative Writing Through the Visual and Performing Arts.* Portsmouth, NH: Heinemann.

Grant, Janet Miller. 1995. *Shake, Rattle, and Learn: Classoom-Tested Ideas That Use Movement for Active Learning.* York, ME: Stenhouse.

Heller, Paul. 1996. *Drama as a Way of Knowing.* York, ME: Stenhouse.

Mantione, Roberta D., and Sabine Smead. 2003. *Weaving Through Words: Using the Arts to Teach Reading Comprehension Strategies.* Newark, DE: International Reading Association.

Miller, Carole, S., and Juliana Saxton. 2004. *Into the Story: Language in Action Through Drama.* Portsmouth, NH: Heinemann.

National Assembly of State Arts Agencies. 1992. *Eloquent Evidence: Arts at the Core of Learning.* Washington DC: National Assembly of State Arts Agencies.

Page, Nick. 1996. *Music as a Way of Knowing.* York, ME: Stenhouse.

President's Committee on the Arts and the Humanities. 1997. *Creative America: A Report to the President: The President's Committee on the Arts and Humanities.* Washington, DC: President's Committee on the Arts and the Humanities.

Robinson, Gillian. 1996. *Sketch-Books: Explore and Store.* Portsmouth, NH: Heinemann.

Roe, Betty, Suellen Alfred, and Sandy Smith. 1998. *Teaching Through Stories: Yours, Mine, and Ours.* Norwood, MA: Christopher-Gordon.

Zakkai, Jennifer. 1997. *Dance as a Way of Knowing.* York, ME: Stenhouse.

ART RESOURCES ON THE INTERNET

ArtsEdge http://www.artsedge.kennedy-center.org, which calls itself the National Arts and Education Network, supports the placement of the arts at the center of the curriculum and advocates the creative use of technology. ArtsEdge offers plans and materials that help educators to teach in, through, and about the arts by providing the tools to develop interdisciplinary curricula that fully integrate the arts with other academic subjects.

At http://aep-arts.org, the Arts Education Partnership makes available the text of their Critical Links studies, which show the social and academic value of arts to students K–12.

The Music Educators National Conference was the lead organization in the consortium that created the national standards. It offers association news, research bulletins, publications, and conference announcements at http://www.uwec .edu/student/mused.

The National Arts Education Association offers papers, news releases, and links to state arts organizations at http://naea-reston.org.

Just as decorative as its new building in California is the website of the Getty Education Institute for the Arts. Find teachers' lesson plans, cross-disciplinary curriculum units, and useful image galleries at http://getty.edu/artsednet.

Americans for the Arts is mainly an advocacy group, lobbying for more arts funding and public support of the arts in school and in civic life at http://www .americansforthearts.org.

Rich examples of the arts as a catalyst of learning across the curriculum and as a tool of whole-school change can be found at http://www.capeweb.org, home of the Chicago Arts Partnerships in Education.

Accomplished teachers who are ready to seek national certification can learn about the rigorous one-year process, find out the benefits of a successful review in their own state, and find a support group at the website of the National Board for Professional Teaching Standards at http://www.nbpts.org.

RECOMMENDATIONS ON TEACHING ART

Increase	Decrease
Art making; more active practice of art, music, dance, drama	Studying other people's artworks
Student originality, choice, and responsibility in art making	Art projects that require students to create identical products or closely mimic a model
Stress on the process of creation, the steps and stages of careful craftsmanship	Concern with final products and displays that neglects learning about process
Art as an element of talent development for all students	Art as an arena for competition, screening, awards, and prizes for a few
Exploration of the whole array of art forms, from Western and non-Western sources, different time periods, cultures, and ethnic groups	Exclusive focus on Western, high-culture, elite art forms disconnected from a wide range of art making
Support for every student's quest to find and develop personal media, style, and tastes	Cursory dabbling in many art forms, without supporting a drive toward mastery in one
Time for art in the school day and curriculum	Once-a-week art classes that lack intensity
Integration of arts across the curriculum	Restricting study to separate arts discipline instruction
Using art as a tool of doing, learning, and thinking	Teaching art as body of content to be memorized
Reasonable classloads and work assignments for arts specialists	Overloading arts specialists with excessive classload
Artists in schools, both as performers and as partners in interdisciplinary work	Arts experiences provided only by school arts specialists
Long-term partnerships with artists and arts organizations	One-shot, disconnected appearances by artists
Teacher, principal, and parent involvement in the arts	Art-phobic, noninvolved school staff members running arts programs for students

Best Practice, Third Edition by Zemelman, Daniels, and Hyde (Heinemann: Portsmouth, NH); © 2005

Chapter 8
The Seven Structures of Best Practice Teaching

W e've already shown that Best Practice is a *philosophy*—a set of harmonious and interlocking *principles of learning*. Whether con-sciously or intuitively (or a little of both), all the teachers we have visited in this book subscribe to a coherent philosophy of learning that is student-centered, experiential, expressive, reflective, authentic, holistic, so-cial, collaborative, democratic, cognitive, developmental, constructivist, and challenging. But what do Best Practice teachers *do?* How do they enact, im-plement, and live out their principles, their paradigm? Do they drive to school with national curriculum standards on their laps, deciding at the last stoplight which methods to use today?

Although the wonderful classrooms we have described so far may look quite complex, in some ways they're simpler than they first appear. Under the surface of these elegant lessons are just a few recurrent structures, some basic ways of organizing kids, time, materials, space, and help. Actually, these ex-emplary teachers orchestrate a surprisingly *small* repertoire of basic, recur-rent activities in their search to embody Best Practice. Among these basic structures are:

- Small-Group Activities

- Reading as Thinking

- Representing-to-Learn

- Classroom Workshop

- Authentic Experiences

- Reflective Assessment

- Integrative Units

Most of these structures are simple, familiar, and time-tested. While these elements can profoundly shift the classroom balance from teacher-directed to student-centered learning, many of them are actually quite easy to implement; they are easy to begin, easy to slot into the existing teaching day, easy to experiment with incrementally. Indeed, far from requiring teachers to master a huge inventory of newfangled, technical instructional methods, Best Practice largely means returning to some old, perhaps prematurely discarded approaches, and fine-tuning them until they work. But these simple activities are also very powerful: they can effectively take the teacher off stage, decentralize the classroom, and transfer responsibility for active learning in any subject to the students.

Each of these seven key structures has a robust literature of how-to's and implementation guides: in fact, several contain within their very design the management features necessary to make them work. But many of them do require careful training of students, and the more complex a structure is, the more time and training it will require—happily, of course, the learning and social skills acquired during this training are valuable in themselves. Many of these key structures are the subject of recent articles or whole books that explain in detail how they can be adapted for different subjects and grade levels. Harvey and our colleague Marilyn Bizar have recently added to that literature with *Teaching the Best Practice Way: Methods That Matter, K–12* (2004), a book-length treatment of these seven building blocks of excellent pedagogy. In the next few pages, we offer a brief description and a few examples of each major structure, along with recommended readings that can provide more detailed information and guidance about each of these seven "methods that matter."

SMALL-GROUP ACTIVITIES

Best Practice means big changes in the way classrooms operate. Across all content areas, the new curriculum calls for much less teacher presentation and domination, far more active student learning, and constantly shifting, decentralized groupings. In Best Practice classrooms, students work together effectively in small groups—in pairs, threes, ad hoc groups, and long-term teams—without constant teacher supervision. Teachers all across the country have been discovering and adapting the powerful versions of collaborative learning described by William Glasser (1990), David and Roger Johnson (1998), Shlomo Sharan (1999), and others. They have been reassured and excited by research showing that, even using the customary standardized measures, students of all grade levels show significant achievement gains across the curriculum when they are organized into collaborative groupings and projects. It works.

But we must be sure to apply these effective collaborative structures to an elevated conception of curriculum. Some trendy cooperative learning applications are merely study teams that harness the power of social interaction to help kids memorize the same old curriculum content. In fact, kids *can* teach each other dates and facts and formulas quite effectively when they study as a group, but why bother? Far more powerful and appropriate uses of collaboration occur when students set up and pursue group investigations, read and discuss novels in literature circles, or generate their own crafted pieces of writing with the input of peer response and editing groups. Following are a few structures for collaborative learning that move kids toward higher-order thinking.

Partner/Buddy Reading. Paired reading activities with many variations. Two students may take turns reading aloud to each other from a story or textbook, either passing a single book back and forth, or with the listener following the text in her own copy. Pairs can read the same section outside of class and join to discuss the reading, or they can jigsaw the text, reading different sections and sharing their respective pieces of the puzzle.

Peer Response and Editing. Ongoing groups in which students give diplomatic and critical feedback on drafts of each other's writings. Training students to help each other with their work requires both management tools (e.g., how to use your "twelve-inch voice" so that everyone in the room can hear their own partner) and process skills (e.g., how to pose questions that help an author make her own decisions, instead of just giving criticism).

Literature Circles/Book Clubs. Groups of four or five students choose and read the same article, book, or novel. While doing their reading inside or outside of class, they make notes about topics or questions they want to bring up later with their friends. Then, student-led groups meet every few days, using everyone's notes as sources of discussion topics. When they finish a book, the circle may report briefly to the whole class; then they trade members with other finishing groups, select more reading, and move into a new cycle (Daniels 2002; Daniels and Steineke 2004).

Study Teams. Where it is absolutely necessary for kids to memorize volu-minous or complex material, Slavin's "Team Games Tournament" and related strategies help students bring energy to the task (1985). These struc-tures help kids form interdependent groups that parcel out tasks, share the work, stop to help members who fall behind, and provide an interlocking re-ward system where everyone gets maximum benefits if everyone in the group succeeds. As we have warned, if such small-group activities merely harness collaborative learning to an archaic, irrelevant, teacher-dominated curricu-lum, they are a pretty mundane application of Best Practice.

Group Investigations. One useful legacy of the 1960s is the wide assortment of group inquiry models developed in different fields, including the Biologi-cal Science Curriculum Study, the Social Science Curriculum Project, and the Group Investigation Model (all described in Joyce, Weil, and Calhoun 2003). In all these models, a learning cycle begins when the class encounters or identifies a problem for study. As a first step, the whole class discusses the topic, shares prior knowledge, generates hypotheses, poses questions, sets goals, and makes a plan for studying the topic. Tasks are parceled out to dif-ferent groups of students based on their curiosities and skills. Then the in-quiry proceeds in the small groups, with the teacher serving as facilitator and resource along the way. When the investigations are completed, the teams re-convene to share and discuss their findings.

Centers. This form of small-group work is usually thought of as relevant mainly for elementary teachers, though we see many secondary applications as well. Centers are learning stations set up by the teacher around a class-room, where students can visit and explore ideas in an organized sequence. Centers are meant to replace passive whole-class presentations with active exploration by individual kids and small groups; they also include an ele-ment of student choice, in that kids can decide when to visit each center, traffic permitting.

Good centers are natural. A writing center might be mainly a computer or two and a supply depot with a variety of paper, pens, markers, tape, white correction fluid, and a table for editing. A reading center would include a classroom library of enticing books of various levels of difficulty, hand-published books by other students, comfortable corners for reading, and a table and chairs for quiet group discussion. Listening centers, with a couple of tape recorders and a good collection of tapes, offer kids a chance to listen to books read aloud (either familiar ones or ones they can't yet handle independently) or to hear interviews with favorite authors. Math centers can present a variety of manipulatives and problem-solving activities, so that as students cycle through all of them over a period of weeks, they are involved in a variety of tasks—some review previously taught ideas, some work with topics currently being discussed, and others provide challenging inquiry into more advanced concepts (as in Mary Fencl's classroom, pages 128–132). A science center might be the location where a classroom pet is kept, along with books about that creature, and a set of observational activities to be recorded in each child's learning log. A room with centers offers kids variety in the day, a chance to engage content actively, natural occasions for quiet talk, opportunities for spontaneous collaboration, and the responsibility for making choices. Centers also put the teacher in a helper-observer role, providing a splendid time to give help to kids who need it and to observe carefully the ways in which different kids approach the work of different centers.

Teachers who want to successfully implement all these promising new student-centered small-group activities may need to begin with some whole-class training first. If students are inexperienced with small-group structures, the starting point may be developing a productive, interdependent, cooperative classroom community. After all, if the climate isn't right, small groups will fail, and instruction inevitably will regress toward the old teacher-centered, lecture-test model. At the whole-class level, teachers must help students to join in effective, democratic meetings during which the group can brainstorm ideas, set goals, make plans, learn new structures for working, solve problems, and evaluate their own work. While this kind of session may sound routine, most teachers are experienced in giving whole-class presentations and instructions, not in chairing meetings that invite genuine interchange and decision making by the students.

William Glasser (1990) outlined a recurrent cycle of classroom meetings that builds both content learning and democratic involvement. The class (1) meets regularly to talk about its own learning activities and social processes; (2) identifies learning goals or group problems; (3) prioritizes its goals or problems; (4) proposes and discusses alternative courses of action; (5) makes a formal, group commitment to action; and (6) regularly meets to share and review the outcomes of group decisions. While this pattern of whole-class meetings obviously can nurture the socioemotional development of the classroom community, its academic uses are just as vital: at these meetings, students can decide what to study, divide into working groups, plan how and when to report their learnings with others, and more.

Whole-class meetings are also important for sharing completed work that students are proud of or for which they want feedback to help them revise further. Many elementary teachers end their daily writing workshop time with ten minutes for a few students to occupy the "author's chair," read their work aloud, and call on peers who ask questions, offer specific praise, or explain where they felt confused. A whole science class can profitably talk through the qualities that characterize an effective lab explanation, report, or small-group presentation—so that everyone participates in setting criteria for meaningful evaluation. And when any small-group project is finished, the teacher can help her class internalize the underlying concepts by outlining together not only the major ideas explored, but also the activities the class used, and how groups overcame various obstacles and solved problems in the course of their learning.

SUGGESTED FURTHER READINGS

Daniels, Harvey. 2002. *Literature Circles: Voice and Choice in Book Clubs and Reading Groups*. York, ME: Stenhouse.

Girard, Suzanne, and Kathlene Willing. 1996. *Partnerships for Classroom Learning: From Reading Buddies to Pen Pals to the Community and the World Beyond*. Portsmouth, NH: Heinemann.

Glazer, Susan Mandel. 1997. *The Literacy Center: Contexts for Reading and Writing*. York, ME: Stenhouse.

Johnson, David, and Roger Johnson. 1998. *Learning Together and Alone*. New York: Allyn and Bacon.

Samway, Katharine, Gail Whang, and Mary Pippitt. 1995. *Buddy Reading: Cross-Age Tutoring in a Multicultural School*. Portsmouth, NH: Heinemann.

Sharan, Shlomo. 1999. *Handbook of Cooperative Learning Methods*. New York: Praeger.

Steineke, Nancy. 2002. *Reading and Writing Together: Collaborative Literacy in Action*. Portsmouth, NH: Heinemann.

READING AS THINKING

In Chapter 2, we talked about the nature of reading, the research about how it is learned, and the standards documents that guide reading teachers from primary grades through high school. As we noted, all young readers have two overlapping and ongoing tasks: learning to read and reading to learn. As kids move up through the grades, they encounter steadily more difficult kinds of texts, and must develop increasingly sophisticated reading-as-thinking strategies along the way.

Smart teachers use a special family of methods to ensure kids' comprehension of literary, scientific, historical, mathematical, and all the other kinds of text encountered in school. Sometimes known as *strategic reading* or *reading-as-thinking strategies,* these highly structured and interactive activities use discussion, writing, and drawing to help students engage with, understand, and apply the reading that they do. These distinctive activities help students use their minds more effectively by supporting the mental strategies proficient readers use. In this section we'll draw on our own recent work in describing a few of these "content-area" reading activities (Daniels and Zemelman 2004; Daniels and Steineke 2004.) These activities are usually organized in three categories that cover the stages in the reading process, which, of course, is not merely linear but also recursive.

INTO: Activities that prepare students before they read. This includes (1) helping students get focused on and excited about the reading, (2) developing purposes for reading, (3) involving students in issues and concepts in the reading, and (4) making connections with students' prior knowledge to help make sense of the reading.

THROUGH: Activities that help students construct, process, and question ideas as they read. Good readers *visualize* what is happening in a story or historical situation or science experiment. They may realize they have more *questions* about the topic. They make *connections* between various parts of the piece and their own lives as well as the larger world around them. They draw *inferences,* going beyond the information given to the implications it offers. They notice which are the *important ideas* and which are minor elements or digressions. And they *monitor* their comprehension, noticing when they understand and when they've lost the thread. The mind of a proficient reader is agile and active, and nothing like a passive sponge.

BEYOND: Activities that guide students to reflect on, integrate, and share the ideas after they're finished. This is when readers *synthesize* ideas within their reading and between what they've read and what they already knew about a topic, to make larger *inferences* and *connections.* They follow up on the *questions* and *purposes* they had and consider whether they've learned answers, found surprises, or developed a new perspective on the topic. And they share their thoughts to help others with this process.

As you can foresee, dividing the tasks of reading into these stages and providing students with support at each step takes more time than traditional teaching. It would be easier to simply command kids to "read this for Friday" and then pop a quiz on the appointed day. But, as all of us ex-students know, with that kind of reading assignment, the kids generally won't understand or remember material two minutes after the test—and sometimes not even that long. The new approach to content-area reading invests time in having students deeply understand some important texts in the field rather than skimming over everything. The family of into-through-and-beyond strategies includes several dozen related structures. Here, we'll offer just three examples, each one tied to a different stage of reading, and encourage readers to explore further in the resources listed later.

Before Reading: KWL

This widely used strategy, developed by our National-Louis University colleague Donna Ogle (1986), is a sophisticated brainstorming process that works for students of all ages and in all content areas. Everything is built around an *upcoming topic,* a subject (whales, photosynthesis, Navajo culture, global warming, folktales) that students will soon read about. In successive stages, the teacher leads students, usually as a whole class, to first list what they think they already **Know** about the topic, then what they **Want** to find out about it—and later, after reading, what they've **Learned.**

The initial **K** step asks students to access their prior knowledge. As students brainstorm what they already know or "think they know" about the topic, the teacher lists the items on chart paper or an overhead. Why is evoking this "prior knowledge" so crucial? Because when their knowledge base is surfaced, students have an easier time making connections between new information and what they already know, which in turn helps make sense of the new material. It doesn't even matter if kids brainstorm misconceptions during a **K** session; this can actually be actually helpful, because incorrect ideas will be challenged by the upcoming reading, a much more effective kind of feedback than having the teacher simply say "you're wrong."

While the **K** step usually goes smoothly, students sometimes need help getting started on the **W** questions—perhaps because they are hesitant to reveal their lack of knowledge, or because they're too infrequently asked to pose their own questions in school. To overcome any reticence, teachers can use items in the **K** column to tease out the questions: *I notice that you said Iraq was a desert. So what do you wonder about how people live in such a place?* This **W** process, generating questions about the topic, explicitly sets purposes and goals for the reading to come. Kids—and adults—read better and comprehend more when they enter the text thinking, with specific questions in mind. After completing the **K** and **W** columns, students can group and label the items in categories they decide on, to streamline their goals for reading.

Later, after the reading is done, students return to **L**, "what we've learned," and record how they achieved the reading goals they set for themselves. When completing the **L** list, teachers make sure to compare it to the **K** and **W** columns. Students should not only become more aware of what they've learned but also realize—as is often the case in learning—that some questions didn't get answered, while unexpected new ideas turned up. Used in this full form, KWL is really a complete into-through-and-beyond strategy, one of its elegant attributes. Developer Donna Ogle has written about elaborated versions of KWL (KWL+) that take this valuable idea even further (Carr and Ogle 1987).

During Reading: Text Coding

Veteran readers often have ways of marking or coding text they want to remember. Maybe they use a yellow highlighter, underline or box words, or put marks in the margins to flag questions, exclamations, or wonderment as they read. Indeed, marking up the text may be the most simple, practical, and widespread thinking tool that real-life readers use. In school, however, students often are discouraged from making any marks in the books they're using. In fact, the more challenging the material (like science or history textbooks), the less likely that kids will be allowed to use this effective tool for enhancing comprehension. Too bad.

When books or other reading materials *can* be marked up, it's important for students to have a useful set of response codes. This is especially helpful with dense, content-loaded texts where every single word matters, like poetry or fact-filled nonfiction books. When addressing such tough text, students need to attack the page, penetrate the surface, and dig out the meaning. Symbols help students notice their responses as they read, and allow them to quickly mark spots in the text where that thinking occurred. Many teachers we know use the INSERT system of text coding with their students (Vaughan and Estes 1986).

"INSERT" Text Codes

✓ Confirms what you thought

x Contradicts what you thought

? Raises a question

?? Confuses you

★ Seems important

! Is new or interesting

Teachers don't just hand out these codes; they *show* kids how to use them. Placing a short story or news article on an overhead transparency, the teacher reads aloud and puts down marks where she herself is stopping to think. The teacher tries to vocalize her thinking process: "Well, I already knew that."(check) "What? I don't understand this." (question mark) "Now that's really important." (exclamation point) Next, students can begin using the coding system on short class readings. If a student, while reading, notices something he already knows, he'll put a check in the margin. If another is confused by a new formula, she'll jot a "?" beside it. Words can be part of text coding, too. Students may jot words or brief phrases in the margins to flag big ideas, note strong reactions, or highlight puzzling questions. If the book belongs to the school or a library, the codes can be placed on small $1\frac{1}{2}$ × 2-inch Post-it notes, with a little edge sticking out for easy locating.

Once students become skilled at coding text, these special notes can be used to feed classwork in a variety of ways. Many teachers send students into small groups for reading discussions, using the coded sections of the text as conversation-starters (e.g., "I was really puzzled here on the bottom of page 23 where Romeo says, 'What light from yonder window breaks?' How can light break?"). The teacher can also lead whole-class discussions using prompts like these: Who had a question mark in the first section? Exactly where was it? What puzzled you?

After Reading: Written Conversation

We often use class discussion as a key after-reading activity. But when you think about it, what is a class discussion? It is usually one person talking and twenty-nine others sitting, pretending to listen, and hoping that their turn never comes. Not quite what the standards documents call "engaged learning." In fact, whole-class discussions may be routine, but they are a pretty passive form of instruction, since most kids at any given moment are not actively engaging the material. With written conversation, we can have a "discussion" where everyone is actively talking at once—though silently, in writing.

Here's how it works in practice. After students have completed a key piece of reading, they identify partners for a written conversation. The teacher explains the activity first: students will be writing simultaneous notes to one another about the reading selection, swapping them every two or three minutes at the teacher's command, for a total of three exchanges (or two or four, depending on time constraints), and keeping quiet as they work. They are to write for the whole time allotted for each note, putting down words, phrases, questions, connections, ideas, wonderings—anything related to the passage, or responding to what their partner has said, just as they would in out-loud conversation. Spelling and grammar do not count—after all, these are just notes.

The teacher can leave the topic open ("whatever struck you about this reading") or can give an appropriate open-ended prompt: "What do you understand and not understand in this selection?" "What are the most important ideas here?" "Do you agree or disagree with the author, and why?" Then both students in each pair start writing a note. Meanwhile, the teacher watches the time, and after two or three minutes, asks students to exchange notes. The teacher reminds: "Read what your partner said, and then take two minutes to answer, just as if you were talking out loud. You can write responses, feelings, stories, make connections of your own, or ask your partner questions—anything you would do in a face-to-face conversation." Here's part of a recent in-class written conversation between two high school boys on the topic of global warming.

Dear Jerry,

People's beliefs about how the world will be affected in the future I think are totally non-realistic. The fact is the United States never really focuses on environment b/c they are too busy w/ stupid wars over oil or resources that just hurt the environment. Every war adds to environmental problems. Also the President of the US never speaks of the environment or ways to help it. We follow our president and no environmental progress is being made. What do you think?

Randy

Dear Randy,

Well I agree with you that our president, probably the most influential and powerful man in the world is doing very little to reduce environmental problems. Perhaps this coming November (and before then) the public should be informed of how their choice for leaders of their nation could effect the entire world's future. I also agree that our nation is preoccupied with silly wars that may or may not directly affect the future of our world. Like I said before, education is the most important thing to get the majority of America informed.

Jerry

 Dear Jerry,

I agree that education is a key to reducing the tragedy known as global warming. However, as individuals we can only do so much with our surroundings b/c the minute you fix something, someone else is probably there to ruin it. I think in order to eliminate problems of global warming our nation needs to take a step individually, and later a step has to be taken by the world as a whole. If the world can work together, peace will be brought, and our environment can be a clean one, not just parts being cleaned.

Randy

After the planned two- or three-note exchange is complete, the teacher says: "OK, now you can talk out loud with your partner for a couple of minutes." There should be a rising buzz in the room, because all the partners, like Jerry and Randy, now have plenty to talk about. Following pair sharing, a whole-class discussion will then be much more engaged and productive, because everyone has fresh ideas about the topic. A simple way to kick this off is to ask a few volunteer pairs to "share one highlight or thread of your written conversations, something that you spent time on, agreed or disagreed about."

The first time teachers try this activity, kids will tend to shift into oral conversation when papers are passed (adults also do this—it's a normal human response when bonding with a partner). The reminder to keep it in writing may have to be reiterated during the transitions. And, even with the best instructions, some kids will write two words and put their pens down, wasting two good minutes of writing time with each pass. The teacher just keeps stressing that "we write for the whole time," and if necessary, provides additional prompts to the class or to individuals to help them keep going. Finally, when kids are done writing and they are finally allowed to talk out loud with their partners, teachers may find it very hard to regain their attention. This happy little "management problem" shows that students are connecting to each other and the material they have read.

SUGGESTED FURTHER READINGS

Allen, Janet. 2004. *Tools for Teaching Content Literacy*. Portland, ME: Stenhouse.

Beers, Kylene. 2003. *When Kids Can't Read, What Teachers Can Do*. Portsmouth, NH: Heinemann.

Blachowicz, Camille, and Donna Ogle. 2002. *Reading Comprehension: Strategies for Independent Learners*. New York: Guilford.

Daniels, Harvey, and Steven Zemelman. 2004. *Subjects Matter: Every Teacher's Guide to Content-Area Reading*. Portsmouth, NH: Heinemann.

Harvey, Stephanie, and Anne Gouvdis. 2000. *Strategies That Work: Teaching Comprehension to Enhance Understanding*. Portland, ME: Stenhouse.

Keene, Ellin Oliver, and Susan Zimmerman. 1997. *Mosaic of Thought: Teaching Comprehension in a Reader's Workshop*. Portsmouth, NH: Heinemann.

Serafini, Frank. *Lessons in Comprehension*. 2004. Portsmouth, NH: Heinemann.

Tovani, Chris. 2004. *Do I Really Have to Teach Reading?* Portland, ME: Stenhouse.

Wilhelm, Jeff. 2001. *Strategic Reading: Guiding Students to Lifelong Literacy 6–12*. Portsmouth, NH: Heinemann.

REPRESENTING-TO-LEARN

Many teachers are already familiar with the notion of *writing-to-learn*, developed in the 1970s and 1980s and widely disseminated in National Writing Project in-service programs. The idea is simple: writing can be a tool of thinking as well as a finished product. There are many quick and simple writing activities that help students to encounter, probe, explore, and remember the content of the curriculum. While schools typically act as though finished, polished compositions are the only form of worthwhile writing, modern learning theory shows us that when students act on information by using informal, spontaneous writing, they actually understand and recall more of what is taught in school.

Since the early days of writing-to-learn, we've discovered that writing down *words* is not the limit of this activity. Drawing, sketching, jotting, mapping, and other artistic and graphic representations are equally valuable—and when combined with words, in strategies like clustering, semantic mapping, or cartooning, they can powerfully leverage students' thinking about the curriculum. Indeed, research is quickly accumulating (see Chapter 7) that documents the contribution artistic expression offers to the development of basic-skills learning in subjects like math, science, and literature. So, to acknowledge this important broadening of writing-to-learn, we've renamed the category *representing-to-learn* (Daniels and Bizar 2004).

Representing-to-learn strategies help overcome the passivity of the traditional classroom, making students more active and responsible for their own learning. Teachers of all subjects and grade levels can have students keep sketchbooks or learning logs in which students regularly do short, spontaneous, exploratory, personal pieces of writing or drawing about the content they are studying. Instead of filling in blanks in worksheets and jotting short answers to textbook study questions, students respond to fewer, broader, more open-ended prompts: What would have changed if Lincoln had been shot six months earlier? What are the advantages of an indicator over a meter? What are three questions from last night's reading that we ought to discuss in class today? In logs, teachers ask students to react, record, speculate, compare, analyze, or synthesize the ideas in the curriculum. Students aren't writing to be graded on grammar or artistic ability, but rather to pursue ideas and try out thoughts. These notebooks are a way of running your brain, monitoring your thinking, and making reflection habitual and concrete. This is writing and drawing for thinking, not as a polished product.

As a cognitive tool, learning logs can work for learners in any content field. After all, whatever the subject matter, learners can always jot down their responses, record their own prior knowledge, probe their own thinking patterns, map predictions, diagram connections, or sketch plans for what to do next. When they are shared, notebooks also open a private channel of communication between the teacher and each student. In learning logs, teachers report, students will often share things that they would never announce out loud, thereby providing teachers a new and valuable kind of feedback.

Teachers also use student representing-to-learn products in class, reading them aloud, feeding them into group discussions, parceling them out to teams for review or action. Many teachers, like our friend Wayne Mraz, assign "admit slips" and "exit slips," short bits of writing used to start and end a class. Others run classroom discussions about a topic—a poem or a Civil War battle or a chemical process—in the kind of written conversation we just described (pages 236–238). For teachers who use these representing-to-learn strategies regularly, the compiled entries become an increasingly thick record of what each student has done and learned.

One of the surprising and pleasant side effects of representing-to-learn is that, sometimes, the classroom is *quiet*. While many people anticipate chaos in progressive classrooms, the opposite is often the case. For example, if you visit the kind of reading workshop described by Nancie Atwell (1998) and implemented by teachers around the country, you typically will find a room full of teenagers working quietly, without overt supervision, for forty-five minutes at a stretch. Students may be reading novels of their own choice, which they will occasionally put aside at a good stopping place to write a "literature letter" to the teacher or a designated student partner. Or they may draw their own vision of a scene from a story in response to a "lit letter" received from their partner. In this quiet but hard-working classroom, the teacher and the students are all industriously reading books and using special kinds of writing and drawing to channel their responses and enhance their comprehension.

Although these logs are often called journals, they are *not* diaries. Some teachers are wary of trying journals because of the confessional connotations of that word, but academic journaling (which we prefer to call learning logs, notebooks, or sketchbooks) is expressly for recording and advancing subject-matter learning in school. Other teachers worry about implementation problems, perhaps because they have seen too many ill-advised English teachers trudging home from school on Friday afternoon, lugging a sky-high stack of student spirals that they "have to" respond to over the weekend. But learning logs needn't increase the workload of either students or teachers. They are supposed to *replace* textbook study questions, ditto sheets, or other low-level, memorization-oriented activities. Students should spend the same amount of time working and teachers the same amount of time responding, with everyone engaged in higher-order, more valuable thinking. In fact, many teachers find that when the students' representing-to-learn pieces are used as the starting point for class activities and discussions, they don't even need to collect and read the work separately; hearing the ideas discussed aloud provides plenty of feedback about what kids are thinking.

Some teachers wonder whether their content is too technical or their students are too young for notebooks to work. We have seen learning logs effectively integrated into everything from preschool classes, where kids draw their entries, to animal husbandry courses at a technical college. Other teachers worry that if students are assigned learning logs in all school subjects, they will either become confused or "burn out" from the overuse of this teaching novelty. One answer to this: in Terrie Bridgman's first-grade class at Baker Demonstration School in Evanston, Illinois, all the six-year-olds are keeping a math journal, a reading journal, and a personal "news" journal within the first few days of school, with gusto and without any confusion. On a deep level, treating representing-to-learn as a gimmick makes no more sense than labeling *reading* in every class a fad. Effective teachers are recognizing that writing and drawing are rightful bookends to reading, too-neglected tools that help students actively process their encounter with ideas to deepen their engagement with the curriculum.

SUGGESTED FURTHER READINGS

Burnaford, Gail, Arnold Aprill, and Cynthia Weiss. 2000. *Renaissance in the Classroom: Arts Integration and Meaningful Learning.* Mahwah, NJ: York: Lawrence Erlbaum.

Countryman, Joan. 1992. *Writing to Learn Mathematics.* Portsmouth, NH: Heinemann.

Daniels, Harvey, and Marilyn Bizar. 2004. *Teaching the Best Practice Way: Methods That Matter, K–12.* Portland, ME: Stenhouse.

Ehrenworth, Mary. 2003. *Looking to Write: Students Writing Through the Visual Arts.* Portsmouth, NH: Heinemann.

Ernst, Karen. 1997. A *Teacher's Sketch Journal: Observations on Learning and Teaching.* Portsmouth, NH: Heinemann.

Fineberg, Carol. 2004. *Creating Islands of Excellence: Arts Education as a Partner in School Reform.* Portsmouth, NH: Heinemann.

Fowler, Charles. 1996. *Strong Arts, Strong Schools: The Promising Potential and Shortsighted Disregard of the Arts in American Schooling.* New York: Oxford University Press.

Gilmore, Barry. 1999. *Creative Writing Through the Visual and Performing Arts.* Portsmouth, NH: Heinemann.

Lambert, Joe. 2002. *Digital Storytelling: Capturing Lives Creating Community.* Berkeley, CA: Digital Diner.

Mantione, Roberta D., and Sabine Smead. 2003. *Weaving Through Words: Using the Arts to Teach Reading Comprehension Strategies.* Newark, DE: International Reading Association.

Miller, Carole S., and Juliana Saxton. 2004. *Into the Story: Language in Action Through Drama.* Portsmouth, NH: Heinemann.

Romano, Tom. 2000. *Blending Genre, Altering Style: Writing Multigenre Papers.* Portsmouth, NH: Boynton/Cook.

Swarz, Larry. 2002. *The New Dramathemes.* Markham, ON: Pembroke.

CLASSROOM WORKSHOP

Probably the single most important strategy in literacy education is the reading-writing workshop. As Donald Graves, Nancie Atwell, Lucy Calkins, Ralph Fletcher, Tom Romano and others have explained, students in a workshop classroom choose their own topics for writing and books for reading, using large scheduled chunks of classroom time for *doing* their own reading and writing. They collaborate freely with classmates, keep their own records, and self-evaluate. Teachers take new roles, too, modeling their own reading and writing processes, conferring with students one-to-one, and offering well-timed, compact mini-lessons as students work. In the mature workshop classroom, teachers don't wait around for "teachable moments" to occur— they make them happen every day.

The workshop model is simple and powerful. It derives from the insight that children learn to read by reading and write by writing, and that schools in the past have simply failed to provide enough guided practice. It recognizes that kids need less telling and more showing, that they need more time *doing* literacy and less time hearing what reading and writing might be like if you ever did them. Even the term *workshop* harks back to the ancient crafts-place, where not only did products get made, but education went on as the master craftsman coached apprentices.

In school, a workshop is a long, regularly scheduled, recurrent chunk of time (i.e., thirty minutes to an hour or more) during which the main activity is to *do* a subject: reading, writing, math, history, or science. Workshops meet regularly, at least once a week; in many classrooms, students have workshop time every day. A defining element of a true workshop is *choice*: individual students choose their own books for reading, projects for investigating, topics for writing. They follow a set of carefully inculcated norms for exercising that choice during the workshop period. They learn that all workshop time must be used on some aspect of working, so when they complete a product, a piece, or a phase, they aren't "done" for the day. Instead, kids must begin something new, based on an idea from their own running list of tasks and topics, or seek a conference with the teacher. While there are regular, structured opportunities for sharing and collaborating in a workshop, students also spend much time working alone; teachers may set up collaborative group or team activities at other times of the day.

Today, pathfinding teachers are beginning to extend the workshop model outward from reading and writing, where many have already found success, into other parts of the curriculum—establishing math workshops, science workshops, and history workshops. Teachers are adapting workshop because they see that deep immersion is the key to mastery, whatever the subject: they want kids to *do* history, *do* science, *do* math. On page 245 is a generic schedule for a single forty-five-minute workshop session that could happen in any subject. It just shows one way that teachers commonly manage time and activities.

Obviously, the workshop classroom is not an entirely new phenomenon. Its decentralized, hands-on pattern, with kids "doing" the subject rather than just hearing about it, is familiar to teachers of art, science, home economics, physical education, and other "doable" subjects. Of these fields, however, only art has traditionally allowed for any measure of student choice in the work. The commitment to student autonomy and responsibility is rooted more in experiments with independent study, classroom contracting, the open classroom, and learning laboratories. This powerful vehicle for student-centered learning—the workshop classroom—works because it addresses the shortcomings of prior experiments: it gives both students and teachers clear-cut roles to perform, it provides for careful balancing of social and solitary activities, and it respects the necessity of detailed training for students to work purposefully in this decentralized format.

Conferences are the heart of the workshop. In a very real sense, they are the main reason we go to all the trouble to set up the norms, structures, and processes of workshop in the first place. What we're trying so hard to create is time and space to sit down with kids, one at a time, and work for a few minutes on just what each student needs. Sadly, these conversations are still too rare in American schools. In spite of decades of research confirming the impact of teacher-student conferences—from Jerome Bruner's scaffolding research in the 1960s to this year's headlines about "reading recovery" tutoring—most American students still spend their school day deployed in groups of thirty, listening to the teacher or doing seatwork. Ironically, most teachers will readily agree that a one-minute private conversation with a child, timed at just the right moment and targeted precisely to that kid's own work, is often more effective than hours of whole-class instruction. But still, few teachers are reorganizing their day to make more one-to-one exchanges happen.

Why haven't conferences caught on more widely? There are several sticking points. Tradition, as usual, provides a first layer of resistance. Teachers' formal training, as well as their own experience as students, strongly conditions them to think of teaching as a one-on-thirty rather than a one-on-one

Five Minutes: Status of the Class Conference. Each student announces in a few words what she will work on this session.

Ten Minutes: Mini-lesson. The teacher offers a short and practical lesson on a tool, skill, procedure, or piece of information potentially useful to everyone.

Twenty to Thirty Minutes: Work Time/Conferences. Students work according to their plan. Depending on the rules and norms, this may include reading or writing, talking or working with other students, going to the library, conducting telephone interviews, using manipulatives or microscopes. The teacher's roles during this time are several. For the first few minutes, the teacher may experiment, read, or write herself, to model her own doing of the subject. Then the teacher will probably manage a bit, skimming through the room to solve simple problems and make sure everyone is working productively.

Then the teacher shifts to her main workshop activity: conducting one-to-one or small-group conferences with kids about their work, either following a preset schedule or based on student sign-ups for that day. The teacher's roles in these conferences are to be a sounding board, facilitator, and coach—rarely a critic or an instructor.

Ten Minutes: Sharing. In many workshop sessions, teachers save the last few minutes for students to discuss what they have done that day. Writers may read a piece of work aloud, readers offer a capsule book review, math students show how they applied a concept to a real-world situation, scientists demonstrate a chemical reaction, social studies teams report the results of their opinion survey.

activity. Experienced teachers already possess banks of lesson plans, some of them developed and polished over years, for teacher-centered classroom activities that seem to work. These treasured whole-class lessons are ready to use, and they don't carry the risks and uncertainties that are inevitably part of anything new.

The second level of reluctance involves classroom management: teachers worry about "what to do with the other twenty-nine kids" while they hold conferences with individual pupils. This is a reasonable concern: until teachers can get a classroom of students working productively without constant monitoring, they won't feel safe to introduce one-to-one activities like conferences. This, of course, is one of the main reasons why it is so important to establish the workshop structure described—not only does it provide practice time in key curriculum areas, but it also creates the basic frame within which conferences can occur. And, working farther backward, building a productive workshop depends on the initial climate-setting, group-building activities we talked about earlier.

The other worry teachers have is that they won't know what to say to a child in a conference. Many think that to have an effective conference, they must first study the learner's work and then ask "the right questions"—or have the right advice ready to give. For teachers just starting to consider instituting such one-to-one conversations, this sounds like a lot of work. But good conferences do not necessarily require extensive teacher preparation. In writing instruction, for example, we have found that kids who have regular three-minute "process conferences" with their teachers gain significantly in writing achievement, even when the teacher does not read the papers or give advice in those conferences.

So what kinds of things can the teacher say? Three simple questions can start a conference in any subject: (1) What are you working on? (2) How is it going? (3) What do you plan to do next? For each of these key questions, teachers will gradually develop some subprompts or helping questions, but the three basic queries serve just fine for starters. In such a process conference, it is not the teacher's job to tell or teach or offer instruction; the task is to help the student talk and to listen. In fact, such process conferences actually can help teachers avoid one conferencing problem that they may not worry about, but should: dominating the student. Too many teachers, when they first begin conferencing, simply offer a kind of knee-to-knee lecture, talking at the student for three or four minutes. The simple, three-question process conference transfers the conversational responsibility from teacher to student, providing the teacher with a good implicit reminder to keep quiet.

How do such short "content-free" conferences actually promote the learning of content? Process conferences work because they teach a habit of mind. They help students learn how to reflect on their own work, to review their own progress, to identify their own problems, set their own goals, and make plans and promises to themselves about steps they are going to take. As we regularly hold conferences with students, leading them through the pattern of where-am-I-and-where-do-I-want-to-go, we are truly modeling a way of thinking for themselves; we are holding out-loud conversations with kids that they can gradually internalize and have with themselves.

Of course, veteran workshop teachers take conferences far beyond the baseline. If you were lucky enough (as Harvey recently was) to observe Nancie Atwell in her middle school classroom, you'd see a dazzling array of quick, carefully targeted, and individualized teacher-student conferences. During a typical forty-five-minute work period, Nancie will sit down with every child in the class for just a minute or two. In some conferences, Nancie asks gentle but probing questions, but in many others she gives very specific *advice,* based on her reading of kids' prior drafts. This is possible only because she reads the kids' work between classes, and jots conference ideas on notecards that she brings to each meeting.

Implementing the workshop classroom, with its core of individual conferences, can be a real challenge for teachers. The structure itself violates the expectations of many students, administrators, and parents; it competes for time with the official curriculum; and it often contradicts teachers' professional training and their own childhood experience in school. Nor do students always take smoothly and effortlessly to the workshop model: on the contrary, implementation can be bumpy, tricky, and slow, even for dedicated teachers in progressive districts. Yet, when the workshop starts to work, it turns the traditional transmission-model classroom upside down: students become active, responsible, self-motivating, and self-evaluating learners, while the teacher drops the talking-head role in favor of more powerful functions as model, coach, and collaborator.

SUGGESTED FURTHER READINGS

Anderson, Carl. 2000. *How's It Going? A Practical Guide to Conferring with Student Writers.* Portland, ME: Stenhouse.

Atwell, Nancie. 1998. *In the Middle: New Understandings About Writing, Reading, and Learning* (Second Edition). Portsmouth, NH: Boynton/Cook Heinemann.

Brown, Cynthia Stokes. 1994. *Connecting with the Past: History Workshop in Middle and High Schools.* Portsmouth, NH: Heinemann.

Buis, Kellie. 2004. *Writing Every Day.* York, ME: Stenhouse.

Calkins, Lucy. 1994. The *Art of Teaching Writing.* Portsmouth, NH: Heinemann.

———. 2003. *Units of Study for Primary Writing: A Yearlong Curriculum.* Portsmouth, NH: Firsthand/Heinemann.

Cruz, M. Colleen. 2004. *Independent Writing: One Teacher—Thirty-Two Needs, Topics, and Plans.* Portsmouth, NH: Heinemann.

Daniels, Harvey, and Nancy Steineke. 2004. *Mini-lessons for Literature Circles.* Portsmouth, NH: Heinemann.

Fletcher, Ralph, and JoAnn Portalupi. 2001. *Writing Workshop: The Essential Guide.* Portsmouth, NH: Heinemann.

Graves, Donald. 1983. *Writing: Teachers and Children at Work.* Portsmouth, NH: Heinemann.

Harwayne, Shelley. 2003. *Learning to Confer: Writing Conferences in Action.* Portsmouth, NH: Heinemann.

Jorgensen, Karen. 1993. *History Workshop: Reconstructing the Past with Elementary Students.* Portsmouth, NH: Heinemann.

Ray, Katie Wood, and Lisa B. Cleaveland. 2004. *About the Authors: Writing Workshop with Our Youngest Writers.* Portsmouth, NH: Heinemann.

Romano, Tom. 2004. *Crafting Authentic Voice.* Portsmouth, NH: Heinemann.

Saul, Wendy, et al. 1993. *Science Workshop: A Whole-Language Approach.* Portsmouth, NH: Heinemann.

Tobin, Lad. 2004. *Reading Student Writing: Confessions, Meditations and Rants.* Portsmouth, NH: Heinemann.

Zemelman, Steven, and Harvey Daniels. 1988. *A Community of Writers: Teaching Writing in the Junior and Senior High School.* Portsmouth, NH: Heinemann.

AUTHENTIC EXPERIENCES

Virtually all the standards documents that have been published over the past decade entreat teachers to "make it real," to involve students in tangible, genuine, authentic, real-world materials and experiences. This challenge is problematic in several ways. To begin with, school itself isn't "real," in the sense that schools are purposely separated from the rest of life and people and work and community. If we want to make education "real," we have to somehow overcome that segregation, either by bringing bits of the world into schools or bringing the kids out into the world. Well, that's OK; the schoolhouse door does swing both ways.

We admit that realness or authenticity isn't exactly a teaching *method,* like workshop or strategic reading, but more of a condition. That means the structure we are calling "authentic experiences" is somewhat asymmetrical with the other six learning methods on our list. But it is worth the difficulty to sort this out. Every story of powerful, transformative learning we've heard (or shared in this book), contains the crucial detail that students were working on something that felt real.

A story in the National Science Education Standards (NRC 1996) provides one vision of "real."

 In Ms. F's classroom, a lesson on collecting data and conducting research began when she noticed the kids' fascination with the earthworms living in an empty lot next to the playground. She suggested that the students figure out what kind of habitat the worms required. The kids eagerly spent a few days examining the living conditions of the earthworms in the empty lot before creating a similar environment in a terrarium, away from the sun and filled with soil, leaves, and grass. Ms. F. ordered some worms from a biological supply house, and the students put them in their new home. For two weeks, students observed the earthworms and recorded their behavior, and began listing questions they wanted to answer: How do they have babies? Do they really like the dark? How big can they get? How long do they live? Children formed into small groups to decide together which question they were most interested in exploring. The groups were given time to decide how they would conduct their investigations and by the following week, the research was under way.

The group that chose to investigate the lifecycle of earthworms had found egg cases in the soil, and while they waited for the eggs to hatch, they read some books about earthworms to add to their knowledge base. Another group wondered what earthworms like to eat and offered test foods. Two other groups wondered what kind of environment earthworms preferred, and they experimented by varying moisture, light, and temperature.

This authentic scientific inquiry started with the interest and natural curiosity of the students and taught them much more than just facts about earthworms. They became researchers: gathering data, manipulating variables, asking questions, discovering answers, and asking more questions. The students worked collaboratively, just as grown-up scientists join in a collaborative enterprise that depends on the sharing of ideas and discoveries.

This exemplary activity actually included several kinds of "realness." Ms. F. began with a real expressed interest of the children; she involved them in real research, doing what real scientists do, in a simplified but complete form; she gave them real responsibility and choice, helping them divide into teams and jigsaw the inquiry; and obviously, she had them working with very real worms. Notice that part of the realness came from getting outside

Making Learning Authentic

Inside School

- Let kids in on curriculum planning, choosing topics and readings, making schedules, keeping records.

- Develop broad, interdisciplinary, thematic units based on student concerns.

- Use tangible, tactile materials, artifacts, and live demonstrations where possible.

- Favor learn-by-doing over learn-by-sitting-there-quietly-and-listening.

- Follow news and current events, connecting them with curriculum.

- Include activities that connect with students' multiple intelligences and cognitive styles.

- Let students subdivide content, form groups, and conduct team projects.

- Assign real, whole books, rather than synthetic basal texts created by publishers.

- Use primary-source documents, not just textbooks, to teach history, science, and other subjects.

- Invite speakers, experts, and interview subjects from the community.

- Bring in parents to give presentations, conference with kids, create materials.

- Mix children through multiage grouping, cross-age projects, buddy programs, and mainstreamed special education.

- Schedule time in flexible blocks that match the curriculum.

- Stress student goal setting and self-assessment.

- Have regular one-to-one conferences across the curriculum.

- Offer frequent performances, fairs, and exhibitions, inviting parent and community audiences.

Beyond School

- Give homework assignments that require interaction with family and community.

- Plan regular field trips and attend arts performances that support the curriculum.

- Visit, study, and investigate local government, services, and businesses.

- Get involved in community issues: recycling, safety, programs for kids.

- Launch family and community history projects.

- Join a community beautification or art project.

- Take children on outdoor education, wilderness, ecology, and adventure programs.

- In conjunction with integrative units, have fact-finding tours where students take notes, make observations, or conduct interviews.

- Conduct survey or opinion research, by mail or in person.

- Develop volunteer relationships with local agencies, nursing homes, and hospitals.

- For older students, create regular student service or work internships.

- Support student service clubs and groups that reach out to the community.

- Invite students to suggest, plan, and evaluate outreach projects.

- Share student work through parent and community newsletters, displays, and events.

- Display student artwork or research projects in off-campus settings.

the school walls, while other aspects of realness came from importing things into the classroom—like worms! The chart above outlines some of these key kinds of authenticity. Keeping in mind that school can be made more lifelike, we first mention steps toward authenticity that can be inside school, followed by ways of taking students out into the community.

SUGGESTED FURTHER READINGS

Beane, James. 2005 (forthcoming). *A Reason to Teach: Creating Classrooms of Dignity and Hope*. Portsmouth, NH: Heinemann.

Bourne, Barbara, ed. 1999. *Taking Inquiry Outdoors: Reading, Writing, and Science Beyond the Classroom Walls*. York, ME: Stenhouse.

Burke, Kay. 1999. *How to Assess Authentic Learning*. Arlington, IL: Skylight.

Chancer, Joni, and Gina Rester-Zodrow. 1997. *Moon Journals: Writing, Art, and Inquiry Through Focused Nature Study*. Portsmouth, NH: Heinemann.

Clyde, Jean Ann, and Mark W. F. Condon. 1999. *Get Real: Bringing Kids' Learning Lives into Your Classroom*. York, ME: Stenhouse.

Fresch, Eula T. 2004. *Connecting Children with Children, Past and Present: Motivating Students for Inquiry and Action*. Portsmouth, NH: Heinemann.

Nabhan, Gary, and Steven Trimble. 1995. *The Geography of Childhood: Why Children Need Wild Places.* Boston: Beacon Press.

Primary Source, Inc. 2004. *Making Freedom.* (five-volume series). Portsmouth, NH: Heinemann.

Roberts, Pamela. 2002. *Kids Taking Action: Community Service Learning Projects K–8.* York, ME: Stenhouse.

Saul, Wendy, and Jeanne Reardon, eds. 1996. *Beyond the Science Kit: Inquiry in Action.* Portsmouth, NH: Heinemann.

Stephens, Lillian. 1995. *The Complete Guide to Learning Through Community Service: Grades K–9.* Des Moines, IA: Allyn and Bacon.

Zemelman, Steven, Yolanda Simmons, Patricia Bearden, and Pete Leki. 1999. *History Comes Home: Family Stories Across the Curriculum.* York, ME: Stenhouse.

REFLECTIVE ASSESSMENT

In Best Practice classrooms, teachers don't just make up tests and put grades on report cards. They are less interested in measuring students' recall of individual facts or use of certain subskills than in how they perform authentic, complete, higher-order activities: reading whole books, drafting and editing stories or articles, conducting and reporting a scientific inquiry, applying math to real problem solving. Because progressive teachers want deeper and more practical information about children's learning, they monitor students' growth in richer and more sophisticated ways. More and more, teachers are adopting and adapting the tools of ethnographic, qualitative research: observation, interviews, questionnaires, collecting and interpreting artifacts and performances. They use information from these sources not mainly to "justify" marks on a report card, but to guide instruction, to make crucial daily decisions about helping students grow. And above all, they see the main goal of assessment to be helping students set goals, monitor their own work, and evaluate their efforts. Nothing more conclusively marks the well-educated person than the capacity to run one's own brain, have clear self-insight, and follow through on projects.

Many teachers now keep anecdotal, observational records, saving a few minutes each day to jot notes about students in their classes—some call this "kid-watching." Instead of using numbers, letters, or symbols, teachers create written descriptions of what students are doing and saying. Some teachers put these observations on a schedule, tracking five particular kids on Monday, another five on Tuesday, and so forth. Some watch just one kid per day; some simply jot notes on any kids who show noteworthy growth, think-ing, problems, or concerns; others prefer to record observations of the class as a community. The common feature of these observational notes is that teachers save time for regularly recording them; they develop a format that works for them; and they consistently use these notes, both to guide their instruction and to communicate with parents and others about children's progress.

Teachers also teach students to become self-observers in increasingly powerful ways. In face-to-face interviews, written questionnaires, or learn-ing logs, teachers ask kids to record and reflect on their own work (e.g., books read, experiments conducted). In Best Practice classrooms, it is com-mon for students to have periodic "evaluation conferences" with their teach-ers, where both parties use their notes to review the child's achievements and problems over a span of time, and then set goals for the upcoming weeks or months. In a curriculum that values higher-order thinking as well as individ-ual responsibility, such self-evaluation teaches multiple important lessons.

One of the most promising mechanisms for authentic evaluation is the student portfolio, a folder in which students save selected samples of their best work in a given subject. The practice of keeping such cumulative records has many benefits. First, of course, it provides actual evidence of what the child can do in writing, math, art, or science, instead of a mark in a grade-book—which represents, after all, nothing more than a teacher-mediated symbolic record of a long-discarded piece of real work. These portfolio arti-facts also invite all sorts of valuable conversations between the child and the teacher, children and peers, or kids and parents: How did you get interested in this? How did you feel while you were working on this? How did you solve the problems you encountered? What would you tell another student about this subject? What are you going to do next? The process of select-ing and polishing items for inclusion in the portfolio invites students to become increasingly reflective about their own work and more skillful at self-evaluation.

When teachers try to add these new, more productive forms of evalua-tion to their classrooms, they will run into a time crunch unless they either subtract some old assessment activities or overlap the new assessments with something else. A good starting point is to review all the forms of evaluation underway in the classroom, terminating those that don't usefully steer in-struction, advance kids' learning, teach students to self-evaluate, or produce artifacts worth saving. For many teachers, this may mean grading far fewer busy-work handouts, workbook pages, study questions, and worksheets. Instead of tabulating the errors in stacks of identical fill-in-the blank worksheets, teachers can spend their precious evaluation time responding to each kid's whole original reports or stories, perhaps writing a personal note of response that gives guidance as well as models solid adult writing.

The other key to implementing better assessments is to overlap assessment with instruction, instead of always relying on evaluations that occur separately, after the work is done (and when it is too late for students to improve their product or learn from the assessment!). Many progressive forms of assessment are integral to learning itself. Reading and writing conferences are a case in point; when sitting down to talk with a child about her writing, the teacher can simultaneously and seamlessly gather information about the child's development as a writer. As the teacher jots down a few notes following each conference, a powerful record of growth is created. Similarly, when students and teachers together design scoring rubrics for class presentations, science experiments, or persuasive essays, they are explicitly being taught the ingredients of a successful performance, right along with creating a mechanism to evaluate their efforts.

All these adjustments mean that teachers are making a time trade: they're not spending any less time on evaluation, but they're also not spending more. They're differentiating their assessment efforts, looking at children's growth in a wider variety of ways. They are committed to the principle that the most valuable assessment activities are *formative,* aimed at understanding a child's development and making instructional decisions about that child. *Summative* evaluation, the process of converting kids' achievements into some kind of ranked, ordinal system that compares children to each other, should happen far less often, if at all.

SUGGESTED FURTHER READINGS

Akhavan, Nancy. 2004. *How to Align Literacy Instruction, Assessment, and Standards.* Portsmouth, NH: Heinemann.

Cambourne, Brian, and Jan Turbill, eds. 1994. *Responsive Evaluation: Making Valid Judgments About Student Literacy.* Portsmouth, NH: Heinemann.

Falk, Beverly. 2000. *The Heart of the Matter: Using Standards and Assessment to Learn.* Portsmouth, NH: Heinemann.

Graves, Donald. 2002. *Testing Is Not Teaching: What Should Count in Education.* Portsmouth, NH: Heinemann.

Harris-Stefanikis, Evangeline. 2003. *Multiple Intelligences and Portfolios: A Window into the Learner's Mind.* Portsmouth, NH: Heinemann.

Hill, Bonnie Campbell, and Cynthia Ruptic. 1994. *Practical Aspects of Authentic Assessment: Putting the Pieces Together.* Norwood, MA: Christopher-Gordon.

Johnston, Peter H. 2004. *Choice Words: How Our Language Affects Children's Learning.* Portland, ME: Stenhouse.

Murphy, Sandra, and Mary Ann Smith. 2001. *A Bridge from Teaching to Assessment.* Portsmouth, NH: Heinemann.

Sunstein, Bonnie, and Jonathan Lovell, eds. 2000. *The Portfolio Standard: How Students Can Show Us What They Know and Are Able to Do.* Portsmouth, NH: Heinemann.

Wiggins, Grant, and Jay McTighe. 2001. *Understanding by Design.* Upper Saddle River, NJ: Prentice-Hall.

INTEGRATIVE UNITS

From the earliest days of elementary school to the waning moments of high school, most American children study a sadly disconnected assortment of facts, ideas, and skills. In the typical first-grade reading program, children are presented with a year-long series of reading "stories" sequenced according to the supposed reading skills that they teach, rather than their meaning or theme. This means that kids may jump from a basal story about fairies in a castle to one about Daniel Boone on the frontier, to another about talking robots in outer space—without any sense of order, connection, or transition among them. At the other end of the educational system, secondary schools are *designed* for incoherence: students' days are chopped into seven or eight segments guaranteed to be discontinuous with each other. A kid may start the day with forty minutes of Greek history in social studies class, then move to English to read some modern American poems, then shuffle off to science where the refraction of light is presented, and then move along to math to do problems connected to no aspect of life whatsoever.

In Best Practice schools and classrooms, teachers refuse to accept this randomness. They believe that content does matter and that for school to work, it must make sense to students—ideally, make sense all day long. Therefore, whether on their own or coplanning with students, teachers identify a few big subjects of interest and importance, and then build extended units around those topics. In elementary grades, we know teachers who've built multiweek chunks of curriculum around topics such as whales, exploring, castles, Australia, fairy tales, or homes. In a whales unit, for example, the children might read (and hear read aloud) lots of different whale stories, build a library of favorite whale books, do a whale readers' theater, study the biology of whales, work in research teams to investigate different kinds of whales (e.g., blue, killer, and beluga), go to the aquarium and observe real whales (in Chicago's Shedd Aquarium, you actually do this), write and illustrate whale stories and reports, do whale mathematics (calculating the days of gestation or the quantity of plankton a baleen whale eats daily), and, of course, do lots of whale art. When teachers design such thematically coherent activities, they usually find that they can quite easily fit in many of the old, mandated curriculum elements; these topics simply come up in a different way, at a different time, and in a different order. But the main benefit of such teaching is that it provides children with the choice, continuity, order, challenge, and genuine responsibility they need to both enjoy school and stay engaged with the work.

Extended lessons like these are often called "themes" or "integrated units," denoting their multidisciplinary nature, but we use the term *integrative* to take the definition one step farther. Often, thematic units are designed by teachers (or published in teacher magazines) and then delivered to students, without kids having any voice or choice in their development. If the teacher guesses right, and lots of kids really are interested in whales, this can be a big step ahead of the old, disjointed curriculum. But it's even better practice to involve students much sooner—identifying topics, developing questions to be pursued, planning the inquiry, dividing up tasks, gathering information, and sharing in the whole process—right from the start.

This kind of negotiated, integrative curriculum, as developed by James Beane (1997, 2005), does more than cross subject areas: it makes students real, responsible partners in curriculum development. An integrative curriculum is designed around real concerns students have about themselves and their world. Inquiries begin with a complex series of brainstorming and listing activities designed to gather students' questions and issues. From these lists of topics, units of the curriculum are developed collaboratively by teachers and students. If needed, teachers can later "back-map" from students' genuine questions to many of the mandated ingredients in district or state curriculum guides. If young people say they want to study racism (as they often do), teachers can plug in plenty of history, math (compiling statistics from racial-attitude surveys), and science (the literature of scientific racism, from phrenology to mental measurement), along with plenty of reading, writing, researching, and representing skills.

Curriculum integration often seems easier in elementary schools, where teachers may have the same thirty kids all day long. Aside from district rules and controls (which may present formidable obstacles), if a self-contained elementary teacher decides to start integrating the curriculum, her own goodwill and resolve can actually get it done. But in high school, things are a little tougher. Creating a truly integrated curriculum for any one student would require the cooperation of six or seven teachers who have no mandate to cooperate nor history of doing so, who have no common planning time, and who all still have on their desks a weighty scope-and-sequence document for their own segment of the school day—a curriculum that they probably have spent many increasingly comfortable years delivering.

Still, in high schools there are many ways teachers can move toward integrated, thematic instruction. If schools are ready to make courageous institutional reform, they can follow the pattern of Addison Trail High School in Illinois, where almost all freshmen now meet in a thematic three-course program that integrates the study of English, science, and social studies. At Best Practice High School in Chicago, teachers develop their own timeshare plan: Tuesdays and Thursdays for block-scheduled integrated curriculum units; Mondays and Fridays are scheduled as regular seven-period, separate-subject days; and on Wednesdays, students attend their community internships.

Even where there's no schoolwide sanction for innovation, teachers still can reform their own forty-five-minute slice of the school day, reorganizing material into more meaningful, coherent, even integrative chunks. If the textbook presents a jumbled or arbitrary sequence of materials, the teachers can rearrange it, finding and identifying organizing themes that the curriculum writers didn't notice or mention. Teachers can help kids by identifying and stressing the few "big ideas" that strand through the welter of seemingly disparate material often presented to students.

For example, at Stagg High School (see Chapter 6), the history teachers decided that the old curriculum presented far too many disparate facts, so the department went on a two-day retreat to hammer out a limited number of major themes in U.S. history. As the teachers testified, this was one of the longest and loudest weekends of their professional lives, but they came back with a list of sixteen themes (they called them "postholes of history") for a whole year's course. This provided every teacher with about two and a half weeks to approach each theme in a way that worked for their own students, even though everyone was still operating within the old bell schedule and framework. The Stagg faculty simply insisted that history make sense to their students.

Sometimes, two secondary teachers can get together to provide integration across more than one period of the day. For years, this has been done in American studies programs, in which history and literature are taught in a combined, two-period, team-taught class. As a next step, several schools we've worked with have begun projects where a group of seventy-five kids and three teachers get a half-day together to pursue a big topic. At Stagg High School, one pilot group studied U.S. history, literature, and German—an approach that, among other things, highlighted the often-overlooked Germanic origins of American colonial culture. Although curriculum integration in high schools is especially problematic, there's increasing hope as schools around the country break down the barriers of student and teacher scheduling, departmental boundaries, ability-grouping, and subservience to standardized test scores.

As helpful as thematic approaches to curriculum can be, teachers also need to be careful not to overload them. Academic subjects are so rich and extensive that in the course of one unit or semester or year, there's simply too much material for anyone to learn in any deep or significant way. Indeed, one of the most counterproductive elements of traditional American schooling has been its relentless emphasis on "covering the material" in a prescribed curriculum guide. Typically, such a mandated curriculum is an overstuffed compendium of facts, dates, concepts, books, persons, and ideas—a volume of material so enormous that no one thing in it can ever be understood if all of it must be mentioned. There's simply not enough time for deep study, and so each ingredient in the curriculum can only be "covered" in the sense that a wall is covered with a microscopic layer of paint. Among the many manifestations of the "coverage curriculum" are lecture-style classes, with emphasis on student notetaking, followed by multiple-choice tests stressing temporary memorization and factual recall.

In Best Practice classrooms, teachers realize that every student needn't study every possible topic, and that not everyone has to study all the same topics. Indeed, it is good educational practice (and solid preparation for adult life) to be part of a community where topics are parceled out to work groups, task forces, teams, or committees. When teachers jigsaw the curriculum, they seek natural ways to divide a given topic, assigning small groups of students to investigate the different parts, each team bringing back its piece of the puzzle to the whole group later on. In U.S. history, for example, not every student needs to learn about every Civil War battle. (Indeed, if everyone had to study every battle, the only choice would be for the teacher to simply talk as fast as she could.) Instead, a Best Practice teacher might let groups of kids each pick a single battle to study—Antietam for one group, Gettysburg for another, Bull Run for a third, and so on. Then the kids' job is to really dig in with reading and researching and talking, taking time to carefully explore and grasp the events involved, pursuing a deep understanding of their particular battle. Later, when the class comes back together, each group has a responsibility to share the highlights that emerged from its study. To pull the whole experience together, the teacher helps students find the similarities, differences, connections, and key concepts in the subtopics all have studied. In following this procedure, everyone learns one subject in detail, while still gaining a familiarity with related topics by way of reports from other classmates.

A final comment: the old "coverage curriculum" dies hard. Because the rote memorization of multiplicitous facts was so much a part of every American adult's education, many grown-ups still confuse factual recall with a good education. This craving for coverage has even given rise to a multimillion-dollar cottage industry. Under the banner of "cultural literacy," E. D. Hirsch and his collaborators are selling the nervous parents of America a series of books that list "What Your First (or Second, Third, or Fourth) Grader Needs to Know." These banal handbooks reiterate what the old school curriculum used to say: that everyone should study the same things at the same time, and that a satisfactory outcome of schooling is the mere recognition of certain key words.

The durability—indeed, the marketability—of this "curriculum of superficiality" is a real challenge to school reformers. The bung-full curriculum has many proponents who use words like *rigor* and *standards* when they defend their view. Yet this advocacy of comprehensive coverage by self-appointed cultural guardians is deeply ironic, since their model of curriculum actually breeds disrespect for learning. After all, most graduates of American schools will testify with remarkably little embarrassment: "I forgot everything they taught me in school." Yet, those of us who want to *raise the standards of learning* by insisting that students study a finite number of topics in much greater depth are labeled "permissivists." This is clearly a long and deeply rooted cultural struggle, one that won't be settled for generations—but it is wise for school reformers to be aware of its dynamic.

SUGGESTED FURTHER READINGS

Alleman, Janet, and Jere Brophy. 2001. *Social Studies Excursions, K–3: Powerful Units on Food, Clothing, and Shelter.* Portsmouth, NH: Heinemann.

Beane, James. 2005 (forthcoming). *A Reason to Teach: Creating Classrooms of Dignity and Hope*. Portsmouth, NH: Heinemann.

———. 1997. *Curriculum Integration: Designing the Core of Democratic Education*. New York: Teachers College Press.

Boomer, Garth, Nancy Lester, Cynthia Onore, and Jon Cook. 1992. *Negotiating the Curriculum*. London: Falmer Press.

Doda, Nancy, and Sue Carol Thompson. 2002. *Transforming Ourselves, Transforming Schools: Middle School Change*. Westerville, OH: National Middle Schools Association.

Five, Cora Lee, and Marie Dionisio. 1995. *Bridging the Gap: Integrating Curriculum in Upper Elementary and Middle Schools*. Portsmouth, NH: Heinemann.

Lake, Jo-Ann. 2000. *Literature and Science Breakthroughs: Connecting Language and Science Skills in the Elementary Classroom*. York, ME: Stenhouse.

Lindquist, Larry, and Douglas Selwyn. 2000. *Social Studies at the Center: Integrating Kids, Content, and Literacy*. Portsmouth, NH: Heinemann.

Manning, Maryann, Gary Manning, and Roberta Long. 1994. *Theme Immersion: Inquiry-Based Curriculum in Elementary and Middle Schools*. Portsmouth, NH: Heinemann.

Short, Kathy G., et al. 1996. *Learning Together Through Inquiry: From Columbus to Integrated Curriculum*. York, ME: Stenhouse.

Stice, Carol F., and Nancy P. Bertrand. 2002. *Good Teaching: An Integrated Approach to Language, Literacy, and Learning*. Portsmouth, NH: Heinemann.

Tchudi, Steven, and Stephen Lafer. 1996. *The Interdisciplinary Teacher's Handbook: Integrated Teaching Across the Curriculum*. Portsmouth, NH: Boynton/Cook.

CAN TEACHERS STILL TEACH?

All of these seven activities have one thing in common: they take the teacher off stage. They do not cast the teacher in the familiar role of information-dispenser, font of wisdom, expert/presenter/lecturer. In each of these key classroom structures, the teacher is somewhere farther in the background, acting as a moderator, facilitator, coach, scribe, designer, observer, model—everything *but* the standard, normal, stereotypical conception of the teacher as . . . well, as a *teacher*. What gives? Does this mean that in the ideal Best Practice classroom the teacher never "teaches" in the old-fashioned sense of the word?

Not at all. But once again, balance is the key. It is fine for teachers to conduct whole-class presentations, to give information, to share and tell and even lecture—*some of the time*. But time-sharing is the key. In the traditional curriculum, we have catastrophically neglected the student-centered side of the "airtime" equation. Indeed, one of the key findings from classroom research across subjects is that students don't get enough time to try out, practice, and apply what teachers are talking about. Kids don't get nearly enough time to do science or writing or math, because the teacher is so busy *talking* that there is previously little time to practice the target activity.

Because it is so deeply ingrained in our culture that teaching means talking at other people who are silent and inactive, we all must police ourselves very closely to make sure we don't regress to that old transmission model. That's one reason why this chapter may seem so unbalanced, giving almost all of its attention to the structures for student-centered classroom time. But teachers already know how to conduct whole-class presentations, probably all too well. It was highlighted in their professional training, it was the core of their personal experience as students, and it probably predominates in their on-the-job experience. Most American teachers simply don't need as much help conducting whole-class presentations as they do with, for example, facilitating a collaborative workshop. So teachers need to fill this gap, to correct this imbalance in their professional repertoire by equipping themselves with all the classroom structures they need to comfortably and safely get off stage, to provide and manage plenty of kid-centered time for practice and exploration.

With this extended disclaimer in place, we can return to the subject of whole-class, teacher-directed activities and see what's valuable about them. There are at least three reasons why teacher-centered, whole-class instruction can and should remain part of the school day. First and most important, teachers have great things to teach—they have knowledge, wisdom, experience, ideas, and content that can be shared through whole-class presentations they design. All of us who teach have developed great units, favorite sequences of activities that engage students, year after year. We have worked to design and refine and enrich these units; they are our treasures, and we're not about to give them up. We also realize that as we present these favorite lessons, we are modeling for students our own passion for the material. Even if they don't understand or remember everything, we hope they'll catch our excitement about ideas.

On a more pragmatic level, some teacher-directed lessons are still necessary because most teachers work within a mandated curriculum. They are responsible for students' learning (or at least briefly remembering) many required elements of an official syllabus of content. We argued earlier that many ingredients of the typical school curriculum can be learned incidentally, amid innovative, student-centered techniques. For example, kids who have regular writing workshops will acquire many English spelling and editing skills even though they are not taught them directly in teacher presentations or workbook drills. However, the average school curriculum still contains much other material that isn't learned collaterally through applied experience in the subject. In language arts, for example, all the writing workshops in the world will not teach students the names of the parts of speech. If kids and teachers are to be held accountable for learning about gerunds, subordinate clauses, and the like, the teacher will probably have to take the initiative to conduct such lessons.

Finally, as learners and as people, teachers deserve to feel safe and comfortable in school too. They need the security of doing something familiar for some of the day: we cannot expect teachers who have been trained and socialized to think of teaching as presenting to suddenly cast aside that whole model for the entire six-hour day. The fact is that teachers *will* continue to present whole-class lessons; the point is for them to get better at it and at the same time start doing it less.

WAYS TO IMPROVE TEACHER-DIRECTED LESSONS

Because good teachers have been creating dramatic and effective individual performances for years, we'll just mention a few valuable examples here. One presentational activity that is especially powerful, but mistakenly neglected above the primary grades, is *reading aloud*. Great writers in every field and subject have hypnotized readers for as long as there has been print. Many of their writings were the very sources that inspired some teachers to enter the profession in the first place. So reading great writing aloud can be one of the most captivating and motivating presentational techniques a teacher can use. Quality children's literature new and old, primary source documents, insightful historical essays, passionate political arguments, biographical and autobiographical accounts of key discoveries in math and science—all are capable of mesmerizing children, adolescents, and adults and drawing them into real engagement with the subject matter. National recommendations on teaching reading advise plenty of reading aloud by the teacher at all levels.

Another strategic way to think about direct teaching is the *mini-lesson*— a very brief explanation or demonstration aimed at helping students the teacher has observed struggling to grasp a skill or concept needed in their work. For example, children who are writing plays may need to understand quotation marks and paragraphing to separate characters' speeches from each other and from stage directions.

Mini-lessons can be given to a whole class before, during, or after more active, experiential activities—or offered to small, selected groups of students as others continue their work. Indeed, one of the fundamental insights of mini-lessons is that teachers' old-style presentations—we might call them maxi-lessons—often were simply too long and too overloaded to be effective. We now find that teachers can convey key content more effectively when they are very selective and present in quicker, smaller bites. Mini-lessons are an integral feature of the workshop classroom; teachers can draw aside small groups of students who are struggling with a particular skill or topic, sit them at a table in the back of the room, give a compact, focused, five- or six-minute lesson—and send them directly back to work, where they will immediately apply the concepts taught. This mini-lesson strategy obviously requires that the teacher be a sharp observer—but handily, the workshop structure itself provides the teacher with the time and the responsibility to monitor students' work closely through conferences and constant observation.

Demonstrations are a closely allied technique, and they are useful in plenty of situations beyond the science lab. A good writing teacher may revise a piece of her own work before the eyes of the whole class, using an overhead projector. Kids can ask questions about her choices as she works. Most students have never watched a competent adult at work on a piece of writing, and all too often their only visual image of the process is from some melodramatic movie in which a struggling poet rips pages out of a typewriter, crumples them, and shoots them despondently toward the wastebasket. Teachers can profitably demonstrate how they go about brainstorming a new writing topic or choosing an appropriate book to read, how they figure out the meaning of a new word from context clues or mentally sort through likely possibilities while working on a geometry proof.

In the most interactive classrooms, many teacher presentations become hybrids. Teachers invite questions and suggestions as the session proceeds. Students know their ideas are valued and don't hesitate to take part. Teachers decide to offer an explanation to just the half or third of the class who need it, while others who don't can continue with more appropriate activities.

CONCLUSION

When we talk about the balance between teacher-directed and student-centered activities, it always boils down to how *time* is spent. Teachers must design days, weeks, years that provide kids a rich alternation between different configurations, groupings, and activities. The schedule must be predictable so students can prepare, mentally and even unconsciously, for what is coming up. This predictability is especially important for poor children, who may lack continuity in their life. The balance in a day's or week's activities must also include things that make teachers reasonably comfortable, and yet teachers need to be challenging themselves, too. In the end, school is more satisfying when everyone is growing and learning daily.

To work toward the goal of Best Practice, to embody the changes recommended in the curriculum reports we have cited, most teachers need to enrich their classroom repertoire in two directions: (1) to set aside time and build classroom structures that support more *student-directed activity,* using the seven key structures outlined in the past few pages; and (2) to make their *teacher-directed* activities both less predominant and more effective. We've seen that when teachers learn practical strategies to manage both of these modes of instruction, the curricular improvements they desire begin to take hold.

WORKS CITED

Atwell, Nancie. 1998. *In the Middle: New Understandings About Writing, Reading, and Learning* (Second Edition). Portsmouth, NH: Boynton/Cook Heinemann.

Beane, James. 1997. *Curriculum Integration: Designing the Core of Democratic Education.* New York: Teachers College Press.

Calkins, Lucy. 1995. *The Art of Teaching Writing* (Second Edition). Portsmouth, NH: Heinemann.

Carr, E., and Donna Ogle. 1987. KWL Plus: A Strategy for Comprehension and Summarization. *Journal of Reading* 30: 626–631.

Daniels, Harvey. 2002. *Literature Circles: Voice and Choice in Book Clubs and Reading Groups.* York, ME: Stenhouse.

Daniels, Harvey, and Marilyn Bizar. 2004. *Teaching the Best Practice Way: Methods That Matter, K–12.* Portland, ME: Stenhouse.

Daniels, Harvey, and Nancy Steineke. 2004. *Mini-lessons for Literature Circles.* Portsmouth, NH: Heinemann.

Daniels, Harvey, and Steven Zemelman. 2004. *Subjects Matter: Every Teacher's Guide to Content-Area Reading.* Portsmouth, NH: Heinemann.

Glasser, William. 1990. *The Quality School: Managing Students Without Coercion.* New York: Harper.

Johnson, David, and Roger Johnson. 1998. *Learning Together and Alone.* New York: Allyn and Bacon.

Joyce, Bruce, Marsha Weil, and Emily Calhoun. 2003. *Models of Teaching* (Seventh Edition). Englewood Cliffs, NJ: Prentice-Hall.

National Research Council. 1996. *National Science Education Standards.* Washington, DC: National Academy Press.

Ogle, Donna. 1986. The KWL: A Teaching Model That Develops Active Reading of Expository Text. *The Reading Teacher* 39: 564–570.

Sharan, Shlomo. 1999. *Handbook of Cooperative Learning Methods.* New York: Praeger.

Short, Kathy, Jerome Harste, and Carolyn Burke, 1996. *Creating Classrooms for Authors and Inquirers* (Second Edition). Portsmouth, NH: Heinemann.

Slavin, Robert. 1985. *Learning to Cooperate, Cooperating to Learn.* New York: Plenum Press.

Vaughan, Joseph, and Thomas Estes. 1986. *Reading and Reasoning Beyond the Primary Grades.* Boston: Allyn and Bacon.

Chapter 9
Making the Transition

Jan calls Steve one night to talk. She's taught many years, but suddenly, she's made a leap: "You won't believe what's happening! Since the books I ordered didn't arrive on time, we interviewed each other, just like you always said we could. We told stories about ourselves and our families, and everyone loved it. When the book did show up, I couldn't even *pretend* I knew what it said, since it was just published. So we're talking over each chapter together, instead of my telling what they're supposed to get from it. They're thinking a lot more that way. And we're trying out those note-books Lucy Calkins recommended. Everything seems to really matter in that room."

Jan had been working towards a more student-centered curriculum for a long time, comparing ideas with Steve, and he'd appreciated her caring for her students. He'd visited her class, modeled a few strategies, and suggested others. But he'd also wondered why she didn't pick up on more of them. Now she was ready. For Steve, it had been difficult to be patient. But in discussions he could tell when he'd gone too far, when the possibilities didn't connect for her or put her on the defensive. Now, Jan was making discoveries on her own. "You've probably been doing this stuff all along, haven't you," she remarked sheepishly.

WHY CHANGE IS DIFFICULT

Teachers, students, parents, and principals go through many learning steps to make new approaches work. They need time, and positive support through structures and relationships as they grow. And they have many questions that must be respected: *What about the math facts? Do the kids still need phonics lessons? Can children really help each other and collaborate in small groups? How do we evaluate children's progress with this kind of teaching?* If change is forced on them, not only will they rebel, but the demand contradicts the very spirit of the changes. The strategies described in this book and advocated by the best of the standards across the country all aim for children to make more thoughtful choices, ask questions, and become invested in learning. *Forcing* teachers to adopt a new pedagogy without developing their ownership of it just about guarantees weak execution, disappointing results, and eventual rejection of the effort.

Many other complexities impede educational change. Much has been written about how the "culture" in a school building—as in most complex organizations—supports or discourages the kind of change Jan experienced. Sociological studies of teachers, such as Dan Lortie's classic *Schoolteacher* (1972), reveal how most spend their careers isolated in cellular classrooms. The trial-by-fire initiation into teaching, the lack of time for interchange, the sense of being "evaluated" rather than helped—all promote teachers' wariness. While there are some wonderful exceptions, not nearly enough principals understand how to balance commitment to high expectations with nurturing and support. This is not meant as a blanket indictment. Each person becomes caught up in this system and is hard put to change without great effort and practice at new kinds of communication.

The now-ubiquitous standardized tests are unfortunately more an obstacle to improved teaching than a means to achieve it. Although the tests may be intended to boost student performance and pressure teachers to do better, the response in too many schools is skill-and-drill, which is not the same as really *doing* science or history or writing. While schools in affluent areas often achieve good scores through Best Practice strategies, poorer districts tend to fall back on the most mechanistic approaches. Teachers under pressure because of low scores begin to disregard kids' spontaneous questions—those "teachable moments." Worse, many standardized tests focus on the rote detail most easily (and cheaply) testable, rather than the important knowledge in a field, thus undermining valuable teaching and learning. As the *National Science Education Standards* document states:

> Many current science achievement tests measure "inert" knowledge—discrete, isolated bits of knowledge—rather than "active" knowledge—knowledge that is rich and well-structured. Assessment processes that include all outcomes for student achievement must probe the extent and organization of a student's knowledge. (NRC 1996, 82)

Increasingly, experts and even the news media critique standardized tests that simply don't *and cannot* test real learning. Nevertheless, we know that politically the tests are not likely to disappear or even change for the better any time soon.

Or consider textbooks. While most teachers depend on them for much of the curriculum, these tomes present a number of problems in addition to their weight, which itself guarantees the next generation's back ailments. Many textbooks are superficial; despite their size, they must cover so many topics that they graze over the material, jam together mountains of detail, and obscure larger concepts. The majority of textbooks are hard to read because they are overloaded with details and short on elaborated examples. Many are badly designed, a patchwork of graphics mimicking the video-game world kids know, making it doubly difficult for those with perceptual disabilities. They are authoritarian, implying that a reader can find reliable answers by consulting just one source, rather than comparing points of view. Textbooks contain a surprising number of errors and inaccuracies, and because they are so expensive, they can't be frequently replaced as new knowledge develops. And finally they invite the most unengaging read-the-section-and-take-the-test approach to instruction.

Meanwhile, the educational world is confusing, a river filled with cross-currents. Conservatives urge programs that march through lockstep curricula and dissociated skills exercises. Principals and politicians worry about standardized test scores, whether or not the drills prepare kids for what they'll really need later. Many reforms seem aimed at teacher-proofing the classroom rather than creating expert nurturers of learning. At the same time, more progressive efforts, such as small schools (Wasley et al. 2000) and nationwide networks like the National Writing Project (Easton 2004), have matured and have highlighted the value of teacher and student and parent voices. Of course, in all sorts of settings, some teachers doggedly resist *every* change that comes along, mumbling about pendulums and muttering, "This too shall pass." Nevertheless, other educators energetically continue seeking to learn and grow.

AT THE CORE: ONE TEACHER AT A TIME

No matter how extensively legislatures and national panels seek control, teachers still learn and grow one at a time; and through their individual interactions the kids, too, learn one at a time. How can we truly facilitate teacher development, then, rather than draft standards that merely list topics to be covered or threaten schools with punishment over test results?

One step is to learn from past mistakes. In many failed efforts, such as "new math," teachers were the last to hear of the experiment. An official goal of "new math" was for kids to become excited about mathematics and to develop understanding that would entice further learning. However, teachers were introduced to the program only at a final "delivery" stage. This left them uncommitted, feeling inadequate about the concepts, and they presented the material in a self-defeating way—so that ultimately nothing changed. True reform must involve teachers from the beginning, not just hand them a new curriculum as an afterthought.

Teachers need to recreate their own understandings of how learning works, and then they need to be involved in decision making. Why is this ownership so vital?

1. The teacher working daily with students knows most concretely what their specific needs, conditions, and obstacles are.

2. No matter what changes are prescribed from the outside, their success depends on teachers' own choices and interpretations. If choice isn't involved sooner, it will inevitably come later, with less likelihood of positive commitment.

3. The most important changes in education are not superficial, but involve teachers' deeply held beliefs, expectations, and relationships.

4. Many key changes give responsibility and initiative to children, which is undermined if teachers don't gain these too.

Andy Hargreaves puts this especially well in his book *Teaching in the Knowledge Society: Education in the Age of Insecurity*:

Deep professional learning involves more than workshops or inservice training in government priorities. . . . Implementing change effectively requires time to understand, learn about, and reflect on what the change involves and requires. Even for the best teachers, changing successfully is hard intellectual work. . . . Learning to teach better, to be a continuously improving professional, involves more than implementing other people's ideas and agendas compliantly. (2003, 108)

AN ILLUSTRATION: HOW ONE TEACHER CHANGED

Delois Strickland teaches second grade in an inner-city building with housing projects on one side and empty lots on the other. She's not the heroine of some pious movie about the valiant inner-city miracle worker who triumphs over all. Rather, Delois is quiet and calm, loves children, and desires continually to improve her craft. Like most good teachers, Delois can do at least three things at once. At lunchtime, she chats uninterrupted with a visitor while preparing materials for an afternoon activity, receiving a steady flow of office messengers, and keeping an eye on the kids who love to hang out in her room.

Delois attended a thirty-hour writing project workshop one fall, where the teachers first interviewed one another and compiled a book of their portraits. They wrote about significant personal moments and shared autobiographical writing in small groups. They talked about journals where children could write without fear of being judged. They explored strategies for small-group work, practiced teacher-student conferences, debated when grammar work is effective and when it's not. They shared food, gossip, disagreements, frustrations, laughs, hopes.

Delois started putting one or two new ideas to work with the help of an Illinois Writing Project consultant, experimenting first with children's journals. Delois understood that these belonged to the children and were not to be graded. Her seven-year-olds were prolific and proud of their work, but there never seemed to be enough time for it. A few enthusiastic weeks passed, and she began to feel pressure to produce the formal essays the principal periodically collected. Delois felt she could teach writing for only two forty-five-minute periods per week at most, so after an initial burst of success, the journals languished on a shelf under the windows.

Next Delois introduced an interviewing activity like one the teachers had enjoyed in the workshop. The children were to interview one another and write portraits to be accompanied by photographs and hung on the bulletin boards. Delois helped the children brainstorm questions to ask one another and copied them on chart paper for easy reference. The kids followed the question list slavishly—but they were writing and having a grand time.

Delois wanted these papers to look good, particularly because other teachers in the building were watching, so she introduced teacher-student conferences to help kids revise and polish their interviews. The students had mostly transcribed literal first-person answers to their questions:

I like ice cream.

I have two sisters.

I will go to college . . . and so on.

At first, she patiently explained to each child how to use the form, "Tyree likes ice cream." This was about a writing skill, but also a concept—was the interviewer an author or a transcriber?—an understandable, in fact a thoughtful, confusion for second graders. Meanwhile, kids waited impatiently in line to have their paper "checked" or fiddled in their seats if Delois shooed the line away. Finally, she shifted to a more efficient whole-class lesson on indirect quotations. She also set up a conferencing sign-up list on the chalkboard and urged children to work on their journals while waiting for a conference. These refinements helped, but her conferences remained focused on proofreading, so the mood was dogged—kids would go back to their seats, try again, and return once more to the teacher, hoping for deliverance. The papers gradually improved, but the work dragged on for weeks and involved too little learning.

Still, that spring, kids began very naturally to help one another. Pieces grew longer. Struggling children made surprising advances. Writing seemed to be a positive, enjoyable activity. And Delois had enough new ideas to digest for one year.

The next fall, Delois requested help from a consultant from Chicago's Erikson Institute who was working in the building. By winter, the whole room looked different. Next to the windows was a large rug where small groups of children could play math games. New children's books occupied one set of shelves. The writing-center desks were cleared of dusty projects and restored to active use. Kids worked industriously in small clusters. "My room used to be so disorganized that my children couldn't use what we had," Delois explained.

She began bringing in her own children's books, which were much more interesting than the hand-me-downs crowding the shelves. Delois realized that if she were clear about rules and responsibilities, the children would treat the books with respect. A mobile hung next to the bookshelves, its dangling parts enunciating the rules. Children took turns serving as classroom librarian. "They're reading much more and enjoying it more," Delois reported, "and they take good care of these books."

The Erikson consultant also modeled good teacher-student conferences. When Steve came by for a visit, Delois handed him an article about using conferences to help children take responsibility instead of simply executing the teacher's corrections. "Teachers ought to read this in your workshops," she urged. If Delois wasn't ready to absorb those ideas a year earlier, they were her own now. She had even added the skillful variation of conducting conferences with groups of four or five children looking on, so they could learn more. Steve asked, with a tinge of guilt, whether he should have provided more ideas the previous year. "No," she said. "I needed to feel my way."

The children were writing far more—four to five days per week. "If you only write once a week you don't really get into it," Delois explained. "But if you enjoy it as a teacher, you'll do it more." Still another improvement: the teacher's aide in the room became much more involved. The previous year, the aide sat off to the side, doing busywork and occasionally scolding an overactive child. Now, with training, she too was helping with conferences. Delois felt the aides should be included in all staff development.

Delois was already thinking about her next innovations. She would use interviewing at the beginning of the year instead of waiting: "That way, they'll get to know one another better at the start." A good refinement, one that made the assignment more purposeful. She'd start group conferences earlier too, to build children's excitement about one another's writing. Kids spent too much time stapling paper into the journal folders, so she planned to purchase spiral notebooks. Every little physical adjustment would mean better use of time. Reading, however, remained a frustration. The children read more, enjoyed it more, and even did better on practice tests. But they still had difficulty with the official subskills-oriented reading tests. "I guess I'm not a miracle worker," Delois sighed.

Gradually Delois Strickland expanded her expertise, refining classroom strategies and sharing ideas with others. She took courses on "The Responsive Classroom," "Math Their Way," and technology in the classroom, and applied the approaches with great thoroughness.

On Steve's last visit, he watched Delois guide her second graders through "morning meeting." The greatest behavioral problem involved several boys who were sitting next to the classroom library and kept grabbing books to read instead of "paying attention." We know teachers who would sell their souls for such a problem. These children, the least advanced of the three second-grade classes in the school, eagerly chose and read books during SSR, listened closely to a mini-lesson on prefixes and suffixes, brainstormed for prewriting about the snow covering the streets that morning, and then turned intently to their journals.

When conflicts arose, Delois calmly but firmly reminded kids about the values taught in their character education class. Each child had a personally made, expandable spelling notebook. The science center drew a steady stream of children checking up on the class snake and trying out the experiments with magnets. Periodic thematic units throughout the year created great excitement. One called "Children as Inventors," funded by a grant from the Chicago Foundation for Education, helped students connect more actively to Delois' history lessons on famous African American inventors. In the larger school context, Delois provided leadership as a powerful example of excellent teaching and respect for children, by working extensively with her grade-level team, giving time for extra school activities, and speaking up when her beliefs called for it.

THE STRUCTURES THAT HELP A TEACHER GROW

What conditions facilitate the kind of evolution we've seen in Delois Strickland's teaching? What helps spread improvements across a school system through support and respect, rather than stifling change through scripted curriculum and lockstep mandates? How do we engender ownership and initiative in a setting built on authority? For answers, we consulted the *Standards for Staff Development* developed by the National Staff Development Council and revised in 2001. These standards are for the most part quite thoughtful and well documented. They call for learning communities and collaboration among teachers in schools, strong and supportive leadership, sufficient time and resources, clear focus on just a few goals at a time, and thoughtful use of a variety of strategies to promote teachers' learning. They support meaningful roles for data and for evaluation of a staff development program's impact. And they set high standards for staff development to promote quality teaching that serves all students. The elaboration of the standards can sometimes go a little overboard, advocating, for example, that teacher learning teams meet every day—when did the authors last visit a busy school with a staff struggling to avoid burnout? So we offer a set of five principles for school change here, drawing on the NSDC standards as well as our own experience and other educators' thinking (e.g., Darling-Hammond 1996; Reitzug and Burrello 1995; Wasley et al. 1997).

1. Clear, Focused, and Supportive Leadership

Significant change needs credible leadership from the top, even as the leader emphasizes teachers' decision making and initiative. When Delois Strickland tried out an interviewing activity, her second graders grew noisy as they worked. What would the principal think if she walked by? With upcoming standardized tests, was it really acceptable to take so much time for writing while other teachers drilled students for the big day? Delois needed to know where her principal stood.

The fact is, we are trying to introduce democratic and collaborative elements in organizations that remain pyramidal. We can try to alter a school's underlying style of operation, but at base there's an element of contradiction that a leader must skillfully negotiate. And so the best staff development effort in the world can fail if school leaders do not consistently support the changes.

This is especially needed in urban schools, where conditions make improvements extra difficult. When the population turns over because families frequently move, when books and materials fail to arrive because of bureaucratic delays, when distant administrative offices suddenly announce new mandates—teachers need protection and support. A strong, encouraging principal is vital—someone who knows curriculum, welcomes innovation, values distributive leadership and group decision making, and who does not impose his or her own sudden arbitrary requirements.

A study of effective principals by Ulrich Reitzug and Leonard Burrello (1995) suggests that school leaders must address four key needs (1) nurturing a supportive school culture—the context in which risk taking and change can take place; (2) acting as a guide and a model, as an instructional leader and thoughtful questioner; (3) marketing change to build support and momentum for it; and (4) supporting change efforts consistently. What matters most, however, are the implicit messages of commitment, openness, and trust that the principal communicates. What this really means is building a healthy adult working community.

Nurture a positive school culture. School researcher Michael Fullan (1999) observes that effective leaders cannot depend on just a few strategies for promoting a new idea; instead they need to develop moral purpose, build relationships, bring fresh knowledge to the work, and establish coherence in a school's programs.

"The single factor common to every successful change initiative is that *relationships* improve," Fullan asserts (1999, 5). A leader who practices listening, who doesn't react defensively or jump to conclusions when events occur, and who seeks maximum feedback will gain a clear picture of teachers' efforts and what obstacles or supports are at work. Student achievement scores alone never yield such information. But administrators' involvement must also be balanced with respect for the sanctity of instructional time. As a teacher once vividly explained:

> An administrator can walk in and interrupt what I am doing with any cockamamie thing. . . . He butts into my classroom with all sorts of nit-picky stuff. The message is clear. What I am doing is not important. The kids can pick this up. (Pfeifer 1986)

Teacher evaluation can especially influence change in the classroom for good or ill. As Boston principal Kim Marshall (1996) explained, frequent brief visits instead of twice-a-year formal observations, teacher evaluation as a dialogue, goal setting by teachers, recognition that new strategies may not go perfectly the first time—all set the stage for change to flourish. Otherwise, it can seem safer for a teacher to stick to what she already knows.

Be a guide and a model. Almost every reform document views the principal as the salesperson for the vision of the school and for any new effort—the "keeper of the dream." A principal's actions will be read very carefully during a school change initiative. The principal who protects faculty from arbitrary district rules or bends a few to help a project along will prove her trustworthiness.

The principal must model the new attitudes and strategies and learn new concepts along with everyone else. We've admired the way Steve DeLapp, principal of Barton Open School in Minneapolis, takes strong, principled, and progressive stances in speeches and articles for all audiences, including the school's families and the central office. At Federal Hocking High School in Southeast Ohio, principal George Wood knows every student by name, spends the majority of his time in the halls and classrooms, and provides the staff development his teachers determine is important, not what the state or district mandates.

We know principals who regularly invite and answer letters from students throughout the school to promote written communication. They are the kind of leaders who attend in-service workshops with their teachers and join in all the activities, risking, doing, and sharing. And sadly, we know others who slip out of the room as soon as the in-service session begins or who sit to one side taking critical notes on participants' behavior. The difference is not lost on teachers.

Develop a "marketing" campaign to build support for any new initiative. In most schools, new ideas don't take hold and blossom simply because a staff development expert comes to town and gives a rousing workshop. Commitment to a new effort needs to be built step by step. This can begin by putting copies of an article in everyone's mailbox or taking a group of teachers to see the new program in another district. It's important to identify potential supporters and skeptics, to get the former involved and convince the latter to give the idea a fair shake. Find a few key, energized individuals to get the planning started, and a few more willing to try the program out. Let people hear about successes as they begin to happen. After informing people thoroughly about the initiative, consult the faculty thoroughly about moving ahead. A workshop by a good staff developer can of course help when the time is right. And teachers begin to feel trust when they see that they will have the resources they need, along with coaching or professional support as they put the new approach into practice.

The National Staff Development Council standards document (2001) outlines some of the major modes for teachers' learning:

- Collaborative lesson design
- Examination of student work
- Curriculum development teams
- Direct experience of new strategies through experiential workshops or observation of model classrooms
- Immersion in the work of mathematicians, scientists, historians, and so forth
- Case studies
- Action research
- Teacher study groups and book clubs
- Professional networks

We watched some of these processes unfold at Federal Hocking High School, mentioned earlier, as the faculty worked to support reading across the content areas, and we saw how enthusiasm and active adoption of new strategies gradually spread throughout the staff.

Support new efforts consistently. We observed one principal who wanted students to do more writing, but marked grammar errors on papers collected from each classroom and nagged teachers incessantly about drilling kids to shore up the test scores. After several months, teachers were assigning *less* writing and were less committed than ever to trying new writing activities. We've watched districts adopt new tests that encouraged rote teaching of isolated skills, just as a committee introduced a higher-order thinking-skills approach to the same subject. It's no surprise when teachers feel whipsawed and grow discouraged. Schools must focus on just a few areas and create a long-range development plan, instead of jumping from one in-service fad to another every year.

Teachers need a strong voice in deciding on that focus and drawing up that plan. At the same time, it's essential to provide constructive guidelines— clarifying the mission, asking staff to choose a reachable goal that addresses clearly identified needs, setting a reasonable timetable, and ensuring that once the faculty has made the decision to move ahead, everyone supports it with a good-faith effort. In some schools, we've seen teachers interpret distributed leadership to mean that everyone can choose whether or not to adopt the new approach that the staff has approved. This only undermines teacher decision making and morale in the long run, so a good leader makes clear that everyone must work with the decision made by the group.

Then there are a myriad of unanticipated ways a good administrator must help. Gene Hall and Shirley Hord outline many of these in their thorough guide, *Implementing Change: Patterns, Principles and Potholes* (2000). We saw a good example of this one day as we waited in a principal's office while she phoned around her building to investigate why the engineer wouldn't unlock the room housing the laminating machine. It was frustrating for the visitor to wait as the drama played out, but she had her priorities right—and teachers were very committed to the school as a result.

We've seen too many promising school change projects come unglued because districts didn't make consistent changes in each of the interlocking elements that combine to make a program work. If you want a true literature-based reading program, you *must* have lots of books in each classroom—period. If the budget for books isn't there, then the program won't take off, no matter what other ingredients may be in place.

So we've used the following checklist. The point is simple: if you really want deep, lasting change across classrooms, it has to be supported by parallel, congruent changes in each factor:

curriculum	faculty hiring
instruction	evaluation/grading/report cards
materials	relationship to state standards and tests

space	administrative leadership
scheduling	parent and community participation
grouping	board support
special education	budget
staff development	

Finally, we realize that not every school system, administrator, or teacher is ready to face real issues or seek change. Some valuable efforts occur under the noses of unsupportive leaders. Much as we care about whole-school improvement, it is important for change agents to help teachers *especially* when circumstances are difficult. More than once, grassroots efforts have ultimately led to wider acceptance. We simply need to be honest about the scope of change likely under such conditions, and not burn out in the process.

2. Common Planning Time

Teachers need regular time together. Make a "concerns" list with any group of teachers and what invariably comes at the top? Time. Teachers need significant chunks of time with their colleagues if they are to plan serious changes in curriculum or school structure. The school that fails to provide this time sends a clear signal that teacher participation and change are not really important. The few days before school begins in August are too hectic for reflection or planning major changes in direction. Two or three in-service days scattered throughout the year, even on the same topic, amount to only a gesture. Fifteen-minute meetings before school do not permit concentration. More extended workshops are often held after school hours, when teachers fight weariness.

Teachers need to talk, encourage, compare ideas, organize cooperation between classrooms, troubleshoot when things don't go as expected, and resolve the conflicts that often come with change. Deep inquiry into reading or math or science requires time to build trust, experience model activities, discuss, disagree, rethink, and work out classroom applications.

Unlike other professions, where planning meetings, "staffings," and conferences at fancy resorts are *de rigueur,* teaching in this country has shockingly little room for professional conversation. With teachers' work carried out almost entirely apart from colleagues, there's little time for informal exchange. Parents and community members who spend many work hours in cooperative tasks and committee meetings (much as they may gripe about them) don't realize how little connectedness teachers have. Linda Darling-Hammond (1997) points out that teachers in many other countries spend fifteen to twenty hours a week in the classroom and the rest of the time on planning, meeting with fellow faculty, continuing their education, contacting parents, and counseling students.

Find time creatively. In Chicago, the district has restructured the school day so that children arrive a few minutes earlier each day, and are then dismissed at midday once every two weeks, to gain planning time for teachers—though that is still not enough. In one school elsewhere that we'll never name, the PTA parents—totally illegally—cover classes one half day each week so teachers can meet in curriculum workshops.

Another part of coping with time is finding funds to pay for extra committee work or after-school in-service time. Although schools are always short of cash, it's surprising how much money can be available if decision makers are clear about priorities. In Chicago public schools, for example, as much as 25 percent of a school's budget may actually be discretionary. Though there are other legitimate needs to be met in each building, devoting some funds to pay for teacher planning time is often possible.

Take time for the long view. Finding time also means working with a longer-range view—easy to say, not always in evidence. Making "science" this year's theme for two in-service days doesn't do the job. The essential steps:

- organizing to study an issue
- conducting a needs assessment and finding internal or outside help
- building interest
- providing in-depth workshops or other learning activities
- identifying and training teacher-leaders
- providing follow-up: follow-up sessions, informal peer support, and classroom consultants for on-the-spot assistance
- arranging teacher visits to other schools and to one another's classrooms to observe new strategies in action
- repeating the cycle to spread the new approaches to more teachers
- revising formal structures (report cards, for example) to support the changes

All this can take three to five years in a school or district. But if it includes teachers in the leadership and decision making, change can become broad and deep.

Taking time, in the long-range sense of coming to new realizations, sometimes means having patience. Teachers new to student-centered approaches usually try one element at a time to gain confidence before moving on, so change requires several school years. It takes time to extend a new concept to all of one's teaching. A school may not be ready for change, perhaps because not enough teachers really seek it or because the administration is ambivalent. An enthusiastic advocate needs to know when it is better—at least temporarily—to focus on her own classroom and share ideas with a few friends. And sometimes it pays to wait. Many a principal or department chair has been known to come back a year or two later and ask blithely for help—because the problem, of course, hadn't really gone away.

3. Collaboration and Teacher Leadership

Significant change requires collaborative, social experiences and extensive, open discussion of issues. In surveying many studies of school change, Michael Fullan concluded that while narrowly defined innovations can work with a top-down approach, complex schoolwide changes need deeper commitment. Meaningful collaboration, where each teacher's voice counts in decision making, is one of the most effective ways to achieve such commitment. That in turn involves regarding teachers as professionals, not just hired workers. In the process, teacher leadership should not devolve to a few senior teachers virtually promoted to become new supervisors. Rather, it's important to find a complementary role for each person's abilities and interests.

Attitudes that must be encouraged in this process include:

- viewing teaching approaches not just as private preferences, but as strategies to be compared, analyzed, and then adapted to one's own style
- regarding a school staff more as a community and less as a hierarchy of leaders and led, or senior people and juniors
- seeking improvement not because a school is "deficient," but because there's always more to learn, which is what keeps us energized for our kids

Most teachers originally entered the profession with a desire to do something of value in their careers. So the impetus toward more professional attitudes is usually just waiting to be reignited.

At the same time, significant forces must be overcome to achieve collaboration. The school culture can reinforce isolation. Teachers often say they hesitate to seek a colleague's help because they fear the word will spread and they'll be negatively evaluated by the principal. Conversely, taking leadership can seem like joining with or seeking favor from the boss.

As new strategies are debated and tried out, there are almost always turf battles, complex organizational dynamics, strong emotions, and normal resistance to change. But a study comparing five high schools in the Coalition of Essential Schools (Wasley et al. 1997) showed that when issues were aired in an atmosphere of mutual respect, changes and improvements went forward much more successfully than when objections were repressed or dealt with either through angry confrontation or covert maneuvering. Thus, while many schools attempt some form of faculty input, *the effort must be approached thoughtfully.* Following are some major areas to consider as collaborative efforts are initiated in a school.

Organize staff or a committee to develop a clear project and/or staff development plan with just a few focused objectives. Teacher leadership and collaboration need not mean endless debates or lack of focus. A staff can be asked to select just a few major goals and then commit to achieving them together. Teachers are encouraged by concrete outcomes to their work; conversely, when they tackle too much and nothing gets completed, people lose faith in the process. The school leader can feed professional materials, program descriptions, and data to a committee to help keep them on track. And he or she can quietly call on any foot-draggers to support the effort. Those who work hard on a project can lose enthusiasm if they see it ignored by half the faculty. And after all, on some other occasion, that less committed individual might wish to have his initiative supported in turn.

Be smart about organizational dynamics and details. Mentoring offers a good case study of pitfalls and solutions. A gathering of high school department chairpersons discussed the following realities: (1) *Time* (again!). Unless mentor and protegé have matching schedules, it is difficult for the two to meet. One chairperson coped by placing the new teacher in a room next to the mentor so that brief informal exchanges could occur. (2) *Arbitrary pairings.* Personalities, styles, and needs differ. Some chairpersons let protegés choose their own mentors, after large-group get-acquainted sessions. Some realized that designating someone as a mentor gave the appearance of favoritism. A solution was to plan the mentoring program collaboratively with the whole department. (3) *Evaluation*. In some locations, mentors are required to conduct evaluations of their protegés. This undermines the entire program, motivating new teachers to conceal rather than share problems.

Effective collaboration depends on the whole school culture, not just an isolated program. Peer coaching, for example, was most positively viewed in settings where a rich variety of communication took place (Little 1988). In the more successful buildings studied among the Coalition of Essential Schools, faculty met at length to compare the vision they had articulated with the strategies they were carrying out. In one school, regular reports from the superintendent and from various faculty groups kept the staff involved and informed.

Allow for differences. Talk isn't automatically productive. Committees can bog down and factions wrangle. The problem is how to keep innovation going *without* alienating the more traditional teachers and turning a building into a battleground. One way to ameliorate this is to avoid absolute mandates for an entire school or district, and to ask instead that each teacher choose among several improvements to work on. This has obviously been one of the great advantages of small schools and small learning communities within schools. Teachers on self-selected teams have a much easier time working together than those thrown together by fiat. And when each group hears about and learns to appreciate the struggles of the other, change is more likely for all.

Build mutual respect. This is so essential to collaborative change that it simply must take priority over installing "correct" practices. A powerful tool for building cohesion among staff is the sharing of individual histories and past learning experiences. This opens communication and builds relationships so teachers can live with their natural disagreements. Group-dynamics theorists assert that every effective group needs plenty of this "maintenance" activity. Good leaders incorporate such self-disclosure, sharing, and storytelling into just about any meeting or in-service session. In a session on lump-sum budgeting, for example, a workshop leader began by asking participants to pair up and describe to each other the gains and tradeoffs resulting from a recent personal purchase. The talk led to principles for analyzing budgets. But the one-to-one exchange was also important to build trust, open channels, and begin the conversation.

All of these strategies help to work *with* teachers' resistance, rather than opposing it head-on. Negative approaches, arbitrary mandates, and punitive labels engender resentment and quiet, passive resistance that, in the long run, can undermine any program.

4. Quality Learning for Teachers

Build staff development around experiential activities, rather than theoretical lectures.

The workshop leaders are starting seventy-five teachers on a writing-reading in-service program. After introductions, the teachers are asked to jot on a four-by-six notecard their own goals and concerns about teaching writing. In pairs they discuss what they've written, and then share their thoughts with the larger group, to be listed on the overhead.

With the list fresh in mind, the group embarks on a reading-writing activity. One leader reads aloud Wednesday Surprise, *by Eve Bunting, a moving story about a child and her grandmother and learning to read. The leaders then guide the group through several rounds of "dialogue journal" writing. Partners each jot down thoughts about the book and then trade papers, responding to the ideas and reactions of the other—a legitimized form of note passing. With this particular book, the teachers invariably write about experiences with literacy—and illiteracy—in their families. People are involved and moved as several volunteers read aloud. The teachers conclude their sharing, and connect the activity with their initial concerns and their thoughts on how to use the strategy.*

These activities are far more than just the demonstrations. We are not simply training teachers to use a new tool. Rather, the best activities provide a mirror in which teachers see themselves in new ways. They draw on teachers' prior knowledge and abilities, and help them construct new approaches of their own, rather than just imitating an instructor. They renew people's enjoyment of their own learning. And they provide space to reconceptualize what learning and teaching can be. Only then are people well equipped—enriched, heartened, drawn into a supportive group—and ready to reflect on the activities and revise their practices accordingly. In the chapters on each curriculum area, we outlined how experts in every field assert that children's learning must be experiential and authentic, reflective and constructivist. Teachers need these ingredients, too.

Furthermore, teachers are a demanding audience, and new ideas must stand up to the rigorous test of everyday application. Therefore, they need to directly experience models of what is possible in the classroom, to end the isolation that cuts them off from alternatives, and to help them work out the many details involved in a new approach.

Teachers need to reflect, to analyze, to compare—to build knowledge and theoretical understandings about their work. Of course, within book covers the knowledge has been there for years—shelves full of studies about classrooms that work and research about what doesn't. However, because research is so often used in the educational world to prove a person's status rather than to really improve schools, teachers often view "theory" with well-justified suspicion. This is just one more reason why they appreciate experiential activity first. Yet when a teacher's natural curiosity has been tapped and she is ready to digest the ideas, it's hard to stop her. Delois Strickland showed *us* the article about conferencing because the information became meaningful to her.

Approach theory authentically. Some academics consider teachers anti-intellectual and unresponsive to theory. But teachers remember their first year teaching, when all that theory seemed to evaporate under the pressures of the moment, since there was virtually no apprenticeship system to help make the connections. We've seen whole districts where few teachers pursue ideas any further than the immediate workshop sessions. They come, let us entertain them, and return to their classrooms to do what they've always done. These are usually places where the teachers hear extremely mixed signals—for example, paying them to attend a summer workshop, but then discouraging individuals from organizing teacher-led groups to keep the new program going.

But we've also watched as a workshop leader unobtrusively leaves stacks of articles on a table at the end of an in-service session and then initiates discussion with individuals as they enter the room the following week. At first, a few teachers read the pieces, then others grow curious, and ultimately the class organizes small-group "literature circles" to compare ideas about the articles they chose to read.

Good administrators encourage interested teacher groups to explore on their own, read about a new approach, meet informally to discuss it, and try it out, critiquing and adjusting both the ideas and their practice. In some schools, one can find a rack with new literature on education in the teacher's lounge—even better when the principal leaves Post-it notes with short comments on some of the articles, to show that she is really reading the stuff. Some schools purchase copies of a key book for everyone who participated in a recent workshop on the subject.

As with Delois Strickland, the process is contagious. At first, a teacher tries one or two new strategies; but when it shows promise, she wants to understand more, to extend the practice, and to troubleshoot the parts that aren't working as well. Just as with children: when teachers rediscover their need for new thinking and see results, their hunger for learning bursts forth, even if long-suppressed.

Use classroom consulting and other follow-up to help teachers translate new ideas into realities. Because we know that inquiry and even guided practice do not lead all teachers to use a new approach, schools can schedule ongoing classroom visits by facilitators to observe, coteach lessons, and meet with teachers who ask for help. Once-a-week visits by a consultant for eight to ten weeks can powerfully launch willing teachers on a new trajectory. Team teaching, peer coaching, inquiry groups that study a new approach together and then try it out are all valuable ways to bring teachers into one another's classrooms and help them support each other as they engage new ideas in practice.

Look for the best in teachers. The lockstep curricula and standardized test scores popular in the news media reflect a distrust in the efficacy of individual teachers, an unwillingness to recognize that, finally, learning means teachers in classrooms who understand, support, and challenge each student. School systems, with their detailed curriculum guides, objectives, and standardized tests in each subject area, seem to expect very little initiative from teachers. Truly changing the relationship means asking the teachers to set their own agenda at the beginning of a meeting or in-service session, asking for their analyses of problems in the school or in children's learning, and respecting the realities within their answers, even when we sometimes disagree with them.

When we visit schools, we begin by asking teachers to talk about their successes and challenges, instead of starting right in to lecture about something or to demonstrate a strategy. We see faces change from glazed to surprised to engaged. When asked, people have plenty to say about what's working and what the obstacles are. Again and again, we observe that when workshops and in-service activities respect teachers—offering ownership and control, immersing them in new perspectives on their own teaching and learning abilities, and providing opportunities to express themselves honestly—most respond with great energy. They start thinking and acting more for themselves. Self-fulfilling prophecy was never more in evidence than here.

5. Sustainability

From the very start, plan ways to ensure that a new effort will endure over the long haul. One of the most troubling phenomena in the world of school reform is that even good, successful new programs rarely last. Visit a school five or ten years after changes were initiated and in all too many cases, there's little or no trace left of the innovation. Leadership changes, and along with it, priorities. New staff don't get the training that the original reformers experienced. Budget cuts wipe out programs that are no longer the new, hot fashion. In the heat of reform, however, it's hard to think about the challenges that will come years later. Some key early steps can help avoid this institutional pattern.

1. Plan for leadership succession. The more successful the program, the more likely the principal or other key administrator will be offered a new, higher-paying job. So train new leaders from the start who understand and support the program and will be ready to take over.

2. Before a new program even begins, bargain for as much autonomy as possible, especially for a school with highly innovative programs, and especially in a large city system. After the effort is launched, it's much harder to gain additional concessions. Large bureaucracies simply aren't designed to support programs that don't fit the mold.

3. Get central office support for the program—in writing. The more the agreement is in the form of a real contract, preferably with an outside partner organization, the more protection you will have. Offer an accountability agreement, a promise to produce specific results within a period of four or five years, to reassure the central administration that you are serious. This helps to keep the whole arrangement clean and clear on all sides.

4. Build community support for the project. It's vital to have teachers on board, of course. But school boards and top administrators are most responsive to their communities. We've seen numerous school programs initiated or saved by highly vocal community groups.

5. Particularly in large city districts, find other innovative schools to work with. Schools tend to be very isolated, just as individual teachers are. But when they work together, their voices grow much more powerful. It becomes easier to advocate for policy changes that are needed to support a program. Conversely, when individual schools make such requests on their own, they often appear to be special pleaders, making excuses when their programs run into difficulties.

Excellent guidance on this issue is provided by Michael Fullan in *Leadership and Sustainability: System Thinking in Action* (2004). Of course, this work is tremendously challenging. Schools and their leaders need to work smart and learn from past failures. And we are learning.

A Five-Year Schoolwide Change Effort

HUNTSVILLE SCHOOL, Huntsville, Ohio

A group of teachers walked into principal Diane Gillespie's office to share their concerns about the kids. It was fall 1999, and Diane was new to the stewardship of Huntsville School, a K–4 building with 335 students in west central Ohio. Gillespie had worked in the district for twenty years, first as a teacher and then as curriculum director, and the teachers clearly trusted her. They had worked hard the previous year and parents had been very supportive, but state test scores were mediocre once again, hovering at 45 percent passing in reading. The children were not getting the skills they would need to succeed in the later grades.

Thus began a five-year process of change. In response to the teachers' concerns, first-grade teachers Becky Grandstaff, Suzanne Headley, and Kris Harper headed to Toledo with the principal in tow to hear about Patricia Cunningham's "Four Blocks" approach to teaching reading—focused on guided reading, self-selected reading, writing, and working with words (Cunningham and Hall 1996). The Ohio-based consultant they'd heard, Marsha Spears, was invited to come work with the first-grade teachers, and returned to the school repeatedly over the year to meet with staff.

To build commitment across the school, the faculty began calling the fourth-grade state test the "K–4 test," reminding themselves that in fact everyone's teaching contributed to the kids' achievement. The fourth-grade teachers themselves decided that their students would simply write and read every day, to prepare them for the test. Meanwhile, the school staff were thrilled when they learned they'd been awarded $60,000 over two years through an "Ohio Reads" grant they'd applied for, and the scope of their effort expanded. Teachers went to work stocking classroom libraries and Gillespie scheduled more training on the Four Block structure.

Testing results in the spring left teachers overjoyed—84 percent passed in reading, the second-highest year-to-year jump in the state. The school received a $25,000 award and the principal and several teachers, along with a former fourth-grade student, drove to Columbus to give speeches at ceremonies there. Nevertheless, anxiety quickly set in: the teachers wondered how they could make sure to keep this up.

What led to this much change? "We weren't yet executing many specific new strategies," Diane observes. "But our children were doing a lot more reading and writing—there were just more books around. And there was a lot of talk going on, informally, every day. In the teachers' lounge and at lunch we talked about our work more. We began to believe in what we were doing." A number of key conditions underlay the effort, as well:

- lots of listening to teachers by the administration districtwide
- strong staff desire to continue their own professional growth and development
- strong expressions of confidence in the teachers and encouragement that they see themselves as professionals—and plenty of trust as a result
- willingness of staff to pull together and come up with ways to tackle whatever issues they faced

In the spring of 2000, teachers Suzanne Headley and Kris Harper attended a conference led by reading expert Regie Routman. On their recommendation, Huntsville was able to bring Routman in for a full week the next September. For three days she conducted demonstration lessons in classrooms and held discussions with observing teachers before and after each demo. The fourth day shifted to coteaching, and on the fifth the teachers took over, with coaching. Each day included Q&A after school. This process filled in many strategies teachers needed, such as group reading conferences, to make the Four Block approach work. "It took a few days to bond," Diane explains, "But by Friday, we were all hugging her and no one wanted to let her go."

Regie returned for a three-day visit in March, and announced on the last day that it was now time to commit to a regular weekly "support group" where teachers could discuss their work and professional readings—and it had to be organized by a teacher, not the principal. After a few moments of silence, Linda Benedict, then a twenty-eight-year veteran second-grade teacher, volunteered. The group's first professional reading was Richard Allington's *What Really Matters for Struggling Readers* (2001). The Wednesday before-school meetings have now become essential for just about the entire staff. Gillespie estimates faculty attendance at 95 percent, and swears teachers will never give up the practice, no matter who their principal is. "If I had to name the one thing besides the staff development that has made the difference for us, it is the support group," Diane asserts—and teachers agree. "It makes us feel like a team. And now we're a model for other schools to follow," says third-grade teacher Deb Hanson. Leadership of the group is now shared between Linda Benedict and reading specialist Karen Contner. In the discussions, teachers are not afraid to take risks or ask for help. They are also more likely to attempt as many interventions as needed to ensure the success of all their students. In addition to the improvements in practice, Kirsten Thomas, also a reading specialist, points out that the camaraderie the staff shares is a direct result of the support group.

Diane credits her staff with bringing compassion, intelligence, and commitment to their work. "This is such an incredibly special group of individuals. I continue to be impressed by the interactions that occur on a daily basis in their classrooms," Diane declares. The staff in turn point to Gillespie's supportive leadership. After we completed interviews with several teachers, the staff compiled a list of the principal's actions that they particularly appreciate. They explain that their principal

- obtains information whenever they request it—and even researches topics on the Internet when they inquire about them
- takes notes when they have individual conversations with her
- updated and personalized the library—she and her husband built a loft for it
- encourages teachers to be more creative with their room schemes
- puts out goodies on the lunch table—often chocolate
- created an extra reading teacher position
- promotes wellness among staff
- finds money to send teachers to conferences
- doesn't miss any opportunity to show appreciation and celebration (example: whenever good news comes in, Gillespie breaks out champagne glasses and bottles of sparkling cider for the staff)
- thanks and praises teachers weekly in the staff newsletter, and drops thank-you notes in people's mailboxes whenever they complete a task for the school

Comments Jo Cook, the district curriculum/instruction director, "Diane Gillespie is low-key, but she's like a bulldog when the issue affects kids."

The school has gone on to seek further staff development, broadened from reading to across-the-curriculum teaching skills. Math began to receive more attention, starting with a districtwide adoption study and the ultimate selection of "Everyday Math." But throughout, the school has maintained a consistent focus. "It's all connected," Diane observes. There's no attraction to passing fads. "And no one-shot staff development sessions, either," Diane makes very clear. Reading scores dipped to 77 percent that second year (not unusual as changes begin at a school)—and then soared back into the 80s and 90s. However, just as important has been everyone's clear recognition that reading has become a more engaged experience for everyone in the school.

Huntsville's faculty is a very experienced group—not a bunch of radical young hotheads, but veteran educators who have embraced profound and thoughtful change. Most have put in more than twenty years at the school. "I'm blessed to have such a caring, child-focused staff," says Diane. "Every single thing that has happened here at Huntsville Elementary is due to the fact that together, we believe in the 'whatever it takes' adage." Teacher Linda Benedict adds, "Instead of one person moaning, 'What can I do?' we now ask, 'What can *we* do?' Before I felt isolated. Now we're a team."

WORKS CITED

Allington, Richard. 2001. *What Really Matters for Struggling Readers.* New York: Longman.

Cunningham, Patricia, and D. P. Hall. 1996. *The Four Blocks: A Framework for Reading and Writing in Classrooms That Work.* Clemmons, NC: Windward Productions.

Darling-Hammond, Linda. 1996. The Quiet Revolution: Rethinking Teacher Development. *Educational Leadership* (March).

Easton, Lois Brown. 2004. *Powerful Designs for Professional Learning.* Oxford, OH: National Staff Development Council.

Fullan, Michael. 1999. *Leading in a Culture of Change.* San Francisco, CA: Jossey Bass.

———. 2004. *Leadership and Sustainability: System Thinking in Action.* Thousand Oaks, CA: Corwin Press.

Hall, Gene, and Shirley Hord. 2000. *Implementing Change: Patterns, Principles, and Potholes.* Needham Heights, MA: Allyn and Bacon.

Hargreaves, Andy. 2003. *Teaching in the Knowledge Society: Education in the Age of Insecurity.* New York: Teachers College Press.

Little, Judith Warren. 1988. Assessing the Prospects for Teacher Leadership. In *Building a Professional Culture in Schools,* edited by Ann Lieberman. New York: Teachers College Press.

Lortie, Dan. 1972. *Schoolteacher.* Chicago, IL: University of Chicago Press.

Marshall, Kim. 1996. No One Ever Said It Would Be Easy. *Phi Delta Kappan* (December).

National Research Council. 1996. *National Science Education Standards: Observe, Interact, Change, Learn.* Washington, DC: National Academy Press.

National Staff Development Council. 2001. *NSDC Standards for Staff Development, Revised.* Oxford, OH: National Staff Development Council.

Pfeifer, R. Scott. 1986. *Enabling Teacher Effectiveness.* Washington, DC: American Educational Research Association.

Reitzug, Ulrich, and Leonard C. Burrello. 1995. How Principals Can Build Self-Renewing Schools. *Educational Leadership* (April).

Wasley, Patricia, et al. 2000. *Small Schools: Great Strides. A Study of New Small Schools in Chicago.* New York: The Bank Street School of Education.

Wasley, Patricia, Robert Hampel, and Richard Clark. 1997. The Puzzle of Whole School Change. *Phi Delta Kappan* (May).

SUGGESTED FURTHER READINGS

Billings, Gloria Ladson. 1994. *The Dream Keepers: Successful Teachers of African American Children.* San Francisco: Jossey-Bass.

Daniels, Harvey, Marilyn Bizar, and Steven Zemelman. 2001. *Rethinking High School: Best Practice in Teaching, Learning, and Leadership.* Portsmouth, NH: Heinemann.

Darling-Hammond, Linda. 1997. *The Right to Learn: A Blueprint for Creating Schools That Work.* San Francisco: Jossey-Bass.

DuFour, Rick, and Robert Eaker. 1998. *Professional Learning Communities at Work: Best Practices for Enhancing Student Achievement.* Bloomington, IN: National Educational Service.

Fullan, Michael, and Andy Hargreaves. 1996. *What's Worth Fighting for in Your School.* New York: Teachers College Press.

Harwayne, Shelley. 1999. *Going Public: Priorities and Practice at the Manhattan New School.* Portsmouth, NH: Heinemann.

Joyce, Bruce, Beverly Showers, and Michael Fullan. 2002. *Student Achievement Through Staff Development* (Third Edition). Alexandria, VA: Association for Supervision and Curriculum Development.

Lambert, Linda. 2003. *Leadership Capacity for Lasting School Improvement.* Alexandria, VA: Association for Supervision and Curriculum Development.

Lieberman, Ann, and Lynne Miller. 1991. *Staff Development for Education in the '90's: New Demands, New Realities, New Perspectives* (Second Edition). New York: Teachers College Press.

———. 1999. *Teachers Transforming Their World and Their Work.* Alexandria, VA: Association for Supervision and Curriculum Development.

Meier, Deborah. 2003. *In Schools We Trust: Creating Communities of Learning in an Era of Testing and Standardization.* Boston, MA: Beacon Press.

Sizer, Theodore. 2004. *The Red Pencil: Convictions from Experience in Education.* New Haven, CT: Yale University Press.

Wasley, Patricia A. 1991. *Teachers Who Lead: The Rhetoric of Reform and the Realities of Practice.* New York: Teachers College Press.

———. 1993. *Stirring the Chalk Dust: Tales of Teachers Changing Classroom Practice.* New York: Teachers College Press.

Wood, George. 1998. *A Time to Learn: Creating Community in America's High Schools.* New York: Dutton.

Chapter 10
Will It Work in City Schools?

Throughout this book, we've described teachers who teach beautifully and are improving. We've pictured ordinary kids who learn and grow. We've visited inner-city and suburban schools that are working. Yet most people conclude that urban schools across the country are *not* working, that so-called at risk kids *aren't* learning, and that too many city schools *haven't* discovered the strategies of Best Practice. Study national achievement scores or, better yet, visit some urban schools, and you realize that the disparity is genuinely catastrophic. While we've seen improvement in elementary education, and innovative high school models that do succeed, the majority of urban high schools have been especially hard to change. And though the rules of No Child Left Behind mainly punish, rather than create improvements that work, many of the deficiencies they highlight are heartbreaking.

In a very real sense, America has two school systems: perhaps three-fourths of our kids attend decent schools in towns and suburbs, while the other fourth attend big-city schools often weighed down with grievous problems. Rather than averaging together these two separate systems to derive the false and misleading picture that America's main educational problem is mediocrity, we really have something much worse: a country of educational *haves* and *have-nots*.

But we've argued throughout this book—and research strongly confirms—that all kids can and do learn well, even under some pretty trying circumstances. So if the children aren't really dumb, and if the teachers and their schools are not really hopeless, then what makes learning and teaching so much harder in the inner city?

We are not looking for excuses or arguments that all city schools are doing the best they can. Rather, if we are ever to get beyond the successes of a few charismatic teachers and principals, if we are to find ways to overcome the challenges, we had better be clear about what stands in the way. In this chapter, we review the factors we believe to be most damaging, and separate some myths from the realities of urban education. Finally, we describe an exemplary program that shows how the state-of-the-art instructional practices described in this book work just as powerfully in inner-city schools as in prosperous suburban ones.

POVERTY

No one questions the deadening effects of poverty. One most unfortunate effect on schools is student mobility. A study by the Center for Urban School Improvement (CUSI) revealed that only two of every five Chicago students stay in the same school from first through sixth grade (1996). Many change schools four to six times, and 48 percent of a sample of sixth graders said they'd switched schools during the year (Consortium on Chicago School Research 1994). The CUSI study identified 118 highly unstable schools, out of 477 on which data were available. Even if a school develops an outstanding program, 40 percent of the children who might benefit are gone before the year is over. A similar number will arrive, forcing teachers to try to bring each new pupil up to speed on what she's missed.

Even if incoming kids achieve at satisfactory levels, the turnover slows the progress of the class and requires repeated readjustment of the group's dynamics. As we've explained, the key structures of Best Practice teaching require a cohesive, interactive, interdependent classroom where students assume high levels of responsibility for their own and their classmates' learning. When the classroom community is constantly reshuffled, teachers are at best driven back to the early stages of group building and at worst constantly preoccupied with discipline.

Outside of school, instability in families and violence in neighborhoods pressure children tragically. In several schools where we've worked, large numbers of children have witnessed shootings and deaths. Younger kids—in grades one to four or five—remain quite open to schooling, although some become withdrawn, overly needy of attention because of threats in the neighborhood, or are untrained in self-discipline and social cooperation. Alex Kotlowitz' moving chronicle *There Are No Children Here* (1991) describes how the brutality of neighborhood violence leaves a child unable to concentrate in school. But it's the older students who are increasingly preoccupied with the magnetism and danger of the streets, especially when they experience repeated failure in school.

Yet the so-called culture of poverty also has been overly blamed and deeply misunderstood. The common belief among many is that poor children speak a defective language and have little exposure to learning outside school, with parents either too overworked, irresponsible, or illiterate to help them. Over the years, researchers—and even court cases—have shown how wrong this is. For example, Black English (African American English Vernacular or Ebonics to sociolinguists) grammar differs from school dialect in relatively minor ways, even if these stand out sharply to the middle-class ear, and it involves forms of expression as rich and complex as in any other language (Labov 1998). Similarly, children of Hispanic background may be limited in English, but may also be well on their way to literacy in Spanish, giving them much to build on.

Further, ethnographic studies of children in poor homes show that many are quite involved in literacy through play, drawing, and even television, which, contrary to the platitudes, is actually full of print (Taylor and Dorsey-Gaines 1988). These children often engage more print at home than during the school day itself. And detailed research on child development during the early years reveals that at age three, they possess all the basic concepts for reading—stability of meaning, representation of reality through symbols, and linear directionality of print. *There are no observable differences of such acquisition at this stage between* any *groups, rich or poor, urban or rural, black or white* (Harste et al. 1984).

Anthropologist Shirley Brice Heath provides one helpful explanation of this puzzle in her classic study comparing different working-class communities. Heath observed that for some cultural groups family patterns of language use harmonize with the usual patterns of student-teacher communication, while for others it does not (1983). Children in some groups get lots of practice using school-type talk at home, answering questions about toys and books, or giving factual information. If the kids in groups with a different communication style don't pick up the new talk quickly in school, they fall behind and stay behind—frustrating their parents, who express strong belief in the importance of education. On the other hand, Heath found that when teachers design learning projects more in tune with their children's cultural language patterns, the kids do far better.

CLASS AND RACE

Because teachers are just about 100 percent middle-class, while many of their inner-city charges are poor, considerable friction and misunderstanding occur. This is not necessarily a matter of race, although race issues can certainly be present. The motives of most of these teachers working with poorer children are positive—they earnestly want to help the next generation escape from poverty, just as they or their parents may have done. But the issue is not so simple, because class in urban America isn't just a matter of how much money you have. Race and class are often reflected in the way you talk, the games you play, the music you listen to—though of course there are also huge differences among the members of any one group. So the cultural gap between teachers and students—already present because the younger generation always needs to distinguish itself—can grow to unfortunate proportions.

Teachers (*and* students) can make dysfunctional assumptions or take damaging actions as a result. One research project showed how some urban teachers grossly underestimated parents' willingness to help their kids or support the teacher's policies. The teachers failed to contact parents whose children were struggling, and when contact was finally made very late in the year, the teachers were surprised at the cooperation and improvement that took place (Allen and Mason 1989). Of course, *every* community has some parents who fail to support their children's education. But the *assumption* that they won't can mean unfortunate lost opportunities.

More heartbreaking is the amount of anger and hostility we sometimes see in urban schools. The kids can seem wild, and the teachers yell and label them harshly to their faces to maintain basic control. In workshops, the teachers assert quite openly that these kids lack discipline in their homes or are accustomed only to such tactics. Some education writers and theorists have argued that only a skills-and-worksheets approach will succeed with some children because of their cultural backgrounds. However, without dismissing the need for culturally sensitive teaching, our experience in good urban classrooms simply doesn't support this conclusion.

Further, in many schools, non-white children, boys especially, are disciplined more frequently and for smaller offenses than other kids. Teachers are often unaware they are doing this, and uncomfortable talking about it. Staffs become divided along racial lines and around various issues, and many school leaders lack the skills to air the issues constructively (Lewis 2003).

What makes these phenomena especially frustrating is that in effective urban classrooms using Best Practice strategies in the poorest areas, we've observed that discipline and relationships aren't a problem at all. The teachers may have to work hard on it, but the kids are industrious and upbeat, the teachers calm and positive. There *are* cultural differences among groups, and it's important for teachers to understand them and listen to them, just as Lisa Delpit has so passionately argued (1995). However, we've observed so many inner-city classrooms (some of which are described in this book) where kids of *all* colors and backgrounds thrive on self-directed and collaborative tasks, that we know the problem must be a deeper, more subtle one.

We've seen some of the forces at work. Students who have experienced years of failure have a lower tolerance for frustration and act out more readily when the learning grows more challenging. And teachers who have weak classroom management skills blame the children, while the teachers' lack of control unwittingly accustoms the kids to chaotic settings.

This sad cycle breeds both danger and irony. If schools decide that "these kids" are already under authoritarian discipline at home and respond only to harsh authority, then the schools actually reproduce dysfunctional behavior right in the classroom. Instead, it's arguable that all these children need to be helped to participate in the mainstream culture in school, to learn self-control, responsibility, self-monitoring, sharing, cooperation, and some deferral of gratification. These things need to be actively taught. But if city kids never get the kinds of experiences that help them internalize these values, how can they ever escape poverty and function in mainstream society?

Other factors can cause problems with learning, but all the difficulty gets ascribed instead to the children's social background. For example, as we observed one teacher trying unsuccessfully to help her third graders with punctuation, she turned to us in frustration, saying, "These kids just don't *want* to learn!" But the explanation was otherwise. When one child read aloud in robotic monotones, it was clear that she had learned to decode words but not to read for meaning—a problem typical of the school's skills-only reading program. She had never been trained to listen to sentences rather than individual words, and couldn't hear where to add punctuation. When we asked for volunteers to try adding meaning, this girl raised her hand again and again, bravely risking embarrassment because she wanted so badly to learn! Thus, in spite of the best of intentions, many teachers and children become embroiled in the endless skirmishes of a class war, a war that eats up all their energy.

Yet—when we work with teachers who have struggled in this saddening whirlpool, they are always desperate to escape it, delighted to discover that meaningful classroom activities result in improved behavior because they communicate respect for children's voices and show the kids they are smarter than they thought. Under the battle-scarred surface of almost every frustrated teacher lives the idealist, the believer who wants kids to grow and learn. The class war does not have to cycle on forever.

RESOURCES

OK, so just throwing money at a problem like education won't solve it. On the other hand, without the funds, how will we ever retrain the thousands of teachers in a city like Chicago, who need to learn new methods of teaching writing, reading, math, science, and social studies (not everyone, of course, since many have excellent skills)? Starting with Jonathan Kozol's *Savage Inequalities* (1991), experts have repeatedly pointed out that city kids, teachers, and schools simply don't get their fair share of the money available for education in this society.

What would it take to deliver staff development on teaching writing, and writing across the curriculum, for a big-city staff of twenty thousand? Our own Illinois Writing Project has trained more than fifteen hundred Chicago teachers in recent years. That same work in the town of Elgin, Illinois, would serve nearly 70 percent of all the teachers. However, in a large city it's a drop in the bucket that can't possibly add up to systemwide change. The cost for retraining just one-fourth of the Chicago staff in one subject area, such as reading or math (i.e., six thousand teachers, a number that, though limited, would create a significant impact, likely influencing even the nonparticipants), would require about $2 million, counting materials, administrative costs, and pay for the time of workshop leaders and teachers. It's a small percentage of the total budget, but ask anyone at the Chicago Board of Education how difficult it would be to find such funds!

"Why didn't the teachers get this training in college, so they wouldn't need it now?" one might ask. Actually, college training has improved in many education fields. However, teachers trained twenty years ago are still working in the system. And most teacher training still lacks the in-depth internship process that allows neophytes in a field like medicine to translate book learning to actual practice in the real world. The resources simply aren't there.

SIZE

The effort to convert large, factorylike, impersonal schools to clusters of small schools is sweeping the country, and for good reason. Large urban high schools are automatically handicapped for serving students in general and for helping struggling students in particular. Overstuffed elementary buildings do little better. Kids fall through the cracks, and receive far too little focused attention from adults. These conditions create problems in schools in communities of all kinds, but students' anonymity in large schools has more of an impact in urban areas, where students need greater individual attention. Small schools have been shown to increase personalization for students and reduce truancy and violence (Wasley et al. 2000). They enable curricular reforms that are often impossible in a larger school. And while smallness does not in itself guarantee a better education, it does open the door to assembling a more cohesive staff, focused more intensely on the school's particular mission and design. At the secondary level, small schools enable the formation of grade-level teacher teams that coordinate curriculum and support for individual struggling students—something mathematically impossible under the scheduling complexities of a large high school.

The conversion of an existing high school into a cluster of small schools is extremely difficult, however. If teachers and kids are arbitrarily shuffled into the new structures without opportunities for choice and planning, the cohesion and commitment that energize a small school simply aren't brought into being. Districts and funders in some areas are turning more to new start-ups to address this concern. But it remains to be seen whether the massive, quick changeover being tried in some cities will really make a significant difference. Districts that mistakenly conclude a school population of six hundred is small enough to make a difference are probably setting themselves up for failure. Rules and mandates that constrict small schools from establishing flexible schedules or providing significant common planning time for teachers can block new schools from ever attaining their full potential.

BUREAUCRACY

Americans love to sneer at it. But bureaucracy represents jobs, so it rarely shrinks. And it almost inevitably resists change. In big-city bureaucracies, programs need to be approved at more levels. People can pass the buck more easily. The system comes to serve the needs of politics and entrenched groups more than the needs of teachers and children. One typical way the politics of a large bureaucracy can undermine change: As a program is launched, an administrator worries that people in one area will raise a ruckus if services are offered elsewhere but not for them. Lacking the money to serve every location adequately, one teacher from each building is ordered to a superficial one-day training session and then expected, unrealistically, to change the practice in her building. The program limps along; isolated change agents get discouraged; it fades away.

One highly visible effort to address the inertia of bureaucracy has been the city of Chicago's system of local school councils. It has quite successfully allowed individual schools to institute special programs and activities on their own. However, the central board office has gradually reasserted control in a myriad of ways, issuing a steady stream of restrictive rules and requirements that narrow the options of even the most courageous principals and shrink the role of the local school councils. Top school leaders may advocate innovation, but they also institute monitoring systems that focus on uniformity and compliance with rules, rather than real improvement in learning. Thus, charter and contract schools operating with more autonomy in exchange for accountability contracts (limited in number thus far) have come to seem the only pathway out of the bureaucratic tangle.

ISSUES OF SUSTAINABILITY AND CONTINUITY

One of the deepest of heartbreaks is to see an exciting, innovative school decline after five or ten years of success. Yet it has happened over and over, for many years. We often sigh philosophically that change is inevitable, and that nothing truly lasts in human affairs. Yet why is it that the traditional structure of schools has been so durable and the more successful innovative schools have not, particularly in big city school systems? We think one answer is that school reformers tend to focus on the shiny new curricula and programs they work so hard to create, often neglecting the organizational structures that could ensure continuity.

We depend on charismatic, risk-taking school leaders and don't plan for what will happen when those wonderful people move up or burn out. Too often, we don't build the community support and organizations that grow to love a school and insist on the preservation of its programs as they see their children blossom. Innovators often choose to work quietly, hiding a good school in a corner of the city and hoping central office bureaucrats won't notice as rules are bent. This works for a while, but sooner or later, especially in large, self-protective bureaucracies, the administrators do notice and clamp down. Or a new principal is put in place who has no allegiance to the program and wants to look good to her superiors. But reformers can learn political and organizational savvy. And they can demand formal autonomies as a price for creating good new schools, so that their work cannot be so easily erased by an inevitably fickle system. These strategies are as important as those we develop for the classroom.

 From our own hard struggles, then, we've learned some key lessons about what innovators and new school developers need to address to increase the long-term viability of their work:

- Start on succession planning from the very start of a new school or innovative program

- Develop a clear definition of teacher leadership and opportunities for its exercise, so future leaders are nurtured within the school

- Get district support in writing for innovations

- Negotiate as much autonomy as possible at the very start for key decision making about programs, personnel, schedules, etc.– asking for it later doesn't work

- Build strong support for the school and its programs among parents and community—central administrators will respond to them more than to teachers

- Build alliances with other schools in the district that feature innovative strategies—it's much harder to survive alone

- Create strategies for self-assessing and adjusting the school's program—even creative and exciting strategies can become rigid or require alteration over time

MISGUIDED CURRICULUM

People outside the educational world assume that teaching is teaching; teachers either have what it takes or they don't. They hear hints of the Reading Wars and figure these are just the battles of academics and big egos. But the fact is that we really have learned more about how learning works, and this isn't a matter of fads or philosophical pendulum swings. Throughout this book, we've marshaled research evidence and expert recommendations asserting that all language learning—speaking, reading, writing—is active and holistic. Children don't learn rules first and then apply them, or sounds first and then words. From the very beginning, toddlers engage in full, actual communication: requests; complaints; expressions of love, surprise, and hurt; questions and answers.

And so we've found that to teach school subjects, creating real purposes and options for real communication works; assigning rote, audienceless topics like "What I Did Last Summer" doesn't. Helping kids with the prewriting and revision that actual writers use works; following arbitrary textbook outlining doesn't. Similarly with reading, practicing whole-group reading with "predictable" stories (i.e., with patterns and refrains children can repeat) works. Teachers reading good children's literature aloud works. Practicing separate sound-decoding skills is of limited usefulness because it leaves many children reproducing sounds but not looking for meaning. Teachers have adopted the more effective approaches to reading and writing in considerable numbers. But larger, older school districts are sometimes the most wedded to lockstep, bureaucratically controlled programs.

The isolated-skills approach to learning, however, is not actually the "traditional" approach. It was, in fact, an innovation of the 1920s. Some nineteenth-century educators actually came closer to Best Practice strategies, though we now understand the rationale and effective application of them far more completely. However, a massive bureaucratic support system, including reams of competency testing, grew up around the isolated-skills method. Tremendous resources were expended on the basal readers, workbooks, and scope-and-sequence plans. These systems were especially embraced by large-city schools looking for ways to ensure uniform, if minimum, performance by huge teaching staffs.

Another phenomenon under great debate is the endlessly expanding focus on standardized testing and the preparation for it. It's a vicious cycle , because more time on effective reading strategies, rather than test practice, especially helps those kids who do poorly on the tests—the very tests meant to ensure that the teachers are doing their job. The result? We've certainly not become a nation of avid readers, as any newspaper circulation manager will tell you, nor are we fluent writers or eager mathematicians. Kids in well-off schools still learn to read tolerably well, partly because children generally will learn what society and families expect of them, barring major disruptions in their lives. The toll exacted on urban children has been far more visible. The kids who need the most effective support suffer the most when they don't get it.

RESISTANCE TO CHANGE

Change is actually slow *everywhere,* because that's just what human beings do—resist change. Think of some new technology you are now comfortable with and recall your feelings just before you tried it. Even for some of the most enjoyable activities, many of us find a dozen reasons to put them off if they're new—until finally some supportive but urgent friend, or perhaps a growing inner need of our own, or the pressure of necessity brings us to take the plunge. At the opposite pole, psychologists tell us that a person who is unhappy or dissatisfied clings to unrewarding situations and behaviors—at least in part because they are predictable, familiar, and part of the definition of self and world the person has depended on for a long time.

Therefore, many of us who work with teachers and school change have learned to be patient, to respect the educators we work with, and to listen supportively. We've found that the most effective path to change is not through labeling and accusing, but through immersing people in activities that are new, enjoyable, and filled with implications about their work, and giving them a chance to talk with each other about what the experience means. This sort of change process takes time, but it's deep and lasting.

IN SPITE OF ALL THESE OBSTACLES

In spite of all these obstacles, we've seen inspiring achievements in many urban schools. A study by the school reform organization Designs for Change showed that 49 percent of Chicago elementary schools posted strong or improving Iowa Test of Basic Skills scores over a period of years, as a result of reform in school governance (Designs for Change 1997, 3). And a series of studies by the Consortium on Chicago School Research identified a number of major factors that influenced student improvement in city classrooms. One was teachers' assignment of "authentic intellectual work." By this phrase, the researchers meant that (1) students were asked to construct knowledge, not just spit back information; (2) they were asked to elaborate their understanding, give supporting arguments, and draw conclusions on topics they studied; and (3) they were encouraged to connect topics to their own lives and the world around them. Classrooms where this kind of work took place showed ITBS gains 20 percent higher than the Chicago average over one year. And classrooms that lacked these kinds of assignments lagged significantly below the average (Newmann et al. 2001). A second study showed that more interactive instruction yielded higher score increases than lectures (Smith et al. 2001). And a third inquiry revealed that strong social support and positive academic press in Chicago classrooms led to better scores than settings where these supports were not in place (Lee et al., 1999).

We cannot delude ourselves that a single institution like the public schools can, without other social services and stronger economic conditions, overcome all the problems facing impoverished groups. And yet we must not allow naysayers to deny the fact that intensive, well-executed efforts in urban schools do pay off. We've seen it happen, over and over.

Whole-School Change at P.S. 126

DARIA RIGNEY
Local Instructional Superintendent, Network 9.10, New York, New York

When Daria Rigney was promoted from literacy coach to principal of Public School 126, on the edge of New York's Chinatown, the school was known as a dumping ground for special education and "behavior-disorder" students. Many kids came from the nearby Alfred E. Smith housing projects, while the middle-class families also close by made sure their homes were zoned into the boundaries of a more distant school all the way across the neighborhood. The student population, 40 percent Latino, 40 percent Asian, and 20 percent African American, was floundering, even though the previous principal was beloved by parents and produced school plays and other engaging activities. While the school was a caring, energetic place where teachers had tried some progressive practices, kids still weren't learning very effectively, and the staff despaired of ever succeeding with them.

Daria came to education from a career buying and selling art in the business world, via training in Lucy Calkins' acclaimed Columbia Teachers College Writing Project. And so she resolved to guide the P.S. 126 kids, including those who struggled most, to love reading and writing. She intended to accomplish this not by waving charts of low test scores or school board warnings at everyone, but by building relationships, looking closely, and communicating extensively. "We had to get away from closed doors and the idea of education as private practice," she explains.

So Daria began to write regular letters to her staff about once every two weeks, or whenever she saw that something needed to be discussed. She worded these as "invitations to think alongside me." "I lived in the classrooms," she says, and she began to simply describe to the faculty the patterns she saw and to ask what they thought they could do about the challenges before them. "Have we noticed how quiet the kids are? How can we get them talking?" She wondered on paper. "Read-alouds are great, but are the kids just sitting too long?" She told stories about her own reading and writing life, and offered to obtain help on strategies teachers were struggling with.

These seeds landed on fertile ground, and the staff initiated a series of key projects. Throughout the halls, pictures were posted of teachers reading, accompanied by short essays they wrote to describe their own reading experiences. When the district sent coaches for literacy and math to the school, Daria made clear that she strongly supported the student-centered instructional approaches they introduced to the staff. Teachers began a series of "lesson studies." They would discuss a need and then design a new classroom activity to address it. Daria would then teach the lesson herself in a classroom as teachers observed (a less adventurous principal might well ask a staff developer or coach to handle this step!), and after debriefing, the observers would head off to try the activity in their own classrooms. Daria also arranged and paid for endless lunches. "Lunch was where we got all our deals done in the business world," she points out, "so why not use them in school?" Teachers hungered for time to talk, and embraced the opportunity to develop common practices and learn from one another.

There were plenty of lessons for a new principal to learn as well. Not surprisingly, some old-guard, discouraged teachers resisted at first. One outspoken staffer accused, "What's wrong with you is, you need to address what the teachers perceive they need, not just what *you* think they need!" So a teacher planning committee was formed in the second year of Daria's stewardship. This group took over professional development planning for the school—and of course enjoyed many of the principal's lunches.

Gradually Daria's letter writing expanded throughout the school. Teachers began writing letters back to the principal and to parents. Daria wrote to the parents frequently herself, and made sure her letters got translated into Spanish and Chinese. She explained the importance of reading and writing, and assured the parents that if kids began to love these things, there would be no need for the uniforms that some thought would bring order to the school. And she began posting letters to the kids by the school entrance. As she started including kids' comments in these letters, the students were drawn in, and the mailbox by her office door began to fill with their responses. Daria wrote to the kids every day for the first three years that she led the school. In her last year there, she tried cutting back on the frequency of these letters, but was called to task by a girl, Raven, who had left the school and returned after more than a year away. Raven demanded to know why the day's letter was missing, and Daria picked up the pace.

Over the four years of Daria's principalship, the students' achievement scores rose steadily. The year before she took over (1999), just 11 percent of the students in grades 3, 5, 6, and 7 tested in the top two levels on the city's math test (out of four levels all together). Four years later, 72.2 percent were in the top two levels. A year later, 2004, the scores bumped up another notch to 74.4 percent in those levels. In reading, students in grades 3 through 8 jumped from 23.4 percent in the top two levels in 1999 to 68.5 percent in 2003.

Daria looked to the future as well, so that this culture of literacy would be sustained by leaders who understood its power. When she was promoted to Local Instructional Superintendent for a group of twelve schools (including P.S. 126), her assistant principal took over. And when he realized this was not the sort of job he really wanted, the capable principal intern Daria had previously trained was ready to step in. P.S. 126 continues to prosper.

Of course, not every principal comes to the position with the background in literacy teaching and leadership that Daria could draw on so effectively. But the essentials can be initiated by any good school leader:

- constant communication about key concerns and personal values among all groups in the school community
- teacher teams with major responsibilities for improving the school
- "lesson study" activities that enable teachers to work together to expand their teaching repertoire
- lots of talk so that teachers can reflect together and themselves become a thoughtful, literate, and mutually supportive community
- extensive, nonpunitive observation of classrooms
- expert coaches who can demonstrate, coteach, and discuss new strategies with teachers
- visible symbols that demonstrate in highly credible ways that the adults in the school value and enjoy reading and writing
- meals and other creature comforts that smooth the way and invite group solidarity for the hard work to be done

We close, then, with the voices of adult and child, writing to one another to make their school a better place—truly a Best Practice.

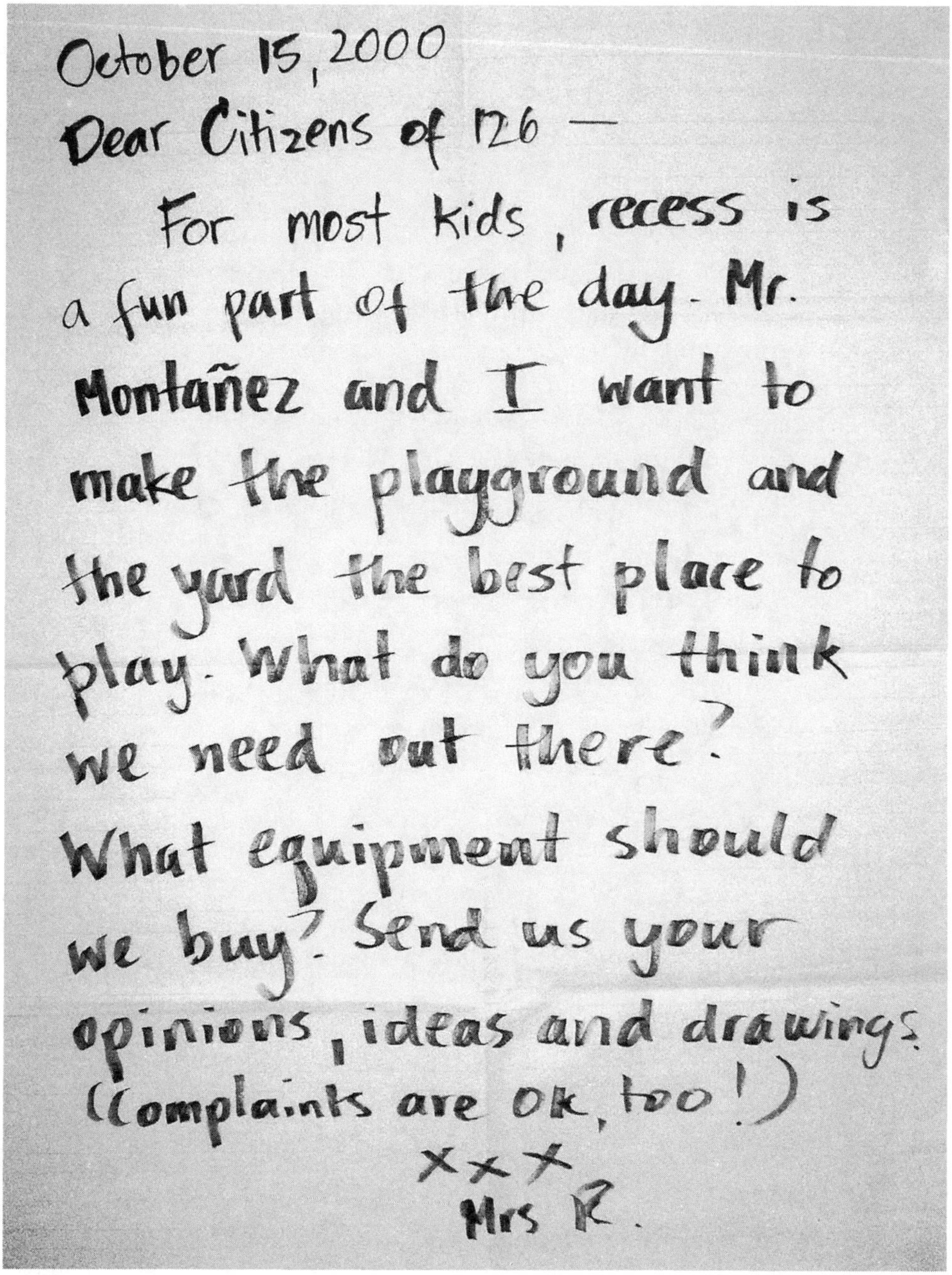

October 15, 2000

Dear Citizens of 126 —

For most kids, recess is a fun part of the day. Mr. Montañez and I want to make the playground and the yard the best place to play. What do you think we need out there? What equipment should we buy? Send us your opinions, ideas and drawings. (Complaints are OK, too!)

xxx
Mrs R.

Figure 10.1: Sample letter from Daria Rigney to P.S. 126 students.

Dear Ms. Rigney,

Jenny and I have the following ideas for a park.

1) To build a jungle gym with a slide attached. With a Math theme. such as using hexqonal shapes to build this figure and various heights for the use of the lower and upper school.

2) Swings for older students and younger students.

3) Also see attached picture of a climbing pyramid made out of rope.

4) A tube slide (see picture with Ms. Rodriquez)

Thank you for considering our ideas.

Jackie Diaz
and
Jenny Wang
7th grade

Figure 10.2: Jackie and Jenny's rely.

WORKS CITED

Allen, Jo Beth, and Jana Mason. 1989. *Risk Makers, Risk Takers, Risk Breakers: Reducing the Risks for Young Literacy Learners.* Portsmouth, NH: Heinemann.

Center for Urban School Improvement and the Chicago Panel on School Policy. 1996. *Pervasive Student Mobility: A Moving Target for School Improvement.* Chicago, IL: Center for School Improvement and the Chicago Panel on School Policy.

Consortium on Chicago School Research. 1994. *Charting Reform: The Students Speak.* Chicago, IL: Consortium on Chicago School Research.

Delpit, Lisa. 1995. *Other People's Children: Cultural Conflict in the Classroom.* New York: The New Press.

Designs for Change. 1997. *Chicago Elementary Schools with a Seven-Year Trend of Improved Reading Achievement.* Chicago: Designs for Change.

Harste, Jerome, Virginia A. Woodward, and Carolyn L. Burke. 1984. *Language Stories and Literacy Lessons.* Portsmouth, NH: Heinemann.

Heath, Shirley Brice. 1983. *Ways with Words: Language, Life, and Work in Communities and Classrooms.* New York: Cambridge University Press.

Kotlowitz, Alex. 1991. *There Are No Children Here: The Story of Two Boys Growing Up in the Other America.* New York: Doubleday.

Kozol, Jonathan. 1991. *Savage Inequalities.* New York: Crown Publishers.

Labov, William. 1998. Coexistent Systems in African-American English. In S. Mufwene et al. (editors) *The Structure of African-American English* 110–153. London: Routledge.

Lee, Valerie, et al. 1999. *Social Support, Academic Press, and Student Achievement: A View from the Middle Grades in Chicago.* Chicago: Consortium on Chicago School Research.

Lewis, Amanda. 2003. *Race in the Schoolyard: Negotiating the Color Line in Classrooms and Communities.* Piscataway, NJ: Rutgers University Press.

Newmann, Fred M., et al. 2001. *Authentic Intellectual Work and Standardized Tests: Conflict or Coexistence?* Chicago: Consortium on Chicago School Research.

Smith, Julia, et al. 2001. *Instruction and Achievement in Chicago Elementary Schools.* Chicago: Consortium on Chicago School Research.

Taylor, Denny, and Catherine Dorsey-Gaines. 1988. *Growing Up Literate: Learning from Inner-City Families.* Portsmouth, NH: Heinemann.

Wasley, Patricia, et al. 2000. *Small Schools: Great Strides. A study of New Small Schools in Chicago.* New York, NY: The Bank Street School of Education.

Chapter 11
Best Practice Works: The Proof and the Pendulum

I t's easy to become cynical and view new (or revitalized) ideas as mere fads, the latest swing of the never-ending pendulum of reform strategies pushed by the latest set of academics trying to build their careers. But as we've shown throughout this book, Best Practice is far more than that. It represents a broad consensus across the subject areas about what is important for children to learn and how they can best learn it. Best Practice draws on a long history of inquiry into the psychology and dynamics of learning. It's confirmed by research and testing that shows greater student achievement and learning as a result of Best Practice strategies. And it reflects the concrete everyday experience of talented teachers across the country.

Nevertheless, advocating for Best Practice approaches—as well as refining and further advancing our understanding of them—requires that we collect the best data possible. We need a steady flow of reliable information—data about individual students, data about whole schools, and research on the effectiveness of particular educational strategies. And we need this data not just to advance our own argument. Rather, each child and each school embodies a fresh human experience. No educational theory or plan or curriculum, however strongly it's shown to be effective, is automatically a success. It's a tool in the hands of thinking people who must always figure out how to make it work with *these* children and *these* teachers in *this* particular culture and setting.

So as we conclude this book, we need to reflect on ways to provide ourselves with the best information on how Best Practice strategies are working with particular kids and schools—and the best research that tests their effectiveness in general. It should be information that not only helps us understand *if* something is effective, but also *what* is needed if it is not.

DATA ON STUDENTS

To be very direct about it, we think teachers and schools evaluate students badly, unfairly, and far too much. American schoolchildren, teachers, parents, taxpayers, politicians, and policymakers are downright fixated on grades and tests. Everyone involved spends far more time worrying about test scores than thinking up ways to increase student learning, which might actually raise achievement scores. We are a country full of measurement-obsessed people who seem to believe that you can raise the temperature by improving your thermometer.

What's so bad about the way we evaluate kids in school? To begin with, the socioeconomic function of evaluation in American education has always been problematic and unsavory. Grading and testing historically have been harnessed to the screening, sorting, and classifying of children into categories of "merit" or "intelligence." These certified categories of students are then allocated certain current or future rewards, such as school prizes, invitations to honors classes, admission to good colleges, or entry to high-paying careers. As scholars like Alfie Kohn (1993), Michael Katz (1968), and Joel Spring (1972) have convincingly shown for decades, this vaunted American meritocracy is largely a sham. School tests and grades are part of a system that camouflages the replication of the existing social hierarchy: kids from wealthy, culturally mainstream homes are certified by schools as "deserving" rewards, while students from poor, culturally different homes are proven by tests and grades to "need" a vocational education or to be "unable to benefit" from a college preparatory program.

The school grading system has been abused, co-opted, and enlisted in the service of some shamefully undemocratic arrangements in our culture. Even today, after the wide distribution of work by social historians and the many exposés of standardized test bias, our two most famous educational exams—the Scholastic Aptitude Test and the American College Test—brazenly continue to show a near-perfect correlation between family income and score levels, and still deliver a huge score penalty for being African American or Hispanic. As the *New York Times* once pointed out, Martin Luther King, "a man who is now viewed as among the nation's greatest orators ever, was in the third quartile or below average [in verbal aptitude on the Graduate Records Exam]. His quantitative score was in the bottom 10 percent, and he was in the bottom quarter for tests in physics, chemistry, biology, social studies, and the fine arts" (November 8, 1997, p. A8).

But even if we admit that educational assessment has been often misused by the society at large, don't we use it more responsibly within the institution of school? Sadly, most teachers are still wedded to evaluation procedures that are ineffective, time-consuming, and hurtful to students. One example from the field of writing is particularly illustrative. Everyone is familiar with the deep-rooted school tradition called "intensive correction," where the teacher marks every error in every paper that every student ever writes. Indeed, in American schools this practice is often considered to be *the* basic, standard treatment for responding to student writing. But George Hillocks' meta-analysis of research (1986) showed that such intensive correction is *completely useless*. Marking all the errors in a student paper is no more effective, in terms of future growth or improvement, than marking none of them. The only difference is the huge expenditure of teacher time and the student demoralization that accompany this practice.

Under pressure to "justify" grades with copious scores and marks in their gradebooks, teachers devote enormous energy to feeding the grading machine—finding ways to quantify, measure, score, compute, and record assorted aspects of kids' behaviors. Coauthor Harvey Daniels has worked to popularize the classroom structure called "literature circles" (2002) and reports that in workshops, the number-one question raised by teachers is: How can I get a grade out of this activity? This frantic quest for quantification should remind us that the main legitimate purpose of evaluation in education ought to be to guide instruction, not to rack up numbers. Anything we do to gather and interpret information about kids' learning should provide accurate, helpful input for nurturing children's further growth.

Back in their preservice educational psychology courses, teachers learned the distinction between summative and formative evaluation. Formative evaluation is the basic, everyday kind of assessment that we continually use to understand students' growth and help "form" their further learning. Summative evaluation doesn't aim to nurture learning at all, but merely quantifies what has been learned up to a given point, translating it into a score or symbol that allows students to be ranked against each other. Summative evaluation isn't actually educational; it is just a way of reporting periodically to outsiders about what has been studied or learned.

It's problem enough when tests are valid but overused or misused, but it's much worse when they don't reflect Best Practice teaching or the skills that the kids are, in fact, learning. Yet over and over, even when communities and news reporters are confronted with studies showing that standardized tests are inaccurate, discriminate against minorities, and reward memorization instead of thinking, school districts opt to retain them anyway. Better, more complex tests are too expensive, they conclude, and besides, how can we compare ourselves to other communities if we don't use the same tests?

Meanwhile, we simply evaluate kids' work too much. We have a norm of grading every piece of work that students ever attempt in any school subject, duly placing a carefully computed number in the gradebook after each attempt. Indeed, in many classrooms the compulsion to evaluate every piece of student work actually becomes an instructional bottleneck, limiting the amount of student practice to a level that the teacher has time to grade. The sad irony here, of course, is that practice—unmonitored practice—is the main way in which humans learn almost every valuable activity in life, from piano playing to roof shingling.

We grade and test and score kids far more than is needed to effectively guide instruction—and ironically, we too often fail to use the data to actually guide the successive help we provide for individual students. In classrooms where teachers are constantly watching, talking, and working with kids, elaborate grading systems are unnecessary, unhelpful, redundant, and sometimes contradictory. As far as the demand for official grades and records is concerned, teachers can produce a perfectly adequate documentation of students' growth through the occasional sampling of their work, periodic observations, and once-in-a-while examination of their products. Especially when records are backed up by a portfolio of students' actual work—the raw material upon which any grade ought to be based—there should be no problem in explaining a given grade. When teachers make this change, substituting descriptive evaluation for grading, they are essentially making a trade: they are swapping time previously spent on scoring, computing, recording, averaging, and justifying grades, in exchange for time to collect, save, discuss, and reflect on kids' real work.

However, in the current climate of preoccupation with test scores and mistrust of teachers and schools, teachers are understandably susceptible to the evaluation obsession themselves. When we lead a workshop with teachers, we always begin by asking what concerns or topics they would like to discuss during the course. Evaluation is usually the first topic to be mentioned, and it almost always ends up being listed as a top priority of every group. To be fair, part of this obsession simply reflects the pressure that teachers feel from the public, taxpayers, the media, state assessments, and so forth. But it also reveals that teachers are, finally, just another group of

Americans—and they have acquired the evaluation fixation just as deeply, and in much the same way, as any other citizens.

But let's return to the bright side. As teachers and schools move toward Best Practice, there is a clear mandate for new forms of assessment, evaluation, grading, and reporting student progress. Across subject fields, Best Practice in evaluation means that teachers assess student learning according to the principles outlined below.

 ## Best Practice Evaluation

- focuses on the knowledge and abilities that are key to Best Practice learning, and on complex whole outcomes and performances of writing, reading, researching, and problem solving, rather than only on isolated subskills

- most of the time, uses assessment that is formative, not summative—and then applies the data to guide individual students' further learning and to adjust our own teaching

- employs evaluation that is descriptive or narrative, not scored and numerical

- involves students in developing meaningful assessments (for example, asks students to describe what makes a good research report), and will call on them to keep track of and judge their own work

- triangulates assessments, looking at each child from several angles, by drawing on observation, conversation, artifacts, and performances, and by looking at learning over time

- operates as a part of instruction (as in teacher-student conferences), rather than separate from it

- allots a moderate amount of time to evaluation and assessment, not allowing it to rule a teacher's professional life or consume lots of instruction time

- where possible, abolishes or de-emphasizes competitive grading systems

- employs parent-education programs to help community members understand the value of new approaches, and then invites parents to participate in the process

DATA ON SCHOOLS

The coin of the realm nowadays is the state-mandated standardized test. Schools that do well or improve markedly are praised and those that don't are threatened with sanctions or even state takeover (though the latter puts us in mind of the dog that finally catches the neighbor's car he's been chasing for years—now what does he do with it?). We've discussed throughout this book the research that unequivocally shows how Best Practice teaching strategies actually improve student performance on such tests. But that doesn't mean we find the tests particularly accurate or meaningful in judging a school's overall performance, or likely to encourage real improvement. In Chicago, for example, high schools are judged on the number of students scoring at or above the 50th percentile on Illinois' "Prairie State" test, which combines the ACT and a test called "Work Keys." Using the test this way means that if your faculty work like demons and improve all their lowest-scoring kids from the 10th to the 49th percentile, they get exactly no credit for their effort; but if you move a bunch of kids from the 49th to the 50th, you look like a miracle worker. You can easily guess which path a principal who is under the microscope is likely to choose, which students will get extra attention and which are likely to be, uh, left behind.

In this atmosphere, it is important for schools to collect and publish data of other kinds, to show parents and the community what they are really accomplishing. Figures on attendance, dropouts versus kids who stay in school, graduation rate, rate of college attendance for high schools, rate of success in college (or success in high school, for graduates of elementary schools)—all reflect important aspects of a school's performance. Schools that use end-of-semester or yearly performance assessments (with jury panels that include community members) can calculate rates of acceptable and high performance and compare them year to year. Regularly publicizing this information can gradually give it credibility and recognition in the community. We know schools that track the number of books and even the number of pages that students read over the course of a year. While this raw data doesn't tell what the student learned, it's still valuable information, compared to the school that doesn't talk publicly about reading at all.

It's also important for schools to seek meaningful *program* evaluation—in other words, to conduct thoughtful reflection on just what sort of teaching is in fact taking place, and whether the school is effectively enacting the programs it has committed to. After all, we've seen so many cases in our profession in which a reform was supposedly "tried" and pronounced a failure, while proponents maintain that it wasn't well enough executed to really determine its efficacy.

One traditional mechanism for program evaluation is the principal's evaluation of individual teachers. But even at its best, this process does not provide a larger whole-school picture of the teaching and learning that is taking place. At the high school level, the regional accrediting agencies around the country make their once-every-five-year visits, but we know of few schools that have truly rethought their curriculum as a result.

One valuable effort to address this has been the "critical friends" strategy. We wish it bore a more felicitous label because the phrase seems uncomfortably self-contradictory and negative. Nevertheless, it's a powerful approach that can both help schools improve and inform people about where they are in the effort. Actually, there are two forms of critical friends work, one internal and the other external. The internal version is a sophisticated form of self-guided reflection: teachers in a school meet regularly and follow a protocol to share and examine their practice (Bambino 2002; Dunne et al. 2000). In the external version, a visiting team provides outside eyes and ears for this process. Both versions receive high praise from teachers who have participated in them.

We'll focus for a moment here on the external version, since it provides more of an explicit report on the school's work. When conducted well, a visiting team asks the school's teachers and administrators to describe their goals and the programs and strategies they are using. Then they spend several days observing classrooms, examining student work, and interviewing kids, teachers, and parents. Finally, the team provides a written report and meets with the school staff to discuss their observations. As a Coalition of Essential Schools guide for this work explains, "The purpose of our evidence-gathering is not to compare or evaluate, but to provide the school with accurate information they can use to decide 'next steps' in their quest to become an excellent school" (Cushman 1998). Clearly, schools that employ such self-reflection can readily demonstrate to the community that whatever the standardized test scores, the school is serious about strengthening teaching and learning for all students.

DATA ON BEST PRACTICE APPROACHES

In many places in this book, we've referred to the research that supports Best Practice, as well as the controversy that has arisen around at least some of that research. We've described some key issues in the Reading Wars, which focus on the narrow question of how to best help beginning readers. We've noted how proponents of differing approaches focus their research on differing aspects of reading or different kinds of reading tests. And we've referred to the important research by Fred Newmann and his associates showing that authentic assignments, interactive teaching, and strong social support in the classroom all lead to higher standardized test scores (see Chapters 1 and 10).

We want to round out the picture by recalling that there is a long history of such research, covering a wide range of Best Practice strategies. Those of us who work with the research understand that all of it is limited because so many variables are beyond control in any classrooms studied, and we don't have much faith in many of the measures for studying them. However, in spite of the more politically motivated statements sometimes heard, the dozens of research studies done and repeated over many years have confirmed over and over the positive outcomes for a wide range of progressive teaching strategies compared to more traditional ones.

For years, for example, cooperative education researchers have published studies confirming significant achievement gains in a wide range of content areas when classrooms include ample cooperative activity—one of the fundamental components of the Best Practice paradigm (Johnson, Johnson, and Holubec 1998). In the teaching of writing, a meta-analysis of numerous statistical studies by George Hillocks (1986) showed that while activities for engaging students with material and ideas for writing have a strong effect on writing quality, lecture presentations and grammar drills are of little use, or even bring down writing scores.

Since reading is the most heavily researched area of the curriculum, we'll briefly list the books and articles that review this vast literature. The learning principles are very similar for other subjects, as this entire book has illustrated. A decades-long body of research on literature-based reading programs shows standardized achievement score gains for students in progressive programs, not just in regular education but among students with ESL, special education, or disadvantaged backgrounds. Michael Tunnell and James Jacobs, surveying studies up to 1989, listed one after another that reached the same conclusion.

Jane Braunger and Jan Lewis compiled a well-organized account of strategies for teaching reading that are supported by research ranging from the 1970s to the mid 1990s. The studies covered in their book, *Building a Knowledge Base in Reading* (1997), confirm that reading is a constructive, active process that involves complex thinking. In 1999, Harvey and Steve, with their partner, Marilyn Bizar, published a sixty-year review of research supporting literature-based teaching of reading, use of independent reading, teaching of the writing process, and other related approaches. Richard Allington's *What Really Matters for Struggling Readers* (2001) marshals the research that supports a simple and clear list of instructional needs:

- Kids need to read a lot.
- Kids need books they *can* read.
- Kids need to learn to read fluently.
- Kids need to develop thoughtful literacy.

Alan Farstrup and Jay Samuels' thorough guide, *What Research Has to Say About Reading Instruction* (2002), presents a range of reading experts who explain the implications of research for teaching reading. The central role of best practice strategies as described in the IRA standards is very clear. Michael Pressley's chapter, for example, examines the importance of above-the-word-level comprehension strategies for good reading. Constance Weaver and coauthors created a very handy research guide in *Creating Support for Effective Literacy Education* (1996), with brief summaries and bibliographies of the studies on topics such as teaching skills in context, teaching phonics, and spelling. However, the third edition of Weaver's *Reading Process and Practice* (2002) is now more up to date, and is encyclopedic in its coverage of the concepts behind a progressive approach to reading and the research that supports each one. Finally, Daniels and Zemelman's *Subjects Matter: Every Teacher's Guide to Content-Area Reading* (2004) contains a summary of research implications for reading in the secondary grades.

But what about the research behind the arguments from the so-called other side in the Reading Wars? The National Reading Panel (2000) has supported a much more conservative view, particularly by defining the acceptability of research so narrowly that many important studies are left out, thereby emphasizing the importance of phonics and direct instruction. Other researchers, like Richard Allington (2001), explain the flaws in this approach. And yet even with all this debate, many of the panel's recommendations firmly support the Best Practice approaches described in this book. The panel affirms that the best research roundly endorses the learning of vocabulary "in rich contexts," the importance of self-monitoring of comprehension, the value of cooperative learning, and the effectiveness of students generating their own questions.

We recognize that no amount of quoted research is likely, by itself, to change educational practice in American schools. Here in Chicago, for example, a major scientific study showed that the effects of retaining students at a grade level were clearly negative (Nagaoka and Roderick 2004), and yet school officials here (and in other cities, like New York) only reaffirmed their commitment to the strategy. Nevertheless, responsible educators want to learn all that they can about what works in their profession, and need to know that they are on the right track. When it comes to Best Practice approaches, we are clearly reassured. And even the schools that try narrower, more traditional strategies frequently end up rethinking and asking for help with new ideas a few years later.

FADS?

Sometimes teachers wonder: *Isn't Best Practice just another educational fad? And is any of this stuff really new? It sounds just like the open classrooms of the 1960s or Whole Language in the early 1990s, and those trends died away, didn't they?* What we are calling the Best Practice movement certainly has a very familiar ring to school veterans from the past thirty years. It's not surprising that earlier waves of progressive reform are scoffed at by some educators, just as newer incarnations are attacked. But we think the educational innovations of the late 1960s and early 1990s were important precursors to today's developments, and it's worth understanding what really happened back then, to comprehend our struggles now.

Let's look at one controversial innovation from this era to help us revalue our heritage. In the 1970s, some American schools plunged into the open-classroom experiment, tearing down walls and offering teachers a one-day in-service at the end of the summer, in which some administrator or outside consultant essentially announced: "OK, next week we want you to throw away the one model of teaching that you were trained for and are experienced in, and instead run your classroom in ten other ways you've never tried and we've never trained you for. Have a nice year." The great open-education movement inevitably collapsed because teachers did not have in their professional repertoire the structures and strategies to run a variety of student-directed, independent, and small-group activities. Kids went bananas, and many teachers who were working in huge rooms with hundreds of kids started sneaking in cardboard boxes, shelves, and other large objects with which they could gradually rebuild a classroomlike space inside the trackless waste of the "pod."

But if you visited Joanne Trahanas' eighth-grade language arts class in Glenview, Illinois, in recent years (as a person who's always growing, she's now moved on to become a principal), you'd have seen something that looks very much like an open classroom. You'd have seen thirteen-year-olds—an age group not usually noted for self-discipline—working industriously and without overt supervision on their writing skills every day. They'd come into Joanne's room, get out their writing folders, and get ready to work. During a quick round of the class, each kid would announce what he or she was planning to work on that day, and then everyone, including the teacher, would go to work. Some were drafting new pieces, others were editing ongoing drafts. A few would quietly seek out a partner for a quick conference. After a while, Joanne would start to see kids one at a time on a schedule she kept, and as she conferred with each student about his or her writing, she would jot a phrase or two in the book where she tracked progress. A couple of times a week, the group would gather for ten minutes to read passages aloud and discuss the progress of their writing.

This was an open classroom—an open classroom that worked. It worked because Joanne set up the structure, the norms, the schedule, the procedures, and the materials in such a way that kids quickly grew into responsible use of this special time and space. What's even more impressive to us is that Joanne had *six* writing workshops each day, with six different sets of kids. Joanne's workshop reminds us that there are important links between contemporary Best Practice ideas and past innovations, but it also demonstrates that we've learned a lot about how to make things really stick this time around.

And here's some more history that helps us understand how change works, or doesn't, in American schools. All those open classrooms of the early seventies were doing open education *wrong* in the first place. In borrowing the idea from British education (where it was more commonly called "integrated day"), many American educators misconstrued open education as an architectural rather than an instructional innovation, believing that the process required big open spaces. They focused on creating huge spaces rather than helping teachers orchestrate the inquiry-oriented, experiential learning that was the true core of the model. Harvey remembers taking one English educator through Chicago's first gigantic open-classroom school in 1972, and the visitor shaking his head in amazement: "They've got this completely wrong," he moaned.

We'll close with a happier but equally important history lesson. At Barton Open School in Minneapolis, progressive reformers got it right the first time. They did not tear down walls or build vast "pods." Instead, inside normal-sized classrooms, they set up spaces where kids' interests were piqued, where exploration and expression were valued, where individual differences were prized, and where teachers could operate as thoughtful facilitators of learning. As a result of this faithful implementation, Barton is still there, still thriving, and has become one of the most celebrated schools in the Midwest. Today, when we visit Barton, we see a Best Practice school in the truest sense. Principal Steve DeLapp and his amazing staff have simply been doing progressive education steadily and genuinely for more than thirty years. No pendulums have swung through Barton.

DOWN WITH THE PENDULUM METAPHOR

One tendency we have pretty successfully avoided in this book is quoting ourselves. But on this subject, we are unlikely to improve on what we wrote in 1988 in *A Community of Writers*:

> A pendulum swinging back and forth . . . seems to be the standard metaphor for changes in our field. How impartial and content free this pendulum image is, tempting us to believe that the fluctuations in educational practice are merely the results of some pointless, random, eternal variation. In fact, this is no impartial pendulum swinging; it is more like the battlefront in a war that moves back and forth with assaults and retreats. This is a historical struggle of one set of ideas against another, continually being fought out in close relation to the social-political-economic issues outside of schools . . . the playing out, over a huge span of time, of a war for the soul of schooling in our society. In the end, the student-centered, humanistic, developmental approach will win out over the authoritarian model because it parallels the direction in which civilization itself progresses. If we look broadly enough, we can see evidence that this direction is already well established: in matters of discipline, teachers no longer whip students in school or crown them with dunce caps; in language arts, we no longer require endless copying of great authors' texts; we no longer have kids stand beside their desks for recitation and enunciation; and sentence diagramming, though far from dead, now occupies far less of the average school day than it did just one generation ago.
>
> Of course there will always be regressions and short-term backslides. Change in schools never follows a straight, steady path, but is more like

three steps forward and two-and-a-half steps back. Perhaps tomorrow a movement will spring up to restore the teaching of sentence diagramming to its "rightful, central place in the English curriculum," and such a trend might even catch on for a few years. Indeed, it is just this sort of event that misleads us, as individuals living in a particular brief here and now, into believing that there's always a pendulum swinging back and forth between two eternal, fixed points, ensuring that nothing ever really changes. (Zemelman and Daniels 1988, 17, 270)

But each time the progressive set of ideas comes back, it gains strength and coherence from the new research and practice that connects with it, and each time it appears, it exerts more influence on the schools. Best Practice, classroom workshop, interdisciplinary studies—if taught in their true, genuine forms, adaptable to the needs of the students involved in them—reflect a set of deep educational ideas. Ideas that are partisan, yes—but they are deeply rooted in an ever-deepening understanding of how human beings learn, and so they will continue to spread. In the words of a courageous Chicago teacher, Joe Perlstein:

It's very difficult to change. It takes a lot out of a person. However, you don't mind if there's a payback, if you feel that the children are growing, that they appreciate what is going on. If you see a light at the end of the tunnel, then you say to yourself, "Don't stop now. Keep pushing, keep pressing." Because it will all be worth it in the end.

WORKS CITED

Allington, Richard. 2001. *What Really Matters for Struggling Readers: Designing Research-Based Programs.* New York: Addison Wesley.

Bambino, Deborah. 2002. Critical Friends. *Educational Leadership* 59:6.

Braunger, Jane, and Jan Lewis. 1997. *Building a Knowledge Base in Reading.* Portland, OR: Northwest Regional Educational Laboratory.

Cushman, Kathleen. 1998. How Friends Can Be Critical as Schools Make Essential Changes. *Horace* 14:5.

Daniels, Harvey. 2001. *Literature Circles: Voice and Choice in Book Clubs and Reading Groups.* York, ME: Stenhouse.

Daniels, Harvey, and Steven Zemelman. 2004. *Subjects Matter: Every Teacher's Guide to Content-Area Reading.* Portsmouth, NH: Heinemann.

Daniels, Harvey, Steven Zemelman, and Marilyn Bizar. 1999. Whole Language Works: Sixty Years of Research. *Educational Leadership* 57: 2.

Dunne, Faith, Bill Nave, and Anne Lewis. 2000. Critical Friends Groups: Teachers Helping Teachers to Improve Student Learning. *Phi Delta Kappa International Research Bulletin* 28 http://www.pdkintl.org/edres/resbul28.htm.

Farstrup, Alan, and Jay Samuels, eds. 2002. *What Research Has to Say About Reading Instruction* (Third Edition). Newark, DE: International Reading Association.

Hillocks, George. 1986. *Research on Written Composition*. Urbana, IL: National Council of Teachers of English.

Johnson, David W., Roger T. Johnson, and Edythe Holubec. 1998. *Cooperation in the Classroom* (Seventh Edition). Edina, MN: Interaction Book Company.

Katz, Michael B. 1968. *The Irony of Early School Reform: Educational Innovation in Mid-Nineteenth-Century Massachusetts*. Cambridge, MA: Harvard University Press.

Kohn, Alfie. 1993. *Punished by Rewards: The Trouble with Gold Stars, Incentive Plans, A's, Praise, and Other Bribes*. Boston: Houghton Mifflin.

Nagaoka, Jenny, and Melissa Roderick. 2004. *Ending Social Promotion: The Effects of Retention*. Chicago, IL: Consortium on Chicago School Research.

National Reading Panel. 2000. *Teaching Children to Read: An Evidence-Based Assessment of the Scientific Research Literature on Reading and Its Implications for Reading Instruction*. Washington, DC: National Institutes of Health.

Spring, Joel. 1972. *Education and the Rise of the Corporate State*. Boston: Beacon Press.

Tunnell, Michael, and James Jacobs. 1989. Using "Real" Books: Research Findings on Literature-Based Reading Instruction. *Reading Teacher* (March).

Weaver, Constance. 2002. *Reading Process and Practice* (Third Edition). Portsmouth, NH: Heinemann.

Weaver, Constance, Lorraine Gillmeister-Krause, and Grace Vento-Zogby. 1996. *Creating Support for Effective Literacy Education*. Portsmouth, NH: Heinemann.

Zemelman, Steven, and Harvey Daniels. 1988. *A Community of Writers*. Portsmouth, NH: Heinemann.

Appendix: Indicators of Best Practice

As we work and grow together in our nation's schools, there are eight areas where we can look for progress toward *Best Practice* teaching and learning. In each of the eight areas, growth does not necessarily mean moving from one practice to another, discarding a previous

PHYSICAL FACILITIES

Set up for teacher-centered instruction (desks) ▶ Student-centered arrangement (e.g., tables)
Rows of desks ▶ Clusters ▶ Centers (varied learning stations for writing, computers, math, etc.)
Bare, unadorned space ▶ Commercial decorations ▶ Student-made artwork/products/displays
Few materials ▶ Textbooks and handouts ▶ Trade books, magazines, artifacts, manipulatives, tools

CLASSROOM CLIMATE/MANAGEMENT

Management by punishments and rewards ▶ Order maintained by engagement and community
Teacher creates and enforces rules ▶ Students help set and enforce norms
No specific time or activities for community-building ▶ Regular class meetings, home base, or advisory
Students are silent/motionless/passive/controlled ▶ Purposeful talk, movement, and autonomy
Students are in fixed groups based on "ability" ▶ Flexible grouping based on tasks and choice
Rigid, unvarying schedule ▶ Predictable but flexible time usage based on activities

STUDENT VOICE AND INVOLVEMENT

Balanced Between Teacher-Directed and Student-Directed Activities

- Students often select inquiry topics, books, writing topics, audiences, etc.
- Students maintain their own records, set own goals, self-assess
- Some themes/inquiries are built from students' own questions; curriculum is negotiated
- Students assume responsibility, take roles in decision making, help run classroom life

ACTIVITIES AND ASSIGNMENTS

Balanced Between Traditional and More Interactive Activities

Teacher presentation and transmission of material ▶ Students actively experiencing concepts
Whole-class teaching ▶ Centers and cooperative small groups ▶ Wide variety of activities
Teacher in front, directing whole class ▶ Teacher hard to find, working with groups
Uniform curriculum for all ▶ Jigsawed curriculum; different topics by kids' needs or choices
Short-term lessons, one day at a time ▶ Extended activities; multiday, multistep projects
Focus on memorization and recall ▶ Focus on applying knowledge and problem solving
Short responses, fill-in-the-blank exercises ▶ Complex responses, evaluations, writing, artwork
Identical assignments for all ▶ Differentiated curriculum for all learners, styles, and abilities

LANGUAGE AND COMMUNICATION

Silence ▶ Noise and conversation alternates with quiet time
Short responses ▶ Elaborated discussion ▶ Students' own questions and evaluations
Teacher talk ▶ Student–teacher talk ▶ Student–student talk
Talk and writing focuses on: Facts ▶ Skills ▶ Concepts ▶ Synthesis and reflection

Best Practice, Third Edition by Zemelman, Daniels, and Hyde (Heinemann: Portsmouth, NH); © 2005

Indicators of Best Practice, Continued

instructional approach and replacing it forever. Instead, teachers add new alternatives to a widening repertoire of choices, allowing them to move among a richer array of activities, creating a more diverse and complex balance.

TIME ALLOCATIONS

Time Allocations ARE BALANCED Between

- Teacher-directed and student-directed work
- Subject-specific lessons and integrated, thematic, cross-disciplinary inquiries
- Individual work/small-group or team work/whole-class work
- Extensive study of wide range of subjects and intensive, deep study of selected topics

Fundamental Activities Happen on Daily/Regular Basis

- Independent reading (SSR, reading workshop, or book clubs)
- Independent writing (journals or writing workshop)
- Reading aloud to students
- Teacher-student and student–student conferences

STUDENT WORK AND ASSESSMENT

Products created for teachers and grading ▶ Products created for real events and audiences
Classroom/hallway displays: No student work posted ▶ "A" papers only ▶ All students represented
Identical, imitative products displayed ▶ Varied and original products displayed
Teacher feedback is scores and grades ▶ Teacher feedback is substantive, varied, and formative
Products are seen and rated only by teachers ▶ Public exhibitions and performances are common
Teacher gradebook ▶ Student-maintained portfolios, with self-assessments and conferences
All assessment by teachers ▶ Student self-assessment an official element ▶ Parents are involved
Standards set during grading ▶ Standards available in advance ▶ Standards codeveloped with students

TEACHER ATTITUDE AND INITIATIVE

Toward Students

Negative, distant, fearful, punitive ▶ Positive, warm, respectful, encouraging
Blaming students ▶ Understanding and empathizing with students
Directive ▶ Consultative

Toward Self

Powerless worker ▶ Risk taker/experimenter ▶ Creative, active professional
Solitary adult ▶ Member of team with other adults in school ▶ Member of networks beyond school
Staff development recipient ▶ Director of own professional growth

Toward Job Roles

Expert, presenter, disciplinarian, gatekeeper ▶ Coach, mentor, model, guide

Best Practice, Third Edition by Zemelman, Daniels, and Hyde (Heinemann: Portsmouth, NH); © 2005

Index